My Memoi:

Volume. I

1802 to 1821

Alexandre Dumas

(Translator: E. M. Waller)

Alpha Editions

This edition published in 2024

ISBN : 9789357961042

Design and Setting By
Alpha Editions
www.alphaedis.com
Email - info@alphaedis.com

Contents

ALEXANDRE DUMAS

BY ANDREW LANG

There is no real biography of Alexandre Dumas. Nobody has collected and sifted all his correspondence, tracked his every movement, and pursued him through newspapers and legal documents. Letters and other papers (if they have been preserved) should be as abundant in the case of Dumas as they are scanty in the case of Molière. But they are left to the dust of unsearched offices; and it is curious that in France so little has been systematically written about her most popular if not her greatest novelist. Many treatises on one or other point in the life and work of Dumas exist, but there is nothing like Boswell's *Johnson* or Lockhart's *Scott*. The *Mémoires* by the novelist himself cover only part of his career, *Les Enfances Dumas*; and they bear the same resemblance to a serious conscientious autobiography as *Vingt Ans Après* bears to Mr. Gardiner's *History of England*. They contain facts, indeed, but facts beheld through the radiant prismatic fancy of the author, who, if he had a good story to tell, dressed it up "with a cocked hat and a sword," as was the manner of an earlier novelist. The volumes of travel, and the delightful work on Dumas's domestic menagerie, *Mes Bêtes*, also contain personal confessions, as does the novel, *Ange Pitou*, with the *Causeries*, and other books. Fortunately Dumas wrote most about his early life, and the early life of most people is more interesting than the records of their later years.

In its limitation to his years of youth, the *Mémoires* of Dumas resemble that equally delightful book, the long autobiographical fragment by George Sand. Both may contain much *Dichtung* as well as *Wahrheit*: at least we see the youth of the great novelists as they liked to see it themselves. The *Mémoires*, with *Mes Bêtes*, possess this advantage over most of the books, that the most crabbed critic cannot say that Dumas did not write them himself. In these works, certainly, he was unaided by Maquet or any other collaborator. They are all his own, and the essential point of note is that they display all the humour, the goodness of heart, the overflowing joy in life, which make the charm of the novels. Here, unmixed, unadulterated, we have that essence of Dumas with which he transfigured the tame "copy" drawn up by Maquet and others under his direction. He told them where to find their historical materials, he gave them the leading ideas of the plot, told them how to block out the chapters, and then he took these chapters and infused into them his own spirit, the spirit which, in its pure shape, pervades every page of the *Mémoires*. They demonstrate that, while he received mechanical aid from collaborators, took from their hands the dry bones of his romances, it was he who made the dry bones live. He is now d'Artagnan, now Athos, now

Gorenflot, now Chicot,—all these and many other personages are mere aspects of the immortal, the creative Alexandre.

Dumas's autobiography, as far as it is presented in this colossal fragment, does not carry us into the period of his great novels (1844-1850). Even this Porthos of the pen found the task of writing the whole of his autobiography *trop lourd*. The work (in how many volumes?) would have been monumental: he left his "star-y-pointing pyramid" incomplete, and no mortal can achieve the task which he left undone.

Despite his vanity, which was genial and humorous, Alexandre Dumas could never take himself seriously. This amiable failing is a mistake everywhere if a man wants to be taken seriously by a world wherein the majority have no sense of humour. The French are more eminent in wit; their masters of humour are Rabelais, Montaigne, Molière, Pascal, and, in modern times, Dumas, Théophile Gautier, and Charles de Bernard. Of these perhaps only two received fair recognition during their lives. Dumas, of course, was not unrecognised; few men of the pen have made more noise in the world. He knew many of the most distinguished people, from Victor Hugo and Louis Philippe to Garibaldi. Dickens he might have known, but when Dickens was in Paris Dumas invited him to be at a certain spot in the midnight hour, when a mysterious carriage would convey him to some place unnamed. Mr. R. L. Stevenson would have kept tryst, Dickens did not; he could not tell what prank this eternal boy had in his mind. Being of this humour, Dumas, however eminent his associates, however great the affairs in which he was concerned, always appeared to the world rather as Mousqueton than as Porthos, a tall man of his hands, indeed, but also much of a comic character, often something of a butt. Garrulous, gay, doing all things with emphasis and a flourish, treating a revolution much in the manner of comic opera, Dumas was not *un homme sérieux*. In literature it was the same. He could not help being merry; the world seemed a very jolly place to him; he never hooted, he said, at the great spectacle of the drama of Life.

His own extraordinary gifts of industry, knowledge, brilliance, ingenuity, sympathy, were playthings to him. He scattered wit as he scattered wealth, lavishly, with both hands, being so reckless that, on occasion, he would sign work into which he had put nothing of his own. To such a pitch did Dumas carry his lack of seriousness that the last quarter or more of his life makes rather sorry reading. "The chase of the crown piece" may be amusing in youth, but when middle age takes the field in pursuit of the evasive coin, the spectacle ceases to exhilarate. Dumas was really of a most generous nature, but he disregarded the Aristotelian mean—he was recklessly lavish. Consequently he was, of course, preyed upon by parasites of both sexes, odious hangers-on of literature, the drama, and the plastic arts. He, who could not turn away a stray self-invited dog, managed to endure persons rather worse than most of that strange class of human beings—the professional friends of men of genius. "What a set, what a world!" says Mr. Matthew Arnold, contemplating the Godwin circle that surrounded Shelley. "What a set!" expresses Lockhart's sentiments about certain friends of Sir Walter Scott. We cannot imagine why great men tolerate these people, but too often they do; a famous English poet was horrified by "those about" George Sand. The society which professionally swarmed round Dumas was worse—the *cher maître* was robbed on every hand. He "made himself a motley to the view," and as all this was at its worst after his great novels—with which we are chiefly concerned—were written, I intend to pass very lightly over the story of his decline.

The grandfather of Alexandre Dumas, Antoine Alexandre Davy de la Pailleterie, was more or less noble. It has not been my fortune to encounter the name of his family in the field of history. They may have "borne St. Louis company," or charged beneath the banner of the Maid at Orléans and Pathay; one can only remark that one never heard of them. The grandfather, at all events, went to San Domingo, and became the father, by a negro woman, of the father of the novelist. As it is hardly credible that he married his mistress, Marie Dumas, it is not clear how the great Alexandre had a right to a marquisate. On this point, however, he ought to have been better informed than we are, who have not seen his parchments. His father at all events, before 1789, enlisted in the army under the maternal name of Dumas. During the Revolution he rose to the rank of General. He was a kind of Porthos. Clasping his horse between his knees and seizing a beam overhead with his hands, he lifted the steed off the ground. Finding that a wall opposed a charge which he was leading, he threw his regiment, one by one, over the wall, and then climbed it himself. In 1792 he married the daughter of an innkeeper at Villers-Cotterets, a good wife to him and a good mother to his son. In Egypt he disliked the arbitrary proceedings of Napoleon, went home, and never was employed again. He had mitigated, as far as in him lay, the sanguinary ferocities of the Revolutionaries. A good man and a good sportsman, he died while Alexandre, born July 24th, 1802, was a little boy. The child had been sent to sleep at a house near his father's, and was awakened by a loud knock at the moment of the General's death. This corresponds to the knocks which herald deaths in the family of Woodd: they are on record in 1661, 1664, 1674, 1784, 1892, 1893, and 1895. Whether the phenomenon is hereditary in the House of la Pailleterie we are not informed. Dumas himself had a firm belief in his own powers as a hypnotist, but thought that little good came of hypnotism. Tennyson was in much the same case.

Madame Dumas was left very poor, and thought of bringing up her child as a candidate for holy orders. But Dumas had nothing of Aramis except his amorousness, and ran away into a local forest rather than take the first educational step towards the ecclesiastical profession. In later life he was no Voltairean, he held Voltaire very cheap, and he believed in the essentials of religion. But he was not built by lavish nature for the celibate life, though he may have exaggerated when he said that he had five hundred children. The boy, like most clever boys, was almost equally fond of books and of field sports. His education was casual; he had some Latin (more than most living English novelists) and a little German. Later he acquired Italian. His handwriting was excellent; his writing-master told him that Napoleon's illegible scrawls perplexed his generals, and certainly Napoleon wrote one of the worst hands in the world. Perhaps his orders to Grouchy, on June 17-18th, 1815, were indecipherable. At all events, Dumas saw the Emperor drive through Villers-Cotterets on June 12th, and drive back on June 20th. He had beaten the British at 5.30 on the 18th, says Dumas, but then Blücher came up at 6.30 and Napoleon ceased to be victorious. What the British were doing in the hour after their defeat Dumas does not explain, but he expresses a chivalrous admiration for their valour, especially for that of our Highlanders.

After the British defeat at Waterloo the world did not change much for a big noisy boy in a little country town. He was promoted to the use of a fowling-piece, and either game was plentiful in these days or the fancy of the quadroon rivalled that of Tartarin de Tarascon. Hares appear to have been treated as big game, the huntsman lying low in ambush while the doomed quarry fed up to him, when he fired, wounded the hare in the leg, ran after him, and embraced him in the manner of Mr. Briggs with his first salmon. The instinct of early genius, or rather of the parents of early genius, points direct to the office of the attorney, notary, or "writer." Like Scott and other immortals, Dumas, about sixteen or eighteen, went into a solicitor's office. He did not stay there long, as he and a friend, during their master's absence, poached their way to Paris, defraying their expenses by the partridges and hares which they bagged. Every boy is a poacher, but in mature life Dumas is said to have shot a large trout in Loch Zug—I find I have written; the Lake of Zug is meant. This is perhaps the darkest blot upon his fame.

His escapade to Paris was discovered by his employer, who hinted a dislike of such behaviour. The blood of de la Pailleterie was up, and Dumas resigned his clerkship. He had made at Villers-Cotterets the acquaintance of Auguste de Leuven, a noble Swede, "kept out of his own" for political reasons. De Leuven knew Paris and people about the theatres; he also tried his own hand at playwriting. Dumas in his society caught the stage fever, and he happened also to see the *Hamlet* of Ducis acted—a very French *Hamlet*, but Dumas divined somehow the greatness of Shakespeare through the veil of Ducis. He knew no more English than most Frenchmen of letters know. Like M. Jules Lemaître, he read Shakespeare and Scott, "in cribs," I suspect, but he read them with delight. Homer, too, he studied only in cribs, but he perceived the grandeur of the Greek epics, the feebleness of the cribs, and vowed that he would translate Homer himself. He did not, however, take the preliminary step of learning Greek. The French drama of the period is said by those who know it to have been a watery thing. The great old masters were out—Dumas and Hugo were not yet in. Dumas began by collaborating with young de Leuven in bright little patriotic pieces. Thus his earliest efforts were collaborative, as they continued to be, about which there is much to be said later. Just as Burns usually needed a keynote to be struck for him by an old song or a poem of young Fergusson's—by a predecessor of some sort—so Dumas appears to have needed companionship in composition. It is a curious mental phenomenon, for he had more ideas than anyone else. He could master a subject more rapidly for his purpose than anyone else, yet he required companionship, contact with other minds engaged on the same theme. I am apt to think that this was the result of the pre-eminently social nature of Dumas. Charles II., as we learn from Lord Ailesbury's *Memoirs*, could not bear to be alone, and must have Harry Killigrew to make him laugh, even on occasions when privacy is courted by mankind. Most people like to write alone; not so Dumas. Comradeship he must have, even in composing, and this, I conceive, was the true secret of his inveterate collaborativeness.

At all events, he began, as a lad, with de Leuven. Through him, after poaching his way to Paris for a day or two, he made the acquaintance of Talma, the famous actor. Returning to Paris after that escapade, he instantly became known to all sorts of useful and interesting people. This gift of making acquaintances stood him in great stead: one often wonders how it is done. In a recent biography of a Scot of letters we find the hero arriving in town, not, it would seem, an eminently attractive hero, but he is at once familiar with George Lewes, George Eliot, Tennyson, Browning, and other *sommités*. How is it done? Dumas's father had known General Foy, General Foy knew the Duc d'Orléans (Louis Philippe), and got a little clerkship in his service for the young quadroon. A few days later he goes to a play, and to whom must he sit next but Charles Nodier, then celebrated, and Nodier must be reading the Elzevir *Pastissier Français*, of which I doubt if a dozen copies are known to exist. How Nodier made friends with Dumas, and hissed his own play, is a most familiar anecdote. It sounds like a dream, a dream that came through the ivory gate. Shifted from one clerkship to another, now snubbed, now befriended by officials, Dumas did certainly read a great deal of modern literature at this time, especially Schiller and Scott. Without Scott he might never have written his great novels, for the idea of historical novels, based on a real knowledge of history, and on a vivid realisation of historical persons as actual men and women, is Sir Walter's own. Scott's daring and Turneresque composition was also bequeathed to Dumas. Sir Walter had no scruples about bringing Amy Robsart to life some fifteen years or more after her death, or about making Shakespeare a successful dramatist fifteen years before he came upon the town.

But plays, not novels, at this time occupied Dumas. Chance brought him acquainted with the history of Christine of Sweden, and with that of Henri III. of France. A little collaborative comedy was acted, a volume of *contes* was published, but was not purchased. A son was born to Dumas in 1824, the celebrated Alexandre Dumas *fils*, whose talent was so unlike that of his sire. The parent tried, with Soulié, to dramatise *Old Mortality*, to "Terrify" it, as Scott would have said. They did not finish their attempt, but Dumas now saw Shakespeare acted by Kemble, Liston, and an English company. He found out "what the theatre really was," and he proceeded to evolve many "parts to tear a cat in." More "in Ercles' vein" than in the vein of Shakespeare were the romantic plays which now arose in France: passions and violent scenes of intrigue were within the compass of Dumas: humour, too, he had, and great skill in effect and in *charpentage*. The style, the charm, the poetry, are absent, *carmina desunt*.

Christine and the murder of Monaldeschi furnished the first topic. After troubles and complications innumerable (there were three *Christines* in the field), Dumas's play was written, and re-constructed, and accepted. In the interval he had made, for the joy of mankind, the acquaintance of Henri III. and Saint-Mégrin, of Catherine de Medici and Chicot, and Guise, in the *Mémoires* of L'Estoile. The time was now 1828-30. Dumas left his official work; the authorities did not think him a model clerk, he was a good deal interrupted by actresses while *Henri III.* was being rehearsed. Just before the first night his mother suffered a shock of apoplexy; his attention was divided between the stage and her bedside. With colossal self-confidence, he invited the Duc d'Orléans to his play. The Duc had a dinner-party, but what of that? The party must meet earlier; the play must begin earlier than the usual hours, and all the party must come. But the adventure of the Duchesse de Guise and Saint-Mégrin, the appearance of that Elagabalus of the Valois, Henri III., with his *mignons*, and cup and ball, his foppery and asceticism, thrilled and entertained a large and distinguished audience in the Théâtre Français. Dumas triumphed; unhappily his mother was unable to share his joy. His fortune was made, and he took pleasure in his publicity. He was probably better known for the time and more spoken of than Victor Hugo, whose really sonorous fame scarcely dates before the first night of *Hernani*.

Though Dumas thus led the *Romantiques* of 1830 through the breach, though he was first in the forlorn hope that took the acropolis of the old classical drama, one does not think of him as a *Romantique*. For one reason or another, he stands a little aloof from Hugo, Gautier, Alfred de Musset, and the set of Pétrus Borel, however intimate he may have been with Augustus Mackeat (Maquet).

Dumas's next play, "classical" in form, was *Christine*, the long-deferred *Christine*, for the Odéon. The anecdotes about the difficulties with the classical actress, Mlle. Mars, are familiar. Dumas was now one of the most notable men in Paris, and in the July days of 1830 he added to his notoriety, conducting himself much like Mr. Jingle on the same historic occasion. He was prominent, with a fowling-piece, in the street-fighting, and it seems that he really did seize the powder magazine at Soissons, by that "native cheek" which never failed him at need. The details are as good as anything in his novels, but Dumas surely invented the lady who, beholding him armed with pistols, declared that it was "a revolt of the blacks." His unlucky colour and his crisp thick hair gave people so many opportunities for jests, that Dumas anticipated the world and made the jokes himself. Perhaps the accident of blood and complexion was one of the reasons that prevented him from taking himself seriously. We need not linger over his political adventures: they led him into La Vendée, where he found the elements of romance. Dumas, I think, was by nature as Royalist as Athos, who, in his advice to Raoul, expresses the very creed of the great Montrose. He ought to have fought for the Duchesse de Berry and the Queen of Naples, but circumstances threw him with the Orleanists and Garibaldi, though he loved Louis Philippe no more than other gentlemen did. He tried to be elected for the Assembly: he might as well have tried to get into the Academy, he was not *un homme sérieux*.

Dumas's career as a novelist was brightest in the forties of the nineteenth century. In the thirties he was much more occupied with plays, whereof *Antony* caused most noise. He went on producing plays of the most various types—he travelled, he married, but soon "went by," he made historical compilations, and glided into the field which chiefly concerns us, that of historical romance. Omitting *Le Capitaine Paul* (Paul Jones) of 1838, and *Le Capitaine Pamphile*, a most amusing book (1840), we find *Le Chevalier d'Harmental* (1843), *Les Trois Mousquetaires* (1844), *Vingt Ans Après* (1845), *La Reine Margot* (1845), *Le Comte de Monte Cristo* (1845), *La Dame de Monsoreau* (1846), *Joseph Balsamo* (1846-1848), *Les Quarante Cinq* (1848), *Le Vicomte de Bragelonne* (1848-1850), not to specify dozens of others, including unavailing things like *Jeanne d'Arc*, charming things like *La Tulipe Noire,* and the novels on the Regency, and the long series on the French Revolution.

Consider the novels of 1844-1850. The *Mousquetaire* cycle, the Valois cycle, *Monte Cristo*! Did Scott, or even Dickens, at their best and most prolific, ever equal this rate of production? Perhaps we must give the prize to Scott for the work of 1814-1820, including *Waverley, The Antiquary, Old Mortality, The Heart of Midlothian, Rob Roy*, and so on. That record cannot be broken, and Scott worked in his odd hours, or in his holidays, while he worked *alone*. But in all the great novels of Dumas, Maquet, the *ci-devant* Augustus Mackeat, collaborated. Yet who can deny that the work is the work of the Dumas of the *Mémoires* and of *Mes Bêtes?* It is the same hand, the same informing spirit, the same brilliant gaiety, the same honest ethics, the same dazzling fertility of resource. Maquet did something—there is no doubt on that head, the men constantly worked together.

But what did Maquet do? He may have made—he did make—"researches." Heaven knows that they were not very deep. Perhaps he discovered that Newcastle is on the Tweed, and that the Scottish army which—shall we say did not adhere to Charles I.?—largely consisted of Highlanders. Perhaps he suggested that Charles I. might want to hear a Mass on the eve of his execution. Perhaps he depicted jolly Charles II. as *un beau ténébreux*, in the *Vicomte de Bragelonne.* I think that there I find the hand of Maquet. Whatever he did, Maquet did something. I suggest that he made these remarkable researches, that he listened while Dumas talked, that he "made objections" (as the *père* invited the *fils* to do), that sometimes he "blocked out" a chapter, which Dumas took, and made into a new thing, or left standing, like that deplorable Charles II. at Blois. On the whole, I conceive that (as regards the great novels) Maquet satisfied Dumas's need of companionship, that he was to the man of genius what Harry Killigrew was to the actual Charles II.

Before the law, in 1856 and in 1858, M. Maquet claimed his right to be declared fellow-author of eighteen novels, all the best of them. It was recognised by the law that he had lent a hand, but he took no more than that by his legal adventures. M. Glinel publishes two of his letters to his counsel: "It is not justice which has won the day, but Dumas," exclaims Augustus. He also complains that he is threatened with a new law-suit *"avec l'éternel coquin qu'on appelle Dumas."* Time kills many animosities. According to M. About, M. Maquet lived to speak kindly of Dumas, as did his legion of other collaborators. "The proudest congratulate themselves on having been trained in so good a school; and M. Auguste Maquet, the chief of them, speaks with real reverence and affection of his great friend." Monsieur Henri Blaze de Bury describes Dumas's method thus:—

"The plot was considered by Dumas and his assistant. The collaborator wrote the book and brought it to the master, who worked over the draft, and re-wrote it all. From one volume, often ill-constructed, he would evolve three volumes or four. *Le Chevalier d'Harmental* by Maquet at first was a tale of sixty pages. Often and often Dumas was the unnamed collaborator of others." M. Blaze de Bury has seen a score of pieces, signed by other names, of which Dumas in each case wrote two-thirds. M. About confirms M. Blaze de Bury's account. He has known Dumas give the ideas to his collaborator. That gentleman then handed in a sketch, written on small leaves of paper. Dumas copied each leaf out on large paper, expanding, altering, improving, *en y semant l'esprit à pleines mains.*

By this method of collaboration Dumas really did the work himself. He supplied the ideas and the *esprit*, and gave the collaborator a lesson in the art of fiction, much as a tutor teaches composition in Greek or Latin. In other examples, such as *Le Chevalier d'Harmental*, the idea, we know, came from Maquet, who had written a *conte* on the subject. Nobody wanted the *conte*, and Dumas made it into the novel, whereby Maquet also benefited. In England collaboration in novel-writing is unusual. In the case of Mr. Rice and Sir Walter Besant we have Sir Walter's description of "how it was done," and it appears that he did most of it. In another case familiar to me, A, an unpopular author, found in his researches a good and dramatic historical subject. On this he wrote a tale of seven chapters, and placed that tale in a drawer, where it lay for years. He then showed it to B, who made a play out of it. The play was nibbled at, but not accepted. B then took the subject, and, going behind the original story, worked up to the point at which it began, whence B and A continued it, and now the thing was a novel, which did not rival in popularity the works of Dumas. Probably in each case of collaboration the methods differ. In one case each author wrote the whole of the book separately, and then the versions were blended.

These are legitimate practices, but in his later years Dumas became less conscientious. There is a story, we have seen, that Maquet once inserted sixteen *ques* in one sentence, and showed it to his friends. Dumas never looked at it, and the sentence with its sixteen *ques* duly appeared in the *feuilleton* of next day's newspaper, for in newspapers were the romances "serialised," as some literary journals say. I have never found that sentence in any of the novels, never met more than five *ques* in one sentence of Dumas's, or more than five "whiches" in one of Sir Walter Scott's. As his age and indolence increased, the nature of things revenged itself on the fame and fortunes of Dumas. The author of the later novels, as M. Henri Blaze de Bury says, is "Dumas-Légion."

The true collaborators of Dumas were human nature and history. Men are eternally interesting to men, but in historical writing, before Scott, the men (except the kings and other chief actors) were left much in the vague. They and their deeds and characters lay hidden in memoirs and unprinted letters. Such a man as the Cavalier, Edward Wogan, "a very beautiful person," says Clarendon, was briefly and inaccurately touched on by that noble author. More justice is done to him by his kinsman, the adventurous Sir Charles Wogan, in a letter to Swift. He did not escape Scott, who wrote a poem to his memory. Now, such a character as Wogan, brave, beautiful, resourceful as d'Artagnan, landing in England with the gallows before his eyes, and carrying a troop of cavalry through the hostile Cromwellian country, "wherever might lead him the shade of Montrose," to join the Clans and strike a blow for King Charles, was precisely the character for Dumas. Such men as Wogan, such women as Jane Lane and Lady Ogilvy, Dumas rediscovered, and they were his inspiration. The past was not really dull, though dull might be the books of academic historians. They omitted the human element, the life, the colour, and, we are told, "scientific history" ought to be thus impartially jejune. The great public turns away from scientific history to Dumas and to modern imitators, good and bad, and how inordinately bad some of his followers can be! An American critic half despairs of his country because some silly novels, pretending to be historical, are popular. The symptom is good rather than bad. Untrained and undirected, falling on the stupid and ignorant new novels most loudly trumpeted, the young Americans do emancipate themselves from the tyranny of to-day, and their own fancy lends a glamour to some inept romance of the past. They dwell with tragedy and with Mary Stuart, though she be the Mary Stuart of a dull, incompetent scribbler. They may hear of Scott and Dumas, and follow them.

Dumas has been blamed by moralists like Mr. Fitzgerald for depraving the morals of France! That he set an example of violence and frenzy, crime and licence on the stage, cannot easily be denied. But in the *Musketeers* he decidedly improves on the taste and morals of the France of 1630-1660, whether tested by d'Artagnan's *Mémoires* or by the more authentic works of Tallemant and de Retz. He is infinitely more delicate, he apologises for what he justly calls the "infamies" of certain proceedings of his heroes, and he puts heart and sentiment even into the light love of Milady's *soubrette*. If d'Artagnan "had no youth, no heart, only ambition," he acquires a heart as he goes on: and, indeed, never lacked one—for friends of his own sex.

Dumas was at the opposite pole from a Galahad or a Joseph. His life, as regards women, was much like that of Burns or Byron. His morality on this point is that of the camp or of the theatre in which he lived so much. This must be granted as an undeniable fact. But there are other departments of conduct, and in the virtues of courage, devotion, fortitude, friendship, and loyalty, the Musketeers are rich enough. Their vices, happily, are not those of our age but of one much less sensitive on certain points of honour, as Dumas remarks, and as history proves. But the virtues of the Musketeers are, in any age, no bad example.

Dumas never writes to inflame the passions, to corrupt, or to instruct a prurient curiosity. The standard of his work is far higher than that of his model or of the age about which he writes. His motto is *sursum corda*; he has not a word to encourage pessimism, or a taste for the squalid. He and his men face Fortune boldly, bearing what mortals must endure, and bearing it well and gaily. His ethics are saved by his humour, generosity, and sound-hearted humanity. These qualities increase and become more manifest as this great cycle rolls on to its heroic culmination in the death of d'Artagnan, the death of Porthos, the unwonted tears of Aramis.

For many years "high sniffing" French critics have sneered at Dumas as a scene-painter, a dauber, a babe in psychological lore, and so forth. But of late we have seen in the success of M. Rostand's *Cyrano de Bergerac,* that France looks lovingly back on her old ideals of a frank and healthy life in the open air—a life of gallant swordsmen, kind friends, and true lovers. In Major Marchand, of the Fashoda affair, we may recognise a gentleman and soldier of the school of Dumas, not of Maupassant, or Flaubert, or Zola. To know his task and to do it despite the most cruel obstacles; to face every form of peril with gaiety; to accept disappointment with a manly courtesy, winning the heartiest admiration from his political opponents, these are accomplishments after Dumas's own heart; and this is a morality which the study of Dumas encourages, and which our time requires.

The authors who relax, and discourage, and deprave may be thought better artists (an opinion which I do not share), but they are less of men than the author of *The Three Musketeers.* Who reads it, but wants to go on reading the sequel, and the sequel to that, and, were it possible, yet another sequel? But Aramis alone of the four is left on the stage, and we pine for another sequel— with Aramis as Pope.

I have dwelt on the *Musketeers* and their historical sources as a type of the powers and methods of Dumas. As much might be said in detail as to the sources of the other great novels, especially those of the Valois circle. History gives little more than the name of Chicot, and his ferocity in the St. Bartholomew massacres. La Mole, Coconnas, and *le brave Bussy,* were really "rather beasts than otherwise," as the lad in Mr. Eden Philpotts's *Human Boy* says about pirates. Catherine de Medici is the Catherine of the *Mémoires,* which are probably truthful on the whole, whatever criticism may say. Dumas fills with gaiety these old times of perfidy and cruelty; he adds Gorenflot and Chicot; he humanises Coconnas; he even inspires regret for Henri III.; he has a Shakespearean love and tolerance for his characters. The critics may and do sniff, but Dumas pleased George Sand, Thackeray, and Mr. Stevenson, who have praised him so well that feebler plaudits are impertinent, Thackeray especially chooses *La Tulipe Noire* as a complement and contrast to the *Musketeers.* Monte Cristo, rich and revengeful, has never been my favourite; I leave him when his treasure hunt is ended, and the Cagliostro cycle deals with matters too cruel for fiction.

In brief, though the rest of the life of Dumas was full of labour, the *anni mirabiles* of 1844-1850 are the prime of his harvests. In 1844, on a tour with the son of Jérôme Napoleon (who certainly had a strange bear-leader), Dumas saw the actual isle of Monte Cristo; it dwelt in his boyish fancy, and became the earliest of all Treasure Islands; but its use as the first part of a tale in the manner of Eugène Sue was an afterthought—like the American scenes and Mrs. Gamp in *Martin Chuzzlewit*. In 1843-44, Dumas, being rich, built his Abbotsford, Monte Cristo, between Saint Germain and Marly le Roi. Thenceforth it was the farce of which the real Abbotsford is the tragedy. It was open house and endless guests, very unlike the guests who visited the villa on the Tweed. At both houses many dogs were kept, at Monte Cristo only were piles of gold left lying about for everyone to help himself. The Théâtre Historique was also founded, that road to ruin Dumas could not leave untrodden, and he abandoned all his schemes to visit Spain and Algiers with the Duc de Montpensier, like Buckingham with Prince Charles. The celebrated vulture, Jugurtha, was now acquired and brought home, to fill his niche in the gallery of *Mes Bêtes*, one of the most delightful books in the world.

On returning Dumas found, like Odysseus, "troubles in his house," angry editors clamorous for belated "copy." Then came the parasites, and then the Revolution of 1848, exciting but expensive to a political man of letters. The Théâtre Historique was ruined, and Dumas chose another path to financial collapse, the ownership of a newspaper. In 1851 Dumas went to Brussels, quarrelled with Maquet (one creditor among many), wrote his *Mémoires*, tried to retrench, but embarked on a new newspaper, *Le Mousquetaire*. He was the reverse of a man of business; *Le Mousquetaire* was not profitable like *Household Words*. The office was a bear garden. More plays were written, more of every kind of thing was written, a weekly paper was attempted, and as the star of Alexandre *fils* was rising, the star of Alexandre *père* descended through shady spaces of the sky. Dumas travelled in Russia, and wrote about that; he joined Garibaldi in 1860, and obtained in Italy an archæological appointment! The populace of Naples did not take Dumas seriously, any more than the staff of the British Museum would have done. For reasons known or unknown to the mob they hooted and threatened the Director of Excavations: the editor of a Garibaldian newspaper, the father of the god-daughter of Garibaldi, a child whose mother had accompanied Dumas in the costume of a sailor. At this time the hero was fifty-eight, and perhaps the Neapolitans detected some incongruity between the age and the proceedings of the Director of Excavations. Perhaps *la vertu va se nicher* in the hearts of the lower classes of "the great sinful streets" of the city of Neapolis.

In 1864 Dumas and the new Italian Government were not on harmonious terms. He left his Liberal newspaper and his meritorious excavations in Pompeii; he returned to Paris accompanied by a lady bearing the pleasing name of Fanny Gordosa. The gordosiousness, if I may use the term, of Fanny far exceeded her capacities as a housekeeper and domestic manager, and the undefeated veteran had to pursue that hunt for the *pièce de cent sous* whereof we have spoken. *La jeunesse n'a qu'un temps*, but Dumas was determined "to be boy for ever." Stories are told about him which, whether they be true or untrue, are better unrepeated. Senile boyishness, where the sex is concerned, cannot be seemly. Money became more scarce as work ceased to be genuine work. Dumas fell to giving public lectures. A daughter came to attend him, as the Duchess of Albany presided over and more or less reformed the last years of her royal father. In 1869-70 the strength of this Porthos of the pen was broken: *c'est trop lourd!* In the autumn of 1870, about the time of the disaster of Sedan, the younger Dumas carried his father to a village near Dieppe. They kept from him the sorrows of these days: his mind dwelt with the past and the dead. He died on December 5th, and on the same day, at Dieppe, the Germans reached the sea. His body lies at Villers-Cotterets, beside his father and mother.

ANDREW LANG.

BOOK I

CHAPTER I

My birth—My name is disputed—Extracts from the official registers of Villers-Cotterets—Corbeil Club—My father's marriage certificate—My mother—My maternal grandfather—Louis-Philippe d'Orléans, father of Philippe-Égalité—Madame de Montesson—M. de Noailles and the Academy—A morganatic marriage.

I was born at Villers-Cotterets, a small town in the department of Aisne, situated on the road between Paris and Laon, about two hundred paces from the rue de la Noue, where Demoustier died; two leagues from La Ferté-Milon, where Racine was born; and seven leagues from Château-Thierry, the birthplace of La Fontaine.

I was born on the 24th of July 1802, in the rue de Lormet, in the house now belonging to my friend Cartier. He will certainly have to sell it me some day, so that I may die in the same room in which I was born. I will step forward into the darkness of the other world in the place that received me when I stepped into this world from the darkness of the past.

I was born July 24th, 1802, at half-past five in the morning; which fact makes me out to be forty-five years and three months old at the date I begin these Memoirs—namely, on Monday, October the 18th, 1847.

Most facts concerning my life have been disputed, even my very name of *Davy de la Pailleterie*, which I am not very tenacious about, since I have never borne it. It will only be found after my name of *Dumas* in official deeds that I have executed before a lawyer, or in civil actions wherein I played either the principal part or was a witness.

I therefore ask permission to transcribe my birth certificate, to allay any further discussion upon the subject.

Extract from the Registers of the Town of Villers-Cotterets.

"On the fifth day of the month of Thermidor, year X of the French Republic.

"Certificate of the birth of Alexandre Dumas-Davy de la Pailleterie, born this day at half-past five in the morning, son of Thomas-Alexandre Dumas-Davy de la Pailleterie, lieutenant-general, born at Jérémie, on the coast of the island of Saint-Domingo, dwelling at Villers-Cotterets; and of Marie-Louise-Élisabeth Labouret, born at the above-mentioned Villers-Cotterets, *his wife*.

"The sex of the child is notified to be male.

"First witness: Claude Labouret, maternal grandfather of the child.

"Second witness: Jean-Michel Deviolaine, inspector of forests in the fourth communal arrondissement of the department of Aisne, twenty-sixth jurisdiction, dwelling at the above mentioned Villers-Cotterets. This statement has been made to us by the father of the child, and is signed by

"Al. Dumas, Labouret, and Deviolaine.

"Proved according to the law by me Nicolas Brice-Mussart, mayor of the town of Villers-Cotterets, in his capacity as official of the Civil State,

Signed: MUSSART."

I have italicised the words *his wife*, because those who contested my right to the name of *Davy de la Pailleterie* sought to prove that I was illegitimate.

Now, had I been illegitimate I should quietly have accepted the bar as more celebrated bastards than I have done, and, like them, I should have laboured arduously with mind or body until I had succeeded in giving a personal value to my name. But what is to be done, gentlemen? I am not illegitimate, and it is high time the public followed my lead—and resigned itself to my legitimacy.

They next fell back upon my father. In a club at Corbeil—it was in 1848—there lived an extremely well-dressed gentleman, forsooth, whom I was informed belonged to the magistracy; a fact which I should never have believed had I not been assured of it by trustworthy people; well, this gentleman had read, in I know not what biography, that it was not I but my father who was a bastard, and he told me the reason why I never signed myself by my name of Davy de la Pailleterie was because my father was never really called by that name, since he was not the son of the marquis de la Pailleterie.

I began by calling this gentleman by the name usually applied to people who tell you such things; but, as he seemed quite as insensible to it as though it had been his family name, I wrote to Villers-Cotterets for a second birth certificate referring to my father, similar to the one they had already sent me about myself.

I now ask the reader's permission to lay this second certificate before him; if he have the bad taste to prefer our prose to that of the secretary to the mayoralty of Villers-Cotterets, let him thrash the matter out with this gentleman of Corbeil.[1]

Certificate of Birth from, the Registers of the Town of Villers-Cotterets.

"In the year 1792, first of the French Republic, on the 28th of the month of November, at eight o'clock at night, after the publication of banns put up at the main door of the Town Hall, on Sunday the 18th of the present month, and affixed there ever since that date for the purpose of proclaiming the intended marriage between citizen *Thomas-Alexandre Davy de la Pailleterie*, aged thirty years and eight months, colonel in the hussars du Midi, born at la Guinodée, Trou-Jérémie, America, *son of the late Alexandre-Antoine Davy de la Pailleterie*, formerly commissary of artillery, who died at Saint-Germain en Laye, June 1786, and of the late Marie-Cessette Dumas, who died at la Guinodée, near Trou-Jérémie, America, in 1772; his father and mother, of the one part;

"And citizen Marie-Louise-Élisabeth Labouret, eldest daughter of citizen Claude Labouret, commandant of the National Guard of Villers-Cotterets and proprietor of the hôtel de *l'Écu*, and of Marie-Joseph Prévot, her father and mother, of the other part;

"The said domiciled persons, namely, the future husband in barracks at Amiens and the future wife in this town; their *birth certificates* having also been inspected and naught being found wrong therein; I, Alexandre-Auguste-Nicolas Longpré, public and municipal officer of this commune, the undersigned, having received the declaration of marriage of the aforesaid parties, have pronounced in the name of the law that they are united in marriage. This act has taken place in the presence of citizens: Louis-Brigitte-Auguste Espagne, lieutenant-colonel of the 7th regiment of hussars stationed at Cambrai, a native of Audi, in the department of Gers;

"Jean-Jacques-Étienne de Béze, lieutenant in the same regiment of hussars, native of Clamercy, department of la Nièvre;

"Jean-Michel Deviolaine, registrar of the corporation and a leading citizen of this town, all three friends of the husband;

"Françoise-Élisabeth Retou, *mother-in-law* of the husband, widow of the late Antoine-Alexandre Davy de la Pailleterie, dwelling at Saint-Germain en Laye.

"Present, the father and mother of the bride, all of age, who, together with the contracting parties, have signed their hands to this deed in our presence:

"*Signed at the registry*:

"MARIE LOUISE ÉLISABETH LABOURET; THOMAS-ALEXANDRE DUMAS-DAVY DE LA PAILLETERIE; widow of LA PAILLETERIE; LABOURET; MARIE-JOSEPH PRÉVOT; L. A. ESPAGNE; JEAN-JACQUES-ÉTIENNE DE BÉZE; JEAN-MICHEL DEVIOLAINE, and LONGPRÉ, Public Officer."

Having settled that neither my father nor I were bastards, and reserving to myself to prove at the close of this chapter that my grandfather was no more illegitimate than we, I will continue.

My mother, Marie-Louise-Élisabeth Labouret, was the daughter of Claude Labouret, as we saw, commandant of the National Guard and proprietor of the hôtel de l'*Écu*, at the time he signed his daughter's marriage contract, but formerly first steward of Louis-Philippe d'Orléans, son of that Louis d'Orléans who made so little noise, and father of Philippe-Joseph, later known as Philippe-Égalité, who made so much!

Louis-Philippe died of an attack of gout, at the castle of Sainte-Assise, November the 18th, 1785. The Abbé Maury, who quarrelled so violently in 1791 with the son, had in 1786 pronounced the funeral oration over the father at Nôtre-Dame.

I recollect having often heard my grandfather speak of that prince as an excellent and on the whole a charitable man, though inclined to avarice. But far before all others my grandfather worshipped Madame de Montesson to the verge of idolatry.

We know how Louis-Philippe d'Orléans, left a widower after his first marriage with that famous Louise-Henriette de Bourbon-Conti, whose licentiousness had scandalised even the Court of Louis XV., had, on April the 24th, 1775, married as his second wife Charlotte-Jeanne Béraud de la Haie de Riou, marquise de Montesson, who in 1769 had been left the widow of the marquis de Montesson, lieutenant of the king's armies.

This marriage, although it was kept secret, was made with the consent of Louis XV. Soulavie gives some curious details about its celebration and accomplishment which are of sufficient interest to confide to these pages.

We feel sure these details are not unwelcome now that manners have become so different from what they then were.

Let us first impress upon our readers that Madame de Montesson was supposed by Court and town to hold the extraordinary notion of not wishing to become the wife of M. le duc d'Orléans until after he had married her.

M. de Noailles has since written a book which opened the doors of the Academy to him, upon the resistance of Madame de Maintenon to the solicitations of Louis XIV. under similar circumstances.

Behold on what slight causes depends the homogeneity of incorporated associations! If the widow Scarron had not been a maid at the time of her second marriage, which was quite possible, M. de Noailles would not have written his book, and the Academy, which felt the need of M. de Noailles' presence, would have remained incomplete, and in consequence imperfect.

That would not have mattered to M. de Noailles, who would always have remained M. de Noailles.

But what would have become of the Academy?

But let us return to M. le duc d'Orléans, to his marriage with Madame de Montesson, and to Soulavie's anecdote, which we will reproduce in his own words.

"The Court and capital were aware of the tortures endured by the duc d'Orléans and of Madame de Montesson's strictness.

"The love-lorn prince scarcely ever encountered the king or the duc de Choiseul without renewing his request to be allowed to marry Madame de Montesson.

"But the king had made it a matter of state policy not to allow either his natural children or those of the princes to be legitimatised, and this rule was adhered to throughout his reign.

"For the same reasons he refused the nobility of the realm permission to contract marriages with princes of the blood.

"The interminable contentions between the lawful princes and those legitimatised by Louis XIV., the dangerous intrigues of M. de Maine and of Madame de Maintenon, were the latest examples cited to serve as a motive for the refusals with which the king and his ministers confronted M. le duc d'Orléans. The royal blood of the house of Bourbon was still considered divine, and to contaminate it was held a political crime.

"In the South the house of Bourbon was allied on the side of Henry IV., the Béarnais prince, to several inferior noble families. The house of Bourbon did not recognise such alliances, and if any gentleman not well versed in these matters attempted to support them it was quite a sufficient ground for excluding him from Court favour.

"Moreover, the minister was so certain of maintaining supremacy over the Orléans family, that Louis XV. steadfastly refused to make Madame de Montesson the first princess of the blood by a solemn marriage, forcing the duc d'Orléans to be contented with a secret marriage. This marriage, although a lawful, conjugal union, was not allowed any of the distinctions belonging to marriages of princes of the blood, and was not to be made public.

"Madame de Montesson had no ambition to play the part of first princess of the blood against the king's wishes, nor yet to keep up hostilities over matters of etiquette with the princesses: it was not in her nature to do so.

"Already accustomed to observe the rules of modesty with M. le duc d'Orléans, she seemed quite content to marry him in the same way that Madame de Maintenon had married Louis XIV.

"The Archbishop of Paris was informed of the king's consent, and allowed the pair exemption from the threefold publication of their banns.

"The chevalier de Durfort, first gentleman of the chamber to the prince, by reversion from the comte de Pons, and Périgny, the prince's friend, were witnesses to the marriage, which was blessed by the Abbé Poupart, curé de Saint-Eustache, in the presence of M. de Beaumont, archbishop of Paris.

"On his wedding-day the duc d'Orléans held a very large Court at Villers-Cotterets.

"The previous evening, and again on the morning of the ceremony, he told M. de Valençay and his most intimate friends that he had reached at last an epoch in his life, and that his present happiness had but the single drawback that it could not be made public.

"On the morning of the day when he received the nuptial benediction at Paris he said:

"'I leave society, but I shall return to it again later; I shall not return alone, but accompanied by a lady to whom you will show that attachment you now bear towards myself and my interests.'

"The Castle was in the greatest state of expectation all that day; for M. d'Orléans going away without uttering the word *Marriage* had taken the key to the mysteries of that day.

"At night they saw him re-enter the crowded reception chamber, leading by the hand Madame de Montesson, upon whom all looks were fixed.

"Modesty was the most attractive of her charms; all the company were touched by her momentary embarrassment.

"The marquis de Valençay advanced to her and, treating her with the deference and submission due to a princess of the blood, did the honours of the house as one initiated in the mysteries of the morning.

"The hour for retiring arrived.

"It was the custom with the king and in the establishments of the princes for the highest nobleman to receive the night robe from the hands of the valet-de-chambre and to present it to the prince when he went to bed: at Court, the prerogative of giving it to the king belonged to the first prince of the blood; in his own palace he received it from the first chamberlain.

"Madame de Sévigné says in a letter dated 17th of January 1680 that:

"'In royal marriages the newly wedded couple were put to bed and their night robes given them by the king and queen. When Louis XIV. had given his to M. le prince de Conti, and the queen hers to the princess, the king kissed her tenderly when she was in bed, and begged her not to oppose M. le prince de Conti in any way, but to be obedient and submissive.'

"At M. le duc d'Orléans' wedding the ceremony of the night robe took place after this fashion. There was some embarrassment just at first, the duc d'Orléans and the marquis de Valençay temporising for a few moments, the former before asking for it, the latter before receiving it.

"M. d'Orléans bore himself as a man who prided himself upon his moderation in the most lawful of pleasures.

"Valençay at length presented it to the prince, who, stripping off his day vestments to the waist, afforded to all the company a view of his hairless skin, an example of the fashion indulged in by the highest foppery of the times.

"Princes or great noblemen would not consummate their marriages, nor receive first favours from a mistress, until after they had submitted to this preliminary operation.

"The news of this fact immediately spread throughout the room and over the palace, and it put an end to any doubts of the marriage between the duc d'Orléans and Madame de Montesson, over which there had been so much controversy and opposition.

"After his marriage the duc d'Orléans lived in the closest intimacy with his wife, she paying him unreservedly the homage due to the first prince of the blood.

"In public she addressed him as *Monseigneur*, and spoke with due respect to the princesses of the blood, ceding them their customary precedence, whether in their exits or their entrances, and during their visits to the state apartments of the Palais-Royal.

"She maintained her name as the widow of M. de Montesson; her husband called her *Madame de Montesson* or simply *madame*, occasionally *my wife*, according to circumstances. He addressed her thus in the presence of his friends, who often heard him say to her as he withdrew from their company: 'My wife, shall we now go to bed?'

"Madame de Montesson's sterling character was for long the source of the prince's happiness, his real happiness.

"She devoted her days to the study of music and of hunting, which pastime she shared with the prince. She also had a theatre in the house she inhabited in the Chaussée d'Antin, on the stage of which she often acted with him.

"The duc d'Orléans was naturally good-natured and simple in his tastes, and the part of a peasant fitted him; while Madame de Montesson played well in the rôles of shepherdess and lover.

"The late duchesse d'Orléans had degraded the character of this house to such a degree that no ladies entered it save with the utmost and constant wariness. Madame de Montesson re-established its high tone and dignity; she opened the way to refined pleasures, awakened interest in intellectual tastes and the fine arts, and brought back once more a spirit of gaiety and good fellowship."

Sainte-Assise and this château at Villers-Cotterets wherein, as related by Soulavie, this ardently desired marriage was brought about, were both residences belonging to the duc d'Orléans.

The château had been part of the inheritance of the family since the marriage of Monsieur, brother of King Louis XIV., with Henrietta of England.

The edifice, which was almost as large as the town itself, became a workhouse, and is now a home of refuge for seven or eight hundred poor people. There is nothing remarkable about it from an architectural point of view, except one corner of the ancient chapel, which belongs, so far as one can judge from the little that remains, to the finest period of the Renaissance. The castle was begun by François I. and finished by Henri II.

Both father and son set their own marks on it.

François I. carved salamanders on it, and Henri II. his coat of arms with that of his wife, Katherine de Médicis.

The two arms are composed of the letters K and H, and are encircled in the three crescents of Diane de Poitiers.

A curious intermingling of the arms of the married wife and of the mistress is still visible in the corner of the prison which overlooks the little lane that leads to the drinking trough.

We must here point out that Madame de Montesson was the aunt of Madame de Genlis, and through her influence it was that the author of *Adèle et Théodore* entered the house of Madame la duchesse d'Orléans, wife of Philippe-Joseph, as maid of honour; a post which led to her becoming the mistress of Philippe-Égalité, and governess to the three young princes, the duc de Valois, the duc de Montpensier and the comte de Beaujolais. The duc de Valois became duc de Chartres upon the death of his grandfather, and, on the 9th of August 1830, he became Louis Philippe I., to-day King of the French.

---

[1] We ought to say that this incident, which occurred in 1848, is interpolated in MS. written in 1847.

CHAPTER II

My father—His birth—The arms of the family—The serpents of Jamaica—
The alligators of St. Domingo—My grandfather—A young man's
adventure—A first duel—M. le duc de Richelieu acts as second for my
father—My father enlists as a private soldier—He changes his name—Death
of my grandfather—His death certificate.

My father, who has already been mentioned twice in the beginning of this
history—first with reference to my birth certificate and later in connection
with his own marriage contract—was the Republican General Thomas-
Alexandre Dumas-Davy de la Pailleterie.

As already stated in the documents quoted by us, he was himself the son of
the marquis Antoine-Alexandre Davy de la Pailleterie, colonel and
commissary-general of artillery, and he inherited the estate of la Pailleterie,
which had been raised to a marquisate by Louis XIV., in 1707.

The arms of the family were three eagles *azure* with wings spread *or*, two
wings across one, one with a ring *argent* in the middle; clasped left and right
by the talons of the eagles at the head of the escutcheon and reposing on the
crest of the remaining eagle.

To these arms, my father, when enlisting as a private, added a motto, or
rather, he took it in place of his arms when he renounced his title: this was
"*Deus dedit, Deus dabit*"; a device which would have been presumptuous had
not Providence countersigned it.

I am unaware what Court quarrel or speculative motive decided my
grandfather to leave France, about the year 1760, and to sell his property and
to go and establish himself in St. Domingo.

With this end in view he had purchased a large tract of land at the eastern
side of the island, close to Cape Rose, and known under the name of la
Guinodée, near Trou-Jérémie.

Here, on March 25th, 1762, my father was born—the son of Louise-Cessette
Dumas and of the marquis de la Pailleterie.

The marquis de la Pailleterie, born in 1710, was then fifty-two years old.

My father's eyes opened on the most beautiful scenery of that glorious island,
the queen of the gulf in which it lies, the air of which is so pure that it is said
no venomous reptile can live there.

A general, sent to re-conquer the island, when we had lost it, hit upon the
ingenious idea of importing from Jamaica into St. Domingo a whole cargo

of the deadliest reptiles that could be found, as auxiliaries. Negro snake-charmers were commissioned to take them up at the one island and to set them free on the other.

Tradition has it that a month afterwards every one of the snakes had perished.

St. Domingo, then, possesses neither the black snake of Java, nor the rattlesnake of North America, nor the hooded cobra of the Cape; but St. Domingo has alligators.

I recollect hearing my father relate—when I must have been quite a young child, since he died in 1806 and I was born in 1802—I recollect, I say, hearing my father relate, that one day, when he was ten years old, and was returning from the town to his home, when he saw to his great surprise an object that looked like a tree-trunk lying on the sea-shore. He had not noticed it when he passed the same place two hours before; and he amused himself by picking up pebbles and throwing them at the log; when, suddenly, at the touch of the pebbles, the log woke up.

The log was an alligator dozing in the sun. Now alligators, it seems, wake up in most unpleasant tempers; this one spied my father and started to run after him. My father was a true son of the Colonies, a son of the seashores and of the savannas, and knew how to run fast; but it would seem that the alligator ran or rather jumped still faster than he, and this adventure bid fair to have left me for ever in limbo, had not a negro, who was sitting astride a wall eating sweet potatoes, noticed what was happening, and cried out to my already breathless father:

"Run to the right, little sah; run to the left, little sah."

Which, translated, meant, "Run zigzag, young gentleman," a style of locomotion entirely repugnant to the alligator's mechanism, who can only run straight ahead of him, or leap lizard-wise.

Thanks to this advice, my father reached home safe and sound; but, when there, he fell, panting and breathless, like the Greek from Marathon, and, like him, was very nearly past getting up again.

This race, wherein the beast was hunter and the human being the hunted, left a deep impression on my father's mind.

My grandfather, brought up in the aristocratic circle of Versailles, had little taste for a colonist's mode of life: moreover, his wife, to whom he had been warmly attached, had died in 1772; and as she managed the estate it deteriorated in value daily after her death. The marquis leased the estate for a rent to be paid him regularly, and returned to France.

This return took place about the year 1780, when my father was eighteen years of age.

In the midst of the gilded youth of that period, the Fayettes, the Lameths, the Dillons, the Lazuns, who were all his companions, my father lived in the style of a gentleman's son. Handsome in looks, although his mulatto complexion gave him a curiously foreign appearance; as graceful as a Creole, with a good figure at a time when a well-set-up figure was thought much of, and with hands and feet like a woman's; amazingly agile at all physical exercises, and one of the most promising pupils of the first fencing-master of his time—Laboissière; struggling for supremacy in dexterity and agility with St. Georges, who, although forty-eight years old, laid claim to be still a young man and fully justified his pretensions, it was to be expected that my father would have a host of adventures, and he had: we will only repeat one, which deserves that distinction on account of its original character.

Moreover, a celebrated name is connected with it, and this name appears so often in my dramas or in my novels that it seems almost my duty to explain to the public how I came to have such a predilection for it.

The marquis de la Pailleterie had been a comrade of the duc de Richelieu, and was, at the time of this anecdote, his senior by fourteen years; he commanded a brigade at the siege of Philipsbourg in 1738, under the marquis d'Asfeld.

My grandfather was then first gentleman to the prince de Conti.

As is generally known, the duc de Richelieu was, on his grandfather's side (whose name was Vignerot), of quite low descent.

He had foolishly changed the *t* of the ending of his name to *d*, to confute pedigree hunters by making them think it was of English origin. These heraldic grubbers claimed that the name Vignerot with a *t* and not with a *d* at the end of it had originally sprung from a lute player, who had seduced the great Cardinal's niece, as did Abelard the niece of Canon Fulbert; but, more lucky than Abelard, he finished his course by marrying her after he had seduced her.

The marshal—who at this time was not yet made a marshal—was, by his father, a Vignerot, and only on his grandmother's side a Richelieu. This did not, however, prevent him from taking for his first wife Mademoiselle de Noailles, and for his second Mademoiselle de Guise, the latter alliance connecting him with the imperial house of Austria, and making him cousin to the prince de Pont and the prince de Lixen.

Now it fell out one day that the duc de Richelieu had an attack of colic, and therefore had not taken the usual pains with his toilet; it fell out, I say, that he returned to the camp with my grandfather, and went out hunting, covered with sweat and mud all over.

The princes de Pont and de Lixen were hunting at the same time, and the duke, who was in haste to return home to change his clothes, passed by them at a gallop and saluted them.

"Oh! oh!" said the prince de Lixen, "is that you, cousin? How muddy you are! But perhaps you are a little bit cleaner since you married my cousin."

M. de Richelieu pulled up his horse and leapt to the ground, motioning to my grandfather to do the same, and he advanced to the prince de Lixen:

"Sir," said he, "you did me the honour to address me."

"Yes, M. le duc," replied the prince.

"I am afraid I misunderstood the words you did me the honour to address to me. Will you have the goodness to repeat them to me exactly as you said them?"

The prince de Lixen bowed his head in the affirmative, and repeated word for word the phrase he had uttered.

It was so insolently done that there was no way out of it. M. de Richelieu bowed to the prince de Lixen and clapped his hand to his sword.

The prince followed suit.

The prince de Pont naturally was obliged to be his brother's second, and my grandfather Richelieu's.

A minute later M. de Richelieu plunged his sword through the body of the prince de Lixen, who fell back stone dead into the arms of the prince de Pont.[1]

Fifty-five years had gone by since this event. M. de Richelieu, the oldest of the marshals of France, had been in 1781 appointed president of the Tribunal of Affairs of Honour, in his eighty-fifth year.

He would therefore be eighty-seven when the anecdote we are about to relate took place.

My father would be twenty-two.

My father was one night at the theatre of la Montansier in undress, in the box of a very beautiful Creole who was the rage at the time. Whether on account of the lady's immense popularity or because of his imperfect toilet, he kept at the back of the box.

A musketeer, who had recognised the lady from the orchestra, opened the box door and, without in any way asking leave, seated himself by her and began to enter into conversation.

"Pardon me, monsieur," said the lady, interrupting him at the first words he uttered, "but I think you are not sufficiently aware that I am not alone."

"Who, then, is with you?" asked the musketeer.

"Why, that gentleman, of course," replied the lady, indicating my father.

"Oh! pardon me!" said the young man; "I took monsieur for your lackey."

This piece of impertinence was no sooner uttered than the ill-mannered musketeer was shot forth as from a catapult into the middle of the pit.

This unexpected descent produced a great sensation.

It was a matter of interest both to the falling body and to the people on whom he fell.

In those days people had to stand in the pit, therefore there was no need for them to rise up; they turned to the box from which the musketeer had been hurled, and hooted loudly.

At the same time my father, who naturally expected the usual sequel to such a proceeding, left the box to meet his enemy in the corridor. But instead he found a police constable, who touched him with an ivory-headed ebony baton and informed him that by order of the marshals of France he was attached to his person.

It was the first time my father had encountered the arm of the law. Brought up in St. Domingo, where there was no marshals' tribunal, he was not versed in the practices of that institution.

"Pardon me, monsieur," he said to the guard, "am I right in assuming that you are going to stick to me?"

"I have that honour, monsieur," replied the guard.

"Will you have the kindness to explain to me what that will mean?"

"It means, monsieur, that from this moment until the Tribunal of Affairs of Honour shall have settled your case, I shall not leave your side."

"You will not leave me?"

"No, monsieur."

"What! you will follow me?"

"Yes, monsieur."

"Everywhere I go?"

"Everywhere."

"Even to madame's house?"

The guard bowed with exquisite politeness.

"Even to madame's house," he replied.

"Even to my own?" continued my father.

"Even to your house."

"Into my bedroom?"

"Into your bedroom."

"Oh! this is too much!"

"It is even so, monsieur."

And the guard bowed with the same politeness as at first.

My father felt a strong inclination to disengage himself of the constable as he had of the musketeer; but the whole of the replies and injunctions we have above reported were made so courteously he had no reasonable excuse for taking offence.

My father escorted the lady to her door, saluted her as respectfully as the constable had saluted him, and took home with him the representative of the marshals of France.

This gentleman installed himself in his apartment, went out with him, came back with him, and followed him as faithfully as his shadow.

Three days later my father was summoned to appear before the duc de Richelieu, who then lived at the famous pavilion de Hanovre.

This was the name by which the Parisians had dubbed the mansion Richelieu had built at the corner of the boulevard and of the rue Choiseul (Louis-le-Grand), thereby hinting, and perhaps not without some show of reason, that the war with Hanover had supplied the requisite funds.

My father then styled himself the comte de la Pailleterie; we shall soon relate the reason for his renouncing this name and title. It was under this name and title, therefore, that my father was introduced to the marshal.

The name awoke a recollection alike in the mind and in the heart of the conqueror of Mahon.

"Oh! oh!" he exclaimed, as he turned round in his armchair, "are you by any chance son of the marquis de la Pailleterie, one of my old friends, who was my second in a duel in which I had the misfortune to kill the prince of Lixen during the siege of Philipsbourg?"

"Yes, monseigneur."

"Then, m'sieur (this was the way the duc de Richelieu pronounced the word *monsieur*), you are the son of a brave gentleman and ought to have a fair hearing; relate your case to me."

My father told what had happened just as I have given it.

There was too close a resemblance between this affair and the one the duc de Richelieu had had with his cousin for the marshal not to be struck with it.

"Oh! oh!" he said, "and you swear that was exactly what occurred, m'sieur?"

"Upon my word of honour, monseigneur."

"You must have reparation, then, and if you will to-day accept me as a second, I shall be delighted to render the same service to you that your father rendered me forty-six or forty-seven years ago."

As may well be imagined, my father accepted the offer, which was thoroughly characteristic of Richelieu.

The meeting took place in the very garden of the pavilion de Hanovre, and my father's adversary received a sword-cut across the shoulder.

This event reunited the two old friends; the duc de Richelieu asked news of the father from his son, and learnt that the marquis de Pailleterie, after having lived in St. Domingo nearly twenty years, had returned to France, and now lived at Saint-Germain en Laye.

An invitation was sent to the marquis de la Pailleterie to come and visit the duke at the pavillon de Hanovre.

Of course my grandfather accepted willingly enough. The two heroes of the Regency held long conversations over their campaigns and their love-affairs. Then over dessert the talk fell on my father; and the marshal proposed to take the first opportunity that offered to place his old friend's son in the army.

It was decreed that my father's military career should begin under less illustrious auspices.

About this time my grandfather married again, and took his housekeeper to wife, Marie-Françoise Retou; he was then seventy-four years of age.

This marriage caused an estrangement between father and son.

The result of this estrangement was that the father tied up his money bags tighter than ever, and the son soon discovered that life in Paris without money is a sorry life.

He then had an interview with the marquis, and told him he had made up his mind to a course of action.

"What is that?" asked the marquis.

"To enlist."

"As what?"

"As a private."

"In what regiment?"

"In the first regiment I come across."

"That is all very fine," replied my grandfather, "but as I am the marquis de la Pailleterie, a colonel and commissary-general of artillery, I will not allow you to drag my name in the mire of the lowest ranks of the army."

"Then you object to my enlisting?"

"No; but you must enlist under an assumed name."

"That is quite fair," replied my father. "I will enlist under the name of Dumas."

"Very well."

And the marquis, who had never in any sense been a very tender parent, turned his back on his son and left him free to go his own gait.

So my father enlisted under the name of Alexandre Dumas, as had been agreed.

He enlisted in a regiment of the Queen's Dragoons, 6th of the Army, as Number 429, on June 2nd, 1786.

It was the duc de Grammont, grandfather of my friend the real duc de Guiche, who entered his enlistment under the name of Alexandre Dumas; and, as a verification of this enlistment, a certificate was drawn up which the duc de Guiche brought me only two years since as a souvenir of his father the duc de Grammont.

It was signed by four noblemen belonging to Saint-Germain en Laye, and stated that although enlisting under the name of Alexandre Dumas the new recruit was really the son of the marquis de la Pailleterie.

As for the marquis, he died thirteen days after his son's enlistment in the Queen's Dragoons, as became an old aristocrat who could not endure to see the fall of the Bastille.

I give his death certificate from the civil registers of Saint-Germain en Laye.

"On Friday, June 16th, 1786, the body of the high and mighty Seigneur Alexandre-Antoine Davy de la Pailleterie, knight, seigneur and patron of Bielleville, whose death took place the preceding day, aged about 76, husband of Marie-Françoise Retou, was interred in the cemetery, and mass was sung in the presence of the clergy, of sieur Denis Nivarrat, citizen, and of sieur Louis Regnault, also citizen; friends of the deceased, who have signed this at Saint-Germain en Laye."

By this death the last tie that bound my father to the aristocracy was severed.

[1] There are different versions of this anecdote, but I give it as I found it related among my father's papers, where this note is added in another handwriting: *The general had this story from the duc de Richelieu himself.* I cannot, then, do other than adopt or rather retain this version of it.

CHAPTER III

My father rejoins his regiment—His portrait—His strength—His skill—The Nile serpent—The regiment of the King and the regiment of the Queen—Early days of the Revolution—Declaration of Pilnitz—The camp at Maulde—The thirteen Tyrolean chasseurs—My father's name is mentioned in the order of the day—France under Providence—Voluntary enlistments—St. Georges and Boyer—My father lieutenant-colonel—The camp of the Madeleine—The pistols of Lepage—My father General of Brigade in the Army of the North.

The new recruit rejoined his regiment, which was quartered at Laon, towards the end of the month of June 1786.

My father, as already stated, was twenty-four, and as handsome a young fellow as could be found anywhere. His complexion was dark, his eyes of a rich chestnut colour, and his well-shaped nose was of the kind only found in the crossing of Indian and Caucasian races. His teeth were white, his lips mobile, his neck well set on his powerful shoulders, and, in spite of his height of five feet nine inches, he had the hands and feet of a woman. These feet were the envy of his mistresses, whose shoes he was very rarely able to put on.

At the time of his marriage the calf of his leg was the same width as my mother's waist.

His free colonial life had developed his strength and prowess to an extraordinary degree; he was a veritable American horse-lad, a cowboy. His skill with gun or pistol was the envy of St. Georges and Junot. And his muscular strength became a proverb in the army. More than once he amused himself in the riding-school by passing under a beam, grasping it with his arms, and lifting his horse between his legs. I have seen him do it, and I recollect my childish amazement when I saw him carry two men standing up on his bent knee and hop across the room with these two men on him. I saw him once in a rage take a branch of considerable toughness in both his hands and break it between them by turning one hand to the right and the other to the left. Another time I remember going out one day from the little château des Fossés where we lived, and my father found he had forgotten the key of a gate: I recollect seeing him get out of the carriage, take up the gate crosswise, and at the second or third attempt break down the stone pillar in which it was fixed.

Dr. Ferus, who served under my father, has often told me that when about eighteen he, Ferus, was sent as assistant-surgeon to the Alpine army. On the first evening of his arrival, by the camp firelight he watched a soldier who, among other trials of strength, amused himself by putting his finger into the mouth of a heavy musket and lifting it up not by, his arm but on his extended finger.

A man wrapped in a cloak mingled among the onlookers and watched with them: then, laughing and flinging back his cloak, he said:

"That is not bad—but now bring four guns."

He was obeyed, for he was recognised as the commander-in-chief.

He then put his four fingers in the four gun holes and lifted the four guns with as much ease as the soldier had lifted one.

"See how easy it is," said he, placing them gently on the ground—"when one is in training for such exercises."

When Ferus told me this incident, he said he still marvelled how any man's muscles could bear such a weight.

Old Moulin, landlord of the Palais-Royal at Avignon, where Marshal Brune was murdered, was also possessed of immense strength. When trying to defend the marshal from assassination he took up one of the assassins, to use his own expression, "*by putting his hand under his ribs*, and threw him out of the window." This same Moulin told me once, when I was passing through Avignon, that when he was serving under my father in Italy orders were given forbidding the soldiers to go out without their sabres, under penalty of forty-eight hours in the guardroom.

This order was issued on account of the number of assassinations that had taken place.

My father was riding out, and met old Moulin, who was then a handsome, strapping fellow of twenty-five. Unluckily this handsome, strapping fellow had not his sword on.

Directly he caught sight of my father he set off at a run to try and slip down a side street; but my father had spied the fugitive and guessed the cause, so he put his horse to a gallop and, catching up with the culprit, he sang out, "You rascal, so you want to be murdered?" Then, seizing hold of him by his coat-collar, he raised him completely off the ground without either urging on or slackening his horse's pace, and carried him thus in a tight grip, just as a hawk swoops down on a lark, until, meeting a patrol, he threw down his burden and exclaimed:

"Forty-eight hours in the guardroom for this scoundrel!"

Old Moulin had his forty-eight hours in the guardroom, but it was not the forty-eight hours in prison that lived longest in his memory, it was that ten minutes' ride.

My father's skill as a hunter was equal to his strength; I have come across veterans who had hunted with him, when serving in the Alps, where, as we have just seen, he had been in command, and they preserved many traditions of his almost inconceivable agility as a good shot.

One example will suffice.

My father had selected from among his aides-de-camp Captain d'Horbourg de Marsanges, commandant of the crack company of the 15th regiment of dragoons, as an excellent and indefatigable sportsman.

He was my father's regular hunting companion.

One day my father and his aide-de-camp left Cairo, by the Nile Gate, to go hunting on the isle of Rhodes; they had not gone more than five hundred steps from the walls before they met a captain of dromedaries, who, sinning against all the accepted codes of hunting, wished success to their expedition.

"Devil take the brute!" exclaimed Captain d'Horbourg, who was steeped in all the hunter's superstitions. "Our day is ruined, and I expect we had better turn back."

"What!" said my father. "Are you mad?"

"But, General, you know the proverb?"

"Of course I know it, but it is a French proverb and not an Arabian one. Now, if we were hunting over the plain of St. Denis I should not say anything. Come, let us go on."

They embarked, and reached the island.

Usually so abounding in game, the isle seemed barren.

Captain d'Horbourg consigned the captain of dromedaries to the infernal regions every five minutes.

Suddenly he stopped short, his eyes fixed and his gun arrested in his hand.

"General!" he cried to my father, who was about twenty-five paces from him.

"Well, what's the matter?"

"A snake!"

"What! a snake?"

"Yes, and such a size! It is thicker than my arm."

"Where is it?"

"In front of me!"

My father took a few steps forward, but although he looked most attentively, he could not see anything.

He shrugged his shoulders to indicate his inability.

"Why, there, there! Can't you see it?" said the captain. "It is curled round and round, sitting up on its coils with its head poised, hissing."

"Well, then, fire at it as quickly as you can, or it will spring."

Captain d'Horbourg rapidly raised his gun to his shoulder and drew the trigger.

Only the priming went off.

At the same moment the snake sprang, but before it had covered the distance that separated it from the captain, the gun went off, and the ball shattered its head.

The serpent fell at the captain's feet and coiled round his legs in its death convulsions, writhing in its agony.

The captain shrieked, for he did not see for the moment the state the snake was in.

When he had recovered himself and was somewhat reassured, Captain d'Horbourg took the snake to Cairo, skinned it and had the skin made into a sword-belt as a souvenir of his narrow escape.

But the whole way back he kept reiterating to my father—

"Ah! General—didn't I tell you that devil of a rider would bring us ill luck!"

As a matter of fact the two hunters shot nothing but the snake, and it could not be described as a good bag.

In the month of July 1843, on my return from Florence, I lodged at the hotel de *Paris*, in the rue de Richelieu, where I received a letter signed "Ludovic d'Horbourg," wherein the writer begged an interview with me to unburden his mind of a dying request made him by his father.

The next day was to be the first representation of *Les Demoiselles de Saint-Cyr*, so I put off the interview till the day after.

General Dumas's old Egyptian aide-de-camp had, on his deathbed, as a sign of his gratitude, ordered his son Ludovic d'Horbourg to give me after his death the skin of the serpent my father had killed so quickly and cleverly on the isle of Rhodes. It seems he had often related this adventure with the Nile serpent to his son, for, amidst the innumerable dangers Count d'Horbourg had encountered throughout his long military career, this one had remained the most deeply imprinted on his memory.

Thanks to this verbal account, I am able to give the story here in all its details.

My father had hardly rejoined his regiment before an occasion for displaying his skill as a pupil of Laboissière presented itself.

The King's and Queen's regiments, which had always been in rivalry with each other, both happened to be stationed in the same town. This afforded a grand opportunity for constant skirmishes between them, and you may be sure such worthy opponents were not going to lose their chances.

One day a soldier of the King's regiment passed one belonging to the Queen's regiment.

The former stopped the latter and said—

"Comrade, I can tell you something you do not know."

"Well," replied the other, "if you tell it me I shall know it."

"All right I the king ... the queen."

"That is a lie," replied the other,—"it is the other way round, the queen ... the king."

One insult was as gross as the other, and could only be wiped out by duels.

About a hundred duels took place during the next twenty-four hours—three fell to my father's account.

In one of them he was cut across the forehead. Luckily his head was as tough as Duguesclin's.

He took no notice of this wound at the time, but it led to grave complications later, which nearly drove him out of his mind.

My father took no part in the earlier events of the Revolution. The National Assembly was constituted, the Bastille fell, and Mirabeau sprang into fame, thundered and died. Meanwhile my father served as private soldier or corporal in provincial barracks.

About 1790 he came with a detachment to Villers-Collerets, and there he met my mother, whom, as we have stated, he married November 28, 1792.

In the meantime the Revolution was spreading throughout France, and coalitions were being formed between the foreign Powers. On August 27,

1791, four days after the first insurrection of the negroes at St. Domingo, Leopold I., Emperor of Germany, and Frederic-William II., King of Prussia, met at Pilnitz and, in the presence of M. de Bouillé, who enjoyed such a terrible celebrity in the affair of the Swiss at Nancy, drew up the following declaration:—

"Their Majesties, having listened to the petitions and remonstrances of their Royal Highnesses Monsieur and the comte d'Artois, brothers of the king, have jointly agreed in considering the present position of the King of France a question of common interest throughout Europe. They hope that this interest will not fail to be recognised by the Powers whose aid has been solicited, and that in consequence they will not withhold the use of the most efficacious means within their power, in conjunction with the undersigned Majesties, for the re-establishment of the King of France in a more stable position, within the limits of the most perfect freedom consistent with the basis of a monarchical government, equally befitting the rights of the sovereigns and the welfare of the French nation. Then, and in that case, their said Majesties the Emperor and the King of Prussia are mutually resolved to take prompt measures with the forces necessary to obtain the end proposed in common. In the meantime, they agree to give orders to their armies to prepare for active service."

These were the lines that kindled the fire at Quiévrain, which was not to be extinguished before the battle of Waterloo.

On January 14, 1792, an edict of the National Assembly invited King Louis XVI. to demand in the name of the nation explanations from the emperor. The 10th of February was the date fixed for his reply. "And, in default of such reply," the edict went on to say, "the silence of the emperor will, after the declaration of Pilnitz, be looked upon as an infraction of the treaties of 1756, and considered hostile."

On March 1st following, the Emperor Leopold died, worn out by debauchery, at the age of forty-five years, and his son François succeeded to the Hereditary Estates.

As no satisfactory reply was returned, the troops proceeded to the frontier, and the regiment of the Queen's Dragoons, in which my father always served (though since February 16th, 1792, in the rank of brigadier), was placed under the command of General Beurnonville.

It was while in camp at Maulde that my father found his first opportunity to distinguish himself. Commanding as brigadier a reconnoitring party of four dragoons, he unexpectedly encountered a patrol of the enemy, comprised of thirteen Tyrolean chasseurs and a corporal.

Despite his inferiority in numbers he did not hesitate for a second to order his men to charge as soon as he saw them. The Tyroleans, who were unprepared for such a sudden attack, retired into a small meadow, surrounded by a ditch large enough to arrest the progress of the cavalry. But, as I have said, my father was a first-rate horseman; he mounted his good horse Joseph, gathered up the reins, urged him on, and they leapt the ditch after the fashion of M. de Montmorency. My father instantly landed alone in the very midst of the thirteen chasseurs, who, completely dumbfounded by such boldness, delivered up their arms and surrendered. The victor piled up the thirteen carbines in a heap, placed them on his saddle-bow, made the thirteen men march to meet his four dragoons, who had stopped on the other side of the ditch, over which they could not jump, and, being the last to cross the ditch, he led his prisoners into the camp.

Prisoners were rare in these days and the apparition of four men leading in thirteen produced a great sensation in the camp. This proof of the courage of the young officer was much talked of. General Beurnonville desired to see him; made him *maréchal des logis*, invited him to dinner, and mentioned his name in the order of the day.

This was the first mark of distinction attached to the new name of Alexandre Dumas, adopted by the son of the marquis de la Pailleterie.

From that moment General Beurnonville promised my father his good-will, a promise he never failed to keep: he used to say when my father was on duty over the general's quarters:

"Oh! Dumas is watching over us, so I shall sleep peacefully to-night."

This was the time of Volunteer enrolment, and France set a unique example to the world.

Never had a nation been so near its downfall as was France in 1792, unless it were the France of 1428.

Two miracles saved this dearly loved daughter of God. In 1428 the Lord raised up a maiden to save France, as Christ by His death saved the world.

In 1792 He roused and inspired a whole nation.

Xerxes, on the rock of Salamis, was not more sure of Athens, when its fortunes rested on the waves and on the fleet of Themistocles; Louis XIV. at the gates of Amsterdam was not more sure of Holland, who was ready to drown herself to escape his conquest, than was King Frederic-William of conquering France at Longwy and at Verdun.

France felt the hand of death pressed on her, but, by a terrible and powerful convulsion, although her feet were already wrapped in her grave-clothes, she struggled out of her tomb.

She was betrayed on all sides.

By her king, who attempted to fly to Varennes to rejoin Bouillé at Montmédy; her nobility, who fought in the enemy's ranks and urged the Prussians on France; the priests, more terrible still, who spread abroad a spirit of civil war, not merely between citizens of the same country, province, or town, but between members of the same family, between husband and wife, between son and father, between brother and sister.

At this period, when French Rome was struggling, we will not say against the world, but against Europe, there was scarcely a house which did not contain its Camille cursing her brother or weeping for her lover.

Oh! it is at such moments as these that France is great, and it is evident she has a true mission from Providence, since she rose up, struggled and triumphed, when all other nations would have succumbed.

All historians refer to Paris at this period as though it were Paris that did everything and sent the army of the Revolution to march to the frontiers.

Of course Paris did much, Paris with its enlistment offices in every public square, Paris with its recruiting sergeants going from house to house, Paris with its roaring cannons, its beating drums, its clanging bells, Paris with its proclamations of the country's danger, Paris with the great folds of its flag of distress floating from the windows of the hôtel de Ville, Paris with the stentorian tones of Danton calling the people to arms; but the provinces did quite as much as Paris, and they had not passed through those terrible days of the 2nd and 3rd of September.

Two departments alone, le Gard and le Haute-Saône, levied two armies among themselves.

Two men unaided, each equipped and armed a squadron of cavalry.

One village gave every single man it had, and offered besides a sum of three hundred thousand francs.

The mothers did more than give themselves or their money, they gave their sons, a more terrible and heartrending travail than that of giving them birth.

Eight hundred thousand men enlisted; France, which had been under great difficulty to raise an army to defend her Thermopylæ of the Argonne and to win the battle of Valmy, had a dozen armies at her command, and a year later began the march to conquer Europe. Frederic-William and Leopold made a grave error when they declared war against the Revolution; had they been satisfied with drawing a kind of protective cordon round France and with surrounding her with an armed girdle, France would in all probability have preyed upon herself. The volcano which threw up such fire and lava would have engulfed everything in the heart of that deep crater called Paris, wherein such days as the 5th and 6th October, as the 20th June, as the 10th August, as the 2nd and 3rd September, as the 21st January, had seethed and burst forth. But they broke open the mountain with two strokes of their swords, and laid bare a channel by which the Revolution flowed out over the whole world.

New regiments, whose very existence had been unsuspected hitherto, kept pouring into the army daily, regiments whose names were not entered on any list.

Only created the day before, they were totally inexperienced, but on they marched against the enemy.

St. Georges had been made colonel of the Free Legion of American cavalry in the South.

Boyer raised the regiment of the hussars *de la Liberté et de l'Égalité* as his contribution.

They both knew my father, and both wanted to have him under their orders.

St. Georges took him first, as second lieutenant, on the 1st September 1792.

Boyer made him a lieutenant the next day.

Finally St. Georges, wishing to keep him at any price, made him lieutenant-colonel on January 10th, 1793.

My father was in reality in command of the regiment, for St. Georges, who was no fire eater, remained at Lille under the pretext of superintending the organisation of his troops (using for his own purposes the money given him to buy horses). Placed, as I have said, at the head of the regiment, my father saw before him a vast field for the display of his sagacity and his courage. The squadrons of men trained by him were noted for their patriotism and their good military discipline. Always under fire, very few engagements took place in the camp of la Madeleine without his squadrons taking part, and wherever they went they left an honourable, and often a glorious record behind them. Once, for example, the regiment was in the van-guard when suddenly it came across a Dutch regiment hidden in the rye which, at that season and in that part of the country, grew as high as a man. The presence of this regiment was revealed by the movement of a sergeant who was about fifteen paces from my father, and who raised his gun to fire. But my father saw this movement, realised that at such a distance the sergeant could not fail to hit him, drew a pistol from his holster and pulled the trigger with such rapidity and good luck that before the weapon was levelled its barrel was pierced clean through by the pistol bullet.

This pistol shot was the signal for a magnificent charge, in which the Dutch regiment was cut to pieces.

My father picked up the bullet-pierced firelock on the battlefield, and it was only held together on both sides by two fragments of iron. I had it in my possession a long time, but in the end it was stolen from me in a house-moving.

The pistols which had wrought this miracle of accuracy had been given by my mother, and came from the workshops of Lepage. They acquired further renown in the Italian campaign, and we shall have more to say concerning them when we come to that chapter in our history.

My father received his commission as brigadier-general of the Army of the North on July 30, 1793.

On September the 3rd of the same year he was appointed general of division of the same army.

Finally, five days later, he was made general commander-in-chief of the Army of the Western Pyrenees.

So when my mother married my father, on November 28th, 1792, he was lieutenant-colonel of hussars; and in less than a year afterwards he had been appointed general-in-command.

It had taken him but twenty months to rise from the lowest rung of the ladder, where he was nothing but a simple soldier, to one of the highest positions in the army.

CHAPTER IV

My father is sent to join Kléber—He is nominated General-in-Chief in the Western Pyrenees—Bouchotte's letters—Instructions of the Convention—The Representatives of the People who sat at Bayonne—Their proclamation—In spite of this proclamation my father remains at Bayonne—*Monsieur de l'Humanité.*

With the grade of brigadier-general, my father was sent to join Kléber at the siege of Maestricht, but he remained only a short time under his orders. Later, in Egypt, Kléber became his intimate friend.

Created divisional general of the same army on the 3rd of September, he was given the command of the Western Pyrenees, and five days later he received news of his nomination from Bouchotte, minister of war, in these terms:—

"PARIS, *11th September 1793, Year II of the Republic, one and indivisible.*

"THE MINISTER OF WAR to CITIZEN DUMAS, General of Division of the Northern Army.

"I have to inform you, General, that the Executive Provisional Council, relying upon your patriotism, your courage, and your experience, has appointed you to the position of general-in-chief to the Army of the Western Pyrenees, rendered vacant by the death of Delbecq. The National Convention has approved this nomination, and I hasten to send you your credentials, and to ask you to lose no time in taking up the post committed to your charge.

"This appointment will afford you fresh opportunities for showing your devotion to the public welfare in beating down its enemies: the zeal for the Republic you have hitherto shown is a sure guarantee that you will not spare her enemies.

J. BOUCHOTTE."

On the 24th, his instructions were sent him.

We transcribe these instructions here, because they seem to us to be important, in that they emanated direct from the Revolutionary Government, at the most revolutionary epoch of that Government, that is to say, on the 24th of September 1793, and yet did not prescribe any of those rigorous measures in which the Representatives of the People indulged in the departments. Perhaps it may be these Representatives of the People had particular instructions, and suffered the soldiers to play the most prominent parts in that bloody tragedy.

We shall see the rôle that was laid out for my father.

"WESTERN PYRENEES.

"PARIS, 24*th September, Year II.*

"Notes for General Alexandre Dumas.

"The Army of the Western Pyrenees is composed (according to article 2 of the decree of 30th April 1793) of the Republican forces that are situated along the frontier and in fortified towns or ports, in the whole of the territory that borders the left bank of the Garonne, including the departments of the Basses-Pyrénées, Hautes-Pyrénées, the Landes and Gers, as well as the whole of the country along the left bank of the Garonne, in the departments of the Haute-Garonne, of Lot-et-Garonne, and of la Gironde.

"It is thought best that the general should go immediately to Bayonne by Bordeaux. He had better interview the Representatives of the People, the constituted authorities and the military heads, as he goes along. He must consult together with them upon every matter that concerns the defence and the tranquil settlement of the portion of the Republic comprised in his command; as well as upon the most convenient means to be employed in making necessary requisitions, which should be demanded in the troop-centres indicated by the Representatives of the People.

"He will reach Saint Jean-de-Luz as soon as possible, where his headquarters will be made. He will carefully examine his staff and head employés of the different branches of the army.

"He will make himself acquainted with every detail concerning his sphere of administration.

"He must examine all books of orders, plans, charts, and memoranda relative to the defence of the frontier and the seaboards. He must give ear to the chief engineer and other authorised personages.

"He must pay a visit to the camps, cantonments, and stations, in order to regulate the order and discipline that ought to exist throughout the service.

"He must take cognisance of the most important passes, ports, and highways, and if they are occupied by the Spanish he must use his best endeavours to expel them and to take possession of them, if it is desirable from a military point of view, and possible without unduly risking the troops.

"Their actual position is in four divisions.

"1st. That of Saint-Jean-de-Luz, consisting of twelve thousand men, with its van-guard stationed at Bruges and its outposts extending from Trouber in Borda as far as Coulin Baïta.

"The main body is encamped in front of the fort of Socoa de Saint-Jean-de-Luz, upon the heights of la Chapelle de Boudagain de Belchéséa, as far as the river Nivelle.

"The purpose of this division is to keep the enemy behind la Bidassoa and to defend the pass of Reza.

"2nd. The division of Serres and of Saint-Plée, of from four to five thousand men, is stationed at Ascain, Serres, Saint-Plée, and Aintroevé, with its outposts protecting Helbaren and Notre-Dame-de-Bon-Secours.

"It prevents entrance into France by way of Tugarro, Murdé, and Ordache, and harasses the enemy in the valley of Bastan; furthermore it can throw forward troops to Souzarde, Espelette, and Itlassu.

"3rd. The division of Saint-Jean-Pied-de-port consists of about ten thousand men, of which two battalions and three Basque companies are at Baygorry, to defend the valley, and one battalion at Anhaix. The rest covers the town, which is a most important pivot. Furthermore, it threatens the enemy in les Bloules, the valley of Bastan, and the road from Pampelune by Roncevaux.

"4th. The division of the cantonments of Pau includes Pau, Navarreins, Oleron, the Basse-Burice, the valleys of Barettoux, Ayret, Ossan, Oevar, and Saint-Savin.

"This division numbers five thousand men, and can be increased by requisitioning the departments of Hautes-Pyrénées, of Gers, Haute-Garonne, Lot-et-Garonne, Gironde, and the Landes.

"Its object is to defend the valleys and to be the reserve from which the whole army should be supplemented.

"The Spanish have a formidable artillery from Fontarabia to Biriatou.

"Their forces, it is said, consist of fifteen thousand men from Fontarabia to Cerdac, and as many round Saint-Jean-Pied-de-port, everywhere intrenched.

"Their military arrangements seem excellent.

"In time of peace, our posts on the extreme frontier were stationed at Andaye, at Saint-Jacques de Souberang, Pas-de-Béhobie, Biriatou, and other places a league from the frontier, in the neighbourhood of the Ruhne, and on the banks of the Bidassoa.

"The great camp to be occupied is la Croix des Bouquets and Andaye, with outposts at Serres and at Joliment, to restrain the Spanish, whose flanks and rear will thereby be endangered.

"Beyond Saint-Jean-Pied-de-port is the post of Castel-Mignon, which the Spanish have taken from us. We ought to try to recapture this, and even the pass of Baguette, which is the way into Spain at that point.

"These items of local information have been extracted from memoranda, particulars of which will be found at the headquarters of the general army and at the engineer's office, with transcripts of the military reconnoitrings that have been carried on along the frontier.

"The general will acquaint himself with these details, and he will direct his operations according to the strength of his active and reserve forces, and to those of the enemy and their positions, taking advantage of every circumstance that may promise an advantageous attack, without running risks.

"He will keep a controlling hand over all movements and instructions given to the troops, and especially over the officers, who shall be suspended if they are not found fulfilling their proper duties.

"Military schools shall be open to common use; they shall deal with all branches of the service: police, account-keeping, and Republican discipline.

"A general officer and an officer from the chief staff shall be specially set apart for this object.

"The general will find the army in excellent spirits, and he will only have to keep it so.

"He must watch and arrest suspected men, who might escape from the army.

"All communication with the enemy must be avoided.

"No one must be allowed to penetrate into his camp under any pretext whatever.

"Deserters must be sent to the rear to some suitable place.

"He must maintain an accurate correspondence with the minister of war, independently of that from the headquarters.

"In short, his sense of patriotism and his courage render him worthy of the confidence of the nation. He will not keep back anything, and he will set his brothers-at-arms an example of every Republican virtue."

It is clear that these instructions had nothing very revolutionary about them.

But when he reached Bayonne, serious differences broke out between my father and the Representatives of the People sitting in that town.

These Representatives of the People were citizens Monestier, Pinet senior, Garreau, d'Artigoyte, and Cavaignac.

This Assembly had gained for itself a sorry notoriety in the south; and when the above-mentioned members heard that my father was coming, knowing his moderate views, they tried to ward off the blow.

On the 3rd Brumaire, before my father had actually arrived, they issued the following proclamation:—

"IN THE NAME OF THE FRENCH REPUBLIC, ONE AND INDIVISIBLE:

"The Representatives of the People within the sphere of the Army of the Western Pyrenees and the adjoining departments, being informed that the minister of war has promoted to the rank of divisional generals in the Army of the Western Pyrenees certain citizens who have not the confidence of Republicans; appointments which have raised a sense of uneasiness among the democratic people of Bayonne; fearing, in the first place, that the *sans-culotte* officers placed in their posts by the Representatives of the Montagnards may be deprived by them; and, secondly, fearing that they will see a recrudescence of intriguers and military spies at work misleading the soldiers; have been impelled to communicate their fears to their colleague Garreau, who has already on their behalf drawn up the following provisional measures:

"Being informed that citizen Dumas has been appointed by the Executive Council general of the Army of the Western Pyrenees, that he is on his way to Bayonne, and that he has been announced by his aide-de-camp Darièle, who has already arrived in the said town;

"Taking note of the fact that when the minister of war made the above-mentioned appointments he could not then have been acquainted with the *important operations* which the Representatives of the People have carried out by means of the Army of the Western Pyrenees;—operations rendered imperative on behalf of the public safety, of which the minister and the Executive Council will warmly approve as soon as they are acquainted with them;

"Also having regard to the interests of the army, which require that nominations made by Representatives of the People of generals and officers who have merited the confidence of the soldiery by their courage, their talents, and their Republican opinions, shall be maintained;

"It is resolved:—

"*Art.* 1. The appointments made up to this date by the Representatives of the People in the Army of the Western Pyrenees, whether that of general in command or those of any other officer, shall hold good.

"*Art.* 2. Citizen Muller, general commanding the Army of the Western Pyrenees, is forbidden to deliver letters of commission to officers who have just been or who are about to be promoted by the Executive Council to any rank in the said army whatever, or to recognise them in the rank the minister may have conferred or proposes to confer on them.

"*Art.* 3. It is decreed that citizen Dumas, who has been nominated general of the Army of the Western Pyrenees by the Executive Council, and also all other officers who shall be or have been promoted to any sort of rank in the said army by the above-named Council, shall on their arrival remain outside the walls of Bayonne and of Saint-Esprit, until such time as the Representatives of the People of this town shall have arrived.

"General la Roche, commandant of the town of Bayonne and of the fort of Saint-Esprit, will see that this command is strictly adhered to. Those officers, however, who were already in the army when they were appointed by the minister, are exempted from this order, and will remain at their posts in the ranks they have held previously.

"*Art.* 4. The Representatives of the People will frequently visit Bayonne to confer together as to what action shall be taken relative to the nominations of the Executive Council.

"In the meantime they request their colleague, citizen Garreau, at present at Bayonne, to adhere strictly to this proclamation, and to look to it that its regulations are enforced.

"Drawn up at Mont-de-Marsan, 1st of the second month of the year II of the French Republic, one and indivisible.

"J. B. B. MONESTIER (of Puy-de Dôme),

"J. PINET (senior), and D'ARTIGOYTE.

"The above-signed Representatives, approving this decree, declare that it does not and cannot apply to citizen Fregeville, general of division so long attached to this army, whom the Representatives of the People have summoned to them both at Toulouse and at Bordeaux. They therefore consider that General Fregeville should exercise his functions as general of division whether at Bayonne or in the army, from the time of his arrival.

"At Bayonne, 3rd of the second month of the year II of the French Republic, one and indivisible.

"Authenticated copy.

GARREAU."

If you would know how these famous Representatives of the People occupied their time at Bayonne and in the surrounding country, and in what way my father's presence was distasteful to them, glance through their correspondence. That will explain why it was decreed that General Dumas should depart outside the walls of Bayonne as soon as he reached the town.

Unfortunately, my father was not the type of man who could be made meekly to go out of a town when he believed he had the right to remain in it.

So he stayed at Bayonne.

This refusal to obey the order of the Representatives of the People led to a fresh proclamation, which was issued the day after his entrance, on the 9th Brumaire:—

"IN THE NAME OF THE FRENCH REPUBLIC, ONE AND INDIVISIBLE:

"The Representatives of the People, in the sphere of the Army of the Western Pyrenees and the neighbouring departments,

"Assured that the Committee of Public Safety and the National Convention are neither aware of the urgently needed reforms which have been brought about in this army, nor of the fresh appointments that had taken place in it, when the minister of war or Executive Council, supported by the National Council, promoted General Dumas;

"And in view of the fact that General Muller has received from these Representatives the position of provisional commander-in-chief of this army by reason of the proofs he has already given of his abilities, of his activity, of his courage, and of his pronounced Republican opinions; and in consideration of his tried experience of four months' laborious work in conducting war in countries and localities where it is impossible to exercise the same methods of warfare as among the armies of the Republic; work which takes considerable time and requires great intelligence in order to unite all the scattered forces employed at a multitude of different points, and to weld them into one harmonious army corps; and finally, on account of his services to this army and of his high moral character, which have won for him the respect, affection, and confidence of its officers and men;

"Seeing that General Muller is still in full enjoyment of this esteem, of this friendship, and of this confidence; that he alone can carry on the campaign to its completion as he alone has the clue to its workings; and finally, that this campaign and war can hardly last more than another three weeks, or even less;

"Considering that General Dumas (against whom, let it be understood, the Representatives of the People have no personal objections) cannot obtain a knowledge of these localities, of the plans and of the positions, in a less period than six weeks, as he himself admitted in the *friendly* Conference which the Representatives of the People have had with him;

"And as order and discipline, harmony and concord have reigned more forcibly and with more marked success since the provisional election of General Muller and the reforms made in the army;

"It is resolved, in the highest interests of the Republic, that temporarily, and until a definite command comes from the National Assembly, General Muller shall retain the command-in-chief of the Army of the Western Pyrenees;

"But it is also resolved that General Dumas be left at liberty to serve in this same army as general of division until a definite decree is received.

"At Bayonne, 2nd day of the 2nd month in the year II of the Republic, one and indivisible.

"*Signed*:

"J. B. B. MONESTIER (of Puy-de-Dôme), D'ARTIGOYTE, GARREAU, CAVAIGNAC, and PINET (senior.)"

My father had obtained the satisfaction he desired.

The Representatives of the People had declared that they had no complaint to make against him, and had withdrawn the clause in their decree that had enjoined him to leave Bayonne.

As to the sanction they granted him to serve as general of division, it may easily be guessed he meant to ignore it altogether.

So he installed himself and his staff in the square where lodgings had been taken for him in advance. Unluckily, all the executions took place in this square.

When the ghastly hours arrived, and all other windows were filled with spectators, my father closed his, pulled down the blinds and drew his curtains.

Soon a terrible commotion began under his closed windows—all the *sans-culottes* of the countryside gathered below and yelled:

"Hah! *Monsieur de l'Humanité!* Come to your windows! Show yourself!"

But in spite of these yells, which were of such a threatening character that my father and his aides-de-camp stood sword and pistols in hand, fearing, more than once, matters would develop into an attack, not one of the windows were opened, not one of the officers belonging to my father's general staff appeared at the balcony.

After this affair, the new general appointed by the Executive Powers was no longer addressed as citizen Alexandre Dumas, he was known only by a name sufficiently compromising at that time—especially among the people who had dubbed him with it—that of *Monsieur de l'Humanité*.

Dispute if you wish, gentlemen, my name of Davy de la Pailleterie; but what you cannot dispute is the fact that I am the son of a man who in face of the enemy was called *Horatius Cocles*, and before a scaffold *Monsieur de l'Humanité*.

CHAPTER V

My father is appointed General-in-Chief of the Army of the West—His report on the state of La Vendée—My father is sent to the Army of the Alps as General-in-Chief—State of the army—Capture of Mont Valaisan and of the Little Saint-Bernard—Capture of Mont Cenis—My father is recalled to render an account of his conduct—What he had done—He is acquitted.

It can be seen that such a state of things could not last: moreover, my father by his resistance risked his life in a far more dangerous game than that of the battlefield.

The Committee of Public Safety replied on the 10th of Frimaire in the following terms:—

"The Committee of Public Safety decrees:

"That the Provisional Executive Council shall immediately send 10,000 men of the Army of the Western Pyrenees into la Vendée to join the portion of the Army of the West which is acting against the rebels of that department and its neighbouring tracts on the left bank of the Loire. This division is to be under the command of General Dumas.

"The Executive Council is to take the most active steps to carry out these orders, and must forward its despatches by special courier.

"*Signed in the Records*:

"ROBESPIERRE, LINDET, RIVIÈRE, CARNOT, BILLAULD-VARENNES, and C. A. PRIEUR.

"Authenticated copy.

"J. BOUCHOTTE, Minister of War."

My father went to la Vendée.

There he found an entirely different state of things.

As soon as he arrived General Canclaux was recalled to Paris under suspicion.

Everything fell on my father's shoulders; and he received the chief command of the Army of the West.

He began his work by taking stock of the men at his disposal, as a good workman before setting to work examines the tools in his hands.

The tools were bad, according to my father's report. If we read it attentively in the light of to-day, if we take careful note of the time it was penned (17 Vendémiaire, year II), we shall see that there was sufficient matter in this report to have guillotined him twenty times over.

It was miraculous that he escaped.

Here is the report:—

"REPORT ON THE ARMY OF LA VENDÉE.

"WESTERN ARMY.

"GENERAL QUARTERS AT FONTENAY-LE-PEUPLE, 17*th Vendémiaire, Year II of the Republic, one and indivisible.*

"*The Commander-in-Chief to the Committee of Public Safety.*

"I have delayed my report on the state of the war and army at la Vendée, so that I might be able to make quite sure of my information from personal observation; otherwise it would have been but an echo of the various accounts which have been told me by persons who had each his own particular point of view. Now, on my return from my tour of inspection, it will be quite another matter; I shall speak of facts which have come to my personal knowledge, and of irregularities which I myself have witnessed.

"Well, to speak plainly, there is no part of the Army of the West, whether in its military or administrative departments, which does not need the hand of a martinet. The battalions have no sort of cohesion. The old muster-rolls are reduced to a hundred and fifty men.

"By that you can judge of the small number of recruits there has been, of the incapacity of its regiments, the efficient portions of which are paralysed by the inexperience of the majority, whilst the officers themselves are so undisciplined it is quite hopeless to expect them to train fresh men.

"But there are worse evils than these.

"The evil lies deeper, in the spirit of lawlessness and pillage that prevails through the whole army, a spirit fostered by lack of punishment and produced by long-standing habit. This spirit has been carried to such a pitch that I have ventured to say it is quite impossible to put it down, except by transferring these corps to other armies and in replacing them by troops that have been trained to subordination.

"To convince you of the truth of this it will be sufficient to tell you that the soldiers have threatened to shoot their officers for trying to stop pillage according to my orders. You may at first be amazed at such outrages; but you will cease to be surprised when you reflect that it is the necessary consequence of the system carried on till now during this war. When once *an impulse to plunder and pillage* has been indulged in, it is difficult to stop it at will, as you, citizen Representatives, know; la Vendée has been *treated just like a town taken by assault: everything in it has been sacked, pillaged, burnt.* The soldiers do not understand why they are forbidden to do to-day what they did yesterday. You will not find even among the general officers any means of recalling the rank and file to a love of justice and more decent behaviour. I do not doubt that there are some who have higher principles and desire to return to a better state of things. Some of these men served in this army when pillage was in practice; witnesses to the defeat of our arms, these men have lost, by their participation in these past defeats, the requisite authority to put a stop to the state of disorganisation I have pointed out; the remainder are lacking in intelligence, in firmness, in proper methods for reducing the troops to order and discipline. Therefore, after careful examination, I have found but few general officers capable of doing any good. Their influence is usually bad, and a deplorable spirit of pillage, of lawlessness, and of license reigns throughout the army. There is no spirit of activity, no supervision, no teaching. One night I walked right through the whole camp without being so much as observed, let alone recognised. Is there, then, any wonder at our recent defeats?

"And this, notwithstanding that military virtues are never more needed than in civil warfare. How can we fulfil your orders without such virtues? How are we to convince these country-people of your just dealings when justice is violated by your own troops? of your respect for persons and property *when the men* who are charged to proclaim that respect publicly pillage and murder unpunished? Your designs and their carrying out constantly contradict one another, and there can be no successful outcome unless this is all changed: to change the system we must change the men. It is above all urgently necessary to support precepts by example, as the inhabitants of these parts have so often been deceived by false hopes and broken promises.

"I shall, however, have expressed myself badly if you infer from my report that la Vendée is still a source of danger to the Republic and threatens her liberty.

"That is not my opinion at all, for I fully believe the war could be quickly ended if such measures as I propose were adopted. These are:

"1. A complete reorganisation of the army.

"2. A thorough change in the staff officers.

"3. A carefully sifted selection of officers intended for la Vendée. They should be able to maintain the strictest discipline and to stop the tendency to pillage, by their tried experience, their intelligence, and their integrity, and, finally, by their own steady and determined conduct.

"Citizen Representatives, must I speak out? So many difficulties confront me that I prefer to make this admission to you rather than fall short of your expectations. I should be proud to be able to end this disastrous war and to help to deliver the Republic at last from the perils with which it is threatened; but desire for glory does not make me blind to facts; the materials at my disposal are not adequate to satisfy your views, to reorganise the army, to make up for the inefficiency of the general officers, to restore the confidence of the inhabitants of the revolted provinces; in short, to rouse new life and infuse a better spirit all round.

"Whilst, therefore, matters remain in this condition it will be quite impossible for me to respond to your hopes and to assure you of a speedy termination to the war in la Vendée."

Could not the reader fancy he was studying the report of an old Roman warrior of the time of Regulus or of Cato the Elder, who had had to be sent into a revolted province as a result of the proconsulship of a Calpurnius Piso or a Verres?

This report was equivalent to a resignation, and, considering the spirit of the time, seemed pretty certain to lead to that end; but some good genius always seemed to protect my father; and, instead of forfeiting his head as the penalty for declaring such terrible truths, he was made commander-in-chief of the Army of the Alps on 2nd Nivôse, year II. He took up his new command on the 2nd of the following Pluviôse.

Let us here say a few words about the situation of the Alpine army at the time my father was appointed commander-in-chief.

In the first place, the defeats of Quiévrain and of Marchain and the taking of Longwy and the bombardment of Lille were such comparatively ancient history as to have been almost forgotten. At the end of a year France, who had been so near a foreign invasion, had carried war into the enemy's territory. Belgium was entirely conquered; our soldiers were examining the mountains of the Savoy which they were soon to scale; and our old enemy Austria was already threatened on the one hand by Germany and on the other by Italy.

Three fresh enemies, England, Spain and Holland, rose against us, in response to Francis's and Frederic William's cry of distress. The old Allies, who had placed the old monarchy within an ace of destruction at Fontenoy and at Rosbach, threatened the young Republic; but, as we have said, to the chant of *la Marseillaise*, a miracle was wrought, the whole of France rose simultaneously, and seven armies confronted their enemies on all sides.

When the Prussians had penetrated as far as la Champagne and the Austrians had invaded Flanders, the King of Sardinia made sure that France was lost; he did not hesitate to join the Coalition and to prepare his army for war. The Government, alarmed by these demonstrations, sent General Montesquiou South to prospect. He had not been there a month before, becoming convinced that France ought to reckon the King of Sardinia henceforth among her enemies, he sent the Government a plan for the invasion of Savoy. After untold difficulties, including even a temporary disgrace, General Montesquiou received orders to put his project into execution. He transported his camp to Abrelles, and ordered General Anselme, who was in command of the camp of Var, to make ready to invade the district of Nice towards the end of September, and to combine his forces with those of the fleet then under the command of Admiral Truguet at the port of Toulon.

As soon as the Piedmontese were aware of our preparations to invade, they hastened to make ready for our attack. Three forts had been built, one near Champareille, and the other two at Miaux. Montesquiou allowed these preparations to grow and intrenchments to be thrown up. Then, just when he knew the Piedmontese were about to mount guns in them, he sent Major-General Laroque with the 2nd battalion of light infantry and some grenadiers to take them by surprise. The Piedmontese, whose preparations for defence were not yet complete, made no attempt to resist the attack, and, abandoning the half-finished fortifications which they had raised with such labour, they fled without firing a single shot. The evacuation of the bridges, the marches from Bellegarde and Nôtre-Dame-de-Miaux and Apremont, were the result of this retreat. The French followed the Piedmontese a half-day's march behind. Montmeillan opened its gates.

Public opinion, checked until now by the Sardinian occupation, began to wake up. The French were welcomed on all sides as liberators. The Piedmontese fled to the sound of the cheering which greeted the tricoloured flag. Deputations from all the villages hurried up to General Montesquiou; his march was a triumphal procession; deputies came to him even to the château des Marches to bring him the keys of Chambéry, and the next day he entered the town with an escort of a hundred cavalry, eight companies of grenadiers and four pieces of cannon. There a grand banquet awaited him, his staff, and his soldiers, given by the Municipal Council.

Savoy was now incorporated into France under the name of the department of Mont-Blanc, a title retained until 1814. This first conquest was brought about without the firing of a single rifle—solely by the superiority of the tactics of the French general over those of his enemy.

In the meantime, General Anselme took possession of the district of Nice and added the department of the Alpes-Maritimes to France; the principality of Monaco soon followed.

But here the French invasion ended. Civil war began to rage at home. Jean Chouan had raised la Vendée by his nocturnal whisperings; the scaffold, ever ready in the squares of Revolutionary towns, claimed its ghastly toll; General Montesquiou was proscribed by the Convention, but succeeded in escaping to Switzerland, where he found refuge. Anselme was arrested and beheaded for the conquest of Nice. Biron took his place, and followed him to the scaffold. Finally Kellermann, whom my father was to succeed, took a turn as commander-in-chief in a post known to be under suspicion, and more dangerous than grapeshot; but Kellermann soon found himself between the Piedmontese army, eager to assume the offensive, and Lyon, which was in a state of revolt. He kept his eyes on Italy and France alternately, and divided his small army into two corps, leaving one under General Brunet's command, and leading the other up to the walls of Lyon himself.

Directly the Piedmontese discovered Kellermann's departure, they took advantage of the reduced numbers of the French troops, and fell upon them with 25,000 men. For eighteen days that handful of brave men fought incessantly, only falling back step by step, losing but a matter of twenty leagues of ground, and saving all their magazines.

However, General Brunet could not hold out much longer, and he notified his position to Kellermann. Kellermann immediately raised the siege of Lyon, and joined the army with a reinforcement of three thousand men, bringing up the total of his forces to eight thousand men. He placed three hundred of the National Guards in the second line, and with these trifling numbers he began the attack on 13th September 1793.

His plan of attack was most cleverly contrived, and was carried into execution with equal skill by his lieutenants and men. It was a complete success, and, from October 9th following, the enemy was chased from Faucigny, from Tarantaise, and from la Maurienne; the Piedmontese were driven from post to post till they reached St. Maurice, which they hoped to hold, since they had mounted there several pieces of cannon. The advance guard reached it at seven o'clock on the morning of October 4th; the cannonade lasted until ten o'clock, till the bulk of the army appeared on the scenes with its artillery. Whilst the French guns were silencing the enemy's battery, Kellermann ordered the 2nd battalion of light cavalry to outflank the Piedmontese. The eight hundred men who composed this battalion were accustomed to mountain warfare, and dashed over the boulders, leaped the precipices, climbed down the abysses and attacked the Piedmontese with such impetuosity that they could not withstand the onslaught, but fled in disorder, abandoning St. Maurice.

When Kellermann left this village he wrote to the Convention as follows:—

"Mont Blanc was invaded several days ago by a considerable number of the enemy, but to-day it is evacuated; the frontier from Nice to Geneva is open, and the retreat of the Piedmontese from la Tarantaise will necessitate their retiring from la Maurienne. The taking of Mont Blanc has cost the enemy two thousand men and a vast quantity of money."

Kellermann's reward was a warrant for his arrest and a summons to appear before the Convention.

It was to replace him whilst he went to give an account of his victories, that my father was called to the Army of the Alps.

His first care on arrival was to reconnoitre the enemy's lines and to re-establish the broken communications between the Army of the Alps and the Army in Italy; while busied over these preliminary operations he sent the Convention a plan of campaign which was adopted.

All this time my father was making friends with the boldest chamois-hunters; he made one or two excursions with them to show them that he was capable of making one of their party, and, when he had gained their confidence, or rather their devotion, by hunting with them among the snows, he converted his hunting comrades into guides.

One morning the general left his army in command of General Bagdelaune, took provisions to last several days, and set out with three of his faithful hunters.

He was absent five days; during these five days he examined all the passes by which it might be possible to reach the redoubt on Mont Cenis. This work was no easy task, for the passes could only be examined by night; and the least false step would have hurled a reckless scout into the precipices.

He returned on the fifth day.

Mont Cenis was the strategic point, the pivot on which all his plans had to turn; Mont Cenis, with its everlasting snows, its bottomless abysses, and its impracticable paths, was reckoned impregnable.

As he re-entered the camp my father remarked:

"In a month Mont Cenis will be ours."

It should be pointed out that the men who had to second him in this enterprise were used to mountain warfare; they stuck at nothing short of the impossible; now they were about to overcome the impossible: the soldiers would have to pass where no mountaineer had ever passed, paths whose snows the foot of man had never trodden, where only the hoofs of chamois or the eagle's talons had pressed.

My father had three thousand iron *crampons* (frost-nails) made for distribution among his soldiers, and they were bidden to practise the use of these in crossing the most difficult places.

Spring came, and with it the possibility of action; but the Piedmontese too had been busy, and were preparing to give their enemies a warm reception. Mont Cenis, the Valaisan, and the Little St. Bernard bristled with guns. My father decided he must begin by seizing St. Bernard and the Valaisan. The enemy he wanted to get at were bivouacking among the clouds. It was a war with Titans: and the heavens had to be climbed.

On the evening of April 24th General Bagdelaune received instructions to scale the Little St. Bernard and to be ready by daybreak to attack it.

My father reserved Mont Valaisan to himself.

General Bagdelaune set out at nine at night; he marched for six hours in the region of precipices without the least sign of paths, trusting in guides who themselves several times got confused in the darkness and misled our soldiers. At last, at break of day, they reached the redoubt, and attacked it with that courage and fury of which his men had so many times before given proof; but the redoubt was a hard nut to crack. The mountain seemed like a flaming volcano; three times Bagdelaune rallied his men to the attack and three times they were driven back. Suddenly the muzzles of the cannon of an outlying fort, which my father had just stormed, were turned on them; a hail of bullets overwhelmed the defenders of St. Bernard; my father had been the first to succeed in his enterprise, he had turned the Piedmontese cannon against themselves. Mont Valaisan, which should have protected St. Bernard, now destroyed it. The French, seeing the help that had so unexpectedly come to them, made a fourth dash. The Piedmontese, intimidated by this effectual diversion, did not even attempt to offer resistance, but fled on all sides; General Bagdelaune sent two battalions of new recruits from the Côte d'Or with the 2nd battalion of light infantry in pursuit of them; for three leagues the Piedmontese were followed and hunted down like chamois in bloody tracks; twenty pieces of cannon, six howitzers, thirteen pieces of mountain artillery, two hundred muskets, and two hundred prisoners were the trophies from this twofold victory.

But there was still Mont Cenis to take.

The possession of this last redoubt would complete the effective occupation of the whole of the Savoy, and to gain it the commander-in-chief of the Army of the Alps concentrated all his attention. The Piedmontese would thus be cut off from all means of pouring down the defiles into this duchy at their own sweet will, and they would be compelled to camp in the plains of Piedmont.

Several attempts had been already made and proved abortive; in one of these attempts, tried in the month of February, General Sarret had lost his life. His foot slipped, and he fell to the bottom of a precipice, where his body was buried beneath the snows.

This accident had suggested to my father the precaution of having crampons made for himself and his men.

Mont Cenis was only assailable from three sides; the fourth was so well defended by Nature that the Piedmontese simply protected it by a stockade.

To get up from this side meant a climb from the very bottom of a precipice.

My father made a pretence of attacking the other three sides; then, on the 19th Floréal (8th of May), he set out at night with three hundred men.

He had to turn the mountain, climb the inaccessible rock-side, and give the signal for attack to the other corps by his own attack.

Before beginning the ascent my father showed his men the rock they had to climb.

"Understand beforehand," he said, "that any man who slips is a dead man, for nothing can save him if he falls from such a height. It will therefore be useless to call for help; his cry will not save him, and may imperil the enterprise by giving the alarm."

Three men fell; their bodies were heard bounding from rock to rock; but no cry, not a groan, not a murmur, escaped them.

The climbers reached the plateau. Although it was a dark night, the long line of soldiers, clothed in blue uniforms, could have been perceived outlined against the snow from the fort. But my father had foreseen this contingency; each man had a cotton cap and a shirt rolled up in his knapsack.

This was the ordinary dress my father adopted at night when he hunted chamois.

They reached the foot of the palisade without having roused a single challenge. The men began climbing the palisades as soon as they reached them; but thanks to my father's herculean strength he thought of a better and quieter way—namely, to take each man by the seat of his trousers and the collar of his coat and throw him over the palisades. The snow would break the fall, and also deaden the noise. Surprised out of their sleep, and seeing the French soldiers in their midst without knowing how they had come there, the Piedmontese hardly offered any resistance.

So just a month to the day, after it had been predicted, Mont Cenis became ours!

Whilst my father was taking Mont Cenis, another column of the Army of the Alps crossed the pass of Argentière, near Barcelonnette, seized the post at the Barricades, invaded the valley of la Hure, and thereby put the Army of the Alps in close connection with the Army of Italy, the extreme left arm of which had advanced as far as the little village of Isola, near San-Dalmatio-Salvatico.

My father had just reached the stage at which the commanding generals of the Army of the Alps were recalled to be guillotined.

He expected this reward, and he was not therefore surprised to receive this communication:—

6th Messidor, Year II.

"CITIZEN GENERAL,—You are commanded to leave the Army of the Alps instantly and to present yourself in Paris, to answer the accusations which are being made against you."

"COLLOT D'HERBOIS."

The accusations, or rather the accusation, which my father had to answer was this:

My father had entered the little village of St. Maurice in mid-winter.

The first thing he saw in the open square of the village was a guillotine ready prepared for an execution.

He was informed that four wretched men were going to be executed for trying to steal and smelt down the church clock.

The crime did not seem to my father deserving of the penalty of death, and he turned to Captain Dermoncourt—the same who was soon to become his aide-de-camp:—

"Dermoncourt," he said to him, "it is horribly cold, as you can see and feel for yourself; we may not find any wood where we are going, let that devilish red-coloured machine you see there be pulled down and taken away to make firewood for us."

Dermoncourt, accustomed to implicit obedience, obeyed implicitly.

This proceeding, put into execution with truly military rapidity, very much embarrassed the executioner, who had four men to guillotine and no longer a guillotine to do it with.

My father, perceiving the poor man's dilemma, took pity on him, relieved him of his four prisoners, gave him a quittance for them, and let them go, with the advice to flee to the mountains as fast as their legs could carry them.

It need hardly be said that the prisoners did not wait for a second bidding.

By nothing short of a miracle my father escaped paying for the four heads he had saved by his own; but, thanks to his conquest of the St. Bernard, of Valaisan, and of Mont Cenis, he was pardoned for this insult to patriotism.

But the nickname of "M. de l'Humanité" was now more applicable than ever, and was more often than ever applied to him.

I have already said how lucky my father was.

CHAPTER VI

The result of a sword-stroke across the head—St. Georges and the remounts—The quarrel he sought with my father—My father is transferred to the Army of Sambre-et-Meuse—He hands in his resignation and returns to Villers-Cotterets—A retrospect over what had happened at home and abroad during the four years that had just elapsed.

My father was glad enough to find himself once more in Paris, as soon as he saw they were not going to guillotine him. He had been troubled for long by a wen on his forehead, which had caused him great pain. This wen had grown upon the old sword-cut he had received in one of those three army duels he fought to sustain the pre-eminence of the queen over the king. The wen was found to have adhered to his skull, and its removal meant a rather critical operation.

The operation was very successfully performed by M. Pelletan.

On the 15th of Thermidor this year, an order from the Committee of Public Safety appointed my father as commandant of the military school established at the camp of Sablons.

This appointment did not last long.

On the 18th Thermidor, three days, that is, after this appointment, he was ordered to join the Army of Sambre-et-Meuse.

But before quitting Paris my father had an account to settle with his old colonel, St. Georges.

We mentioned previously that instead of joining his regiment St. Georges had found it more convenient to settle at Lille, where he induced the Government to place him in charge of a remount depot; in addition to this, by virtue of the powers which regimental heads arrogated to themselves at this period, he requisitioned an immense number of pleasure-horses, in which he traded.

The price these horses fetched was estimated at upwards of a million francs.

Although people were not very strict in those days at this kind of peccadillo, St. Georges went to such lengths that he was summoned to Paris to show his accounts. As St. Georges' books were very badly kept, he hit on the idea of throwing the blame upon my father, by saying it was Lieutenant-Colonel Dumas who had had charge of the regimental remounts.

The minister of war therefore wrote to my father, who immediately proved that he had never ordered a single requisition, nor bought nor sold a single horse.

The reply of the minister entirely exculpated my father from blame. But this did not lessen his grudge against St. Georges, and as his wen caused him horrible suffering and kept him in a perpetual state of irritability of temper, he positively swore he would fight a duel with his old colonel.

Brave though St. Georges was with pistol or sword in hand, he much preferred to choose his own duels. Fortunately or unfortunately, this one was noised abroad. My father called three times at St. Georges' house without finding him at home; he called again another three times, each time leaving his card. At length he wrote such a pressing threat in pencil on the last of these cards, that, the day but one after he had undergone his operation, my father, who was in bed and nursed by Dermoncourt (the captain who had turned the guillotine of St. Maurice into faggots), received a visit from St. Georges, who, on being told that the invalid was ill in bed, was about to leave his card and withdraw, when Dermoncourt, who had heard a great deal about him, seeing a magnificent specimen of a mulatto, who stuttered in his talk, recognised St. Georges, and ran after him.

"Ah! M. de St. Georges," he exclaimed, "is it you? Do not go away, I beseech you; for, ill though he is, the general is quite capable of running after you, so anxious is he to see you."

St. Georges at once made up his mind what part to play.

"Oh! dear good Dumas!" he cried. "I know how very much he longs to see me; and I him. We were always such great friends. Where is he? where is he?"

And darting into the room he flung himself upon the bed, clasped my father in his arms and hugged him almost to suffocation.

My father endeavoured to speak, but St. Georges did not give him time.

"Ah!—and you wanted then to kill me, Dumas?" he said. "To kill me—me? To kill St. Georges? Is it possible? Why, you are my own son! Were St. Georges dead, no other man but you could replace him. Be quick and get up! Order me a cutlet, and let there be an end to all this nonsense."

At first my father was strongly inclined to pursue the quarrel to the bitter end; but what could you say to a man who threw himself on your bed, embraced you, called you his son, and invited himself to lunch?

My father held out his hand and said:

"Ah! you ruffian, you may well be pleased to call me your successor instead of being the successor of the former minister of war; for I promise you I would have hung you!"

"Oh! but surely you would have guillotined me," said St. Georges, laughing at the wrong side of his mouth.

"Not a bit of it, not a bit of it! Only honest folk are guillotined nowadays; thieves are hung."

"Now tell me frankly what were your intentions in coming to see me?" said St. Georges.

"First of all to find you."

"Certainly, but what next?"

"Next?"

"Yes."

"I should have gone into the room I was told you were in, I should have shut the door behind me, I should have put the key in my pocket, and whichever of us two remained alive at the end of five minutes would have had to open it."

"In that case," replied St. Georges, "you see I was very wise not to be found at home."

But as at that moment the door opened to announce that lunch was ready, the discussion ended and the meal began.

With that rapidity of movement with which the Convention manoeuvred its generals at this period, my father was changed from the Army of Sambre-et-Meuse to the chief command on the coast of Brest; but he had grown disgusted with these factitious moves, and, sixteen days after his appointment, he sent in his resignation, and retired to Villers-Cotterets, to be with my mother, who, a year or two before, had given birth to my eldest sister.

Many things had happened since the 28th November 1792, when Lieutenant-Colonel Thomas-Alexandre Dumas Davy de la Pailleterie had married Marie-Louise-Élisabeth Labouret.

In the first place, to look abroad, a speedy vengeance had succeeded the defeats of Marchain and the taking of Longwy and of Verdun, in the victories of Valmy and of Jemappes. Charleroy had been occupied by General Montesquiou, and Nice by General Anselme. The siege of Lille was raised;

and Mayence was taken by General Custine. Our troops had entered Frankfort-on-the-Maine. Brussels had been occupied by General Dumouriez, and Savoy restored to France. The citadel of Anvers had been taken by General Labourdonnaye, Namur by General Valence. England, Holland and Spain had declared war. Breda and Gertruydenberg had been taken by Arçon. The First Coalition against France was formed, comprising Prussia, Austria, Germany, Great Britain, Holland, Spain, Portugal, the two Sicilies, the Papal States, and the King of Sardinia. The battle of Nerwinde had been lost, which led to the emigration of Dumouriez and of the duc de Chartres. Porentruy was restored to France. The English took Tobago from us. Spain invaded le Roussillon. Lyons rose in arms. Negroes massacred the whites at St. Domingo. Mayence surrendered to the Prussians, Valenciennes to the Austrians, and Pondichéry to the English. Toulon was handed over. Le Quesnoy capitulated. But Jourdan blockaded Maubeuge, Toulon was retaken, and Bonaparte appeared on the scenes.

The year 1794 opened under brighter auspices. Jourdan, Marceau, Lefebvre, Championnet, and Kléber won the battle of Fleurus. Ypres was re-captured by Moreau. A second battle of Fleurus opened up Belgium once more to the French armies. The taking of Ostende and of Tournay by General Pichegru, and the occupation of Mons by General Ferrand, had freed our frontiers and made way for the besieging of Condé, Valenciennes, le Quesnoy, and Landrecies, which were taken—Condé on June 15th, Valenciennes on the 28th July, le Quesnoy the 11th of September 1793, and Landrecies the 30th April 1794. Finally we re-entered Ghent, Brussels, Landrecies, Nieuport, Anvers, Liège, Fontarabia, St. Sébastien, Valenciennes, Condé, and Aix-la-Chapelle. We invaded Roncevaux, that valley of poetical associations. We took by force Andernach, Coblentz, Venloo, Maestricht, Nimègue, Figuières. We gained the battle of Escola, which lasted five days, from the 15th to the 20th October 1794, and in which the two generals commanding were killed; Dugoummier on the 18th; and la Union on the 20th. We took possession of Amsterdam, and the Stadtholder fled to London. We took the Dutch fleet (which was blocked up in the ice of the Texel) with a charge of cavalry. Berg-op-Zoom surrendered to Pichegru. Ross was taken after a seventy days' siege. Holland was conquered; and finally a treaty was concluded between Tuscany and France; which openly recognised the French Republic as a part of the political system of Europe.

Prussia imitated Tuscany's example, and concluded a treaty of peace with France at Bâle. It was signed by baron de Hardenberg and François Barthélemy, nephew of the author of the *Voyages du jeune Anacharsis*. By April 5th, 1795, the two Powers had nothing further to restore to each other.

A third treaty of peace was signed on May 16th between France and the United Netherlands. The United Netherlands ceded the whole of the

Batavian provinces along the left bank of the eastern Escaut, and on both banks of the Meuse to the south of Venloo.

The United Netherlands paid France 100,000,000 florins sterling, Dutch currency, to indemnify the cost of the war.

Finally, on July 22nd, Spain in her turn treated for peace with France; France surrendered to Spain her conquests in Biscay and in Catalonia. Spain ceded to France the portion of St. Domingo which she possessed.

Such was our position with regard to Europe towards the middle of the year 1795.

Now a word about our home politics.

On all sides were signs of arrest and change.

The old world was tottering and dragging down into the débris with it the very people who had undermined it. A new world was springing into being.

The age of Louis XV. was at an end. The age of Napoleon was beginning.

The great event which occupied the mind of France was the trial of Louis XVI. on the 28th November 1792.

On the 7th November the Convention had decreed, upon the report of the Mailhe (Deputy of the Haute-Garonne) that Louis XVI. could be tried and that the Convention should try him. The same day Robespierre demanded that the king should without further delay be pronounced a traitor to his country, a criminal towards humanity, and that he should be sentenced to death to set a good example to the world.

On December 4th it was decreed that whoever should attempt to reinstate royalty in France, or any other power which might assail the supremacy of the people, should suffer the penalty of death.

On December 6th a decree was issued nominating a Commission of twenty-one members, with instructions to accelerate the examination and trial of Louis XVI.

On December 11, Louis XVI. appeared before the Convention.

On the 25th he made his will.

On the 15th January the nominal appeal turned upon these two queries:

1. *Was Louis guilty of conspiracy against liberty and of an attempt against the safety of the State?—YES or NO.*

Out of 719 members present, 683 voted in the affirmative.

2. Should the sentence to be passed upon Louis be submitted to the sanction of the people in their primary assemblies?—YES or NO.

Out of 749 members present, 424 refused an appeal to the people.

A third question was put; vital, supreme, final.—*What penalty had Louis incurred?*

Three hundred and eighty-seven votes out of seven hundred and thirteen replied: *The penalty of death.*

Finally they proceeded to promulgate a fourth nominal appeal, couched in these terms:

Should the execution of the sentence on Louis Capet be reprieved?—YES or NO.

Three hundred and eighty votes were against reprieve.

Three hundred and ten for it.

There could not then be any reprieve.

On January 20th the sentence was declared to Louis XVI.

On the 21st January at ten o'clock Louis XVI. was executed.

The Convention created ten armies to meet the outburst of indignation that rose throughout the whole of Europe: the Army of the North and of the Ardennes, commanded by General Custine; the Army of the Moselle, commanded by Houchard; the Army of the Rhine, commanded by Alexandre Beauharnais; the Army of the Alps, commanded by Kellermann; the Army of Italy, commanded by Brunet; the Army of the Eastern Pyrenees, commanded by Defiers; the Army of the Western Pyrenees, commanded by Dubousquet; the Army of the Coastline of Rochelle, commanded by General Canclaux; the Army of the Shores of the Channel, commanded by Félix Wimpfen; the Army of the West, commanded by Westermann.

At the same time, Representatives of the People were appointed in connection with each army, selected by the Convention, and invested with absolute powers.

Three of the generals we have just named died on the scaffold: Custine, Houchard, and Alexandre Beauharnais.

The Girondists, who had voted with the Jacobins at the king's trial, now split off from them.

On the 18th April a Commission was formed to restrain the Terrorist party.

This Commission was elected on the 18th, dissolved on the 27th, re-established on the 28th, and definitely suppressed on the 31st.

The result was to bring about a total separation between the two parties.

On the 31rst of May the Girondists were proscribed.

On the 13th June Charlotte Corday stabbed Marat.

On August 1st, Marie-Antoinette was accused by the Revolutionary Tribunal.

On the 5th August an itinerary Revolutionist army was created to survey the departments, bearing the guillotine and artillery with them.

On September the 3rd the trial of Marie-Antoinette began.

On the 5th the decree which abolished the Christian Calendar and dated the beginning of the French Era from the 22nd September 1792 was issued.

On the 12th, Marie-Antoinette underwent her first examination.

On the 16th, Marie-Antoinette was condemned to death.

At eleven o'clock the same morning she ascended the scaffold.

On the 31st October the execution of the Girondists followed.

On the 6th November it was Philippe-Égalité's turn.

On the 11th, Bailly's.

On the 1st December the prisoners were reckoned up: they numbered 4130 in the various prisons of Paris.

On March 1st, 1794, there were 6000.

On April 27, 7200.

On April 5th, Danton, Charbot, Bazire, Lacroix, Camille Desmoulins, Hérault de Séchelles, and Fabre d'Églantine were guillotined.

Robespierre ruled without opposition as master of France, aided by Barère, Merlin de Douai, Saint-Just, Couthon, Collot d'Herbois, Fouché de Nantes, Vadier, and Carnot.

On the 16th the following decrees were issued:—

1. That all individuals warned of conspiracy, or who are under suspicion, shall be conducted to the Revolutionary Tribunal at Paris from any part of the Republic.

2. That all so-called nobles and foreigners shall leave the frontier and sea-board towns within ten days under penalty of death.

On the 22nd they guillotined Malesherbes, who defended Louis XVI. They made the martyrdom and holocaust complete by conducting to the scaffold at the same time his daughter, his sister, his son-in-law, his granddaughter and her husband.

The number of prisoners grew and grew. On the 1st May they mounted to 8000.

On the 8th, Lavoisier was executed; and twenty-seven other tax-collectors, whose names are now forgotten, were executed with him.

On the 10th, Princess Élisabeth ascended the scaffold; and, as her neckerchief was pushed aside, she exclaimed to the executioner:

"In the name of modesty, monsieur, cover up my bosom."

She died as she had lived, a Christian, a saint, a martyr.

On the 8th June, Robespierre celebrated the Feast of Supreme Reason. He was the high priest of the new religion. Standing on a platform raised against the walls of the Tuileries, and surrounded by his disciples, he made a speech in which he condescended to recognise the Supreme Being and the immortality of the soul; after which he set fire to two mannikins representing Atheism and Fanaticism.

Still the prisoners went on increasing. 11,400 were incarcerated in Paris prisons.

There were thirty-two prisons in Paris—twenty-seven more than in the time of the Bastille.

A 2nd and 3rd of September was expected.

A 9th and 10th of Thermidor arrived, and it was high time. At Bicêtre the experiment of a guillotine with nine blades was tried. The former machine, it seemed, could not work fast enough. By the 25th, 26th, and 27th July they had only managed to execute some 135 persons in all by means of the guillotines between the Place de la Révolution and that of the faubourg St. Antoine.

The Thermidorians next reigned; their rule was milder, but it nevertheless had its special events.

On the 26th July the two Robespierres were executed, with Couthon, St. Just, Lebas, Henriot, and seventeen other Jacobins.

On August 10th a decree lessened the power of the Revolutionary Tribunal, which the nation did not yet dare to abolish altogether.

It issued regulations more favourable to the accused: they were now allowed to have legal counsel to defend their cases. True, the queen had been allowed two; but they had received orders not to defend her.

Executions no longer occurred daily, and each execution accounted for only a small number of victims.

In former times, when they guillotined the condemned in batches of twenty-five and thirty, the blades grew blunt by the time the last person's turn arrived. They had to fall two or three times before they finished their task; this method spilt such a quantity of blood that it set up an epidemic in the faubourg St. Antoine, caused by the smell of the blood. In the Place de la Révolution the blood flowed into a ditch which was dug round the scaffold. A child fell into this ditch and was drowned.

After the Revolutionary Tribune came the Committee of Public Safety. Here cause followed effect instead of preceding it. The Committee of Public Safety indeed! A name of terrible omen. The Committee of Public Safety might, indeed, have saved France; but you will remember the saying of Pyrrhus after the battle of Siris:

"Another victory like that, and we are lost."

Another Committee of Public Safety, and there would be no France left.

On August 24th a decree was made to limit its prerogatives. Barère, Billaud-Varennes, Collot d'Herbois, and Carnot were turned out of this formidable institution; Barère after having sat there seventeen months, and Carnot fourteen.

On October 8th seventy-three of the proscribed deputies re-entered the Convention. They were proscribed after the 31st of May; they returned to office after the 9th Thermidor. Chief among these were Lanjuinais, who sat last on 31st May; Boissy-d'Anglas, who saluted the head of Féraud on 1st Prairial, Daunou and Henri la Rivière.

On the 16th, Carrier was accused by a majority of 418 votes out of 500, and condemned to death.

On the 2nd February 1795, Barère, Billaud-Varennes, Collot d'Herbois and Vadier were impeached, and on the 1st April they were sentenced to banishment.

Barère took refuge in Belgium, returned to France in 1830, and died in the bosom of his family.

Billaud-Varennes was transported to Cayenne with Collot d'Herbois, but managed to escape to Mexico, where he entered a monastery of Dominicans, under the name of Polycarpe Vareñas. He fought on the side of the settlers against the mother country, twice narrowly escaped being shot, and died at Haiti in 1820.

Collot d'Herbois, an indifferent comedian and poet, nearly always half drunk, mistook a bottle of nitric acid for brandy, and died in horrible agony at Cayenne in 1796.

And last on the list, Vadier disappeared completely, and was never afterwards heard of.

On May 3rd a decree restored confiscated goods to the families of all those who were condemned for *any reason whatsoever save emigration.*

Two families were excepted from the operation of this beneficial law, those of Louis XVI. and Robespierre.

What a strange turn of fortune's wheel it was which subjected these two names to the same punishment!

Lanjuinais and Boissy-d'Anglas marked their return to the Assembly by this decree.

On the 6th, Fouquier Tinville and fifteen judges or members of the ancient Revolutionary Tribune were executed *en Grève* in Paris. Do you understand the significance of that term *en Grève?* Public order was now restored, for had not the scaffold itself resumed its place?

Notwithstanding all that had happened, means for defending France, as we have seen, had sprung up on all sides as if by miracle. France, which scarcely had an army in 1789, had had six in 1792, ten in 1793, and fourteen in 1795.

On the 3rd October 1793, Carnot drew up a report for the Convention, wherein he advocated the setting up of workshops, and suggested that measures should be taken to facilitate as rapidly as possible the formation of divers and formidable means of defence against the enemy.

Science, in fact, placed herself at the disposition of the Committee of Public Safety; she took her part in the Revolution in busying herself about the provision of special methods of defence. She was confronted with almost insoluble problems, and she succeeded in solving them.

France was short of gunpowder, of guns, and of cannons. In nine months the scientific Commission had extracted soil out of France which yielded

900,000 pounds of gunpowder per annum—12,000,000 pounds of gunpowder.

Before the French Revolution there were but two foundries for making pieces of bronze ordnance and four for making iron gunnery; these six foundries turned out 900 cannon annually.

Fifteen foundries were built to turn out bronze cannon, and thirty for iron ones.

The former produced 7000 cannon per annum, and the latter 13,000. An enormous firearms factory had even been improvised at Paris, which made 140,000 muskets per annum, that is to say, more than all the other factories together were capable of turning out previous to the Revolution. There was only one manufactory for side arms before the war.

Twenty factories were now opened and directed their attention to fresh processes.

A manufactory of rifles was founded and set to work; these arms were unknown in France; air-balloons and the telegraph became organs of war.

And, thanks to a new process, hides, which ordinarily took several years to be cured, were made fit for use in a week.

Thus, whilst the Convention was evolving its fourteen armies, science was providing the material for their use; and the members of the Committee of Public Safety boasted loudly.

"These fresh triumphs, and all those which signalised the immortal campaign of 1794, belong to us. They are the outcomes of measures for which we have been reproached as though they were crimes, it is with these successes we pay back to you all the blood we have shed."

These terrible words, so profoundly true, were not uttered by an Attila nor a Genseric, but were pronounced by Carnot.

Yes, you terrible heroes of the Convention, you have wielded the hammer of God and made the sword which was to deliver the world!

What a dark and melancholy creed you formidable Titans reared; you who from 1793 to 1795 piled up June upon August, September on January, Prairial on Thermidor, and who, from the height of the ruins of the monarchical Olympus which you scaled, have confounded all Europe!

CHAPTER VII

My father at Villers-Cotterets—He is called to Paris to carry out the 13th Vendémiaire—Bonaparte takes his place—He arrives the next day—*Buonaparte's* attestation—My father is sent into the district of Bouillon—He goes to the Army of Sambre-et-Meuse and to the Army of the Rhine, and is appointed Commandant at Landau—He returns as Divisional General in the Army of the Alps, of which he had been Commander-in-Chief—English blood and honour—Bonaparte's plan—Bonaparte appointed Commander-in-Chief of the Army of Italy—The campaign of 1796.

Such are the events which took place in the period which elapsed between my father's marriage and his return to Villers-Cotterets, after his resignation as commander-in-chief of the Army of the coast near Brest.

He was very happy, very comfortable, and hoped to be left in peaceful oblivion by the side of his young wife, when, on the morning of the 14th Vendémiaire, he received this letter:—

"PARIS, 13 *Vendémiaire of the Year IV of the French Republic, one and indivisible.*

"The Representatives of the People in charge of the Army of Paris and of the Army of the Interior

"Order General Dumas to present himself at once at Paris to receive instructions from the Government.

"J. J. B. DELMAS,

"LAPORTE."

What, then, had happened in Paris?

We must explain.

The 13th Vendémiaire had taken place. Bonaparte had fired grapeshot on the rebels on the steps of the church of Saint-Roch.

The Convention had settled on my father to defend it, my father was not in Paris. Barras proposed Bonaparte, and Bonaparte was accepted.

That momentous hour that comes, so people say, once at least in the life of every man, and decides his future, had struck inauspiciously for him.

My father accepted the position instantly, but he did not arrive till the 14th. He found the rebels conquered, and Bonaparte general of the Army of the Interior.

This is the certificate that was given my father; we have copied this precious document from the original.

"LIBERTY—JUSTICE—EQUALITY.

"We, general officers and others, certify and attest that citizen Alexandre Dumas, general in the army, arrived in Paris on the 14th of Vendémiaire, and that he immediately joined his brothers-in-arms in defence of the National Convention against the attack of the rebels; who have this day laid down their arms.

"PARIS, 14*th Brumaire, Year IV of the French Republic.*

"Signed:

J. J. B. DELMAS; LAPORTE; GASTON; BERNARD, Aide-de-Camp; HUCHÉ, General of Division; TH. ARTEL, Captain Adjutant—General; BERTIN, Brigadier-General; PAREIN, General of Division; ROINAY, *Commissaire-Ordonnateur.*

Then, at the bottom of all these signatures, in his illegible writing, every letter of which was like a Gordian knot, the man who was going to weld the Revolution by bloodshed wrote these three lines:—

"Certified correct.

"BUONAPARTE, Commander-in-Chief of the Army of the Interior."

He dropped the *u* which Italianised his name three months later, and then signed himself *Bonaparte.*

It was doubtless during these three months that he had his Macbeth-like apparition, when the three witches addressed him, "Hail! thou shalt become commander-in-chief; Hail! thou shalt become First Consul; Hail! thou shalt become Emperor."

The Convention which Bonaparte saved, ended its three years' session on the 26th October (1792), by a decree of amnesty for all the Revolutionary misdemeanants who had not been concerned in theft or assassination.

Then, when it had delivered 8370 decrees, it dissolved or rather reorganised itself, to reappear under the triple form of Council of Elders, Council of Five Hundred, and the Directory.

The five directors were: La Reveillère-Lepaux, Letourneur de la Manche, Rewbell, Barras, and Carnot.

They were, every one of them, members of the Convention.

Each of them had voted for the death of the king.

These Revolutionist appointments caused a rising in the district of Bouillon. On the 23rd Brumaire, year IV, my father was again in active service, and was sent to repress this insurrection—an end he accomplished without the shedding of blood.

From Bouillon my father rejoined the Army of Sambre-et-Meuse and the Army of the Rhine. He was made commandant at Landau, on the 21st Nivôse, year IV, returned to Villers-Cotterets on furlough in the month of Ventôse, and finally, on the 7th Messidor, he returned to the Army of the Alps as general of division. This army, of which he had formerly been commander-in-chief, was intended to guard the frontier and to keep a watch on Piedmont, with which we were at peace.

My father at first wanted to decline the post. In times of war he was always ready, even to act a common soldier's part; but in times of peace he was not in his element.

"Nevertheless, accept it, General," Dermoncourt advised him. "You will be close to Italy. From Chambéry to Suze there is only Mont Cenis to cross."

"In that case," replied my father, "I had better take it."

And he went.

At this time, as we have said, war had ceased between us and Spain, Prussia, Tuscany, Piedmont, and Holland; we were only at war with our two eternal enemies, Austria and England.

On the 17th November 1795, the English, who were vainly expected at Quiberon, evacuated l'Ile Dieu. Sombreuil and twelve hundred French emigrants were condemned to military executions. The rattle of this fusillade echoed as far as London, where Pitt exclaimed: "At least no English blood has been spilled."

"No," retorted Sheridan, "but English honour oozed out at every pore."

We continued warfare with Austria in the north and south simultaneously. Masséna won the battle of Loano in the south, and Bernadotte gained one in the north, at Crutznach.

Nevertheless, nothing seemed to be gained by these victories. Using Barras as an intermediary, Napoleon submitted a gigantic plan to the Directory, which was carried.

The war of la Vendée was tending towards its conclusion, and Hoche had shot Stofflet and Charette. France, therefore, freed from her internal strife and completely settled within her own borders, was now able to concentrate all her energies upon Germany and Italy.

This was the plan laid before the Directory.

When la Vendée was quelled, the forces were immediately to assume the offensive. Our armies of the Rhine were to blockade and besiege Mayence, to subjugate the princes of the empire one after another, to transfer the theatre of war into the Hereditary States, and to establish themselves in the noble valleys of the Mein and Necker.

From this time forward the armies would not cost France anything, the war would defray the expenses of the war.

As for Italy, a great victory was needed to force the King of Piedmont to make peace, or to compel him to give up his kingdom. This end achieved, the kingdom of Piedmont wiped off the map of Italy and joined to France under the title of the department of the Po, they would cross the river, skirt Pavia, wrest Milan from Austria, then break through into Lombardy, and penetrate up to the very gates of Vienna by way of the Tyrol and Venice.

As in the case of Germany (and certainly as well able to do it as Germany), Italy would feed our armies.

In consequence of this scheme, and in order to put it into execution, Hoche was to unite under his command the three armies of the coasts of Cherbourg, the shores of Brest, and of the West, a hundred thousand men all told, to achieve the pacification of la Vendée.

Jourdan was to keep the command of the Army of Sambre-et-Meuse.

Moreau was to replace Pichegru on the Rhine.

And Bonaparte was appointed commander-in-chief of the Army of Italy.

On the 21st March 1796, Bonaparte left Paris, taking with him in his carriage two thousand louis. It was all he had been able to get together, and it included his own fortune, the contributions of his friends, and the subsidies of the Directory.

Alexander took seven times more when he set out to conquer the Indies.

It should be stated that each louis d'or, in the time of Bonaparte, was worth seven thousand two hundred francs in assignats.

Why did Bonaparte prefer the 25,000 naked and famished soldiers of the coastline of Genoa to those grand armies of the Rhine, to those 80,000 well-armed, well-equipped men who had been put under the orders of Jourdan and Moreau, whose command could have been his, had he wished it? Because Italy is Italy—the country of wonderful memories; he chose rather the Éridan and the Tiber to the Rhine and the Meuse, the Milanese country to the Palatinate; he preferred to be a Hannibal rather than a Turenne or the Marshal of Saxony.

When he reached Nice, he found an army minus food, minus clothing, minus shoes, striving with great difficulty to keep to its posts, facing 60,000 Austrian troops and the most famous generals of the empire.

The day after his arrival Bonaparte distributed the sum of four louis to each general, in respect of his entry upon the scene; then, pointing to the plains of Italy, he said to the soldiers, "Comrades, you starve among these rocks! Cast your eyes over those fertile plains which spread out below your feet; they belong to you, take them."

Hannibal had made a similar remark nineteen hundred years before to his Numidian troops, as they crouched like sphinxes on the highest pinnacles of the Alps and gazed with eager eyes down into Italy; and during those nineteen hundred years there had only risen two men—Cæsar and Charlemagne—worthy to be compared with these two.

Bonaparte, as we have stated, had nearly 60,000 men against him: 22,000 were stationed at Céva, on the other side of the mountains, under Colli; Beaulieu, he of the boy's courage beneath his white hairs, had advanced with 38,000 upon Genoa by the passes of Lombardy.

Bonaparte moved his army to Albenga, and on the 11th April he made a dash against Beaulieu, near Voltri.

From this concussion flashed the spark which before eleven days had elapsed set fire to Italy; the young commander-in-chief beat his enemy five times—at Montenotte, at Millesimo, at Dego, at Vico, and at Mondovi. In eleven days the Austrians were cut off from the Piedmontese, Provera was taken, the King of Sardinia was forced to sign an armistice in his own capital, to surrender the three fortresses of Coni, Tortona, and Alexandria, and Bonaparte issued the following proclamation to his soldiers:—

"Soldiers, in fifteen days you have won six victories, taken twenty-one flags, fifty-five pieces of cannon, several fortified places, and have conquered the richest half of Piedmont. You have taken 15,000 prisoners, killed or wounded more than 10,000 men; your courage would have overcome the sterile rocks, had we not deemed the sacrifice useless to the country; your services, to-day, equal those of the armies of the Rhine and of Holland. Deprived of everything, you have managed without anything; you have won battles without cannons, crossed rivers without bridges, made forced marches without shoes on your feet, bivouacked without your allowance of spirits, often without bread; the phalanxes of the Republic and the soldiers of Liberty alone were capable of suffering what you have suffered. All thanks are due to you, soldiers! The country owes a debt of gratitude to you for her prosperity. Conquerors of Toulon if you foreshadowed the immortal campaign of 1793, your actual victories predict still finer things to come. The two armies which recently had the effrontery to attack you, fled before you in terror; wicked men, who mocked at your misery and rejoiced in their hearts at the thought of your enemies triumphing over you, have been put to shame, and they tremble before you. But, soldiers, whilst there still remains something not yet accomplished, your duties are not at an end. Neither Turin nor Milan are ours. The ashes of the conquerors of Tarquin are still being scattered by the assassins of Basseville! I have heard it whispered that there are those among you whose courage is ebbing, who would rather return across the Apennines and Alps. But I cannot believe it—no, the conquerors of Montenotte, of Millesimo, of Dego, and of Mondovi are burning to carry the glory of the French people still farther afield."

Bonaparte next advanced to Northern Italy, and, predicting his future successes by those of the past, he wrote to the Directory:—

"To-morrow I march upon Beaulieu. I shall compel him to recross the Po, I shall cross it forthwith, I shall take possession of the whole of Lombardy, and before a month is past I hope to be on the mountains of the Tyrol, there to join forces with the Army of the Rhine, and in conjunction with it to carry the war into Bavaria."

Beaulieu was, in fact, overtaken. He returned in vain to try to oppose the passage of the Po; the Po was crossed; so he returned to shelter behind the walls of Lodi. A battle, lasting three hours, chased him from his position; and he formed a line of battle along the left bank, defending with all his artillery the bridge he had not had time to destroy. The French army, drawn up in serried columns, dashed at the bridge, scattering all before it, dispersed the Austrians, and went on its way over what was left of the enemy's army. Pavia was the next to submit, Pizzighitone and Cremona fell, the castle of Milan opened its gates, the King of Sardinia definitely accepted peace; the dukes of Parma and of Modena followed his example, and Beaulieu only just managed to shut himself up in Mantua.

It was at this moment that news of Wurmser's advance reached him: he came with 60,000 men, 30,000 taken from the Army of the Rhine, 30,000 drawn from the interior of Austria.

These 60,000 men advanced through the Tyrol.

Let us now examine the state of the French army and of its adversaries.

The French army had entered Italy with a strength of 30,000 to 32,000 men, of which they had lost 2000; nearly 9000 men had joined from the Army of the Alps, 4000 or 5000 had been added from the military centres of Provence and the Var. The army therefore numbered 44,000 to 45,000 men—disposed about the Adige or grouped round Mantua.

In addition to these, two divisions could be reckoned on, drawn from the Army of the West, now that la Vendée was pacified. But these two divisions had yet to journey across France.

The Austrian army comprised from 10,000 to 12,000 men, not including the sick and wounded shut up in Mantua; 12,000 or 15,000 men, the remnants of the various battles fought since the commencement of the campaign and dispersed through Northern Italy, and 60,000 men headed by Wurmser.

The fame of this 60,000 men was spread abroad, and rumour boldly doubled its numbers. This time, so rumour had it, Bonaparte was not only going to encounter an army four times stronger than his own, but a general who was a match for him. Hannibal was to meet his Scipio; people repeated the old proverb, *L'Italia fu e sarà sempre il sepolcro dei Francesi.*

Italy had been, and always would be, the grave of the French.

That is what people said.

Wurmser then, as we have said, had 60,000 men; of these 60,000 men he had detached 20,000, whom he had given to Quasdanovitch, with orders to march by the road which runs along by the lake of Garda, by the tiny lake of Idra and, after crossing the Chiesa, comes out at Salo.

The remaining 40,000 he took with him, dividing them between the two roads which run by the Adige—one portion marched on Rivoli, the others were directed towards Verona.

In this way the French army, concentrated round Mantua, would be surrounded, attacked in front by Wurmser's army, attacked in the rear by Beaulieu's garrison and by the remaining scattered 10,000 men which were being rallied together.

The whole of this stratagem of Wurmser's was revealed to Bonaparte by its very execution.

Step by step he learnt:

That Quasdanovitch had attacked Salo and routed General Sauret, and that General Guyeux was left there isolated, in an ancient building into which he had withdrawn himself with a few hundred men;

That the Austrians had stormed Corona between the Adige and Lake Garda;

Finally, that they were in front of Verona.

On the morrow they were at Brescia. From all these points they would cross the Adige.

Whether doubtful of his chances, or whether on the contrary he wished to show the superiority of his genius, Bonaparte called together a council of his generals; all of whom advised a retreat. Augereau alone, the Parisian soldier, a son of the faubourg St. Antoine, declared that the rest might do what they liked, but that neither he nor his division would fall back a step.

Bonaparte knit his eyebrows, for from the first that had been his own intention; how did it happen that Augereau was of his opinion? Was it boldness or genius? He looked at his head, finely carved but depressed at the temples and enlarged at the back. It was simply and solely from temerity.

Bonaparte dismissed this council of war without openly deciding anything, but, when alone, his mind was made up.

Bonaparte's headquarters were at Castelnovo, almost at the end of the lake of Garda; he gathered as large an army round him as possible, raising the siege of Mantua; he abandoned the Lower Mincio and the Lower Adige, concentrating all his forces at Peschiera, to beat Quasdanovitch and Wurmser separately before they had accomplished their junction.

He began with Quasdanovitch, who was the nearest and weakest.

On the 21st Thermidor (July 31), while Serrurier was abandoning the siege of Mantua, burning his watch-towers, spiking his guns, burying his projectiles, and throwing his powder into the water, Bonaparte crossed the Mincio at Peschiera, and defeated Quasdanovitch at Lonato, whilst Augereau entered Brescia without striking a blow, and General Sauret, ascending as far as Salo, relieved Guyeux, who had been fighting for two days without bread or water, in his old building.

Quasdanovitch, who thought to surprise and beat us, was himself surprised and beaten; he stopped, dismayed, and decided not to engage in another battle until he knew what had become of Wurmser.

Bonaparte also pulled up: Wurmser was the real enemy to be wary of. Wurmser must be confronted: his rear-guard must become his van-guard, and *vice versâ*; it was high time to reverse the position.

Wurmser's generals had crossed not only the Adige, but also the Mincio, in order to effect their conjunction with Quasdanovitch at Peschiera: Bayalist advanced on the road to Lonato, and Lilpay drove General Varelle out of Castiglione; whilst Wurmser moved towards Mantua, which he believed was still blockaded, with his two divisions of infantry and two of cavalry.

When he reached General Serrurier's quarters, he found the watch-towers in ashes and the guns spiked.

Bonaparte was afraid, he had fled. To the Austrian general's mind the calculations of genius looked like fear.

But Bonaparte, whom Wurmser thought had flown, was engaged in cutting Bayalist's army in two at Lonato, forcing one portion upon Salo, which Junot pursued and scattered, himself pursuing the other, which he drove on Castiglione. The Austrian fugitives were caught between two fires, General Sauret being at Salo, and General Augereau at Castiglione.

They took 3000 prisoners at Salo and 1500 prisoners at Castiglione, they killed and wounded 3000 or 4000 men, they took twenty pieces of cannon, and Bayalist's fugitives were thrown amongst Quasdanovitch's.

Wurmser saw his mistake when he had scarcely got into Mantua: he rushed off with 15,000 men at the noise of the firing, managed to rally 10,000 of Bayalist's and Lilpay's forces, and drew up in line of battle.

Bonaparte accepted the challenge, but he needed all his troops; he galloped off to Lonato; in three days he personally inspected and organised everything; he rode five horses to death in those three days. He arrived at Lonato; a portion of the troops in that town were to advance on Salo and on Gavado to settle with Quasdanovitch; whatever troops besides were unengaged he took with him to Castiglione; he gave the command for the various troops to march forth, each to its destination; he remained at Lonato with 1000 men; he took a few moments' rest, and at night he intended to set out for Castiglione to fight a battle with Wurmser at break of day.

Bonaparte had just dismounted from his horse and sat down to table when news was brought to him to the effect that Lonato was surrounded by 4000 men, and that an Austrian bearer of a flag of truce was waiting to demand him to surrender.

With his 1000 men Bonaparte might manage to face 4000, and perhaps to conquer them. But he was urgently needed elsewhere, and he had resource to another method. He gave orders to the whole of his general staff to mount on horseback, caused the envoy to be brought in, and then ordered his eyes to be unbandaged.

The envoy, who little knew with whom he was dealing, was amazed to find himself before a general staff, when he expected but to find a few officers; nevertheless, he delivered his message.

"So, my poor fellow," Bonaparte said to him when he had finished, "you neither know who I am nor where you are? I am Bonaparte, commander-in-chief, and you and your 4000 men have fallen right into the midst of my army; go back to those who sent you and tell them I give them five minutes to surrender, and if they refuse I shall put every one of them to the sword, to punish them for the insult offered me."

A quarter of an hour later, the 4000 men had laid down their arms.

When night fell, Bonaparte was at Castiglione.

On the following day Wurmser was defeated, and left 2000 men on the field of battle, where our soldiers, worn out with fatigue, slept pell-mell among the dead.

In five days' time Bonaparte with 30,000 men had beaten 60,000; Wurmser had lost 20,000 men, killed, wounded, or taken prisoners. He had recaptured the Rivoli road between the Adige and the lake of Garda, which was the key to the Tyrol.

Bonaparte collected 28,000 men and dashed in pursuit of Wurmser, who, gaining Quasdanovitch's force, had still 40,000 men left; he won the battle of Roveredo, entered Trent, the capital of the Tyrol, left Vaubois to guard it and threw himself into the gorges of the Tyrol in pursuit of Wurmser; he chased 30,000 men before him with his 18,000, covering twenty leagues in two days, caught up Wurmser upon the banks of the Brenta, gave him battle at Bassano, took 4000 of his men prisoners, took all his war-material, drove him back upon the Adige, and left him and his remaining 14,000 men no other resource but to retire for shelter within the walls of Mantua, the blockade of which he had essayed to raise with 60,000 men.

This was the third Austrian army that Bonaparte had destroyed since he entered Italy.

Wurmser entered Mantua resolved to defend it to the last extremity, and, to add to his provender, he slew and salted his 7000 cavalry horses, converting the cavalrymen into foot-soldiers.

Then, infuriated at the way his men had been led, he condemned his officers as a punishment to parade the streets of Mantua for three months with distaffs in their hands instead of walking-sticks.

The officers obeyed this singular punishment without a murmur.

Bonaparte allowed Serrurier to blockade Mantua, and, turning back to Milan, he awaited fresh supplies from the Directory, employing his time until they came in founding the Cis-Alpine Republic.

CHAPTER VIII

My father in the Army of Italy—He is received at Milan by Bonaparte and Joséphine—Bonaparte's troubles in Italy—Scurvy—The campaign is resumed—Discouragement—Battle of Arcole.

Whilst these wonders were being performed in Upper Italy my father was still commanding a division of the Army of the Alps: as we have pointed out, since it was a post of observation, he had placed the brigadier-generals Dufresne and Pailloc respectively at the foot of Mont Cenis, and at St. Pierre d'Albigny in the Tarantaise, whilst he established his own headquarters at la Chambre, a little village comprising a dozen houses, situated at the base of a chain of peaks which abounded in chamois. Herein lay his predilection for la Chambre, where, besides, he knew he would meet again one of his old guides from Mont Cenis, a most ardent hunter, with whom he spent days and nights on the mountains.

One night, on his return after three days' grand sport, my father found a letter commanding him to go to Italy and put himself at the disposal of General Bonaparte. This order was dated 22 Vendémiaire (October 14th).

Bonaparte no longer signed himself "Buonaparte."

It was exactly what my father had been hoping for, although to some extent he shared the same dislike felt by his colleagues, who considered themselves experienced generals at the age of thirty-two and thirty-four years, and who objected to serve under a general aged twenty-six; yet the roar of the cannons and the sound of many battles had been ringing in his ears for a year, until he was quite ready to ask for service in Italy, no matter in what rank.

My father reached Milan, October the 19th, 1796.

Bonaparte gave him a cordial welcome, and Joséphine an even warmer reception; she had just joined her husband, and, as a Creole, was passionately attached to anything that recalled her beloved Colonies.

He found Bonaparte in a state of great uneasiness, and very angry because of the conduct of the Directory, which had deserted him. The Austrian generals were beaten, but Austria herself was not beaten.

The troops at the emperor's disposition in Poland, thanks to the promises Catherine had given him, were able to march to the Alps; many troops, too, were stationed to watch over the Danube and to keep an eye on Turkey; moreover, all the reserves of the Austrian monarchy were being prepared for

Italy; a new and splendid army therefore was being equipped in Friuli, made up of the remnant of Wurmser's troops, those from Poland and Turkey, with reserves and recruits. Marshal Alvintzy was charged to take command of this fourth army, intended to avenge the honour of Colli, Beaulieu and Wurmser.

Bonaparte had not more than 25,000 men of the troops which had accompanied him to Italy, or had joined him there, with which to meet this new army; for the Austrian cannon had made great gaps in our ranks, in spite of their defeats. Some battalions had reached him from la Vendée, but they were greatly reduced by desertion; Kellermann, who had just despatched my father, sent word by him that he could not weaken the line of the Alps, as he was compelled to keep a watch on Lyons and the banks of the Rhone, where the Compagnies de Jésus were given over to all kinds of brigandage. Bonaparte clamoured vehemently for the 40th and the 83rd brigades with their 6000 men, and, if they should arrive, he would be equal to anything.

He wrote thus to the Directory:—"I am unwell, I can hardly sit my horse; there is nothing left me but courage, and that alone is not enough for the position I am in: our prestige is regarded as evaporated; send troops or Italy is lost."

Indeed, my father found Bonaparte very ill. The malady of which he complained was scurvy, which he had caught at Toulon in doing a very heroic act, in himself cleaning out a gun with the sponge of an artillery-man who had just been killed; he had neglected the disease, and it was wearing him out; he was frightfully thin, he looked like a walking skeleton with nothing alive about him but his eyes.

Nevertheless, he did not despair; he recommended my father to exercise the utmost vigilance and incessant industry; and, informing him of his next plan of campaign, he sent him to take command of the first division before Mantua.

So, eleven days later, the campaign re-opened.

The fourth hydra-head was scotched; Marshal Alvintzy had thrown bridges over the Piave and advanced to Brenta with 40,000 men.

The struggle was terrible. It lasted from the 1st to the 17th of November; Bonaparte, with 20,000 men, attacked 50,000; once his army was reduced to 15,000; once Bonaparte, discouraged by the indecisive battles of Bassano and Caldiero, addressed the following cry of distress to the Directory.

It was the 14th November; on the 13th Bonaparte had reached Verona after ten days of struggle, not only against the Austrians, but against mud, rain, and hail.

"All our superior officers," he wrote, "are *hors de combat*; the Army of Italy, reduced to a mere handful, is exhausted; the heroes of Millesimo, of Lodi, of Castiglione and of Bassano have died for their country or are in the hospital; there is nothing left the corps but their pride and their reputation; Joubert, Lannes, Lamart, Victor, Murat, Charlet, Dupuis, Rampon, Pigeon, Menard, Chabadon are wounded; we are abandoned in the heart of Italy; the brave men who remain to us have to face inevitable death in the very midst of continual hazards and with inferior numbers. Perhaps the fatal hour for the brave Augereau and the dauntless Masséna is on the point of striking; then, then what is to become of these brave men? This thought keeps me back. I dare no longer court death to the discouragement of those I value so highly; had I only received the 83rd and been strengthened by 3500 tried men, I would have dared anything; perhaps in a few days 40,000 men will not suffice to save us.

"To-day our troops are resting; to-morrow, subject to the movements of the enemy, we will take action."

Here we have the complaints, or rather the gloomy predictions, of a tired-out, discouraged, and depressed man: the strongest of constitutions succumb to such moments of doubt, and experience these hours of despair: after great fatigue the body overrides the mind, the sheath tarnishes the blade.

Two hours after having penned this letter Bonaparte had devised a new plan.

The battle of Roneo took place on the following day, being the beginning of the famous battle of Arcole, which lasted three days.

By the third day the Austrians had lost 5000 men as prisoners, 8000 or 10,000 killed or wounded, and, although still 40,000 strong, they withdrew to the mountains, pursued by 15,000 French.

They retreated into the capital of the Tyrol: 15,000 French had accomplished the gigantic undertaking of fighting against and conquering 50,000 men.

But they had only repulsed the army of Alvintzy, they had not destroyed it, as they had destroyed the three others.

Bonaparte advised Serrurier to continue the blockade of Mantua, to harass Wurmser as he had harassed Beaulieu (Cauto d'Irles), and took up his winter quarters at Milan, a centre for negotiations with all the little princedoms of Italy, which through fear alone became our allies.

About three weeks after, an event occurred during the blockade which was to have a great influence on the course of events of this terrible campaign.

One night—either the 23rd or 24th December, which corresponded to that of the 2nd or 3rd Nivôse—my father was awakened by the visit of three or four soldiers, who brought a man before him who had been captured by one of our advanced sentinels just as he was going to leap over the first barricade at Mantua.

My father was at Marmirolo.

The colonel in command of our outposts at St. Antoine sent this man to my father with the message that he was a Venetian spy and he believed he carried important intelligence.

The man's replies were astonishing. He was in the Austrian service, and one of the garrison of Mantua, which town he had left on account of a love affair; he was just returning when he was challenged and arrested by the sentinel, who had heard the noise of his footsteps on the frozen snow.

Although he was searched all over, nothing was found on him.

But, in spite of the apparent frankness of his answers and his ease of manner during his examination, my father thought he detected certain quick glances, certain nervous twitches, which denoted a man who was not quite sure of his ground. Moreover, the word "spy" when used before him confused him, and made the reasons he gave for his going out and returning hard to believe. Furthermore, when a general is watching' a town of the importance of Mantua, and hopes he has caught hold of a spy, he does not easily renounce his hopes.

But there seemed nothing further to be said: the man's pockets were perfectly empty, and his replies mathematically precise.

Favourite books of my father's were Polybius and Cæsar's *Commentaries*. A volume of the *Commentaries* of the conqueror of Gaul lay open on the table near his bed, and the passage my father had just been re-reading before going to sleep was where Cæsar relates how, in order to pass his lieutenant through to Labienus with valuable information, he had enclosed his letter in a little ivory ball about the size of a child's toy; how the messenger when he came to the enemy's pickets, or to any place where he feared being taken prisoner, was to carry the ball in his mouth, and to swallow it if he were pushed to extremes.

This passage from Cæsar flashed across my father's mind as a ray of light.

"Very well," said my father; "since this man lies, he must be taken out and shot."

"What! General," the Venetian exclaimed in terror. "Why am I to be shot?"

"To cut open your stomach and find the despatches you have swallowed," said my father with as much certainty as though the matter had been revealed to him by his familiar spirit.

The spy trembled.

The men hesitated.

"Oh! it is not a joke," said my father to the soldiers who had taken the prisoner; "if you wish it, I will give you a written order."

"No, General," replied the soldiers; "if you are serious—"

"Perfectly serious; take him away and shoot him."

The soldiers moved forward to lead off the spy.

"One moment!" he said, seeing that matters had taken a grave turn.

"Will you confess?"

"Yes, yes, I confess," said the spy, after a moment's hesitation.

"You confess you have swallowed your despatches?"

"Yes, General."

"And how long ago did you do that?"

"About two hours and a half ago, General."

"Dermoncourt," said my father to a young aide-de-camp who slept in the next room to his, and who had been listening and looking on since the beginning of this scene with the greatest attention, not seeing what it was going to lead to.

"Here I am, General."

"You have heard?"

"What, General?"

"That this man has swallowed his despatches?"

"Yes."

"Two and a half hours ago?"

"Two and a half hours ago."

"Very well, go and find the chemist of the village and ask him whether it is a purgative or an emetic that should be given to a man to make him get rid of what he has taken two hours and a half ago; he is to tell you which will have the quickest result."

Five minutes later Dermoncourt returned, his hand at the salute and, with wonderful command of his features, he replied:

"A purgative, General."

"You have brought one with you?"

"Yes, General."

They gave the purgative to the spy, who swallowed it with a grimace; then they took him to Dermoncourt's room, where two soldiers kept him in view, whilst Dermoncourt passed a very bad night, being waked up by the soldiers each time they thought the medicine was going to take effect. At last, towards three in the morning, he was delivered of a tabloid of wax, as large as a filbert. This little ball of wax was washed in one of those irrigating canals which are to be found in thousands in the meadows round Mantua, steeped in a liquid the spy carried for the purpose in a tiny flask hidden in his waistcoat pocket which the soldiers had not thought necessary to take from him, and handed to my father; he passed it on to be opened by Dermoncourt, who, in his capacity of secretarial aide-de-camp, had to open despatches.

One fear alone remained to them—the despatch might be in German, and not a single man in the general's quarters could speak German.

In the meantime, Dermoncourt was performing the Cæsarian operation on the wax pellet with his pen-knife; and he drew from it a letter written on vellum in such small characters that, when rolled between the fingers, the letter was not larger than a big pea.

Great was the delight of the two operators when they perceived that the letter was written in French; one might almost have said the emperor and his commander-in-chief had foreseen the possibility of this letter falling into my father's hands.

I give the tenor of the letter, which I take from a copy in my father's handwriting; the original, as we shall see presently, was sent to Bonaparte:—

"TRENT, 15*th December 1796.*

"I have the honour to transmit to your Excellency His Majesty's commands, dated 5th of the month, literally, and in the same language in which I received them.

"You will take care to advise Field Marshal Vurmser without delay not to discontinue his operations; you will inform him that I am expecting him valorously and zealously to defend Mantua to the last extremity; that I know him, and the brave officers of his staff who are with him, too well to fear they will give themselves up as prisoners; moreover, he must try to transport the garrison into France rather than to send it back into my realm; I desire that in the event of his being reduced to the last extremity and without means of subsistence, he will take measures to destroy as far as possible anything in Mantua that would be serviceable to the enemy, and, in leading out the portion of his troops that are fit to follow him, to make for and to cross the Po, and then to march to Ferrara or to Bologna, holding himself ready, if the need arises, to go towards Rome or into Tuscany; he will find very few of the enemy in those regions, which are *favourably disposed* towards the provisioning of his troops, on whose behalf, if needful, he must use force, as he would to surmount any other obstacle.

"FRANÇOIS.

"A reliable man, a cadet from the Straroldo regiment, brings this important despatch to your Excellency. I would add that the actual situation and the requirements of the army do not allow of attempting any fresh operations for *three weeks or a month*, without exposing it anew to the danger of non-success.

"I cannot too strongly urge upon your Excellency to hold on in Mantua as long as you possibly can, His Majesty's commands acting as your general instructions; whatever happens, I beg of your Excellency to send me news by some safe means, in order that I may keep in touch with you.

"ALVINTZY.

"*P.S.*-In all probability the next action I am arranging will take place on the 13th or 14th January. I shall march with 30,000 men to the plateau of Rivoli, and I shall despatch Provera with 10,000 men along the Adige to Legnago, with a considerable convoy. When you hear firing, make a sortie to cause a diversion in favour of his movement."

CHAPTER IX

The despatch is sent to Bonaparte—Dermoncourt's reception—Berthier's open response—Military movements in consequence of the despatch—Correspondence between my father and Serrurier and Dallemagne—Battle of St. Georges and La Favorite—Capture of Mantua—My father as a looker-on.

My father's joy was great, and so was Dermoncourt's; the despatch was clearly of the greatest importance. For one thing it proclaimed Tuscany and the Venetian and Pontifical States as countries *favourably disposed*. Moreover, it revealed Alvintzy's intention of taking no action *for three weeks or a month*.

The despatch must be taken to Bonaparte post haste.

Dermoncourt instantly mounted his horse and rode off to Milan.

He reached there the next day but one, at seven in the morning, and dismounted at the steps of the hôtel Serbelloni, where General Bonaparte lodged. He had made part of his journey on horseback and part in a kind of *calessino* called a *sediollo*.

But here Dermoncourt met an unexpected difficulty: the aide-de-camp on duty had received instructions that no one was to be admitted to Bonaparte until nine o'clock.

Dermoncourt grew angry.

"But, monsieur," he said, "you can see clearly by my muddy condition that I have not come from a ball, and why I insist on seeing the commander-in-chief is because I have important news to give him."

The aide-de-camp persisted in his refusal. Dermoncourt grew furious in his wish to see Bonaparte; the aide-de-camp barred the passage; Dermoncourt was a bulldog of the Republican school; he took the aide-de-camp by both shoulders, twisted him round, and passed in; but all this scuffle had not been accomplished quietly, and Dermoncourt found Bonaparte standing at the door of his room.

"Now, what is the matter?" asked Bonaparte, frowning.

"Upon my word, General," replied Dermoncourt, "it is not very pleasant after travelling thirty leagues in twenty-six hours to have to force one's way across the bodies of your aides-de-camp to get at you."

"But what if those were the given orders?"

"If those were the orders given, General," Dermoncourt replied lightly, "have me shot for transgressing orders; only, I entreat of you not to send for the picket before you have read this despatch."

Bonaparte read the despatch.

Then turning to his aide-de-camp he said, "You have forgotten, monsieur, that the order is not meant for any officer attached to the staff who may arrive from Mantua, and that no matter whether they come at noon or at midnight the door is open. Place yourself under arrest."

The aide-de-camp saluted and went out.[1]

"How did Dumas get hold of this despatch?" Bonaparte demanded.

Dermoncourt related the incident with full details.

"Berthier! Berthier!" shouted Bonaparte.

Berthier appeared with his accustomed air of importance and gravity.

"Here, Berthier," exclaimed Bonaparte, handing the despatch to him, "smell that and tell me what the scent is."

"Why, General," said Berthier, "it smells of dung."

"Not so bad that; you have not minced matters. Now read it." Berthier read.

"Oh! oh!" he exclaimed.

"Do you see, Berthier? The next battle will be called the battle of Rivoli, and, if I am not greatly mistaken, it will decide the campaign. At all events, as Alvintzy says, we have quite three weeks before us."

"And as one man forewarned is worth two," said Dermoncourt, "and as even when you are not forewarned you are worth a hundred, there is surely cause for laughter."

"Meanwhile," said Bonaparte, "as you are probably hungry, you had better just brush the mud off you,—don't bother to do more than that,—and you shall breakfast with us. Have you met Joséphine?"

"No, General, I have not had that honour."

"Very well, I will introduce you to her: go and come back quickly."

Dermoncourt did not wait to be told twice. He breakfasted and dined with Bonaparte, who insisted that he should stay and sleep at the palace.

Next morning he sent a letter by him to my father loaded with compliments, and told him he might set off when he liked, a carriage being at his disposal.

Dermoncourt entered the carriage in the courtyard; Bonaparte and Joséphine were at one window, and Berthier at the next.

"A good journey to you!" cried Bonaparte to Dermoncourt.

"Thank you, General," he replied; "do not forget the 13th of January, and be careful with those delicacies of Capua."

"Rest easy," cried the commander-in-chief; "I will not act as Hannibal did."

Here is Bonaparte's letter to my father:—

"ARMY OF ITALY—THE FRENCH REPUBLIC.

"*Liberty—Equality.*

"FROM THE HEADQUARTERS AT MILAN, 7 *Nivôse* (*Sunday, 28th December*), *Year V of the Republic, one and indivisible.*

"BONAPARTE, Commander-in-Chief of the Army of Italy, to GENERAL DUMAS.

"I am in receipt of the letter brought[2] me by your aide-de-camp; it would have been impossible to have acquired more opportune or more valuable information. You will receive an order to the effect that all the inhabitants of the countryside are to be sent a league away from Mantua; I do not doubt that you will faithfully carry out this order; although somewhat harsh, it is extremely necessary.

"I give this order because precautions are being taken on the other side of the Po; this project from the Court of Vienna seems to me very mad. I beg you to send the spy you have arrested under a good escort to Milan.

"I congratulate you on your good fortune and augur better to come.

BONAPARTE."

It will be seen that, though a year had hardly elapsed, after the battles of Montenotte, Millesimo, Dego, Mondovi, Lonato, Castiglione, and Arcole, Bonaparte recognised so clearly that his fate was bound up with that of France that he suppressed the *u* in his name.

Dermoncourt reached my father's camp, and gave him the commander-in-chief's letter; my father read it, and probably the observation we make in the light of to-day did not then occur to him, namely, that by suppressing the *u* Bonaparte had suppressed that which gave an Italian flavour to his name.

The same day that Dermoncourt left Milan, the French army received the order to occupy the positions of Montebaldo, Corona, and Rivoli.

On the 5th of January, General Alvintzy left Bassano.

On the 6th, Bonaparte occupied Bologna with 7000 men.

On the 11th, Bonaparte advanced to the walls of Mantua.

On the 12th, the Austrian army gave battle at Saint-Michel and Corona, and encamped at Montebaldo.

On the 13th, Joubert evacuated Corona and took up his position at Rivoli, whilst the Austrians occupied Bevilacqua.

Finally, on the 14th, Bonaparte visited the plateau of Rivoli, which he reached at two o'clock in the morning.

Here it was that the final battle took place, as he had predicted.

We know the results. At eight in the morning 45,000 Austrians invited battle.

At five in the evening they were nowhere to be seen; it was as though an earthquake had swallowed them up; Alvintzy had been wiped out at a single stroke.

There was still Provera to be dealt with.

Provera followed the plan indicated in the letter intercepted by my father; he slipped away from Augereau and threw a bridge over Anghiari, a little above Legnago. He marched on Mantua, which he intended to reinforce with nine or ten thousand men.

Augereau had obtained knowledge of his crossing; falling upon his rear, he took 2000 of his men prisoners; but Provera continued his march with the remaining 7000.

Luckily, Bonaparte learnt these details at Castelnovo. He was about the same distance from Mantua, he had Frenchmen under his command, and he would therefore reach it before Provera.

If he did not arrive, and if the garrison attempted the sortie Wurmser had been ordered to take in Alvintzy's letter, the blockading corps would be caught between two fires.

Masséna's division received orders to march at double quick pace to Mantua, where it should arrive the same evening. The reserves from Villa-Franca were to take the same route and march at the same speed.

Finally, Bonaparte himself galloped off to reach Mantua before nightfall.

Now let us see from General Serrurier's letters to my father what was going on round Mantua, and what action was taking place in the French camp.

"HEADQUARTERS AT ROVERBELLA,

"20 *Nivôse, Year V.*[3]

"SERRURIER, General of Division, in command of the blockade, to GENERAL DUMAS, in command of the 2nd Division.

"MY DEAR GENERAL,—I have just received a letter from Divisional-General Augereau, dated from Porto-Legnago, on the 19th inst.; wherein he informs me that the enemy attacked his outposts with a force greatly superior to his own, and that Adjutant-General Duphot has abandoned the Castle of Bevilacqua, to prevent himself from being outflanked. He will write and tell me the various movements of the enemy that night. All our troops are thoroughly on the alert; but I do not believe the enemy at Mantua will undertake any big action unless its army has a very marked advantage, or unless they try to slip away. As soon as I receive news from General Augereau I will let you know it.—Yours, with all good wishes, SERRURIER."

Provera was the enemy referred to who was attacking Augereau, in carrying out his instructions to march on Mantua.

"HEADQUARTERS AT ROVERBELLA,

"22 Nivôse.

"SERRURIER, etc.

"In consequence of the letter you sent me yesterday, General, relative to the disembarking carried out by the enemy, I believe the means for the defence of the Mincio. I have therefore just written off to General Victor to send to-day a battalion of his reserve to Formigosa, to be held in readiness to send immediately where help is most needed; although I have asked this general to communicate with me direct, I have at the same time requested him to keep you and General Dallemagne informed of all important news.

"The remainder of the 57th battalion, to which you previously referred, will stay in reserve at Goïto.—Yours, etc.

SERRURIER."

"23 Nivôse.

"SERRURIER, etc.

"This is to inform you, General, that the enemy has attacked our lines; they began fighting at nine in the morning. I do not doubt that the garrison of Mantua will aid them by some movement; as we are ready to receive them, we shall send them back pretty quickly within their walls. In event of any emergency, I beg you to communicate with me and with the generals near you; it may possibly be that some part of the line of army will be compelled to yield ground; for this reason it is more than ever necessary to watch the approaches, to prevent any troop or convoy entering the town.—Yours faithfully,

SERRURIER."

At ten o'clock on the morning of the 25th Nivôse my father received this letter:—

"HEADQUARTERS AT ROVERBELLA,"

25 Nivôse.[4]

"SERRURIER, etc.

"I have to advise you, General, that the enemy crossed the Adige last night at Anghiari, near Porto Legnago; I do not know in what strength; but we must be prepared, for it is quite likely we shall be attacked to-night: do not forget, I beg you, to warn General Miollis; tell him to send out a reconnoitring party by Castellaro—or at all events near Due-Castelli.— Faithfully yours,

SERRURIER."

"I have ordered the commandant of the 64th, who is at Formigosa, to fall back on General Miollis, if he cannot hold out. In case of need I shall withdraw to Goïto."

Two hours later my father received another letter:—

"SAINT-ANTOINE,

"25 Nivôse.

"SERRURIER, etc.

"I hazard the opinion, General, that there will be no sortie on General Dallemagne's side.[5] I believe the enemy mean to present themselves in force on Governolo and Formigosa, to make sure of those two bridges and to secure the Po, in order to relieve Mantua. It is quite certain they will not have so far to march if they go there, instead of coming here. But I think we must protect ourselves on all sides; that will not prevent us from availing ourselves of any opportunity that may arise.

"General Beaumont has no cavalry left. I withdrew them all to-night to send to Castelnovo.—Yours,

SERRURIER.

"I am counting greatly on General Miollis and on a battalion I have sent to Governolo. On second thoughts, to save time, I am returning to Roverbella, where I hope to receive news from the commander-in-chief."

My father sent on copies of these two letters to General Miollis, who was at St. Georges.

The day was employed in keeping a strict look-out. My father spent the night at the outposts.

At nine o'clock on the morning of the 26th, he received this despatch:—

"GENERAL SERRURIER, etc.

"I advise you that the enemy is appearing on the Due-Castelli side.

"Issue your orders in accordance with this.—Yours,

"SERRURIER.

"ROVERBELLA, 26 *Nivôse.*"

Two hours later he received this second letter:—

"SERRURIER, etc.

"It is imperative, General, that you should prevent the enemy from disembarking: to effect this, take as many as 1500 men to that quarter.

"We are not short of troops at present, so do not be anxious.—Yours,

SERRURIER.

"*26 Nivôse*, ROVERBELLA."

If 1500 men had to be taken to the place appointed by General Serrurier, it was necessary to have that number to take. My father therefore wrote to his friend Dallemagne at Montanara to spare as many men from his division as he could and to send them him.

Dallemagne replied immediately:—

"MONTANARA, 26 *Nivôse, Year V*.

"DALLEMAGNE to his friend DUMAS.

"Although I do not expect to be attacked, my dear friend, yet the means at my disposal are too weak to allow of my sending much of a force to

Formigosa; a third of my division is unable to get on its feet, and its whole strength is but 2000 men. Judge therefore, my dear fellow, if I have any to spare. Nevertheless, directly I got your letter I gave orders to General Montant to hold a few troops ready to march. Moreover, I must inform you that General Serrurier gave me notice in his letter of last night that he was about to give orders to destroy the bridge at Formigosa. If, therefore, he executes this order, it will be impossible for me to send you aid; furthermore, if the enemy, which has crossed the Adige, succeeds in the attack on St. Georges, the sortie from Mantua is certain to take place, and we shall be forced to succumb in spite of all our efforts to withstand the shock, because the enemy will engage without running great risks where he has the stronger force. Good-bye, my dear friend. Rely upon it that I shall always eagerly seek every opportunity to serve you, as to serve my country.—With affectionate regards,

"DALLEMAGNE."

Nevertheless, the worthy Dallemagne was very reluctant to refuse my father the men he asked for, for he knew that, if he asked for them, it was because he believed himself to be hard pressed.

So, towards noon, he wrote him from Casanova:—

"GENERAL DALLEMAGNE to GENERAL DUMAS.

"I have just heard, General, that the bridge of Formigosa is still standing; so I have given General Montant orders to start off for Formigosa with 500 men and two pieces of artillery, and have given him the necessary instructions to take the enemy in the rear, in the event of your being attacked.—Yours,

DALLEMAGNE."

The following copy, which was attached to this letter, explains why the bridge at Formigosa had not been destroyed:—

"Copy of the letter written by CITIZEN DORÉ, Head of the 1st Battalion of the 64th Demi-Brigade, to GENERAL DALLEMAGNE.

"I have to inform you, General, that in accordance with the instructions I received last night from General Serrurier, I went this morning to Governolo with my battalion; the general had instructed me to break the bridge at Formigosa before I left Governolo.

"When I began to carry out his order, the commandant of a detachment of the 45th demi-brigade, who occupied that position, opposed the execution of this order, as being contrary to the instructions you gave him, saying that we ought at all events to make sure the enemy was in sight first. I yielded to his argument, which seemed to me reasonable.

"*Signed:* DORÉ.

"Authenticated copy.

DALLEMAGNE."

At six o'clock my father received this third letter:—

"HEADQUARTERS AT MONTANARA,

"26 *Nivôse, 4.30 o'clock.*

"GENERAL DALLEMAGNE to GENERAL DUMAS.

"Fearing that General Montant and his 500 men have not yet reached Formigosa, I have just written to him to hasten his march. As General Serrurier notifies me that in case of attack we must hold out to the last extremity, if the enemy attacks me, as I quite expect he will, and you see that those 500 men will not be of much use to you, do me the kindness to send them back to me; so that if the enemy attacks us we shall be better able to meet them.—Ever yours,

"DALLEMAGNE."

We see how anxious this worthy Dallemagne was at the thought of my father incurring any danger.

But it was Miollis who was to bear the brunt throughout that day, not my father.

Provera had marched straight before him, and, by way of Cevea, Sanguinetto, Torre, and Castellaro, had drawn up in front of St. Georges, where Miollis was in command.

The Austrian general knew what a bad state the fortifications of St. Georges were in, so he was in good hopes that Miollis would not even attempt to dispute his passing, therefore he simply asked him to surrender.

Miollis replied by a terrible cannonading. My father not only heard the firing at St. Antoine, but he could even see the smoke of it.

My father despatched Dermoncourt in hot haste to obtain definite news. Dermoncourt was very young, thoroughly active and full of courage; he rode across hedge and ditch till he reached St. Georges, where he found General Miollis facing both Provera and Wurmser at the same time.

Just as he got up to Miollis, through the firing, and saluted, a bullet carried the general's cap off.

"Ah! is it you, my lad?" said Miollis. "Have you come from Dumas?"

"Yes, General; he heard your cannonade, and, knowing the rotten condition of your fortifications, he was very uneasy about you."

"Very good. Tell him not to worry about me; I have made my headquarters here in the citadel, and, if there is one thing more certain than another, it is that the enemy will have to pass over my grave if they enter the citadel."

"But what about Provera?" asked Dermoncourt.

"Bah! Provera is in a trap. My friend Augereau, who let him pass by, is following him, and, while I stay here, he has gone to drive him into a corner. So tell Dumas that to-morrow will see Provera despatched."

Dermoncourt had seen enough; he returned to St. Antoine, which my father had made his headquarters so as to be more within reach of the enemy.

He arrived there at five o'clock, and reported that all was going forward satisfactorily. Victor had rejoined my father with his brigade and he was dining with him, when Dermoncourt entered.

This was the third sleepless night they had passed. My father and Victor flung themselves clothed as they were upon their beds. Dermoncourt remained up to draw out the report to General Serrurier of his excursion to St. Georges. He was in the full tide of his narrative when he felt someone place a hand on his shoulder.

He turned; it was Bonaparte; he had arrived.

"Well!" he said, "we have won the battle of Rivoli; here I am; the head of Masséna's division is following me at top speed. What is Miollis doing? Where is Provera? From what I hear, Augereau let him slip by. Surely he followed him? What is Wurmser doing? Has he attempted any move? Do you hear? Speak."

"General," Dermoncourt replied, as laconically as Bonaparte had interrogated him, "Augereau was overpowered, but he fell back on Provera's rear, and took two thousand prisoners and twelve pieces of cannon."

"Good."

"Provera is now before St. Georges, which Miollis has held all day long, and means to hold until he and his men are exterminated."

"Good."

"Wurmser has tried to make sorties, but he has been forced back into Mantua."

"Good. Where is Dumas?"

"Here I am, General," replied my father, appearing at his bedroom door.

"Ah! there you are, monsieur," said Bonaparte, who looked rather black at him.

My father could not pass by such a look without asking an explanation of it.

"Yes, it is I! Well, what is wrong?"

"General Serrurier wrote two letters to you yesterday, monsieur."

"Well! what then?"

"In the first he notified you that in certain events he should withdraw to Goïto."

"Yes, General."

"Did you reply to that letter?"

"Certainly."

"What did you reply?"

"Do you wish to know?"

"I should like to hear what you said."

"Very well! I replied, 'Retreat to the devil, if you like; I don't care; but I'll shoot myself rather than retire.'"

"Do you know that if you had written me such a letter as that I would have had you shot?"

"May be; but you would probably never have written me such a letter as General Serrurier wrote me."

"That is true."

Then, turning to Dermoncourt, he said to him:

"Go and have the troops drawn up in three columns, and come back and tell me when it is done."

Dermoncourt went out; then, turning to my father, who was about to return to his room, he said:

"Stay, General; I was obliged to speak to you as I did before your aide-de-camp; deuce take it, when a man writes such letters to his chief, he should at least write them himself, and not dictate them to his secretary. But we will say no more about it. Who are your commanding officers here?"

"The first column, General, is composed of the 57th demi-brigade, under its own leader, Victor; the second is under the command of Adjutant-General Rambaud, our chief staff officer; the third, of Colonel Moreau, commandant of the 11th demi-brigade."

"Very good. Where is Victor?"

"Oh! he is not far off," said my father; "listen and you will hear him snoring."

"Go and wake him."

My father went into the room close by and shook Victor, who could not be induced anyhow to wake up.

"Come, my lad!" said my father, "you must wake up."

"What the deuce do you want?" he growled.

"I want to make you general of division."

"What, me?"

"Yes, Bonaparte is here, and has given you the command of a column in to-morrow's battle."

"Goodness me!"

Victor shook himself awake and ran out.

Dermoncourt entered at the same time.

"Well?" asked Bonaparte.

"Your orders are executed, General."

"Good. Now go to the outskirts of la Favorite and find out the position of the enemy."

Dermoncourt went.

It was eight in the evening, and our troops occupied la Favorite. Dermoncourt went beyond the outposts, and, venturing towards Mantua, fell up against a sortie which Wurmser was making.

So, three-quarters of an hour after his departure, they heard him shouting a long way off:

"To horse, General, to horse! The enemy is following me."

Indeed, he narrowly escaped being caught, and feeling himself almost overtaken, he called out for help.

My father leapt to his saddle, dashed out at the head of the 20th regiment of dragoons and fell upon the enemy, whom he drove back to their base, holding them in check till day; whilst Masséna's division, which was completely disorganised by the forced march and immense distance it had had to traverse, reached Marmirolo and St. Antoine, where it re-formed.

Bonaparte's intention in making such speed was to finish off Provera at a blow, as he had finished Alvintzy.

Indeed, Provera was lost from the moment he had failed to enter Mantua. Augereau was at his heels, Miollis in front of him, Bonaparte on his flanks, with Masséna's division.

Bonaparte spent the night in making his plans for the morrow.

My father remained where he was; it was an important post, as he was deputed to drive Wurmser back into the town with his 15,000 or 20,000 men—a garrison which, without reckoning Provera, was much stronger than the enemy which blockaded them.

During the night Provera managed to communicate with Wurmser, by means of a boat, and to plan for the next day a combined attack with that general upon la Favorite and Montada. No one in Mantua or in Provera's camp knew that Bonaparte had arrived with the troops that had fought on the previous day at Rivoli.

Had they been told, it would have sounded to them too incredible for belief, and they would not have believed it.

My father was attacked by Wurmser at five in the morning; it was a terrific struggle. After his letter to Serrurier of three days back he could not, and did not, retreat; he held his ground with two or three regiments and his own regiment of dragoons, till Bonaparte had time to send him the 57th demi-brigade under Victor, whose troops cut such a fearful gap in the enemy's ranks to get to my father's relief that from that day forth they went by the name of "the *Terrible.*"

They found my father with 700 or 800 men, surrounded by dead; he had had one horse killed under him, a second had been slain by a cannon-ball, but its rider, whom they took for dead, rose triumphantly out of his glorious tomb.

Wurmser thus repulsed, fell back upon la Favorite; but la Favorite, defended by 1500 men, withstood Wurmser's efforts, and even made a sally. What with this sally, the repeated charges of my father and his dragoons, and Victor's heroic stubbornness, whose fresh troops fought with pent-up fury after being condemned to inaction whilst the rest of the army had been covering itself with glory at Rivoli, Wurmser was beaten back, and forced to re-enter the town.

From that time Provera, abandoned by his ally, was lost; caught between Bonaparte, Miollis, Serrurier, and Augereau, he and his 5000 men laid down their arms,—the rest of his troops had all been killed.

So the battles of Rivoli and la Favorite had been won in two days, two armies had been destroyed, and 20,000 men taken prisoner. All their guns and ammunition had been captured, and the Austrians rendered too demoralised to continue the campaign without raising a fifth army. All these events had resulted from the lucky chance of my father's taking the spy, combined with the fertile genius of Napoleon.

My father's brigade alone captured six standards. And on the following day, 28 Nivôse, my father received this letter from General Serrurier:—

"HEADQUARTERS AT ROVERBELLA,

"28 *Nivôse, Year V of the Republic, one and indivisible.*

"SERRURIER, etc. etc., to DUMAS, Divisional General.

"Will you please give orders, General, for the colours which you took from the enemy yesterday to be brought here to General Berthier, or if he is away, to me.

"The general-in-chief grants four louis to each man who takes a standard.— Faithfully yours,

SERRURIER."

On the same evening after the battle, my father received a despatch from General Serrurier, containing a letter for Wurmser.

This letter was virtually a demand for the surrender of Mantua.

General Serrurier's letter was as follows:—

"ROVERBELLA, 27 *Nivôse, Year V.*

"GENERAL SERRURIER, etc., to DIVISIONAL-GENERAL DUMAS.

"This is to inform you, General, that I have just issued orders to the 18th and 57th demi-brigades to proceed to la Favorite, with instructions to put themselves at your service. I must tell you, however, that these two corps must not form a permanent part of your division, therefore do not send them to a distance unless in case of urgent necessity.

"The general-in-chief has been informed that you have captured a considerable convoy of bullocks and grain; if so, give orders for it to be taken to Porto Legnago under a strong escort.

"Also let all the artillery and ammunition waggons taken from the enemy be forwarded to our artillery park immediately. See that there is the strictest surveillance throughout the military stations. It is suspected that General Wurmser will take advantage of our rejoicings to make good his escape.— With sincere regards, yours,

SERRURIER.

"*P.S.*—I beg you, General, to hand over the enclosed letter to General Wurmser at Mantua as soon as possible.

"SERRURIER."

The convoy of bullocks and grain was sent off at once to Legnago, and the letter went to Wurmser the same night.

The army was in great want of that convoy of grain and meat, as we learn from the following letter which General Serrurier wrote to my father on the 20th Nivôse:—

"I am informed, General, that you are short of meat; I have not mentioned it before, because I could not supply the deficiency. We areas badly off as the troops at Verona. I have given orders to the army commissariat to deliver rice instead, until we can supply something better.

"You need never be afraid of wearying me, General, with any matter concerning the soldiers; those who have served with me know how interested I am in their welfare.

"I have asked for some fresh equipments of clothing and outfits; and they have sent word that since my arrival a thousand *roupes*[6] and some shoes for the whole of the division are on their way, but nothing has come yet.

"Remind our adjutant-general of the list of officers I asked for; I must have it before I can fill in the general-in-chief's inspection list.—Faithfully, etc.,

SERRURIER."

The garrison was, as we can quite understand, in a deplorable condition with regard to provisions: famine had reached such a pitch that a fowl cost ten louis, and a cat fifteen; rats might be procured with the greatest difficulty for two louis.

Wurmser went to confession once a fortnight, and every time he confessed he sent Canon Cavallini, the priest of the Collegiate Church of St. André, a joint of horse, at the same time inviting himself to dinner. These were fête-days, and they lived on the remains of that dinner the whole week after.

In consequence of the letter my father passed on to Wurmser on the night of 27th-28th Nivôse, that general decided to capitulate on the 2nd Pluviôse

(January 22nd, 1797). But the surrender did not actually take place until the 14th, and the entry of the French army into the town was not till the 16th of that month.

He was allowed to go out of Mantua free, with his staff, 200 cavalrymen, 500 persons of his own choice and six pieces of cannon.

The soldiers of the garrison, which was 13,000 or 14,000 strong, were made prisoners, and taken to Trieste to be exchanged.

Victor was made commander of a division, as my father had predicted when he woke him, and Adjutant General Vaux was made brigadier-general. Bonaparte singled out Generals Brune, Vial and Bon as having especially distinguished themselves, and also chiefs of brigades Destaing, Marquis, and Tournery.

As to my father, his name was not even mentioned.

It was a known fact that this was Bonaparte's custom, he did not like his generals to accomplish too much.

Witness the case of Kellermann at Marengo.

Not merely was my father, who had taken the letter which had revealed Alvintzy's plans, who had kept Wurmser in Mantua, who had captured six colours from a troop three times the strength of his own, who had had two horses shot under him—not only was my father not mentioned, but his divisional rank even was incorporated with Masséna's—and that was equivalent to disgrace.

My father was furious, and wanted to send in his resignation, but Dermoncourt would not let him.

My father next discovered that the general commissioned to report upon the siege had said he merely looked on during the fight at la Favorite.

My father began his defence by obtaining the following testimony:—

"ARMY OF ITALY.

"Division of the blockade of Mantua, 20th regiment of dragoons.

"We, the undersigned officers of the 20th regiment of dragoons, certify that Dumas, general of division, had a horse shot under him in the battle of the 27th of this month before Mantua, and another struck down by a cannon-ball.

"Written at the bivouac at Marmirolo, the 29th Nivôse, year V of the French Republic.

"*Signed*:

"BONTEMS, Adjutant; BAUDIN, Adjutant; DUBOIS, Sub-Lieutenant; L. BONEFROY, Sub-Lieutenant; A. J. BONNART, Chief of Brigade; LE COMTE, Lieutenant; LEBRUN, Lieutenant; DEJEAN, Captain; BOUZAT, Lieutenant."

Then he wrote to Bonaparte:—

"GENERAL,—I learn that the silly fool whose business it was to report to you upon the battle of the 27th states that I only looked on throughout that battle. I have no wish to make similar observations concerning him, although he soiled his trousers.—Respectfully yours,

ALEX. DUMAS."

The fact was that the letter sent to incorporate my father in Masséna's division was curt, and would have wounded a man of much less susceptible nature than his.

It was dated the very day after the battle in which my father had had two horses killed under him.

"HEADQUARTERS, ROVERBELLA,

"28 *Nivôse, Year of the Republic, one and indivisible.*

"General of Division and Head of the Staff.

"The general-in-chief commands Divisional-General Dumas to leave Marmirolo, where he will be replaced by General Chabot, and to proceed to General Masséna's division: he will serve in the active army at Verona, under the orders of that general.

ALEX. BERTHIER."

This time there was no friendly termination, at length or abridged.

[1] This aide-de-camp was Duroc.

[2] I have copied this letter exactly. I shall do the same with all letters I quote.

[3] Four days previous to the battle of Rivoli.

[4] The day of the battle of Rivoli, which took place at the same time; it will be seen how well concerted were the movements of the two generals.

[5] Dallemagne was on the side opposite Montanara, on the road to Milan.

[6] A letter we have just received from an old officer informs us that *roupes* were cloaks similar to the grey cloaks of the dragoons.

CHAPTER X

My father's first breeze with Bonaparte—My father is sent to Masséna's army corps—He shares Joubert's command in the Tyrol—Joubert—The campaign in the Tyrol.

My father was the more exasperated because he knew that with all the will in the world it was impossible for Bonaparte to have believed for one instant those words *looked on*, since it was by reason of the very orders he had received from him that my father had made that heroic defence of the 27th, when he drove the marshal's troop back into Mantua with a force three times less in numbers.

I give below the orders Bonaparte dictated to Berthier at the very moment when, after having left him at the presbytery of St. Antoine, my father had repulsed Wurmser's nocturnal sally at the head of a mere handful of dragoons.

"HEADQUARTERS OF THE GENERAL STAFF

AT ROVERBELLA,

"26 *Nivôse, 8 p.m.*

"The general-in-chief orders you to set off immediately, General, with two pieces of light artillery and all the cavalry you can collect, and particularly the hundred dragoons he sent this evening: you are to reconnoitre the enemy's position,[1] to keep a look-out upon his movements, and to be quite ready to attack him successfully, immediately General Dallemagne, to whom the general-in-chief has transmitted his orders, shall have made his preparations to fall in like manner upon the enemy.

"The troops which arrived this evening at Roverbella are worn-out with fatigue, and need two hours' rest. After this interval they will be ready to start; they will receive the general-in-chief's orders concerning the movements they must undertake after the reconnaissance you are about to make (concerning which you will inform him), as soon as he receives the reports he momentarily expects with regard to the reconnaissances he has ordered of the various positions on the Molinella.

"Whatever happens, you must send everything necessary in the way of men and provisions into Saint-Georges, to enable that post to hold out for forty-eight hours. The general-in-chief has already given you instructions by General Serrurier,[2] to collect a corps of 1500 of the best men out of your division, and place them where the enemy has established his communication with the garrison of Mantua, to be in readiness, if a favourable chance arises, to begin the attack, or on the first order you may receive; you need not be afraid of stripping St. Antoine, your reinforcements must pass through that place.

"Send a report to the general-in-chief of your reconnaissance and of all the arrangements you make.

ALEX. BERTHIER."

It was at St. Antoine indeed that Bonaparte, seeing my father beset by forces four times the strength of his own, sent the famous 57th demi-brigade to his aid; they found him half buried in the same hole in which his horse was completely buried, when shattered by the cannon-ball.

Masséna was acquainted with the reason of this temporary disgrace; so he received my father with the respect due to a man whose military qualifications he admired, and not merely as an ordinary comrade.

Consequently, he gave him the command of his van-guard.

While at the head of this van-guard my father took part in the fight at St. Michel, entered Vicenza, and fought in the battle of Bassano.

In six months, as Bonaparte had himself foretold in his proclamation of war to the pope, the Army of Italy had taken 100,000 prisoners, 400 pieces of cannon, and demolished five armies.

This pontifical war was a joke. On the 16th Pluviôse, we were masters of Romagna, of the duchy of Urbino, of the Marche d'Ancona, of Umbria, and the districts of Perugia and Camerino.

At length, on the 30th Pluviôse (February 19), the French Republic and the pontifical sovereign signed the treaty of Tolentino, by which the Holy Father gave up Avignon and the district of Venaissin to France, renounced the legations of Ferrara and Bologna as well as of Romagna, and sanctioned the occupation of the town, fortress, and territory of Ancona. He was, moreover, compelled to contribute immediately thirty millions to the funds of the Army of Italy, solemnly to disown the murder of Basseville, and to pay 300,000 francs indemnity to those who were sufferers by that murder.

Finally, the pope was obliged to restore the objects of art and the manuscripts mentioned in the armistice of Bologna, and to hand over intact to the French Republic the palace of the School of Arts, which was his property.

The treaty of Tolentino terminated the first Italian campaign, during which the feats of Hannibal and the fortunes of Alexander had been repeated.

Whilst the French Republic, represented by Bonaparte, was signing the treaty of Tolentino with the pope, the Austrians were gathering together among the Tyrolese mountains a sixth army, the command of which was given by the emperor to Prince Charles, who had just made his name in the Rhine campaign.

Prince Charles took up the command of this army during February 1797 (Pluviôse, year V).

By the end of February—about the 8th or 9th of Ventôse, that is to say—the army of the enemy held the following positions.

Its principal position was on the Tagliamento; its right wing, under Generals Kerpen and Laudon, was situated behind the Lavis and the Nos, defending the approaches to the Tyrol. Prince Lusignan, who was so well beaten at Rivoli, occupied the spaces between the two principal arms with his brigade, and had taken up his stand round Feltre; lastly, the van-guard, under command of General Hohenzollern, held the Piave.

Bonaparte, on his side, expected a reinforcement of 18,000 men from the Army of the Rhine, and had mustered four divisions of his army in the Marche of Treviso. Masséna was at Bassano; General Guyeux occupied Treviso; Bernadotte, whose troops were beginning to arrive, was to occupy Padua; Joubert, with his division and those of Generals Baraguay d'Hilliers and Delmas, was to confront Kerpen and Laudon. Lastly, Victor and 7500 men waited in the Marche d'Ancona, whilst Kilmaine, with nearly 6000 men, guarded Lombardy and the frontiers of Piedmont and Genoa.

The Austrian total amounted to 35,000 men, and the French to 36,000 or 37,000.

Towards the middle of Ventôse my father was ordered to leave Masséna's army corps for that of Joubert, and to give up Bassano and Trent.

Joubert, to whom he was sent, was one of the most remarkable men of a time productive of remarkable men. He was one of the fine young thorough Republicans of the school of Marceau, of Hoche, and, I may add, of my father. Like Marceau, like Hoche, and like my father, he died young; but Marceau and he had the good luck to die from Tyrolese bullets, while Hoche and my father died from poisoning.

Joubert was one of the heroes of Rivoli. Like my father at la Favorite, he had had his horse killed under him, and, seizing a grenadier's rifle, he had fought on foot for the rest of the day. That day, during which he took several pieces of cannon, and turned the enemy head over heels into the Adige, won him the rank of divisional general.

We have mentioned that Joubert was at the head of nearly 20,000 men in the Tyrol when my father was sent to him to take command of the cavalry. He received my father in the most affectionate manner.

"My dear Dumas," said he, "if I leave you the command they have given you, you will find it but an empty honour, for you will only have two very incomplete regiments of dragoons, the 5th and 8th, both together hardly making one regiment. And I am quite sure that was not the intention of him who sent you to me. I have 20,000 men, so I will give you 10,000 to command, or rather, we will command the whole army between us."

My father thanked Joubert. Bonaparte's flagrant injustice was so obvious that, as in the case of Masséna, Joubert's one idea, when welcoming him, was to try and make him forget it.

The two generals lodged together; then, as hostilities were about to begin, they visited the outposts and decided to make an attack next day, 21st March 1797 (30th Ventôse, year V).

That same day my father received his official instructions from Joubert, which they had drawn up between them beforehand:—

"LIBERTY—EQUALITY.

"HEADQUARTERS OF TRENT,

"29 *Nivôse, Year V of the French Republic.*

"JOUBERT, General of Division, to Divisional-General DUMAS:—eight o'clock in the morning.

"You will set out to-day, General, to take command of General Belliard's brigades at Segonzano; he has under his orders the 22nd light infantry and the 85th of the line; also the 14th of the main army under General Pelletier.

"You will give General Belliard orders that on leaving the positions he has occupied with the 85th, he is to proceed at nightfall to Segonzano: General Pelletier will also proceed to the same place as soon as the enemy are unable to make out his movements—that is to say, also at nightfall. You will muster all the troops in such a manner as to be able to effect the crossing of the Weiss and to make an attack on Faver and Limbra two or three hours before daybreak.

"Place all the carabineers and grenadiers at the head of your columns.

"In accordance with the plan we agreed upon after our reconnaissance of that point, you must form two columns to cross the Weiss on the right of Faver, and muster upon the road at the head of the ravine, a short fifteen minutes' march to the right of the village, in order to be able to control it, while our attacking columns are being drawn up in the green wood above the village; by this means you will outflank all the enemy's fortifications. When you have taken possession of Faver, proceed to Limbra, and follow up the attack with your light infantry, by taking the ravine first of all, which separates it from Faver.

"Your attention should also be directed to outflanking the enemy's works on the mountain, in order to drive them down into the plain or into the village, where your carabineers and grenadiers, in serried columns, should be ready to attack them vigorously, your light infantry skirmishers supported close at hand by the 85th and 14th: it is hardly necessary to tell you to have a reserve on the road between Faver and Limbra, opposite the ravine.

"To disguise the real attack between Albian and Segonzano, you will give orders to Generals Pelletier and Belliard to cause false attacks to be made by the outposts along the whole line simultaneously with that at Segonzano, seeking to cross the torrent in several places, in order to push forward under the enemy's fire.

"General Baraguay-d'Hilliers will lend you, just for the attack, the 5th of his main army; this, with the two other demi-brigades, will make up your reserve. One battalion should, at night, command the Weiss and Sevignano; the remainder should be at Segonzano.

"I will also send by him to Bedol a battalion and some companies of carabineers to make a false attack upon Sovero. Communicate this to General Belliard, whom I have ordered to place all the information in his power at your disposal, as well as the guides needed for this march.

"If, as we may presume, you take Limbra, you must manage as best you can to take the enemy in the rear, until the columns shall have arrived from the Weiss. You will also look out for the reinforcements which should come from Salurn over the mountains.

"There are three pieces of cannon at Segonzano, under cover of whose fire you could cross the stream by day, if you had not succeeded in doing so by night. You ought also to have 60,000 cartridges there; your troops should have three days' provisions and two rations of brandy with them on setting out.

"Be very stubborn in your attacks; be careful to keep the men well together; sternly forbid pillage; disarm the Tyrolese: such are the instructions of the general-in-chief—you will remember that I showed you them.

"You will distribute and post up the copies of the proclamation I send you.—
I am, etc.,

JOUBERT."

My father left Albian, in accordance with Joubert's instructions, on the 30th
Nivôse, at two o'clock in the morning, and posted himself with the 5th, 14th,
and 85th demi-brigades of the main corps, and the 22nd light infantry, below
the castle of Segonzano, ready for crossing the river Weiss. The first men
who tried to cross the torrent had scarcely put their feet into the water before
they perceived how dangerous the passage would be, owing to the rapidity
of the current. The water was not higher than their waists, but the current
was so strong that when a third of the way across the ford five or six men
had lost their footing, were carried away as by a cataract, and dashed against
the rocks which hemmed in the river.

My father then conceived the idea of making use of these rocks to form a
chain; he took the strongest of his men, placed them under Dermoncourt's
orders, and they succeeded in making a breakwater entirely across the course
of the stream. After that there was no more danger; for the men who were
carried off their feet by the rapidity of the current were stopped by this living
chain. The advance guard, which was composed, as Joubert had advised, of
the grenadiers of the demi-brigade, with my father and Belliard at their head,
soon reached the other side.

My father was quickly master of all the redoubts held by the enemy before
Segonzano. On reaching the heights above the village of Faver, they attacked
it, and, after a vigorous resistance, they took it by assault.

After securing Faver, they marched on Limbra, where the enemy were
intrenched with two pieces of cannon. My father had taken care, on leaving,
to send off a column of troops to the mountains which overlook these two
villages.

The enemy defended themselves vigorously, but the mountain column
arrived, and, returning their fire with interest, they were obliged to make for
the plain. My father soon beat back their advance, and one last struggle
decided the victory: their intrenchments were captured, two pieces of cannon
taken, and 2000 men fell into our hands.

My father mentioned General Belliard and Adjutant-Generals Valentin and
Liébaut as having particularly distinguished themselves in this attack.

A major named Martin, belonging to the 25th of the line with only twenty-
five men, charged and took prisoner 200 of the enemy. My father asked for

promotion for this officer, also for the two aides-de-camp, Dermoncourt and Lambert, and their assistant, Milienk.

Faver and Limbra taken, my father ordered General Belliard to march with his column to Lesignano, where the enemy occupied a strong position; he was to try and take them in the rear, while my father proceeded towards Salurn to protect the movements Joubert was making in that direction.

Next day my father marched on Castello with his column and took a hundred prisoners. At night he conferred with General Baraguay-d'Hilliers, and it was arranged that the villages of Coran, Altrivo, Castello, and Cavaleza should be attacked on the morrow.

The troops bivouacked: at two in the morning of the 2nd Germinal they advanced upon the four villages which they had planned to attack, but the enemy had already evacuated.

General Pigeon was put upon their track by General Baraguay-d'Hilliers, and he pursued them hotly as far as the village of Tesaro; after which a descent was made upon Newmark, in accordance with the instructions of the 30th Nivôse. On the right bank of the Adige the Austrian general, Laudon, who held the villages of Mote and Caldera, withdrew to Bolzano.

Towards two in the afternoon a major of engineers informed my father that the enemy were bearing down for the bridge of Newmark, where they might be harassed in their retreat. This bridge was as important to us for the attack as it was to the enemy for the defence. My father commanded General Belliard to march on this bridge with the 85th demi-brigade, which he commanded: when he reached the bridge he overthrew the enemy and advanced on the village of Mote, which he took by assault. "I," said my father, "at the head of the 5th dragoons, charged the enemy's cavalry, which had advanced to meet me, and put it to flight, although it was superior in numbers. I slashed the commander's face and the neck of one of his horse-soldiers. My regiment took, killed, or wounded, a hundred Austrian cavalry. Adjutant-General Blondeau particularly distinguished himself in this engagement."

We can see how modestly my father referred to any of his own doings. This charge of the 5th dragoons was a magnificent one. Joubert told Bonaparte, in his report, that my father had earned the reputation of being *a terror to the Austrian cavalry*; and this is how Dermoncourt speaks of it:—

"General Dumas crossed the bridge at the head of his cavalry, charged several squadrons of the enemy, and killed with his own hands the commander and a soldier who, seeing his chief in desperate plight, had run to his assistance; he drove the infantry into the vineyards, and continued the pursuit of the cavalry at full gallop with a mere handful of men, charging us to collect what Austrians he left behind him. We took 1900 men."

After this brilliant engagement they marched on Bolzano, chasing the enemy all the time, who kept at a respectful distance; and they entered the town without striking a blow. My father instructed Adjutant-General Blondeau to push his reconnaissances as far as the village of Colman; he left Delmas in position at Bolzano to watch Laudon's troops, and, on the 4th Germinal, at two o'clock in the morning, he himself marched off to follow the enemy which had retreated by the road to Brixen.

This is how my father relates the brilliant encounter which won for him the name of the Horatius Codes of the Tyrol; we shall then see how his aide-de-camp, Dermoncourt, describes it.

"I found the enemy in force, occupying an almost unassailable position at Clausen; he was vigorously attacked, and compelled to abandon the town; our troops occupied it, and were unsuccessfully attacked by the enemy's cavalry.

"At the head of the 5th dragoons, which I at once brought forward, I charged the Austrian cavalry and routed them completely, leaving many dead and wounded: 1500 of their foot-soldiers were taken prisoners, and the rest were pursued as far as Brixen. The remainder of the enemy drew up for battle, evidently intending to wait for us to come on; I rallied my van-guard and prepared to attack them, but they fled at our approach; I followed them with my cavalry more than a league beyond Brixen.

"I received three sword-cuts in these different charges, and my aide-de-camp Dermoncourt was wounded by my side.

"*5th and 6th Germinal.*

"The troops rested on the 5th.

"You charged General Baraguay-d'Hilliers to attack the enemy on the 6th, before Michaelbach, where he is intrenched, and I think I ought to take part in that engagement with my cavalry. You know, General,—for you found it out for yourself,—how well the two regiments of dragoons which I commanded have behaved, and how greatly they contributed to the day's success.

"You are also aware, General, that my horse was killed under me and that I have lost my accoutrements and some very valuable pistols. My aide-de-camp Lambert performed wonders.

"I will send you to-day the reports from the brigadier-generals which have not yet reached me.

"BRIXEN, *7th Germinal, Year V of the Republic.*

"AL. DUMAS.

"*P.S.*—I must really present you with my cloak, I believe it is enchanted; it is riddled with seven bullets, not one of which touched me. It will bring you good luck."

---

[1] It was at the head of his dragoons that my father left the very presence of the commander-in-chief; but Bonaparte took care that everything which was done, no matter what, should at least seem to have been done by his orders, and on his initiative. We shall see an interesting example of the same method in the battle of the Pyramids. Bonaparte was a clever stage-manager; but we may be permitted to believe that Providence, who used him as an instrument, as men of genius are used, had something to do with the success of the pieces he played.

[2] It has been seen that this order reached my father during the day, and well before Bonaparte's arrival.

BOOK II

CHAPTER I

The bridge of Clausen—Dermoncourt's reports—Prisoners on parole—Lepage's pistols—Three generals-in-chief at the same table.

Now let Dermoncourt speak; from his version we shall really see what my father's deeds were; for my father always effaced himself in his own reports, above all when speaking of himself:—

"The army stopped at Bolzano for forty-eight hours, a long halt for this campaign, which was more like a race than a war. General Delmas remained at Bolzano to keep an eye on Laudon's troops, and on the road from Innsbruck. The rest of the army, with General Dumas at its head, prepared to march next day for Brixen, to try and catch up with General Kerpen's army, which had gone in that direction.

"The road we followed skirted a kind of watershed, half stream, half torrent, which had its source among the Noire mountains, and which, swollen by the waters of the Riente, flows into the Adige, below Bolzano. Sometimes the road ran along the right bank of the river; sometimes, crossing the stream, it followed the left bank; then, after several miles, it would cross back to the other side again. The retreat of the Austrians had been so rapid that they had not even blown up the bridges. We marched after them at double quick pace, and we were almost in despair at ever overtaking them, when our scouts came to tell us that they had barricaded the bridge of Clausen with carts, and this time really seemed to intend to dispute our crossing.

"The general at once set off with fifty dragoons, to examine the nature of the ground: I followed him.

"When we reached the bridge of Clausen, we found it effectually barred, with infantry and cavalry behind. We thought that, when the general had examined the position, he would wait for reinforcements; but he never dreamt of such a thing.

"'I Come on, come on,' he said—'I want twenty-five men on foot to clear this bridge for me!'

"Twenty-five dragoons threw their horses' bridles into their comrades' hands, and rushed to the bridge in the very middle of the fire of the Austrian infantry.

"It was not easy work; for, to begin with, the waggons were heavy to move, and the bullets fell like hail.

"'Come along, lazy-bones,' the general called out to me; 'aren't you going to lend a hand to these good fellows?'

"I dismounted and put my shoulder to the waggons; but the general, finding that the bridge could not be cleared quickly enough, leapt from his horse, and he too came to help us. In an instant he did more single-handed with his herculean strength than the twenty-five of us together. When I say twenty-five I exaggerate; the Austrian bullets had made their gaps, and five or six of our men were disabled. Fortunately about sixty foot-soldiers now came up to our assistance at a run. They distributed themselves on both sides of the bridge, and opened hot fire, which soon began to distress the Austrians, and to prevent them from aiming straight. It ended in our overturning the carts into the torrent—an easy matter, as the bridge had no parapet.

"Scarcely was the passage free than the general leapt to his horse and, without waiting to see if he were being followed or not, he dashed down the village street leading from the bridge.

"In vain did I shout after him, 'But, General, there are only the two of us!'

"He did not hear, or rather, he would not hear. Suddenly we found ourselves face to face with a platoon of cavalry, upon which the general fell; and, as the men were all in line, with one single back-handed blow of his sabre he killed the quartermaster, gashed the soldier horribly who was next to him, and with the point of the weapon wounded a third. The Austrians not conceiving it possible that two men would have the audacity to charge them thus, wheeled to the right-about; but the horses stumbled, and horses and riders fell pell-mell. Our dragoons came up at this moment with the foot-soldiers astride behind them, and the whole of the Austrian platoon was captured.

"I paid the general a compliment upon his sabre blow, telling him I had never seen its equal.

"'That is because you are a greenhorn,' he replied, 'but do your best not to get killed, and before the finish of the campaign you will have seen plenty like it.'

"We had taken a hundred prisoners. But he soon descried a considerable body of cavalry climbing a mountain at the other side of the village. No sooner did the general see this body than he pointed them out to his dragoons, and, leaving the prisoners to the care of the infantry, he set off with his fifty men to pursue the Austrians.

"The general and I were so splendidly mounted that we gained rapidly on our soldiers. The Austrians believing that they were being pursued by the whole of our army, fled at top speed. And again it came about that the general and I found ourselves alone.

"At length, when we had reached an inn, at a point where the road curved, I pulled up, and said to him:

"'General, what we are about to undertake, or rather, what *you* mean to undertake, is not reasonable. Let us stop and wait till our men come up. Besides, the look of the ground indicates that there is a plateau behind the house, and we shall perhaps find the enemy there drawn up ready for battle.'

"'All right, my boy; go and see if it is so,' he said. 'Our horses can get their breath in the meantime.'

"I dismounted and walked round the inn, where I soon discovered three trim squadrons all drawn up ready for battle, about two hundred paces off. I returned to tell the general, who, without a word in reply, set off riding in the direction of the enemy's squadrons. I remounted my horse and followed him.

"He had hardly gone a hundred yards before he came within earshot of the enemy. The commanding officer recognised him, and addressed him in French.

"'Oh! so it is you, you black devil!' he said to us.

"*Schwartz Teufel* was the Austrians' nickname for the general.

"'Come on a hundred paces, you scurvy knave,' said the general, 'and I shall make it two hundred.'

"And with this reply, he put his horse to a gallop.

"All this time I was yelling like a demon, following the general, whom I dared not leave, 'Here, dragoons, come on!'

"The enemy accordingly expected to see a considerable force appear at any moment, and, with their commanding officer at their head, they turned and fled.

"The general was on the point of pursuing them single-handed, but I caught hold of his horse by the bridle and compelled him to wait till our forces could come up and occupy the position just vacated by the enemy.

"But when we were once more rejoined, there was no holding the general back, and we set off again to chase the Austrians. I managed, however, this time to arrange that our skirmishers should go in front, as the road was very uneven.

"The skirmishers went on ahead, and we made good use of the time to breathe our horses.

"In an hour's time we heard firing, which indicated that our men were at close quarters with the Austrians. The general sent me ahead to see what it meant.

"I returned in ten minutes.

"'Well!' said the general, I what is going on down there?'

"'The enemy is engaging us, General, but one of our soldiers who speaks German told me it was only a ruse to induce us to cross the bridge of Clausen. The bridge crossed, the enemy intends to take its revenge.'

"'Ah! that is his dodge, is it?' said the general. 'Very well! we will go and have a look. Forward—dragoons!'

"And at the head of our fifty or sixty men we again charged the enemy.

"We reached the famous bridge; there was only just room for three horses to cross abreast, and not the slightest suggestion of a parapet.

"It was as I had told the general: the enemy had merely made a show of resistance to entice us to pursue them. The general crossed the bridge convinced that the Austrians would not dare to turn round upon us. We therefore entered the principal street, following the steps of our skirmishers and the dozen dragoons whom the general had sent on to support them, and we were almost in the middle of the street when we beheld our skirmishers and our dragoons being driven back by a whole squadron of cavalry. It was not a retreat—it was a rout.

"Fear is infectious. It took possession of the dragoons who were with us, or rather, our dragoons took possession of it; they all fled after their comrades, scampering off at full gallop; only about a dozen stayed by us.

"With this dozen of men we checked the enemy's charge, and soon, whether for good or ill, we found ourselves back at the bridge again; but here our few remaining dragoons deserted us, and stampeded as though their salvation lay on the other side of the bridge.

"To tell how the general and I got back to the bridge would be a difficult matter; I saw the general raise his sabre, as a thresher lifts his flail, and each time the sword fell a man was felled. But I was soon so busy looking after myself that I was compelled to lose sight of the general; two or three Austrian cavalrymen made a furious set at me, determined to take me, dead or alive. I wounded one with the point of my sword, I cut open the head of another, but the third dealt me a cut with his sword between the joints of the shoulder, which made me rein in my horse so sharply that the beast, whose mouth was very tender, reared and fell back on top of me into a ditch. This was exactly to my Austrian's mind: he continued to belard me with sword-cuts, and would assuredly soon have spitted me altogether, if I had not managed to draw a pistol out of my holsters with my left hand. I fired at random; I did not know whether I hit the horse or the rider, but I know the horse swung round on his hind legs, set off at a gallop and, when about twenty or twenty-five yards off me, he rid himself of his rider.

"As no one else engaged my attention, I turned round towards the general; he was standing at the head of the bridge of Clausen and holding it alone against the whole squadron; and as the men could only get at him two or three abreast, because of the narrowness of the bridge, he cut them down as fast as they came on.

"I stood there astounded; I had always regarded the story of Horatius Cocles as a fable, and here I saw the very same thing being acted before my own eyes. In a short while, I struggled to extricate myself from under my horse, and succeeded in dragging myself out of the ditch, then I shouted with all my might: 'Dragoons, to your general!'

"I was quite past defending him myself, my right arm being nearly disjointed.

"Luckily, the general's second aide-de-camp, Lambert, arrived just at that moment with a reinforcement of fresh troops. He learnt what was happening from the fugitives, whom he rallied; and together they rushed to the general's assistance; they only just rescued him in time, as he himself acknowledged.

"He had killed seven or eight men, and wounded twice that number, but his strength had begun to wane.

"He had received three wounds, one in the arm, one in the thigh, and the other on his head.

"This last had broken the iron of his headpiece; but, like the other two wounds, it only slightly grazed the outer skin.

"The general had, besides, received seven bullets through his cloak. His horse had been killed under him, but happily its body acted as a barricade across the bridge, and perhaps this circumstance had saved him, for the Austrians had begun to rifle his valise and his holsters, and this gave him time to catch a riderless horse and to recommence his fight.

"Thanks to Lambert's reinforcement, the general was able to take up the offensive and to give the cavalry such a hot chase that we never saw them again throughout the whole campaign."

My father sent the cloak pierced with seven bullets to Joubert as a talisman, but it did not suffice to defend him at Novi.

Dermoncourt's wound was pretty serious, and he was obliged to keep his bed. My father left him at Brixen, and went to lend a hand to Delmas, who, as we have said, was stationed at Bolzano to oppose Laudon.

Laudon, after having reprovisioned his army and being somewhat recovered from our dressing down at the crossing of the Weiss, and from his defeat at Newmark, reinforced also by the Tyrolese peasants, had recommenced serious operations against Delmas, who was isolated at Bolzano with a mere handful of men.

Left to his own resources, and cut off from the main army, which was nine leagues away, Delmas sent a messenger to General Joubert, who had rejoined my father at Brixen on the 7th Germinal. This messenger announced that Delmas feared he might be attacked at any moment, and felt himself too weak to be able to hold out for long.

Joubert showed the despatch to my father, who had hardly dismounted from his horse. My father suggested he should start at once with his cavalry, which he thought would be sufficient to extricate Delmas, and even to settle with Laudon. Joubert accepted his offer, and my father went, leaving Joubert the commission to recover his pistols, no matter at what cost. It will be remembered that my father set immense store by these pistols, which my mother had given him: they had saved his life in the camp of la Madeleine.

He made such good progress that on the following morning he and all his cavalry had reached Bolzano.

The cavalry—men and horses—seem to have caught some of their master's spirit. Their confidence in him had been complete since they had seen his hand-to-hand struggle with the enemy in previous encounters, and they were ready to follow-him to the world's end.

As my father and his men had entered Bolzano by night, the enemy did not know of his arrival, and fancied they had only to deal with Delmas and the few men who were with him. The two generals therefore resolved to take advantage of the Austrians' ignorance, and next day to assume the offensive; so, at daybreak, they attacked the enemy just as they were preparing to make an attack themselves.

My father held the main road with his cavalry; Delmas and his infantry from the heights above attacked the enemy's positions one after another, carrying them all; whilst my father proceeded to cut up the fugitives.

It was a very hot day, and the Austrians, recognising that they were well beaten, disappeared from the neighbourhood of Bolzano, and enabled my father to return to Brixen.

It had taken him but three days to fulfil his mission.

It was quite time he returned, for the peasantry had risen, and had murdered several marauders who had had the audacity to steal out of cantonments. Kerpen had returned, owing to this revolt, and it was soon to be a matter of dealing not only with the regular troops, but also with the terrible Tyrolean chasseurs, whose bullets had already carried off Marceau, and were soon to kill Joubert also.

All was soon in battle array. My father was at the head of his indefatigable cavalry, mounted on a superb steed, the gift of Joubert. Joubert was himself at the head of his own picked regiment of grenadiers.

The same things happened over again. My father, encountering the enemy upon the main road, set to work with the sabre in his usual fashion, carrying everything before him.

I will again let Dermoncourt describe what happened:—

"It was a grand rout. General Dumas and his men slashed away for more than two leagues.

"A great number of Austrians and Tyrolese were killed. The very sight of the general produced on these men the effect of an army corps; nothing could withstand the *Schwartz Teufel*.

"He was mounted on a magnificent horse which General Joubert had just given him in place of the one he had lost a week previously. Again he found himself a quarter of a league ahead of his squadron, and, cutting his way through without looking behind him, he reached a bridge, the planks of which had already been torn up by the enemy, only the cross beams remaining. It was impossible to proceed farther; his horse would neither go through the river nor cross the bridge on the narrow framework. The general drew up in a fury and began flourishing his sword; and when the Tyroleans were conscious that they were no longer being pursued, they turned right about face and began a fearful fire upon this one lonely man; three balls immediately struck down the horse, and in its fall it dragged its rider with it, his leg pinned under it.[1]

"The Tyrolese thought the general was killed, and rushed for the bridge, crying:

"'Ah! The black devil is dead at last!'

"The situation was grave: with the foot that remained free the general pushed off the dead body of his horse, to free his other leg; and when freed he retreated to a little hillock overlooking the road, upon which the Austrians had hurriedly thrown up a rough intrenchment, which they had deserted when they caught sight of the general. It is a known custom among the Austrians to abandon or to throw down their arms before flight; and in this improvised redoubt the general found fifty guns all ready primed. In the general's present situation these were of more value to him than the richest of treasure-trove. He sheltered behind a fir-tree and commenced his solitary fusillade.

"His first care was to pick out the men who had robbed him of his horse; and so good a shot was he that not a single aim was lost: the men fell upon one another in heaps; all who ventured upon those narrow beams fell dead.

"The general's cavalry heard his firing, and as they did not know what had become of him, they guessed he was the cause of the shindy which was being raised a quarter of a league off. Lambert took fifty cavalrymen with twenty-five foot-soldiers seated behind them, and rushed up to find the general holding fast his little redoubt.

"In an instant the bridge was carried, the Austrians and Tyrolese were pursued into the village and a hundred of them taken prisoners.

"Lambert told me he saw over twenty-five Austrians laid dead round the horse they had slain, and that not a single man had had time to cross the space between the bridge and the slight intrenchment.

"The general returned to Brixen on an Austrian horse which Lambert had secured him. He re-entered the room where I lay in bed, looking so pale and exhausted that I exclaimed:

"'Oh, my God! General, are you hurt?'

"'No,' he said, 'but I have killed so many, so many!'

"And then he fainted away. I called for help, and they ran in; the general had not even had time to reach an armchair before he fell unconscious on the floor. This faint was not a dangerous one, it was simply the result of excessive fatigue; and indeed his sabre was so notched and bent it would not go down into its sheath by quite four inches.

"With the help of a dram or two, we soon brought him round; and a bowlful of soup that had been made for me speedily completed the cure. He had eaten nothing since six in the morning, and he had been fighting hard till four in the afternoon. For, quite contrary to the habit of most soldiers, the general always fought fasting, unless he was surprised unawares.

"At this juncture General Joubert came in and flung himself on the general's neck.

"'Really, my dear Dumas,' he said, 'you quite make me tremble; each time I see you leap on your horse and gallop off at the head of your dragoons, I say to myself, "He surely can't avoid coming to grief at that mad pace." It seems you have been working miracles again to-day! Mind you take care of yourself; what the deuce should I do if you got killed? Remember what a distance we have to go yet before we reach Villach.'[2]

"The general was so weak he could not yet speak, but had to be content with putting his arms round Joubert's head to pull his face nearer his own, kissing him as one would kiss a child.

"On the following day General Joubert asked for a sword of honour for General Dumas, as his own was worn out with cutting down the Austrians."

My father was not mistaken; so severe had been the lesson given to the two Austrian generals that neither of them returned to the charge, and, eight days later, General Delmas was easily able to rejoin the bulk of the division stationed at Brixen.

The next day after his arrival the army moved on to Lensk. They had received no news from Bonaparte, and they did not know what position he occupied. However, they acted on their own judgment, and they imagined that if they marched towards Styria they would regain the main army.

They accomplished their march without any other hindrance than was offered by a few squadrons of dragoons belonging to the Archduke John, which were following the main army. Every now and again Joubert detached my father and his dragoons to deal with these gentlemen; and then the army saw a specimen of those charges which Joubert, a man who did not easily flinch at anything, said made him *tremble*.

During one of these charges my father took an officer prisoner, and, recognising him as a man of good family, he let him move about freely on his parole. The Austrian, who spoke French fluently, rode one of Dermoncourt's horses, trotting by and talking with the officers of the staff. The day after his capture he caught sight of his regiment following our rear-guard at about five hundred paces off, doubtless on purpose to gain an opportunity of falling upon us. He asked my father's permission to go just near enough to his old comrades to be able to give them some messages for his family. My father knew he could rely on his word, and let him know that he was perfectly free to do what he wished. The officer set off immediately at a gallop, and quickly covered the space between which separated him from his old comrades before any one of our officers had even thought of questioning where he was off to. After having conveyed his messages, he wished his comrades good-bye and was about to return; but the officer in command of their advance guard pointed out to him that, since he had fallen into the hands of the Austrian soldiery, he was no longer a French prisoner, and invited him to stay with them and to let our troops continue on their journey.

But the officer's only reply to these insidious suggestions was: "I am a prisoner on parole."

And, when his old comrades tried to retain him by force, he drew one of his pistols from his holsters and declared he would blow out the brains of the first man who laid a hand on him.

Then, wheeling round, he galloped back to the French quarters.

On approaching Dermoncourt, he said, "You did well to place such confidence in me as to leave your pistols in your holsters, for it was owing to them I was able to keep my faith with you."

The march continued its same uneventful course, and the two generals were much puzzled by this inertia on the part of the Austrians, until they learnt the successes of the grand army marching on Vienna, and that the heads of the columns of the Army of the Rhine had reached Lensk.

But once more the army witnessed a fight, or rather shall we call it a Homeric contest? Our extreme rear-guard, comprised of a corporal and four men, was caught up by the extreme van-guard of the enemy, composed of an equal number of men under a captain. A conversation began between the two commanding officers. The captain commenced a discourse in French, which our corporal did not find at all to his taste, so he pretended to take affront, and invited him, there being four seconds on each side, to settle the quarrel on the spot. The captain, who was a Belgian, accepted the offer. The two patrols drew up, facing one another, and the champions fought in the space between.

It chanced that the corporal was a fencing-master while the captain was a skilled swordsman, and a most interesting exhibition of skill began between these ably matched rivals. Each blow given was quickly parried, each thrust led to its riposte: after a few minutes' fighting, the champions engaged at such close quarters that the swords clashed hilt to hilt. Then the corporal, who was very active, threw down his sword and seized the captain round the waist; the captain, who was obliged to defend himself by the same form of attack, had to throw aside his weapon also, and to maintain the struggle under the new conditions thrust upon him. But now the corporal proved himself his rival's superior. He lifted the captain out of his saddle, but, unseating himself at the same time by the violence of his exertions, he lost his balance, and they fell together; only, he fell on the top and the captain underneath; moreover, the captain, who was already slightly wounded, dislocated his shoulder in the fall. He could not therefore hold out longer, and had to surrender; but, faithful to the conditions of the fight, he commanded his troop not to stir— an order they were quite disposed to obey, the dragoons with fixed carbines being ready to fire. Each side withdrew, the Austrians returning minus their chief, and the French going off with their prisoner.

We had as a matter of fact taken the superior officer of the lieutenant who was already a prisoner; and the latter, who was on familiar terms with all our staff, introduced his captain to my father.

My father gave him a cordial welcome, and quickly put him into the hands of our surgeon-major.

This warm reception, and the care my father took of these two officers, was to produce consequences which we shall see in due course.

But to return to the main events. The treaty of Léoben was already being discussed, and an armistice had even been agreed upon, when an Austrian dragoon officer reached our staff quarters with a safe conduct from the headquarters of the Rhine army.

This officer was the very same who had turned tail at the farm of Clausen, inciting my father to fight.

Our two prisoners were officers under his command, and he came to bring them money and personal effects.

He thanked my father heartily for his great care of these two officers, and, my father inviting him to dinner, the conversation at table turned to that adventure on the plateau, when a whole regiment had beaten a retreat before two men.

My father had not recognised the commandant.

"Upon my word," he said, "I only regret one thing, and that is that the chief of the squadron who challenged me changed his mind, and did not think fit to wait for me."

At the first mention of this subject Dermoncourt had noticed the officer's embarrassment, and, looking at him more attentively, had recognised him as the commandant with whom my father had had dealings.

He then thought it was about time to cut the conversation short, and said:

"But, General, do you not recognise this gentleman?"

"Upon my word, I don't," said my father.

"He was the commandant—"

"Well?"

Dermoncourt signed to the officer as much as to say that he had better continue the conversation himself.

The officer, understanding his meaning, replied, laughing:

"That commandant, General, was myself!"

"Really!"

"But—did you not see him?" Dermoncourt asked my father.

"The deuce, no," he replied; "I was too much beside myself with rage that day, because I could not manage to cross swords with the person who had incited me."

"Well! I was the man who incited you, General," said the officer. "I meant to give you the chance of fighting, but when I saw you bearing down on me, I remembered the style in which I had seen you *go to work*, and my courage failed me. I wanted to tell you this yourself, General, and that is the reason why I asked leave to bring my officers their money and goods. I wanted to see at close quarters the man for whom I had conceived such a great admiration that I dared tell him to his face, 'General, I was afraid of you, and I refused the fight I had offered you.'"

My father held out his hand.

"Upon my word, Commandant, if that is the case, pray say no more about it. I prefer that our acquaintance should begin at this table rather than elsewhere. Your health, Commandant."

They drank, and the conversation then turned upon other subjects.

But the topic still hovered round my father's fine feat of arms at Clausen; the three officers had heard the story of the bridge; all thought my father had been killed, even as was his horse, and the news had made a profound sensation in the Austrian army.

My father then referred to the famous pistols which he so much regretted, and which he had charged Joubert to regain from the hands of the Austrians if it were possible; they still remained in the hands of the enemy, in spite of that commission.

The three officers took particular note of my father's expressions of regret, each resolving to search for these precious pistols—the commandant directly he returned to camp, and the two others as soon as they were free.

Thanks to my father, the two officers had not long to wait for their liberty: they were exchanged for two French officers of a similar rank. They took leave of the officers' quarters with many expressions of gratitude, and one of them, at any rate, did not lose time in giving proof of this to my father.

A week or so after their departure, an officer came under a flag of truce to the French camp, and, asking to speak with my father, handed him the pistols he had mourned for so long. They had been carried to General Kerpen himself, who, upon the request of the officer whom my father had wounded and taken prisoner, returned them to him with a charming letter. The next day but one my father received the following letter from this officer:—

"MONSIEUR LE GÉNÉRAL,—I hope you have received your pistols by the officer under flag of truce, who left here the day before yesterday; Lieutenant-General Baron de Kerpen has sent them you. I received my cloak, for which I have to thank you, as well as for many other kindnesses you have shown me. Be assured, General, that my gratitude is beyond words, and that my greatest wish is to be able to prove it. My wounds are beginning to heal, and the fever has abated.

"We hear the strongest rumours of peace. I hope as soon as it is concluded that I shall be able to come and greet you before you leave these parts. Frossart,[3] who has lost his heart to you and to General Joubert, charges me with a thousand messages for you both.

"Believe me, Monsieur le Général, with sincerest regards, your very obedient servant,

HAT DE LEVIS, Captain.

"LIENTZ, 20th April 1797."

And that was how my father once more got possession of the famous pistols, the loss of which he had deplored so deeply.

I hope my reader will forgive me these details. Alas! in the rapid movement which carries us along through the time of revolutions, our manners change, become blurred and are forgotten, to be replaced in their turn by other manners as variable as their predecessors. The French Revolution stamped a peculiar seal upon our army; when I come across it I treasure up the impression as one would that of a precious medal fast being obliterated by rust; anxious to make its worth known to one's contemporaries, and to hand down its characteristics to posterity.

And, moreover, we shall misjudge all these men of the Republic if we judge them only by those who survived the Republic and lived on into the period of the Empire. The Empire was an epoch of rude pressure, and the Emperor Napoleon was a rough coiner of new metal. He wanted all money to be stamped with his own image, and all bronze to be smelted in his own furnace; even as he himself had, in some measure, set an example in the transformation of his own character. No one resembled First Consul Bonaparte less than the Emperor Napoleon, the conqueror of Arcole less than the conquered of Waterloo.

Thus the men we must look to to form our ideas of Republican manners are those who by a premature death escaped the birth of the Empire: such men as Marceau, Hoche, Desaix, Kléber, and my father.

Born with the Republic, these men died with her: they knew no change, not even in the cut of the clothes beneath which beat their loyal, brave Republican hearts.

My father, Hoche, and Marceau were all once gathered round the same table: all of them were commanders-in-chief; my father, who was but thirty-one, was the oldest among them. The other two were twenty-four and twenty-six years of age. Their united ages only came to eighty-one. What a promising future seemed before them! But a bullet killed one of them, and the other two were poisoned.

[1] The painter Lethiers painted a picture of my father, representing this scene.

[2] Bonaparte's headquarters and rendezvous.

[3] A Belgian officer.

CHAPTER II

Joubert's loyalty towards my father—"Send me Dumas"—The Horatius Codes of the Tyrol—My father is appointed-Governor of the Trévisan—The agent of the Directory—My father fêted at his departure—The treaty of Campo-Formio—The return to Paris—The flag of the Army of Italy—The charnel-house of Morat—Charles the Bold—Bonaparte is elected a member of the Institute—First thoughts of the expedition to Egypt—Toulon—Bonaparte and Joséphine—What was going to happen in Egypt.

Joubert owed a large share of the success of that fine Tyrolean campaign to my father, and, being a loyal man, he did for his comrade-in-arms what under similar circumstances his comrade-in-arms would have done for him. Each report he sent in to Bonaparte contained my father's name coupled with the highest of praise. To have heard Joubert, one might have thought the whole success of the campaign was owing to my father's energy and courage. My father was the terror of the Austrian cavalry—he was a mediæval Bayard, and if, added Joubert, by one of those miracles which govern the march of the centuries, Italy had produced two Cæsars, General Dumas would have been one of them.

Very different was Berthier's treatment of him—Berthier, who had stigmatised my father as a "looker-on" during a campaign in which three horses were killed under him.

By degrees, as these things were brought to the notice of the general-in-chief, Bonaparte came round to my father's side, and when Joubert was leaving the camp of Grätz, where he had been paying the commander-in-chief a visit, Bonaparte spoke these few most pregnant words: "By the way, send Dumas to me."

Joubert hastened to deliver his commission directly he returned to his army. But my father was sulky, and it took all Joubert's friendly entreaties to persuade him to accede to Bonaparte's invitation. However, he started for Grätz, but with a fixed determination to send in his resignation to the Directory, if Bonaparte did not give him the reception he deserved.

My father was a Creole—with the Creole characteristics, nonchalant, impetuous, changeable. He had no sooner won his heart's desires than he conceived a profound disgust for them. When the energy he had expended in obtaining his desires had died down he fell back into his usual indifference and laziness, and at the first sign of opposition he would talk of the pleasures of country life, as did the ancient poet whose country he had conquered, and would send in his resignation to the Directory.

Happily Dermoncourt was at hand. When he received these letters of resignation to despatch, he slipped them in a drawer of his desk, put the key in his pocket, and quietly waited.

At the end of a week or a fortnight, or even a month, the momentary cloud of disgust which had swept over my poor father's spirits disappeared, and some brilliant charge or daringly successful manoeuvre would arouse his enthusiastic nature, ever eager to aspire after the impossible, and, with a sigh, he would let these words fall: "Upon my word, I believe I did wrong to send in my resignation."

And Dermoncourt, who was on the watch for this, would reply:

"Don't worry yourself, General; your resignation—"

"Well, my resignation—?"

"It is in that desk, ready to send off on the first chance; there is only the date to alter."

Therefore it was only by resolutely determining to send in his resignation himself straight to the Directory this time, at the first hint of any slight that might be put upon him by Bonaparte, that my father went to Grätz to meet him.

As soon as Bonaparte saw my father he opened his arms and exclaimed: "Welcome to the Horatius Codes of the Tyrol!"

My father could no longer retain his ill-feeling in the face of such a flattering reception; he held out his arms likewise, and a fraternal salute was given and returned.

"Oh!" my father exclaimed when, seven years later, Bonaparte proclaimed himself Emperor,—"oh! only to think I held him in my arms and had the chance of strangling him!"

Bonaparte had some end to serve in all he did, and his object in sending for my father was to gain help in organising the fresh cavalry divisions which were required by his army. He gave my father the task of raising these divisions, and also the command of them when organised.

In the meantime my father was appointed governor of the province of the Trévisan, and he and Dermoncourt immediately established themselves there. The new governor was received very favourably in that beautiful province. The finest palaces of the wealthiest of the senators of Venice were placed at his service. The Trévisan was to Venice what ancient Baiæ was to Rome, the country home of a queen.

The Municipality offered my father three hundred francs per day for his household expenses. My father went into his accounts with Dermoncourt (I have his calculations before me, scribbled on the back of a map of the Trévisan), and they decided that a hundred francs would be enough.

He therefore would only accept a hundred francs.

The poor Italians were not used to these methods, neither did they in the least understand the disinterestedness of the motive. They would not believe it for a long time, but continually expected either the imposition of a war tax, or some compulsory levy, or even some gross extortion similar to those said to be exercised in the East.

Once they really believed the fatal hour had come, and great was their alarm! The presence had been announced of an agent from the French Government commissioned to plunder the Italian money-lenders. He called upon my father to offer him a share in the prospective treasure; but only Dermoncourt was at home. That gentleman listened quietly to all the suggested projects made by that bird of prey, and to all his offers to my father of a share in the booty. Then, when he had done, Dermoncourt said:

"How did you come here?"

"Why, by carriage."

"Very well, my advice to you is to go back the same way you came, without even seeing the general."

"Why so?" asked the traveller.

"Why, because he is the very devil when certain proposals are made to him."

"Bah! I will dress these up so fine he will soon listen to them."

"You really intend to try him?"

"Why, certainly I do."

"Then go and try."

My father came in just at that moment, and the agent asked to see him alone.

My father cast a questioning glance at Dermoncourt, who nodded significantly that he had better grant the desired interview.

Alone with my father, the agent of the Directory held forth volubly upon his mission; then, as he noticed that my father listened without making any response, he proceeded from explanation to plans, from plans to peroration.

The peroration contained the offer of my father's share of the plunder: but my father here cut him short. He took him by the collar, lifted him up at arm's length, opened the door into the room where Dermoncourt had summoned the whole of the staff to await the end of the scene:——

"Gentlemen," he said, "look well at this little blackguard, so that you may know him again, and if ever he presents himself at my outposts, no matter in what part of the world I may be, shoot him down without so much as disturbing me to tell me justice has been done."

The agent of the Directory did not stop to hear more; he vanished, and my father reckoned one implacable enemy the more.

These acts of depredation were common in Italy; but raids on money-lenders were usually the most lucrative during those times of distress and misery. Nearly all the jewellery, diamonds and silver belonging to the Italian nobility were in pawn. Many had even deposited therein, as though in a strong-room, everything valuable they possessed, when they were compelled by political events to leave their country.

Then an agent would come from the Directory, whether his authority were true or false (certain of the governors did not inquire too closely), and would make a clean sweep. He would first settle the ruling officer's share, then his own: the rest he sent to the Government.

One of the most notorious of these agents received the sobriquet of "Rapinat." His operations were chiefly confined to Lombardy. This quatrain was composed about him:——

"The Milanese whose goods decline,
Would dearly like to know
If Rapinat does spell *rapine*,
Or rapine—*Rapinat*."

So when, after two months of residence in the country, my father gave up the governorship of the Trévisan to take that of Polesina, situated at the town of Rovigo, he found waiting for him outside the door of the palace a beautiful carriage drawn by four horses, with a coachman sitting on the box. It was a present from the town of Treviso. My father wished to decline it; but the gift was offered so gracefully and so heartily that he felt obliged to accept it. And the neighbouring municipalities sent him dozens of addresses: we will select two specimens haphazard.

"To CITIZEN GENERAL DUMAS, Governor of the Trévisan, and the Municipalities of Mestre, Noale, Castel-Franco, and Asolo.

"We, the undersigned representatives of the above-named municipalities, have been unanimously and specially appointed to present ourselves before you, Citizen General, to bear testimony to our appreciation of, and gratitude towards you for the lenity and equity of your government.

"Would to Heaven they had the means to show their admiration, their affection, and their gratitude! How happy would they be were it in their power to give you tokens worthy your deserts and your virtues!

"But as in their present condition of impoverishment and distress they are prevented from following the dictates of their hearts, they do themselves the honour to hope that you, their protector and their father, will be graciously pleased to accept this slight token.

"Continue your generous protection over us, and cast a fatherly eye on your children; for to you we look for comfort.

"We have the honour to remain

"HENRI-ANTOINE REINATI, President and State Secretary; JEAN ALLEGRI, President of the Municipality of Noale; FRANÇOIS BELHAMINI, President of the Municipality of Asolo; PHILIPPE DE RICOIDI, Vice-President of the Municipality of Mestre.

"CASTEL-FRANCO, *2 Messidor, fifth year of the French Republic and second of Italian Liberty.*"

"LIBERTY—EQUALITY—VIRTUE.

"9 *Nivôse, 1797, Year V of the French Republic, one and indivisible, and II of Italian Liberty.*

"THE MUNICIPALITY OF ADRIA to CITIZEN ALEXANDRE DUMAS, General of Division.

"This Municipality, General, cannot find words in which to express its sense of obligation to you for the kind acts you have condescended to shower upon us under divers circumstances; especially in relieving us by sending away the troops, and still more by refunding the sums unjustly extorted by General L——.

"The Municipality seizes this opportunity to offer you a horse, in recognition of your goodness to us, begging you to accept it as a humble tribute, and in grateful recognition of its many obligations towards you.

"We are, General, with sincere respects and affectionate greetings,

"LUNALI, President; LARDI, General Secretary."

It can easily be seen that the people were in despair when my father left the Trévisan: the whole province mourned, and the town of Treviso wanted to send a deputation to Bonaparte to ask him to allow them to keep their governor. When no hope of keeping him was left them, they asked for ten days longer in order to give him a round of fêtes. When the hour of departure came, all the notables of the town conducted him in a triumphal procession as far as Padua, where there were more festivities.

Here farewells were prolonged another week: the eight leading houses in the town each undertook to provide some form of entertainment; and my father changed his abode daily, spending a day and a night at each house of his various entertainers.

On reaching Rovigo, the seat of his fresh sphere of government, a reception awaited my father quite as complimentary as the farewells. The inhabitants of Polesine had been advised in advance by the inhabitants of the Trévisan, and knew whom they had to expect in their new governor.

Polesine, fertile in corn and pasturage, was the province where Bonaparte had established the squadrons of cavalry of which he wished to form a division, under my father's organisation.

On his arrival, as in the Trévisan, my father at once regulated his household expenses on the basis of a hundred francs a day, giving express orders to the municipalities not to authorise any supplies or to attend to any applications without his consent.

My father remained some time at Rovigo, as the negotiations of the Congress dragged out, until Bonaparte, impatient to conclude matters, decided to collect his army and proceed to the Tagliamento. My father then rejoined his division, and remained near that river until 18th October, 1797, when peace was signed at the village of Campo-Formio. Eight days later he returned to Rovigo.

By the peace of Campo-Formio, which ended the campaign of 1797,—that campaign wherein, thanks to my father and Joubert, the expedition to the Tyrol played so glorious a part,—Austria ceded Belgium and Mayence, Mannheim and Philipsbourg to France, and Austrian Lombardy to the Cis-Alpine Republic.

The Venetian States were divided. Corfu, Zante, Cephalonia, Santa Maura, Cerigo, and their dependent islands, with Albania, were ceded to France. Istria, Dalmatia, the Adriatic isles, Venice, and the Venetian territory on the mainland as far as the Adige, the Tanaro, and the Po were given up to the Austrian emperor, who thus found himself master of the Adriatic Gulf.

The remaining Venetian States on the mainland were given to the Cis-Alpine Republic under the suzerainty of the emperor. And the duc de Modena received Brisgaw as indemnity.

Poor municipality of Adria, which had dated its address to my father Year II of Italian Liberty!

During this sojourn on the Tagliamento—the reason for which, as we have said, was to urge forward the Austrian negotiations—my father dined three times a week at the headquarters of Bonaparte. Here it was that he became more intimately acquainted with Joséphine, whom he had already met at Milan, and who kept a friendly feeling in her heart for him even after his disgrace—the friendship of Creole for Creole.

They also met once a week at Udine. Bernadotte was in command in that town, and after the play they turned the hall into a ballroom and danced all night. Bonaparte danced very little, as might be imagined; but my father, Murat, Clarke, and all the young aides-de-camp danced a great deal.

The day after the signing of the treaty of Campo-Formio the ball was opened by a quadrille. Joséphine danced with Clarke, Madame Pauline Bonaparte with Murat, Mademoiselle Caroline Bonaparte with Dermoncourt, and Madame César Berthier was my father's partner.

Bonaparte set out for Paris directly the treaty of Campo-Formio was signed, and retired to the little house in the rue des Victoires, which he had recently purchased from Talma.

It was there that the Egyptian campaign was conceived and planned.

Bonaparte, with more success than the Carthaginian heroes, had accomplished in Italy almost as much as Hannibal. It remained for him to do in the East what Alexander and Cæsar had done.

But before proceeding to this, Bonaparte acquitted himself of a debt of gratitude that had long been owing to my father and to Joubert. He introduced my father to the acting Directory as the *Horatius Codes of the Tyrol*, and he deputed Joubert to present the *Standard of the Army of Italy* to the heads of government.

This standard of the Italian army was more than a flag: it was a memorial—a wonderful memorial of a wonderful campaign.

On one side it bore the words:

"TO THE ARMY OF ITALY FROM A GRATEFUL COUNTRY."

On the other side was a list of the battles fought and places taken; followed by abridged inscriptions, grand in their simplicity, concerning the campaign that had just been closed.

That second side, alas, so soon to be forgotten by the men who successively headed the affairs of government, forgotten most of all by the nephew of the emperor himself, ran as follows:—

"150,000 prisoners; 170 standards; 550 pieces of cannon; 600 light field-guns; 5 pontoon trains; 9 ships of 64 guns; 12 frigates of 32; 12 sloops of war; 18 galleys: armistice with the King of Sardinia; convention with Genoa; armistice with the Duke of Parma; armistice with the King of Naples; armistice with the Pope; preliminaries of Léoben; convention of Montebello with the Republic of Genoa; treaty of peace with the Emperor at Campo-Formio.

"Liberty given to the peoples of Bologna, Modena, Ferrara, Massa, Carrara, Romagna, Lombardy, Brescia, Bergamo, Mantua, Cremona, to parts of Verona, to Chiavenna, Bormio, la Valteline, and Genoa; to the imperial fiefs; to the peoples of the departments of Corfu, Ægean Sea, and Ithaca.

"Sent to Paris all the principal works of Michael Angelo, Guerchino, Titian, Paolo Veronese, Corregio, of Albano, of the Carracci, of Raphael, and of Leonardo da Vinci."

Bonaparte stopped on his way through Mantua and visited the monument General Miollis had erected to Virgil; he also celebrated a military fête in honour of Hoche, who had recently died—in all probability from poison.

Bonaparte crossed through Switzerland to Moudon, where they gave him a brilliant reception, and where his carriage was broken.

He continued his journey on foot; and when near the charnel-house of Morat, which had not yet been destroyed by Brune, this other *Bold* soldier, who himself was to have his mortuary at Waterloo, asked: "Where is the Duke of Burgundy's battlefield?"

"There, General," said a Swiss officer, pointing out what he wished to see.

"How many men had he?"

"Sixty thousand, sire."

"How was he attacked?"

"By the Swiss rushing down the neighbouring mountains, and, under cover of a wood which then existed, turning the Burgundian position."

"What!" he exclaimed. "Charles the Bold had sixty thousand men and yet he did not take possession of the mountains!" And the conqueror of Italy shrugged his shoulders.

"Frenchmen of to-day fight better than that," Lannes observed.

"The Burgundians were not French in those days," Bonaparte answered shortly; and, as his carriage was now brought up, repaired, he got in and rapidly drove away.

Bonaparte was not altogether easy in the position he had made for himself by this sequence of marvellous conquests. He had indeed received a triumphant ovation in Paris; the whole audience had risen, shouting, "Vive Bonaparte!" when they heard that he was present at the second representation of *Horatius Codes*; but all these ovations did not blind his eyes to facts.

That same night, he said to Bourienne: "Nothing is remembered in Paris. If I remain quiet long without doing something fresh, I shall be lost: one idol quickly replaces another in this great Babylon. If I were to attend the play three times more they would then ignore my presence."

A few days later he was made a member of the Institute, under the Science and Art division—an honour that gratified him extremely. He immediately sent the following letter to the president:—

"CITIZEN PRESIDENT,—I feel deeply honoured by the votes of the distinguished men who compose the Institute. I am very sensible that before I can become their equal I must for a long time yet remain their scholar.

"If there were any more expressive way by which I could express my high regard for them, I would avail myself of it. The true conquests, the only victories which bring no aftermaths of regret, are those that overcome ignorance.

"Those are the most honourable occupations, the most serviceable to all nations, which contribute to the widening of human knowledge. The true strength of the French Republic should from henceforth consist in making every new discovery a part of itself.

BONAPARTE."

There is in Molière's *l'Avare* a phrase which Harpagon thought of inscribing in letters of gold on the walls of his dining-room. Tell me, Prince Louis, if there is not a similar phrase for you to meditate upon in this letter of your uncle's to the Institute?

All these ovations in public places and these receptions by the Institute sufficed for a time to distract a brain so active as Bonaparte's, but they could not satisfy him for long.

Very soon he returned to his favourite idea—the East: it had come to him whilst he was waiting and watching the progress of peace negotiations at Paneriano.

"Europe is a mole-hill," he observed once, when walking with Bourrienne, César Berthier and my father; "it has never had such grand empires or great revolutions as the East, with its six hundred millions of peoples."

He wrote to the Directory as early as August 1797:—"We feel that the time is not far distant when, to destroy England's power thoroughly, we ought to take possession of Egypt."

"Malta is for sale," he said another day, "and it would not be paying too dearly for it if we gave for it half we paid for the peace of Campo-Formio."

Whether to conceal his true motives, or whether Bonaparte really believed in the possibility of invading England, on the 10th of February 1798 he set out for the north of France, and visited Boulogne, Ambleteuse, Calais, Dunkerque, Fumes, Nieuport, Ostend, and the isle of Walcheren. On his return from this journey he said to Bourienne:

"It is too risky a game; I dare not venture it, for I do not want to play wantonly with the fate of our beautiful France."

Was the idea of an Egyptian expedition a conception of Bonaparte's own brain, or had he come across the suggestion in some pigeonholes of ministerial papers belonging to the duc de Choiseul, who proposed a similar project to Louis XV.? It is impossible to say definitely. However that may be, the Directory raised no opposition to the ambitious desires of this second Cambyses.

The Directory was envious of his glory, and it feared the shadows thrown by the conqueror of Arcole and of Rivoli as it would fear the shade cast by the deadly upas-tree.

On April 12th, 1798, Bonaparte was appointed commander-in-chief of the Army of the East.

"How long shall you be in Egypt, General?" his secretary asked, as he offered his congratulations upon the appointment.

"Six months or six years," replied Bonaparte; "it all depends on events. I shall colonise the country, and shall introduce artists, workmen of all kinds, women, actors, poets. I am only twenty-nine years old now, and should then be but thirty-five, which is not such a great age. If all goes as I hope, six years will suffice to penetrate into India as far as Alexander did."

On the 19th April, Bonaparte announced his departure for Toulon. On the 4th May he left Paris, accompanied by Joséphine. On the 8th he reached Toulon.

Seven regiments of my father's division were ordered to Toulon. As my father arrived before either Bonaparte or Kléber, he took command of the troops for the expedition; handing it over to his senior, Kléber, when the latter arrived.

Toulon was full of memories for Bonaparte: it was from Toulon that the Eagle took his flight. The day of his arrival he walked by the sea-shore, and visited the Petit Gibraltar.

He had scarcely had time to see my father before he said: "Come and see me to-morrow morning as early as you like."

At six the next morning my father was crossing the parade-ground to see Bonaparte, when he came across Dermoncourt.

"Where the deuce are you off to, General, at this time of morning?" he asked.

"Come with me, and you will see," said my father. And they proceeded together.

As they approached their destination, Dermoncourt exclaimed:

"You are not going to see Bonaparte, are you, General?"

"I am."

"But he won't receive you."

"Why not?"

"Why, because it is too early."

"Oh! that doesn't matter."

"But he will be in bed."

"Quite likely."

"And in bed with his wife; he loves her as shopkeepers love their wives."

"So much the better! I shall be charmed to see good Joséphine once more."

And my father dragged Dermoncourt after him, half willing, half afraid to see what would happen.

Finally, he came to the conclusion my father had a special audience, and followed him.

My father ascended a staircase, went along a passage, opened a little door, pushed back a screen, and he and Dermoncourt, who still followed him closely, found themselves in Bonaparte's bedroom.

He was in bed with Joséphine, and, the weather being exceedingly hot, they were covered merely by a sheet, which showed the outline of their bodies.

Joséphine was weeping, and Bonaparte was trying to wipe her tears away with one hand, while with the other he laughingly played a military tattoo on the portion of her body which was turned towards the recess between bed and wall.

"Ah! Dumas," he said, as he caught sight of my father; "your arrival is opportune; you must help me to make this silly little woman listen to reason. Ought she to wish to come to Egypt with us? Now, would you take your wife there?"

"Upon my word, certainly not," my father replied. "She would be in my way dreadfully."

"Now, then! you see what I said; and you know that Dumas is not a bad husband, he loves his wife and his daughters. Listen: I may return in six months, or we may be over there several years."

At that Joséphine's tears flowed faster than ever.

"If we stay there some years, the fleet will have to return to fetch some twenty thousand men from the Italian coasts. Return to Paris, tell Madame Dumas, and both of you shall return to us with that convoy. Will that suit you, Dumas?"

"Perfectly," replied my father.

"When there, my dear Joséphine, Dumas, who has only daughters, and I who have not even those, will each of us do our best to produce a boy: if we have a boy, he and his wife shall be its godparents; if he has a boy, you and I will be its godparents. There now, that is a promise; stop crying, and let us talk business."

Then, turning to Dermoncourt, Bonaparte said:

"M. Dermoncourt, you have just heard a word drop which indicates the destination of our expedition. Not a creature knows it yet: do not let the word 'Egypt' escape your lips; you will readily understand the importance of such a secret."

Dermoncourt signified that he would be as dumb as a disciple of Pythagoras.

Joséphine consoled herself: indeed, if we may believe Bourrienne, she managed to console herself too well.

On the 15th May my father again visited Bonaparte, and the departure was fixed for the 19th.

He found Bonaparte just about to dictate an order to Bourrienne; so he was discreetly about to withdraw, when Bonaparte called after him: "No, stay, you are not in the way;—hear what I am going to do."

Then, putting his hand on that giant's shoulder: "What I like about you, Dumas (he said) is, not only your indisputable courage, but your humanity, a rarer quality. I know that Collot d'Herbois wanted to cut your head off because in some little town in the Tarantaise you rescued from the guillotine three or four poor devils who did not wish to let their village bells be melted down. Very well! Would you believe that only six weeks ago they shot an old man of eighty—the butchers—under cover of the law *sur les émigrés*. Now write, Bourrienne." And he dictated.

"HEADQUARTERS AT TOULON,

"*27th Floréal, Year VI* (16*th May* 1798).

"BONAPARTE, Member of the National Institute, to the Military Commissioners of the 9th Division established in consequence of the law of 19th Fructidor.

"I learn with the deepest concern, citizens, that aged people of seventy and eighty years old, poor women who were *enceinte* and needed by their children, have been shot as suspected of wanting to emigrate.

"Have, then, the soldiers of Liberty become executioners? Has the spirit of compassion, which they take even into the very battlefield, become dead within their hearts? The law of 19th Fructidor was a measure providing for public safety; its object was to get at conspirators, not miserable women, and worn-out old men.

"I exhort you, then, citizens, whenever the law brings before your tribunal people above sixty years of age or women, to declare that you have respect for the aged and the women of your enemy even in the midst of fighting.

"The military officer who signs a sentence against any person incapable of carrying arms is a coward.

"BONAPARTE."

As he left Bonaparte's house, my father met Kléber re-entering it.

"You do not know what we are going to do over there?" he said.

"We are going to found a colony."

"No, we are going to re-establish a kingdom."

"Oh! oh!" said Kléber, "we shall see."

"Very well!—you *will* see."

And with these words the two friends parted.

On the 19th of May they set sail.

CHAPTER III

The voyage—The landing—The taking of Alexandria—The *Chant du Départ* and the Arabian concert—The respited prisoners—The march on Cairo—Rum and biscuit—My father's melons—The Scientific Institute—Battle of the Pyramids—Scene of the victory—My father's letter establishing the truth.

Bonaparte sailed in the *Orient*, a fine boat of 120 guns.

As she left the harbour, being very heavily laden, she drew too much water and touched the bottom, causing a short time of confusion among the fleet. The boatswain's mate, Boyer, of the *Guillaume Tell*, in which my father was sailing, shook his head gloomily.

"What is the matter, Boyer?" my father asked.

"Some disaster will happen to the fleet, General."

"Why should it?"

"Because the admiral's flag-ship touched ground. Don't you know it is an infallible omen?"

My father shrugged his shoulders.

Two months afterwards the fleet was destroyed at Aboukir.

The details of the crossing are well known: they took Malta as they passed—Malta the impregnable!

Caffarelli, who visited the fortifications with Bonaparte, could not help saying to him: "Upon my word, General, lucky for you to have someone inside the citadel to open the gates for you! If it had not been for that, I don't think you would ever have got in."

Bonaparte set the Turkish prisoners free—a move to propitiate the Sultan.

The fleet left Malta on the 19th June and set sail for Candia.

Nelson was at Messina with the English fleet when he heard of the taking of Malta. He was convinced Bonaparte intended sailing for Egypt, and immediately set sail for Alexandria.

During the night of the 22nd to 23rd of June, the English and French fleets passed within six leagues of one another. The English fleet did not see ours, and whilst we were bearing north it sailed south, reaching Alexandria three days before us.

As Nelson had not discovered any trace of our passage, and learnt that our fleet had not been signalled by any ship, he thought our expedition was meant to conquer Asia, and rapidly moved off to Alexandretta, in Syria.

This miscalculation saved the expedition, which reached Candia, took advantage of the northerly winds, and immediately sailed due south.

Land was sighted at break of day on July 1st, and high above the ruins and the white houses towered the column of Septimus Severus. Bonaparte realised the danger he had escaped; it was nothing short of a miracle that the English fleet did not catch sight of ours. He gave orders for immediate disembarkation.

The whole day was taken up by this important operation, and it was accomplished without serious accident, although the sea was rough.

But, on landing, about a score of men, thinking they could see a fountain of water, ran off into the interior of the country, were surrounded by a tribe of Bedouins and had their captain killed.

This was a bad beginning! Bonaparte issued very strict orders concerning stragglers, and promised a reward of a hundred piastres to every Arab who should bring back a prisoner.

A hundred Turkish piastres is only equivalent to about twenty-five francs; but Bonaparte did not wish to spoil the Bedouins.

And he was wise, as we shall see presently.

The cavalry were unable, to land on account of the foul weather; Bonaparte decided not to wait for them, and, towards three in the morning, he began to march towards Alexandria, with the three divisions of Kléber, Bon, and Moreau. My father, hunting-rifle in hand, headed the carabineers of the 4th light demi-brigade.

No difficulties were encountered upon the journey until they came up to the walls of Alexandria, which were defended by the Turks.

Kléber received the first blow: a ball struck his head just as he took command of the attack.

The resistance made by the Alexandrians was not serious, and the town was captured at the end of an hour's fighting.

My father was one of the first to enter the town, and his great height, his bronzed complexion almost as dark as those of the Arabs, made a vivid impression upon the native inhabitants. This fact was reported to Bonaparte, who turned everything to account; and accordingly he sent for my father.

"General," he said, "take about a score of my guides and conduct them to the Arab tribe which is to bring me in prisoners. I wish you to be the first general they cast eyes on—the first chief with whom they shall treat."

Off my father set at a gallop, and a quarter of a league from the town he found the people he wanted. Through the agency of his dragoman he quickly gave them to understand that they must present themselves before the general-in-chief, who would be pleased to welcome them and give them the promised reward.

Bonaparte was not mistaken in his calculations: my father at once became a subject of study, curiosity, and admiration on the part of these children of nature, and, as he made no attempt to drive them away, he entered Alexandria with them pell-mell.

Bonaparte received them all in a large hall overlooking the sea, distributed his proclamations among them, which he had had translated into Arabic and offered them a repast which he had taken care should wound none of the customs of their country.

They accepted the repast with evident satisfaction, squatted themselves down, and each man began to snatch his fill.

In the midst of the feast the united bands of the three infantry regiments struck up instantly the *Chant du Départ*.

Although the explosion was both dreadful and unexpected, not a single Arab jumped up; they all continued eating in spite of the deafening din made by the hundred and twenty musicians.

Bonaparte asked them at the conclusion of the air if they liked the music.

"Yes!" they replied, "but our own is better."

Bonaparte desired to hear their music, since it was so superior to that of the French performance. Three Arabs thereupon left off eating, and two took up a kind of drum; the one looked like the pack of a wafer-seller, the other like a pumpkin cut in half. The third took up a kind of three-stringed guitar, and the Arabian concert began solemnly entering into competition with the French one.

Bonaparte complimented them highly upon their music, distributed the promised reward, and vows of friendship were exchanged on both sides.

A dozen or so of men were missing at roll-call. The Bedouins were in full swing of decapitating their prisoners, and had already accomplished a third of their work before they learned that the reward of a hundred piastres was offered for each prisoner brought back alive.

Like men who place business in the front rank before everything else, they immediately stopped killing their prisoners, and contented themselves with a less cruel method of sport, but a more unusual, in the eyes of the captives, than the punishment they had at first feared.

The upshot was, that when Bonaparte had the prisoners up before him to question them, he was amazed to see them all blush, turn their heads away, and stammer like bashful maidens. Finally, when urged by the general-in-chief, who, hearing so much talk of the indignities that had been put upon the captives, was really determined to find out what they had suffered, an old soldier told him, crying with rage, that he and his companions had been treated as the people of Sodom and Gomorrah would have treated the angels if they had not had the advantage over our grenadiers of possessing wings, with which they ascended to heaven without loss of time.

"Idiot," said Bonaparte, shrugging his shoulders contemptuously, "tears ill become you. Come, come, be thankful you got off so cheaply, and stop your blubbering."

This treatment of the prisoners made a great sensation throughout the army, and contributed in a large measure to keep discipline, which would have been more difficult to enforce had the soldiers only been in fear of having their heads chopped off.

Bonaparte stayed a week at Alexandria.

He spent the first day in reviewing his forces.

The second day he gave orders to Admiral Brueys to take the fleet into the old port of Alexandria or to lead it to Corfu.

On the third day he made his proclamation to the inhabitants, and ordered Desaix to march upon Cairo.

The fourth, he had the names of the men who had been killed outside Alexandria carved on Pompey's pillar, and had their bodies buried at the foot of that monument.

On the fifth day General Dugua seized Aboukir.

On the sixth, Rosetta was taken, and whilst the flotilla was being mobilised, the army prepared to march on Cairo.

On the seventh day he made Kléber commandant of Alexandria, assuring the Porte that he desired to keep on good terms with it, and then he left for Cairo himself.

Desaix was the first to set out, and the first to be seized with despondency.

I will quote from Desaix's own words (for his devotion to Bonaparte was beyond dispute).

On the 15th July, Desaix wrote thus to Bonaparte from Bakahireh:—

"For pity's sake don't leave us in this place! The troops are dejected and grumbling; let us either advance or retire as soon as possible. The villages are mere huts, and utterly devoid of provisions."

The army received four days' rations on starting; unluckily, and most unwisely, they had also been allowed four days' supply of rum. The consequence of this addition of liquid to solid provisions was that, during the first hours of the march through the desert that separates Alexandria from Damanhour, the soldiers, parched with thirst, but not yet hungry, attacked the rum, and went so frequently to the canteen where it was kept, that, before half the march was over, the canteen was empty and the men were drunk.

Then the soldiers, imagining with the happy optimism of drunkenness that they would never feel the pangs of hunger, began to lighten their knapsacks by scattering abroad their rice and throwing away their biscuits.

When their commanding officers found out what was going on, they gave orders for a halt.

Now a halt of two hours gave time enough for the first effects of the alcohol to pass off, and they resumed the march, already regretting their indiscreet conduct. Towards five in the morning, the hunger they fancied they had staved off began to attack them cruelly. They could scarcely manage to drag themselves as far as Damanhour, which was reached on the 9th at eight in the morning.

They had some hopes of finding food in that town, but it had been completely evacuated. They ransacked every house, and, as the harvest was just over, they found a morsel of threshed wheat; but the hand-mills wherewith the Arabs ground their corn were broken, having been purposely put out of gear. They managed to put several in order, and succeeded in procuring a small quantity of flour, but if distributed it would not have amounted to above half an ounce per man.

Discontent now began to spread through the troops, and hunger, that evil counsellor, whispered suggestions of rebellion among the men, and even among the officers.

So, amidst dejection and complaints, they began to march towards Rhamanieh.

It was no good the soldiers being impatient, since they had themselves alone to blame for their lack of provisions. Almost dying with hunger, they at last reached Rhamanieh, where they learnt they must halt for the 11th and 12th, to wait for provisions, which had been ordered in the Delta. These duly arrived, and the fresh food and the nearness to the Nile, into which the soldiers plunged the moment they reached it, somewhat restored courage to the army.

My father managed to procure two or three water-melons, and invited several generals of his acquaintance to eat them in his tent. They were not slow to respond to his invitation.

We have seen how badly the campaign had opened and how much the troops had already undergone since they left Alexandria. The Egypt that they had seen from afar, as a large emerald green riband unrolled in the midst of the desert, no longer appeared in its ancient fertility, as the granary of the world, but in its modern poverty, its shifting populations, its ruined and deserted villages.

Desaix's complaints were re-echoed by the whole army.

The gathering under my father's tent, which had met for the purpose of consuming the melons, very soon took a political turn, as each general gave vent to the ill-humour all shared alike.

What had they come to that accursed land for?—a land which had successively devoured all who tried to conquer it, since the days of Cambyses until the time of St. Louis. Had they come to found a colony? What was the good of leaving France, where the sun warmed a man without scorching him up,—France with its lovely forests, its fertile plains,—for this heaven of brass, this shadeless desert, these burning plains? Did Bonaparte want to shape a kingdom for himself in the East, after the fashion of the old Roman proconsuls? He might at least have asked his generals if they were willing to be the heads of this new satrapy. Such schemes might have succeeded with ancient armies composed of freed men and slaves, but not with the patriots of 1792, who were not the satellites of one man but soldiers belonging to a nation.

Were these recriminations simply murmurs wrung from them by their present hardships? Or were they already the undercurrent of rebellion against the ambitious spirit of the hero of the 18th Brumaire? Maybe those who took part in that gathering could not themselves have answered these queries. But they were repeated to Bonaparte as grave attacks upon his authority by a general who had been the loudest in his reproaches against the motives of the general-in-chief and the first to appreciate the good flavour of my father's melons.

Be that as it may, it was at Rhamanieh, beneath my father's tent, that there began that opposition to which Kléber gave so much strength and countenance.

On the 12th the flotilla reached Rosetta, under command of Perrée, chief of the division.

He was on board the *Cerf.*

Bonaparte put on board Perrée's ship a regular Institute of scientific men: Monge, Fourrier, Costa, Berthollet, Dolomieu, Tallien, etc.

They were to ascend the Nile parallel with the French army; their horses would help to complete a small body of cavalry.

We know how that flotilla was driven by the wind faster than the army could march, that it was attacked by the Turkish fleet and fired at from both banks of the Nile by the fellahs. Sussy, who later became comte de Sussy, took a leading part in the conduct of operations, and had his arm broken by a ball during the battle.

Bonaparte, hearing the firing of cannon, intervened just in time to save the fleet from utter destruction, reaching the scene of battle over the bodies of 4000 Mamelukes at Chebreis.

Eight days later, Bonaparte fought the battle of the Pyramids. Four days after the battle of the Pyramids—that is to say, on the 25th July, at four in the afternoon—Bonaparte made his entrance into Cairo.

No one knew better than Bonaparte the value of the dramatic effect of this victory. The sound of a victory increases in volume as it spreads on its way, echoing and re-echoing throughout the world. And none knew better than the coolheaded Bonaparte the value of those sublime sayings he is reported to have uttered before, during, or after his battles, the most celebrated of them being perhaps his—"Soldiers! Forty centuries gaze down upon you from the tops of those great monuments!"

If the reader should wish to learn the extent of exaggeration used by Bonaparte in his despatches, and would form a correct idea of the impression produced by that battle upon those who took part in it, a by no means secondary part, he may permit me to transcribe the following letter from my father. It was addressed to Kléber, who was settled at Alexandria as governor, waiting to recover from his wounds.

"BOULAK, NEAR CAIRO,

"9*th Thermidor, Year VI.*

"At last, my friend, we have reached this long-wished-for country. My God! how different it is from what even a most temperate imagination pictured it! The horrible *villasse* of Cairo is peopled by an idle rabble, squatting cross-legged all day long in front of the vilest of huts, smoking and sipping coffee, or else eating water-melons and drinking water.

"One could easily lose oneself for a whole day in the narrow, stinking streets of this famous capital. Only the quarter where the Mamelukes dwell is at all fit for habitation, and here the commander-in-chief lives in a fairly good house belonging to a bey. I have written to Brigadier Dupuis, who is the actual general and commander in Cairo, to reserve a house for you, but have not yet received his reply.

"The division is stationed at a sort of township called Boulak, close to the Nile, about half a league from Cairo. We are all lodged in filthy houses that had been deserted on our approach; Dugua's is the only passably decent one in the lot.

"General Lannes has just received orders to take up the command of Menou's division, instead of Vial, who goes to Damietta with a battalion. He assures me he shall refuse. The 2nd light battalion, with General Verdier, is in position near the Pyramids, on the left bank of the Nile, waiting until the place is fortified ready for occupation by a guard of a hundred men.

"They ought to build a bridge opposite Gizeh; the place is at present occupied by the reserve of artillery and engineers. Régnier's division is two or three leagues off Cairo; Desaix's is just starting for Old Cairo; Bon's is at the Citadel, and Menou's in the town itself.

"You have no idea of the fatiguing marches we made to get to Cairo—stopping generally three or four hours after noon, after having endured the burden and heat of the day; most of the time without food, obliged to glean what the preceding divisions had left behind in the horrible villages which they had ransacked; harassed the whole march by a thieving horde called Bedouins, who killed our men or officers if they lagged twenty-five steps behind the column. General Dugua's aide-de-camp, Geroret, was assassinated the day before yesterday in that way, when carrying a despatch to a party of grenadiers, within gun-shot of the camp. It is a far nastier war, my friend, than la Vendée.

"We had a battle the very day we reached the Nile, near Cairo. The Mamelukes, who are very cunning, tried to cross the Nile from the right to its left bank. I need hardly say that they were well thrashed, and that we washed their dirty linen in the stream. I believe they called it the battle of the Pyramids. They certainly lost 700 or 800 men without exaggeration; but a great many of that number were drowned in trying to swim across the Nile.

"I am very anxious to hear how you are and when you will be fit to take command of this division, which is in the weakest hands possible. Everybody is longing for you, and discipline throughout is becoming extraordinarily lax. I do all I can to keep each section to itself, but it is rather a hopeless task. The troops are neither paid nor properly fed, and you can readily guess what grumbling this occasions. The officers complain even more bitterly than the men. They hold out hopes to us that in eight days the commissariat will be sufficiently in order to make proper distributions, but that seems a long way off.

"If you come soon—which is my most earnest desire—have an escort even on board ship, say a couple of carabineers, who can reply to the attacks which the Bedouins are certain to make along the banks, to dispute your passage.

"Commissioner Sussy had his arm broken on the flotilla by a shot as he was pointing out Cairo. Perhaps you will be able to return with the gun-boats and djermes which have gone to Alexandria to fetch goods belonging to the troops.

"Come—come—come!—Ever yours,

DUMAS.

"P.S.—Kind regards to Auguste and our colleagues."

CHAPTER IV

Admissions of General Dupuis and Adjutant-General Boyer—The malcontents—Final discussion between Bonaparte and my father—Battle of Aboukir—My father finds treasure—His letter on this subject.

It may perhaps be thought that my father's ill-humour, his vexation at not having the command of a division and his Republican spirit, all combined to jaundice his views. Very well, let us examine the correspondence of the Egyptian Army intercepted by Nelson's squadron, and read a letter from General Dupuis.

He had no grounds for complaint, for he was in command of Cairo, and he owns in the first lines of his despatch that the position was far above his deserts.

"DUPUIS, Brigadier-General in command of the fortress, to his friend CARLO.

"GRAND CAIRO,

"11*th Thermidor, Year VI.*

"I have been in the thick of it both on land and sea, in Europe and in Africa. Yes, my dear friend, on our arrival at Malta I was ordered to disband the military knighthood there and take possession of their effects. Then, after we had taken Alexandria by storm, I was made commander of the fortress. To-day, after a most painful march of twenty-two days across the desert, we reached Grand Cairo, beating the Mamelukes, or rather putting them to flight, for they aren't worth our powder and shot.

"Behold me then, my friend, invested with fresh honours, which I could not refuse, for they have now added the commandership of Cairo. This position, offered me by Bonaparte, was too fine a one to be lightly refused.

"The conduct of the brigade in the skirmish of the Pyramids was unique: it alone destroyed 4000 Mameluke cavalry, took 40 pieces of cannon in position, all their trenches, their flags, their magnificent horses and their richly laden baggage; for there is not a single soldier who hasn't a hundred louis on him, and, without exaggeration, several of them have five hundred.

"Finally, dear boy, I occupy to-day the finest palace in Cairo, belonging to the favourite sultana of Ibrahim Bey, Sultan of Egypt. I live in his enchanted palace in the midst of the nymphs of the Nile, but I am keeping the promise I made to my little European sweetheart.

"This town is atrocious; the very streets reek with the plagues caused by their filthiness: the people are degraded and disgusting.

"Although I work like a horse I have not yet succeeded in finding my way about this vast city; it is much larger than Paris, and so different.

'*Ah! qu'il me tarde de revoir la Ligurie!*

"But, my friend, although I am wonderfully well off here, and in the lap of luxury, I often think of my friends. Where is the worthy Manita? I weep at our separation ... but I hope to rejoin you all soon, yes, soon; I am terribly sick of being so far away from you all.

"Our crossing of the desert and our various fights resulted in very few losses. The army is in good trim, and is now busy preparing for a start. I don't know whether we are bound for Syria: we are ready for any move. I had the ill-luck to lose my ...[1] at the storming of Alexandria.

"Do pray send me all your news.

"You may judge of the cowardliness of this great and vastly overrated people when I tell you that I took this immense city, on the 5th of the month, with only two companies of grenadiers.

"It has a population of 600,000 souls.

"Good-bye, my dear friend! A thousand messages to

Marcellin, his mother, his father, his daddy Carlo, and to all our friends.

"Believe me, ever yours devotedly,

DUPUIS.

"I write by this courier to Pépin and Spinola.

"Tell Pépin he was very lucky to be exiled: would to God I had been too! My kind regards to him and his family, also to poor Pietto; and to Honoria, your brother and your uncle."

We can judge from this letter that the general's enthusiasm did not run high! Here was a man who was governor of Cairo, who acknowledged that the position was far above his deserts, and yet he declares that he would rather have been exiled than enjoy the honours thrust upon him!

"Doubtless, a governor is a very great personage," quoth Sancho; "but I would rather stay in my own village and tend my goats than be governor of Barataria."

To complete our account of the state of affairs, I will place before my readers some extracts from a letter of Adjutant-General Boyer:—

"To return to Alexandria. The town has nothing of antiquity about it beyond its name. Picture to yourself ruins inhabited by an impassive people, who take everything as it comes, whom nothing astonishes; who, pipe in mouth, squat on their haunches all day long before their doors on a bench, taking very little notice of their families or children; the mothers wander about, their faces covered with black rags, offering their children for sale to the passers-by; the men, half naked, with bodies the colour of bronze, and loathsome skins, stirring up the muddy streams, devouring and grubbing up all they find, like pigs; houses hardly twenty feet high, with flat roofs, the insides like stables, the outsides just four bare walls. Such are the houses of Alexandria!

"Then remember that around this sink of squalor and misery are the foundations of the most celebrated city of ancient times, and the most precious monuments of art.

"When we left this town to ascend the Nile we found a desert as bare as your hand, where, every five or ten leagues, we came upon a wretched well of brackish water. Imagine an army compelled to cross those arid plains, which do not afford the soldier the faintest fleck of shade against the intolerable heat. Dressed in woollen, carrying his five days' rations and his knapsack, a soldier is so overcome by the heat and the weight of the things he is carrying that at the end of an hour's march he lightens his burden by throwing away his rations, thinking only of his present sufferings, and regardless of the morrow's hunger.

"He is parched with thirst, and there is no water to drink. Then, to add to the horror of the picture, the men begin to die of thirst, of exhaustion and of heat; others, seeing their comrades' sufferings, blow their own brains out; others, again, throw themselves with all their arms and baggage into the Nile, and perish in its waters.

"Each day our march saw the same sights, with even more unbelievable and unheard-of hardships still! The whole army went without bread for seventeen days. The soldiers lived on pumpkins and *prooils* and what vegetables they could pick up by the way. And that was all the food either general or common soldier had. The generals often fasted for eighteen, twenty, or twenty-four hours, as the soldiers, being the first to reach a village, would pillage everywhere, and the officers had often to satisfy themselves with what the soldiers had refused, or with their wasteful leavings.

"It is useless to tell you of our drinks, as here we have to live under Mahomedan law, which forbids wine, but gives us abundance of Nile water as a substitute.[2]

"If you wish to hear about the country along the banks of the Nile and to form an exact and correct idea of it, you should follow the topographical winding of that river.

"Two leagues below Cairo, it divides into two branches: one flows out at Rosetta, the other at Damietta; the Delta lies between these two tributaries, an extraordinarily fertile tract of land watered by the Nile. At the land end of these two branches is a border of cultivated country sometimes over a league in width, and sometimes less. When you have traversed this, you enter the desert, on the one side stretching away into Lybia, and on the other leading to the plains adjoining the Red Sea. The country round Rosetta and Cairo is densely populated; and quantities of rice, maize, and lentils are cultivated.

"The villages are one and all detestable; they are made of mud worked up by the feet and heaped up with holes scooped out from above.

"To give yourself a better idea, call to mind the snow-heaps children make at home. Their ovens are an exact reproduction of the ancient ones used in the Egyptian palaces. The cultivators, commonly called *Fellahs*, are extremely industrious; they live on very little, and in a state of indescribable filthiness. I have seen them drink the dregs left by my camels and horses in the water-troughs.

"And this is the Egypt so cried up by historians and travellers!

"Nevertheless, in spite of all these abominations and evils, I will admit that the country is quite capable of becoming to France a colony of almost incalculable value; but it will need time, and men. I can see that soldiers are not a suitable class of men to found colonies, and certainly not our soldiers. Ours are terrible in battle, terrible perhaps after a victory, unquestionably the bravest fighters in the world; but they are very little good for distant expeditions, for they are easily discouraged; idle and inconsequent, they are sufficient unto themselves. They have even been heard to say as their generals were passing: 'Look at those killers of French folk!'

"The cup is empty, I have drained it to the dregs: only my resolutions of perseverance are left me, my health, a courage which I trust will never desert me; and, with these, I will struggle to the last.

"Yesterday I saw the Council of Justice Bonaparte has formed: it is composed of nine persons. I saw nine automatons dressed in Turkish garb; their turbans were superb, their beards magnificent, and their robes reminded me of the images of the twelve apostles which my father kept in a cupboard. But, concerning their talent, attainments, genius, and knowledge, I cannot tell you anything: the proceedings are always kept secret, Turkish fashion. Nowhere is there so much ignorance, nowhere so much display of wealth, nowhere such bad and sordid use of temporal power.

"Enough of this chapter: I wished to give you my version, and I do not deny that I have omitted a great deal: but General Bonaparte's report will supply my deficiencies.

"Do not worry over me; I suffer, but so does the whole army. My personal effects have come to hand, so I have every compensation in my troubles. Do not be anxious about me, I am enjoying good health.

"Mind and look after your own. I hope to have the pleasure of seeing you in a year's time: I shall know how to appreciate you by that time, I can tell you! My warm love to my sisters.

"I am, your obedient and affectionate son,

BOYER."

So we see opinion concerning the Egyptian expedition was unanimous: everyone suffered, everyone complained, everyone longed to get back to France.

The recollection of these complainings and the remembrance of the smouldering mutiny followed Bonaparte even to St. Helena.

"Once, when the mood possessed me," he related, "I suddenly appeared in the midst of a group of discontented generals, and, addressing my remarks to the tallest of them, I said to him angrily, 'You are suggesting seditious proposals, take care I do not enforce my prerogative. Your five feet ten inches could not save you from being shot within two hours.'"

The tall general whom he addressed was my father; only Bonaparte was no more exact in relating stories than in the writing of his bulletins.

We will give our own version of the incident.

After the battle of the Pyramids, in which my father fought with his hunting-rifle like a common soldier (there being no cavalry), he went to see Bonaparte at Gizeh. He had noticed that, since the meeting at Damanhour, the commander-in-chief had avoided him, and he wished for an explanation.

That explanation was not hard to obtain. Directly Bonaparte caught sight of my father, he frowned, and, pressing his hat down on his head, he said:

"Ah! it is you. So much the better! Let us go into this room."

With these words he opened a door, and my father went in first. Bonaparte followed him, and bolted the door.

"General," he then went on to say, "you are behaving badly towards me; you are doing your best to demoralise the army; I know all that passed at Damanhour."

My father stepped forward, and placing his hand on Bonaparte's arm, which rested on the sheath of his sword, he said:

"Before I answer you, General, I must ask your motive for locking that door, and your object in according me the honour of this interview?"

"For the purpose of telling you that I consider the highest and the lowest in my army are equal when it becomes a question of discipline; and that, if occasion warrants, I shall shoot a general as soon as a drummer-boy."

"Possibly, General; but I think, nevertheless, there are several men whom you would think twice before shooting."

"Not if they impeded my plans!"

"Wait a bit, General; a moment ago you spoke of discipline, now it is yourself only of whom you are talking.... Very well, then I will give you an explanation.... It is true there was a gathering at Damanhour, and we generals, feeling discouraged after that first march, did question among ourselves the object of this expedition, thinking we detected personal ambition as that object rather than motives of public good; I said that, for the honour and glory of patriotism I would go all round the world, but if it were only just to satisfy your caprice, I would not go another step. What I said that evening I now repeat to your face, and if the sneak who reported my words to you said anything else than what I have told you he is worse even than a spy, he is a liar!"

Bonaparte looked at my father for a moment, then, almost affectionately, he said:

"And so, Dumas, you make a division in your mind: you place France on one side and me on the other. You think I separate her interests and fortunes from my own."

"I think that the interests of France ought to come before those of an individual, no matter how great that man may be.... I do not think that the fortunes of any nation should be subordinated to those of an individual."

"So you are ready to separate from me?"

"Yes, so soon as I am convinced that you are separating yourself from France."

"You are mistaken, Dumas," Bonaparte replied coldly.

"Quite possibly," replied my father; "but I disapprove of dictatorships— whether those of Sulla or of Cæsar."

"And you request—?"

"Leave to return to France, the first opportunity that presents itself."

"Very good. I promise you I will raise no difficulties in the way of your departure."

"I thank you, General: it is the only favour I ask of you;" and, bowing, my father walked to the door, unbolted it and went out.

As he withdrew, he thought he overheard Bonaparte muttering these words:

"Blind fool! not to believe in my fortunes!"

My father met Dermoncourt a quarter of an hour after, and related what had passed between Bonaparte and himself; and a score of times since has Dermoncourt repeated that conversation to me word for word—a conversation which had so momentous an influence on my father's and on my own future.

On August 1st the battle of Aboukir was fought, and the French fleet was destroyed. That put a stop, for the time, to the question of my father's return or that of anybody else.

That terrible battle had a disastrous effect on the army: even Bonaparte was momentarily overwhelmed by it, and exclaimed with Augustus: "Varus! what have you done with my legions?" He cried out several times, "Brueys! Brueys! what have you done with our ships?"

The uncertainty of his return to France troubled Bonaparte more than all. The fleet destroyed, he was no longer master of his actions; and the prospect of remaining six years in Egypt, which he had faced so calmly, now looked unendurable to him. When Bourrienne tried one day to comfort him, by telling him to rely on the Directory, he exclaimed:

"Your Directory! You know well enough it is only a set of damned idiots, who hate me and are jealous of me.... They will leave me to perish here. Don't you see all those faces? It will be a race who shall get away first."

This last outburst was excited by the reports brought to Bonaparte of the general discontent.

Kléber was not spared in these reports any more than my father had been. He knew that Bonaparte spoke of him as an opponent, and, on August the 22nd, 1798, he wrote him the following letter:—

"You would be unjust, Citizen General, if you mistake the vehemence with which I have laid my needs before you, for signs of weakness or of discouragement. It matters little to me whether I live or die, provided that I live for the glory of our arms, and that I die as I have lived. You may rely therefore on me, and on all whom you place under my orders, to stand by you through thick and thin. I have already sent you word that the events of the 14th[3] have had no other effect than to rouse indignation among the soldiers and a desire for vengeance."

To this Bonaparte replied:—

"Rest assured of the value I attach to your esteem and friendship. I am afraid we had drifted a little apart.... You would be doing me injustice were you to doubt the sorrow this has caused me.... When there are any clouds over the land of Egypt they pass off in six hours; with me, if clouds arise, they are gone in three.

"I have just as high a regard for you as you have hitherto shown towards me."

There is a wide distance between these chilly letters and the enthusiastic admiration which Kléber felt when he exclaimed, as he laid his hand on Bonaparte's shoulder:

"General, you are a world in yourself."

Truly it is the poet who makes history, and the history he makes is the finest of all histories. Erase Bonaparte's noble saying at the Pyramids, erase Kléber's words to Bonaparte, and you take away the golden halo which encircled that great Egyptian expedition—the most wild and futile of expeditions, if not the most gigantic and poetic.

Meanwhile a comparatively abundant supply of provisions had succeeded scarcity; and this material well-being made the soldiers forget for the moment their fatigues and sufferings since the beginning of the campaign. But unfortunately another trouble appeared—money was absolutely not to be had.

It was about this time that Bonaparte wrote to Kléber the following letter, which is of earlier date than the one we have just given: it enlightens us concerning the famous insurrection at Cairo, in the suppression of which my father took a prominent part.

"BONAPARTE, General-in-Chief, to KLÉBER, Chief of Division.

"HEADQUARTERS AT CAIRO,

"*9th Thermidor, Year VI.*

"We are badly off for money at Cairo, Citizen General. We want all the bullion we left behind at Alexandria to exchange for some hard cash advanced us by the bankers. I beg you therefore to call a meeting of the merchants who hold the bullion and to ask it back from them. I will give them corn and rice in exchange—we have any quantity of that. We are as rich in provisions as we are poor in cash, and absolutely must withdraw from commerce as much of our bullion and silver as possible in exchange for merchandise.

"We have undergone *greater hardships than the majority of people have courage to endure.* At the present moment we are resting here at Cairo, but it does not afford us much in the way of recompense. All the divisions are here.

"The general staff will have informed you of the military events which preceded our entry into Cairo. It was a brilliant engagement. We threw 2000 well-mounted Mamelukes into the Nile.

"Send us Arabic and French printing outfits. See that they ship all the wine, spirits, tents and shoes, send them all by sea to Rosetta, and when they have crossed the Nile they will have no difficulty in reaching Cairo.

"I await news of your health; I hope it will very soon be re-established and you will shortly be fit to rejoin us.

"I have written to Louis to set off to Rosetta with all my effects.

"I have just found a letter from Louis, dated 21 Messidor: it was in a garden belonging to one of the Mamelukes, which proves that one of your couriers was intercepted by them.

"Greetings,

BONAPARTE."

About the time when paucity of money was being so much felt that Bonaparte was obliged to withdraw the ingots of gold and silver which he had pledged with merchants for money lent, offering them grain in exchange,—a valueless commodity in that fertile land,—my father, while making some improvements to the house he occupied, once the property of a bey, my father, I say, found treasure estimated at nearly two millions (of francs). The owner of the house had left it behind him in his rapid flight.

My father wrote to Bonaparte at once:—

"CITIZEN GENERAL,—The leopard can no more change his spots than the honest man can go against his conscience.

"I therefore send you treasure estimated at nearly two millions (of francs) that I have just discovered.

"If I am killed, or if I die of melancholy here, remember that I am a poor man and that I leave a wife and child behind me in France.

"With friendly greetings,

A. DUMAS."

This letter, which was officially printed among the correspondence of the Egyptian Army, produced a very great effect when certain accusations were being raised against several chief officers. It was reproduced in the New York and Philadelphian papers, and became known throughout that growing Republic. Fifty years later, when called to Holland to attend the coronation of its young king, the United States ambassador at The Hague, the Hon. M. d'Areysas, repeated it to me word for word.

---

[1] We must explain that, the word being apparently illegible, the English could not print it, so we are left to wonder what the important thing could be that General Dupuis had the misfortune to lose.

[2] Some editions read "l'eau du ciel" for "l'eau du Nil."

[3] 14th Thermidor (1st August).

CHAPTER V

Revolt at Cairo—My father enters the Grand Mosque on horseback—His home-sickness—He leaves Egypt and lands at Naples—Ferdinand and Caroline of Naples—Emma Lyon and Nelson—Ferdinand's manifesto—Comments of his minister, Belmonte-Pignatelli.

The want of money, complained of by Bonaparte, was being felt increasingly. There seemed to be no means of paying the troops without having recourse to advances, a miserable method, sure to call to mind the thievish tricks of the famous Mamelukes which the French had ostensibly come to put down. So that remedy was not available. In this embarrassment, Poussielgue, Comptroller-General of Finances, suggested to the general-in-chief to establish the right of registration on all concessions of properties made since their arrival in Egypt, or upon all future concessions. All these concessions were of a temporary character, and could be withdrawn or renewed according to the wish of the commanding general, therefore the scheme was of inestimable value.

This fiscal method was hitherto unknown in the East, where it was looked upon as only another form of lending money; and as it was prejudicial to the interests of the great Turkish or Arabian concessionaires, most of whom lived in Cairo, it turned that capital into a hotbed of revolt.

One of the earliest orders on reaching Cairo had been to keep a watch on the mosque criers. It is the duty of these criers to call the faithful to prayer three times a day. For some time their cries were noted, but by degrees our people grew used to them, and neglected to notice what they said. Seeing this, the *Muezzins* substituted appeals to revolt in place of their sacred formulas; and the French were too ignorant of the language to perceive the difference. This left the Turks every opportunity to conspire and to give orders for delaying or advancing the hour fixed for their insurrection. It was finally fixed to begin on the morning of the 21st October.

On the 21st October at eight o'clock, then, the revolt broke out simultaneously at every point from Syène as far as Alexandria.

My father was still ill and in bed when Dermoncourt rushed in, crying:

"General, the town is in full insurrection. General Dupuis has just been assassinated! To horse, to horse!"

My father did not wait a second bidding, he was too well aware of the value of every moment at such a crisis! He leapt half clad on his horse, not even waiting to saddle it, seized his sword, and rushed into the streets of Cairo at the head of several officers who had followed him.

The news was but too true. General Dupuis, the commander of Cairo, had been mortally wounded under the armpit by a lance-thrust, which had severed the main artery. A Turk who had concealed himself in a cellar had struck the blow. Bonaparte, it was rumoured, was on the isle of Rondah, and could not obtain entrance to the town. General Caffarelli's house had been taken by storm, and all inside put to death. The insurgents in a body were making for the quarters of Paymaster-General Estève.

My father urged his horse in that direction, collecting round him all the French he met on his way, amounting in all to about sixty men.

We know what admiration my father's herculean figure had raised among the Arabs. Mounted on a heavy dragoon horse, which he handled with consummate horsemanship, his head, breast, and arms bare to every blow, he hurled himself into the thickest of the fray with that utter fearlessness of death which always characterised him, this time intensified by the fit of melancholy that preyed on him. He appeared to the Arabs as the Destroying Angel of the flaming sword. In an instant the approaches to the Treasury were cleared, Estève saved and the Turks and Arabs cut to pieces.

Poor Estève! I remember that when I was quite a child he kissed me and said, "Remember what I tell you: if it had not been for your father, this head of mine would be lying to-day in the gutters of Cairo."

The rest of that day was spent in continual strife and fierce fighting. The members of the Egyptian Institute who inhabited the house of Kassim-Bey, in a remote quarter of the city, had barricaded themselves, and fired on the mob like ordinary soldiers. They were at it the whole day until evening, when my father and his brave dragoons came and rescued them.

News came at night that a convoy of sick men belonging to Régnier's division, on its way from Belbeys, had been butchered. Was Bonaparte really at Rondah, as all the official reports said? Or was he at his headquarters, as Bourrienne declared? Did he make fruitless attempts at the gates of Old Cairo, at the gate of the Institute? Could he only effect an entrance by the gate of Boulay towards six in the evening? Was he surrounded at his residence with no means of delivering himself? These questions still remain in obscurity; but it is a perfectly clear and patent fact that he took no part at all that first day, and I can call up living witnesses among the Egyptians[1] who will testify that they saw my father everywhere.

The first orders from Bonaparte were put into execution about five in the afternoon. The sound of cannon roared through the principal streets, the noise of a battery of howitzers, placed on the Mokkan, a noise as of thunder, rare in Cairo, that terrified the insurgents.

Resistance, which had been somewhat desultory and spasmodic in character until now, was increasing everywhere and taking more definite shape.

Nightfall interrupted the struggle, for it is a point of religion with the Turks not to fight in the dark. Bonaparte availed himself of the night to make his plans.

At sunrise the revolt was still alive, but the rebels were lost.

A great number of them had taken refuge with their principal leaders in the great mosque of El-Heazao. My father received orders to go and attack them there, thus striking at the very heart of what remained of the insurrection.

The doors were burst in with volleys of cannon; my father, urging his horse into a gallop, was the first to enter the mosque.

A danger arose at the very threshold, for his horse encountered an obstacle in the way, a tomb about three feet in height, at which he stopped dead, reared, then, dropping his forefeet in front of the tomb, stood for an instant motionless, with bloodshot eyes and smoking nostrils.

"The Angel! the Angel!" yelled the Arabs.

Their resistance was but the struggle of despair in the case of a few, but with the greater number it was continued out of a spirit of fatalistic resignation, and their leaders shrieked "*Amhan!*" and surrendered.

My father sought out Bonaparte to inform him of the fall of the mosque: he was already acquainted with the details of its capture, and, mollified by the treasure my father had sent him, he accorded him a gracious reception.

"Good-day to you, my Hercules," he said. "So you have crushed the dragon?" And he held out his hand.

"Gentlemen," he continued, turning towards his suite, "I shall order a picture to be painted of the taking of the Grand Mosque. Dumas, you have already posed as the principal figure."

The picture was, as a matter of fact, commissioned, but Girodet's principal figure, it will be remembered, was a tall fair hussar, of no name or practically no rank; he it was who took the place of my father, for, eight days after the insurrection of Cairo had been quelled, my father again fell out with Bonaparte, and insisted with renewed vehemence on being allowed to return to France.

He had been for a time distracted from his home-sick despondency by the insurrection at Cairo, but he soon relapsed into it again. A deep disgust with everything, life included, took possession of him, and, in spite of the advice of his friends, he obstinately persisted that Bonaparte should allow him furlough.

Bonaparte made one last attempt during their final interview to endeavour to make him stay, even going so far as to tell him that he meant himself to return to France before long, and promising to take my father back with him. But nothing could allay the desire to go; it had, in fact, become a mania.

Unluckily, Dermoncourt, who was the only man who could influence my father, had returned to his regiment, which was stationed at *Belbeys*. Directly he heard that the departure was settled, he hurried back to Cairo, and went to my father's house. He found the place dismantled and my father selling the things he did not want to take away.

With the proceeds of this sale my father bought 4000 lbs. of Mocha coffee, eleven Arabian horses (two stallions and nine mares), and chartered a small vessel called *la Belle Maltaise*.

Want of news—all of which was intercepted by the English cruisers—cut them off completely from all that was passing in Europe, so we will very briefly recount what was happening in Rome and Naples, for the better understanding of what follows.

Ferdinand and Caroline reigned at Naples. Caroline, a second Marie-Antoinette, hated the French for having killed her sister. She was a woman of strong passions in hate and in love, and she indulged in luxuries both of pleasures and of blood.

Ferdinand was a *lazzarone*; he could scarcely read or write; he knew no other tongue than the Neapolitan dialect. In that patois he composed a slight variation upon the ancient *panem et circenses*. His version was: "The Neapolitans are ruled by three F's:—Forea—Festa—Farina" (gallows—games—grain).

It will be readily understood that a treaty wrung by fear from such sovereigns would only be enforced so long as they lived under the dominion of that fear. Now Bonaparte was to them himself the very embodiment of that terror, but he was away in Egypt, and they soon learnt the news of the destruction of the French fleet at Aboukir. They concluded from that that Bonaparte was lost and the French army annihilated.

Directly the English squadron made ready to stop our course towards the unknown destination of our expedition, the main body of the English fleet, in spite of our treaties with Ferdinand, made for the port of Naples, where it was received with demonstrations that were somewhat ambiguous in the matter of sympathy. It was quite another story after the battle of Aboukir.

Nelson's fleet had hardly been signalled off Naples, tugging the remains of our vessels in its wake, when the king, the queen, the English ambassador, Hamilton, with his beautiful wife, Emma Lyon, embarked on magnificently decorated vessels and advanced to meet the conqueror.

Oh, beautiful and ill-fated Emma Lyon! what historian shall dare to play the Tacitus and write your life? What poet shall presume to lay bare your secret passions? The favourite of Queen Caroline and the mistress of Nelson, who shall dare to be the judge and add up the list of your victims?

This splendid Court went forth in state to honour Nelson: the king offered him a sword, the queen a mistress. The town was illuminated in the evening, and there was a ball at the palace.

Nelson appeared on the royal balcony by the side of Ferdinand, and the people cried, "*Vive Ferdinand! vive Nelson!*"

And all this took place under the eyes of our ambassador, Garat, who witnessed the decline of our influence and the growth of English popularity.

He made due complaints, but he was told in reply that the English fleet had only been received into the port of Naples because Nelson had threatened to bombard the town.

This excuse was, of course, a fallacious one, but our ambassador was obliged to accept it.

The next proceeding he witnessed was the mobilisation of an army of 60,000 men commanded by the Austrian general, Mack, who had won a certain notoriety by his repeated defeats.

From that moment war against France was resolved upon.

The Neapolitan army, under command of the Austrian general, was divided into three camps.

Twenty-two thousand soldiers were sent to St. Germain; 16,000 occupied the Abruzzi; 8000 camped on the plain of Sessa; and 6000 sheltered behind the walls of Gaëte.

Fifty-two thousand men were ready to invade the Roman States, to drive us out of Rome, which we then occupied.

Nevertheless, although war was decided upon, it had not yet been declared, and our ambassador again asked the Neapolitan Government for an explanation of what was passing.

The Government returned answer that they desired the continuation of amicable relations between themselves and the French Government more than ever, and that the soldiery noticed by M. Garat were only in their respective camps for training.

However, a few days later—on the 22nd of November—a manifesto was put forth, wherein King Ferdinand spoke of the "*state of revolutionary disorder in France; the political changes in Italy; the proximity of enemies of the monarchy and of public peace; the occupation of Malta, a fief of the kingdom of Sicily; the flight of the Pope, and the dangers which were threatening religion.*" Then, after this list of troubles, he went on to declare that "*taking into consideration these many and powerful incentives, he was about to lead an army into the Roman States in order to restore to the people their rightful sovereign, the head of Holy Church, and to bring peace to the peoples of his kingdom.*"

He added "*that as he was not declaring war against any monarch, he had persuaded the foreign armies not to oppose the march of the Neapolitan troops, which were intended solely to pacify Rome and the territory of the Holy See.*"

At the same time private letters from ministers of the King of Naples to foreign ministers incited the latter to wage war against the French, not honest, open warfare, but a war of assassinations and poisonings.

It seems incredible, nay impossible, does it not? Read this letter from Prince Belmonte-Pignatelli, minister of the King of Naples, to Chevalier Riocca, minister of the King of Piedmont:—

"We know that in your king's council are several cautious, we might even say timid ministers, *who shudder at the idea of perjury and of murder*, as though the late treaty of alliance between France and Sardinia were to be considered a political act, which could be respected. Was it not dictated by the superior strength of the conqueror? Was it not accepted under the pressure of necessity? Such treaties weigh most unjustly on the oppressed, who in violating them but make amends on the very first opportunity afforded them by good fortune. What! with your king a prisoner in his own capital, surrounded by the enemy's bayonets, you would call it perjury to break promises wrung from you by force against your consciences? You would call the extermination of your tyrants assassination? No, the French battalions are scattered up and down Piedmont full of confidence in the security of peace. Stir up the patriotic feelings of the people to a pitch of enthusiasm and frenzy, until every Piedmontese will pant to tread his enemies beneath his feet. A few *individual murders* will be more useful in Piedmont than victories won on the field of battle, and an impartial posterity will never give the name of treason to the spirited actions of a whole people, who pass over the dead bodies of their oppressors in regaining their liberty.... Our brave Neapolitans, under the leadership of worthy General Mack, will be the first to give the signal of death. They may be already on the track of the enemy of thrones and nations by the time this letter reaches you."

Now it was into the hands of a Government which could write such letters as the above, that my father, a Republican general, was to fall, when he left Egypt on account of his devotion to the Republic, which was threatened, as he thought, by Bonaparte's personal ambition.

And at what a moment, too! When the head of that Government had been defeated on all sides by a mere handful of French troops, chased from his kingdom on the mainland, and obliged to retire to Palermo; carrying in his train feelings of bitter hatred and anger and vows of vengeance, such as always accompany defeat, and fill the minds of the vanquished with desperate and deadly resolutions.

We shall now see how Prince Belmonte-Pignatelli put in practice upon my father and his unfortunate companions the precepts enjoined by him upon his colleague, the Chevalier Riocca, minister of the King of Piedmont.

I will leave my father himself to relate the story of this terrible captivity; his voice shall rise from a tomb closed for forty-five years, and, as did the voice of Hamlet's father, shall denounce the crime and the murderers to the whole world.

[1] All those who took part in the Egyptian campaign are so called.

CHAPTER VI

Report presented to the French Government by Divisional-General Alexandre Dumas, on his captivity at Taranto and at Brindisi, ports in the Kingdom of Naples.

"We left the port of Alexandria on the evening of the 17th Ventôse, year VII, on board the *Belle Maltaise*, with General Manscourt, citizen Dolomieu and many other French military men and civil servants attached to the Egyptian Army, all furnished with leave on furlough from General Bonaparte. I hoped, if the winds favoured us, and with the aid of our excellent sailing vessel, to escape the English fleet and to reach some port in France in about ten or twelve days. That hope was all the better founded as the Maltese captain who commanded the boat (his name was Félix) declared that after some repairs of trifling importance it could hold out against the roughest weather. We had discussed together the price of these repairs, and he had estimated them at sixty louis. I gave him a hundred. I had therefore good reason to believe that these repairs had been conscientiously carried out: unfortunately they were not.

"We had hardly got outside the harbour before the sea was against us, and a high wind buffeted us about from the first night. When day appeared, after a stormy night, we found that our vessel leaked.

"We were already forty leagues from Alexandria; and, as the wind was not favourable, we could not turn the ship's head round for Egypt; we therefore decided to continue our course and to crowd on as much sail as possible.

"But the quicker we went and the more we urged on the boat, the worse became the leakage, until at length it became impossible to cope with it, and on the third day of our voyage the situation became almost desperate.

"During that day we threw overboard our only means of defence, the ten pieces of cannon which armed our vessel. The next day my Arab horses were thrown into the sea; then all the coffee, and, lastly, all our luggage.

"But in spite of this lightening the boat settled down more and more. When the latitude was taken, we found we were in the entrance to the Adriatic Gulf, and, after holding counsel with the seamen and officers on board, it was decided to make for the nearest land and port, without loss of a moment's time.

"The land was Calabria, and the port Taranto.

"On the tenth day we sighted land. It was high time! Another twenty-four hours of navigation and the ship would have foundered with all hands.

"I gave orders to anchor at a small isle which lay about a league from the town. As we came from Egypt, we had to be quarantined, and, thinking Naples was friendly to France, I insisted on conforming to the sanitary regulations, in order to disabuse the minds of the people of Calabria that there was any fear of plague.

"We had hardly cast anchor before I sent the captain of the vessel with a letter to the governor of the town. This letter set forth who we were and our distressed condition, and I begged him, for the sake of our common humanity, to give us all the help he could, as we were in very great need.

"Two hours later the captain returned with a verbal answer from the governor. We were to disembark with confidence; the only condition made was that we should pass first through quarantine.

"We were quite prepared for that, and no one dreamt of opposing it: we rejoiced in such a happy ending to our precarious situation.

"When we entered the harbour, they made us land one at a time, and four Neapolitan captains searched us; the ships of these captains had been burned before Alexandria, and I had given them a passage on the *Belle Maltaise* out of pure humanity.

"To begin by treating us like this seemed somewhat odd; but we were still quite unsuspicious: we put it down to the severity of the sanitary laws, and offered no resistance to their examination.

"After this visitation, they huddled us up together, generals, officers, passengers, and sailors, in so narrow a room that if anyone ventured to lie down he impinged upon his neighbour's rights.

"And thus we spent the rest of that day and night.

"The next day they landed what remained of our goods and effects, and they seized our letters, papers, and arms.

"My two horses were not forgotten in the confiscation, although they made me pay for two months' keep of them, all the while giving me to understand that I should have them returned to me.

"Forty-eight hours more elapsed, and we were still packed tightly in our room. At length, after repeated complaints and offers of money, on the third day they gave General Manscourt, Dolomieu, and myself a room to ourselves, where we could finish the remainder of our quarantine.

"While this was being endured, we had a visit from the son of the King of Naples.

"His Royal Highness questioned us closely concerning the health of Generals Bonaparte and Berthier and on the situation of the Egyptian Army; then he left us abruptly, without wishing us adieux.

"These curious manners, combined with the bad Italian he spoke, caused us to doubt that he was the person he was set forth to be.

"Eight days later the members of the Government came to inform us that by order of Prince François we were declared prisoners of war.

"We had not been deceived—the so-called Prince François was a pretender.

"Four Corsican adventurers had determined to urge the people to revolt in favour of the Bourbons; but, knowing the proverbial cowardice of Prince François, they resolved to act in his name, so one of them, a vagabond named Corbara, an outcast, but a brave man, personated the prince.

"The others, whose names were respectively Cesare, Boccheciampe, and Colonna, were to personate—Colonna the high constable of the kingdom, Boccheciampe the brother of the King of Spain, and Cesare the Duke of Saxe.

"Now who were these men who aspired to such high titles?

"Cesare was once a liveried servant, Boccheciampe a deserter from an artillery corps and Colonna a sort of vagabond like his friend and compatriot Corbara. It was in the house of Intendant Girunda at Montjari that this farcical plot was hatched.

"Girunda in his capacity of intendant was supposed to be personally acquainted with the heir-apparent, and his part, therefore, was to precede the four adventurers, announcing them in their divers assumed names and titles.

"Thanks to these precautions, the tour made by the pretended princes was a triumph; for the entire province rose up before them, behind them, and all round them.

"In the meantime the pretended Prince François was acting as dictator, dismissing magistrates, appointing governors in the towns, raising funds, and doing it all more cleverly, it must be admitted, and certainly more boldly, than the true heir to the throne would have done.

"Two incidents which might have wrecked our adventurers turned out, on the contrary, to increase their popularity. The Archbishop of Otranto knew the prince personally. Duly advised of his coming by Girunda, he received the false Royal Highness as though he were the true prince, and there was an end of the matter. Furthermore, during his sojourn at Taranto, the two old princesses, aunts of Louis XVI., who were coming from Naples on their way to Sicily, were compelled by rough weather to put into port. Learning that their royal relative was there, they naturally asked to see him. The false prince had to make the best of it, and to present himself to his supposed aunts; but the two old princesses had been informed of the reason why Corbara was playing the rôle of prince, and, being desirous of furthering the Bourbon cause, they lent themselves to the lie, and even encouraged its success by the cordial reception they gave to the pretended grandson of Louis XIV.: thus making him still more popular with the Calabrians.[1]

"That was the type of man who controlled our destiny and who made us prisoners of war.

"When they made this declaration to us in the name of the false prince, they promised faithfully that when we were set at liberty our arms, our horses, and our papers should be returned to us.

"They were quite safe in promising all this with such intentions in their minds towards us as they had.

"I insisted on seeing His Royal Highness a second time, to demand an explanation of the captivity; I could not at all understand it, as I did not know of the renewal of hostilities between Naples and France; but I need hardly say that His Royal Highness did not make himself so cheap as to come a second time.

"I then wrote to him; but after the explanations I have just given, it will readily be understood that my letter remained unanswered.

"About a month after this visit, with what object I cannot conceive, they led us to hope that we were soon to be sent back to France, and a letter came from Cardinal Ruffo, the purport of which was as follows: General Manscourt and I were invited to write to the generals-in-chief of the armies of Naples and Italy to negotiate the cartel of our exchange for Signor Boccheciampe, who had just been made prisoner and taken to Ancona. The letter added that the King of Naples set more value on this Signor Boccheciampe than on all the other Neapolitan generals, prisoners of war, either in Italy or in France.

"We accordingly sent the requisite letters to the cardinal; but when the cardinal learnt that Boccheciampe had not been taken prisoner, but killed outright, the negotiations, which could no longer serve the desired end, fell through.

"Soon after this we were visited one morning by the civil and political governor of Taranto and by the military commander, who told us they had orders to take General Manscourt and myself to the Castle at once.

"This order was put into immediate execution.

"After many entreaties, our servants were allowed to join us the day after.

"We were now separated from Dolomieu, who was destined to endure as dreadful a confinement as ours.[2] They put us into separate rooms when we got to the Castle.

"We sent for the governor directly we were installed, and related to him Cardinal Ruffo's proposal, asking him what we should do in the matter.

"He suggested that, as our letter had remained unanswered, we should write again; which we instantly did, and a vessel just setting out was deputed to deliver it to General d'Anciera, commander of Messina.

"It goes without saying that we had no more answer to this than to the first.

"The day but one after my removal to the Castle of Brindisi, as I lay on my bed, the window open, a parcel containing a book was thrust through the bars of my window, and fell on the floor of my room.

"I rose and picked up the packet: it was tied round with string. I cut the knots, and found that the parcel contained two volumes, entitled the *Médecin de Campagne*, by Tissot. A scrap of paper was folded between the first and second page, containing these words:

"'From the Calabrian patriots; read the article on *Poison*.'

"I looked for the indicated word: it was underlined twice; and I knew that my life was threatened. I hid both volumes as best I could, for fear they should be taken from me. I read and re-read the article pointed out to me so often that I nearly knew by heart the remedies prescribed for the different kinds of poison that might be tried on me.

"Notwithstanding all this, our situation for the first eight days was quite tolerable; we enjoyed our walks in front of the door of our quarters, up and down a space of about sixty yards. But, under pretext that the French had just taken possession of Naples, the governor told us, towards the end of the first week, that our walk was henceforth forbidden; and the same day we saw locksmiths put bolts on all our doors, and masons raised the walls of a court a dozen feet long by eight feet wide, where we were in future to take our airings.

"Vainly did we put to ourselves this dilemma: Either we were prisoners of war, and entitled to the treatment allowed to the rank of a general undergoing imprisonment; or we were not prisoners of war, and in that case we ought to be liberated.

"For eight months we were obliged to live at our own expense, fleeced by everybody, and paying double its value for everything we bought.

"At the end of that time we were told that the king had allowed us a grant of ten *carlins* per day, or about four francs ten sous of our French money, and out of this sum we had to pay our servants.

"They might just as well have doubled our allowance, as they had fully determined never to pay us anything.

"I had left Egypt on account of my bad state of health. My friends thought my sufferings were simply from home-sickness and my ailments imaginary; but I knew that my malady was real, and I realised the gravity of my case.

"A stroke of paralysis unfortunately attacked my left cheek a few days after my arrival at the lazaretto, and gave the lie to my friends' incredulity. I had the greatest difficulty in getting permission for a doctor to see me; and he contented himself by prescribing such trifling remedies that the disease remained stationary.

"Some days after I had been taken to the Castle—namely, on June 16th, at ten o'clock in the morning—the same doctor visited me, this time unasked. I was taking my bath. He recommended a biscuit soaked in a glass of wine, and said he would send me the biscuits. Ten minutes later, the promised biscuits arrived.

"I followed his advice, but about two o'clock in the afternoon I was seized by the most violent internal pains and vomitings, which at first prevented me from eating, and which, continually increasing in intensity, soon brought me to the point of death.

"Then I recalled the injunctions sent me by the patriots and the word *poison* which they had underlined; I asked for some milk. A goat that I had brought from Egypt, which had been a diversion to me during my captivity, by good fortune yielded me about a bottle and a half. When the goat ran dry, my servant procured oil and made me swallow thirty or forty spoonfuls; a few drops of lemon, mixed with the oil, counteracted the sickliness of the remedy.

"Directly General Manscourt saw me in such a deplorable state he sent to the governor and informed him what had happened, begging him to send the doctor instantly; but the governor coolly replied that it was impossible, as the doctor had gone into the country. Not until eight o'clock at night, and when the entreaties of my companion in captivity assumed a threatening character, did the governor decide to come with him to my prison: he was accompanied by all the members of the Government, and escorted by a dozen armed soldiers. It was in the presence of this military force, against which Manscourt protested with all the strength of his nature and with the utmost loyalty towards me, that a consultation was allowed me. The doctor no doubt required the support of all this armed force in presenting himself before me, and, even with this aid, when he entered my room he turned deadly pale.

"It was then my turn to question him, and I did it so searchingly that he stammered and was hardly able to reply; his words were so confused that it was easy to see he was not the perpetrator of the crime—why should he be? he had no personal interest in my death, he was but the instrument. He only advised one remedy—namely, to drink iced water, or else to suck snow.

"I mistrusted the alacrity with which they advised me to follow out the wretch's prescription; and indeed, at the end of a quarter of an hour's trial of it, the pain grew so much worse that I hastened to stop it, and returned to my oil and my lemon.

"I was the further confirmed in the belief that I had been poisoned, by other evidence than that of the internal pains and vomiting, which had all the symptoms of arsenical poisoning, and this evidence was as follows:—

"I recollected having seen the doctor through my open door while I was having my bath, before he came to me, go up to General Manscourt, who was reading in the adjoining room, and tell him with an air of great secrecy that he was certain we were going to be robbed as our companions had been;' therefore, if we possessed any valuable belongings, he placed his services at our disposal, and offered to take care of them until we came out of prison, when he would immediately restore them to us.

"He had taken advantage of the absence of a Tarentine gunner, named Lamarrone, to make this communication to General Manscourt; Lamarrone was his accomplice, but the doctor did not mean to share the spoils with him if he could help it.

"My goat died next day. It had saved my life, so it had to be punished.

"Three days later the doctor died. He had missed his blow, so they had to stop his mouth.

"The day the doctor had visited me he prescribed as well for General Manscourt, who was suffering from a scorbutic affection; but the general took good care not to follow his advice when he saw the effect of the biscuits the wretch had ordered me to take; no doubt this abstention saved his life.

"But his death was determined on as well as mine; and they tried different means.

"They mixed a powder with his tobacco, which gave him violent pains in the head, and after a while made him delirious. General Manscourt was puzzled to know what caused these attacks, when it occurred to me to look in his tobacco-box. The powder they had mixed with the tobacco was so corrosive that it had eaten several holes in the bottom of the box, and particles of white lead were mixed with the tobacco in the proportion of about one-twentieth.

"Again I had recourse to my *Médecin de Campagne*, which recommended bleeding. So General Manscourt bled himself in three different places, and was relieved.

"In the meantime, following on the attempt to poison me, deafness attacked me, I completely lost the sight of one eye, and the paralysis was increasing.

"It was an unusual thing that such symptoms of decay should seize any one at the early age of thirty-four, and it proved the presence of some mischievous disease.

"Although the experience I had just had of my first doctor did not inspire me with much confidence in a second, my state of emaciation compelled me to apply to the governor for fresh assistance from medical science.

"I therefore sent for him, and asked him if I might consult a French surgeon who had come from Egypt with a fresh cargo of prisoners; but my request was refused, and I had to be satisfied with a visit from the Castle doctor.

"His name was Carlin, and he spoke French fluently.

"His manner roused my suspicions at his first visit—he began with an outpouring of protestations of devotion and sympathy too profuse to be sincere. He examined me with the greatest attention, declared that there was not the slightest cause for my fears, and that I was only suffering from an attack of languor.

"He entirely disapproved of the treatment I had received from the deceased doctor, characterising it as ignorant and stupid; he ordered injections for my ears, and recommended me to take half an ounce of cream of tartar every morning.

"At the end of eight days of this treatment, my deafness (which had begun to disappear) came back again, and my stomach was in such a highly irritable state that I could not digest anything.

"Carlin visited me regularly, talked a great deal, affected an exaggerated patriotism and much sympathy with the French; but as all his demonstrations, instead of inspiring me with confidence, only made me more and more circumspect, the governor devised a means that he thought would prove efficacious: he forbade Carlin to enter my prison, giving as an excuse that he helped me to carry on communications with the Italian patriots.

"I confess this stratagem took me in. I grew daily worse: I entreated urgently to be allowed to see Carlin; but the governor feigned the greatest strictness in this respect, and, keeping him always away from me, he sent me another doctor.

"This one, like his predecessor, strongly disapproved of the régime I had been following, saying, for example, that the injections in my ears which had been ordered me were only making my deafness worse, by irritating the delicate membrane of the tympanum. Moreover, he himself made up the medicines and brought them to me when he came to see me. I experienced a distinct improvement from his treatment, but unluckily I had the imprudence to confess I was better, and, as my cure was not desired, the good man was dismissed after his second visit. In vain did I ask to have him again, the governor told me that he definitely declined to see me.

"I was obliged to do without a doctor; but, thanks to Tissot's book, I continued to doctor myself with more or less success. My eye, however, grew worse. At last Manscourt recollected having seen a cure effected, in just such a case as mine, by blowing finely ground cane-sugar into the eye seven or eight times a day. We procured the cane-sugar and began the treatment, which at all events was an easy one to follow. It produced a considerable improvement, and to-day my eye is only affected by a slight film, which I hope will finally disappear altogether.

"Unfortunately, my deafness and my internal pains became increasingly worse, and I was obliged to ask for Carlin, who was only allowed to come on condition that he should not utter a single word of French during our conversations, and that he should always be accompanied in his visits by the governor. Carlin found me in such a bad state on his return that he demanded a consultation. I had wanted this for long, and had pleaded for it in vain. Now it was granted me, and Carlin brought a doctor from the town, the Castle surgeon, and a French surgeon whom I obtained by urgent entreaty from the suite of the Marquis de Valvo, Neapolitan minister, at that time on a mission to Taranto.

"At the door the governor stopped the French surgeon before he came in.

'You are going to see your General Dumas,' he said; 'take good care you do not utter a single word of French, or you are lost.'

"Then, drawing back the six bolts which kept us prisoners, he continued: 'You see that door; it opens to you for the first and the last time.'

"They all came into my room and gathered round my bed. I tried to catch sight of the French doctor, eager to see a fellow-countryman. I could hardly believe my eyes when I saw that he was a poor, wretched, attenuated creature, only half clad, his whole aspect as he stood before me betokening suffering and misery.

"I spoke to him, but to my great surprise he did not reply to me: I persisted, but again he was silent. I interrogated the governor, who muttered a few irrelevant words.

"While this was happening the French doctor whispered rapidly and in a low voice to General Manscourt, 'I am forbidden to speak to the prisoner under penalty of death.'

"Carlin then explained to his confrères the nature and developments of my illness, then the treatment he had judged advisable to recommend me; and, after a short discussion, in which the French doctor scarcely joined, partly on account of his ignorance of Italian, and partly intimidated by fear of the governor's threats, it was decided that I should go back to the first treatment, to which they simply added pills, and blisters behind both ears and on my neck and arms.

"I submitted to these remedies; but they reduced me to such a low ebb at the end of a month that I was obliged to give them up. Throughout the month I was the victim of constant insomnia; I was poisoned a second time.

"I called in the doctor. I laid bare every symptom: I made them so evident, so patent, that the governor, who was present at the interview, dared not meet my eye, and turned away his head; but the unabashed Carlin held his ground, assured me that his treatment was the only means of saving me, and, my thirty pills being exhausted, he ordered me another quantity of the same kind.

"I made a pretence of compliance with his wishes, I promised to follow his instructions, and, on the following day, I received ten fresh pills, which I carefully kept in order to submit them to analysis.

"These last were no doubt meant to act more powerfully than the others; for when he left me he said good-bye, saying that he was setting off for the country, and pretending that, in all probability, I should have left Taranto myself before his return.

"Eight days later, although I had completely given up this fatal treatment, I suddenly felt a blow, as though I was struck by a thunderbolt, and I fell senseless in the middle of my room.

"I was seized with a violent fit of apoplexy.

"General Manscourt at once informed the governor of what had happened to me, and begged the help of the Castle surgeon; the governor, without troubling to get up from his dinner, calmly replied that the surgeon was in the country, but that he should be sent me on his return.

"And in that state I had to wait for him for four hours.

"Nature, left to her own devices, had in the meanwhile exerted herself, and I had somewhat regained consciousness; but the rally was only just sufficient to enable me to realise that I was at death's door.

"Therefore, summoning up my small remnant of strength, I told the old woman who cooked our food to go and tell the governor that I knew perfectly well the doctor was not in the country, and that if he did not come to me in ten minutes' time, I gave him fair warning I would drag myself to the window and proclaim to the whole town that I had been poisoned—the news would no doubt cause little surprise, but it might at any rate expose his infamy.

"This threat was effectual; five minutes later my door opened, and the surgeon, who had not been able to come because he was supposed to be away in the country, put in his appearance.

"I had been studying my Tissot, and I had learned that a plentiful letting of blood was the only remedy for the condition I was in. I therefore peremptorily ordered the doctor to bleed me.

"As though he did not dare to obey without orders from his superiors, he went back to the commander of the Castle to obtain leave from him. No doubt it was granted, for he drew a surgical instrument from his pocket; only, instead of this instrument being a lancet, it was a fleam used for bleeding horses.

"I shrugged my shoulders—

'Why not a dagger outright?' I said to him; 'it would be quicker done.'

"I held out my arm. The first incision was, of course, not sufficient, and it was not until the wretch had made three incisions in my arm that he alighted upon a vein and drew blood.

"This first attack of apoplexy was followed by a second, three days later. The same surgeon was again called in, and bled me again with the same instrument; only this time he thought it best to do it in my foot, and he did it either so clumsily or else so cleverly (for they were in constant fear that we should escape through the help of the patriots) that a sinew was cut, and for more than three months my leg swelled to a fearful size whenever I took a dozen steps.

"As the governor feared, the report of this scandalous treatment was noised abroad in the town. One day a stone fell into my room, wrapped in a bit of paper. On the paper was written these words:—

"'They want to poison you, but you ought to have received a book, in which we underlined the word *poison*. If you need any remedy that you cannot procure in your prison, hang a string out of your window, and at the end of the string we will hook on what you want.'

"Between the paper and the stone was rolled a long piece of string with a hook at the end.

"The next night I let down the string, and asked for quinine to dose myself with, and chocolate to sustain me; the night following I received both articles.

"Thanks to this medicine and nourishment, the disease did not make headway, and the apoplectic attacks ceased; but I remained crippled in the right leg, deaf in the right ear, paralysed in the left cheek and the sight of my right eye was almost lost. In addition to all this I was a prey to violent pains in the head and constant buzzing.

"It was an odd spectacle that I was called upon to witness, a struggle taking place in myself between a strong constitution and powers bent obstinately on my destruction.

"We had now been nearly fifteen months prisoners at Taranto, and were of sufficient importance to be talked of about the town. The authorities began to shrink at the thought of the scandal our death would raise. All their attempts at poisoning had leaked out in the town, and the patriots loudly denounced the shameful treatment to which I had been subjected. It was therefore decided between the marquis de la Squiave and the agents of the King of Naples at Taranto to transfer us to the maritime castle of Brindisi. This extraordinary arrangement was carefully hidden from us; but in spite of the strictest secrecy the patriots were warned of the move, and three or four of them made us understand, by gestures when passing in front of our windows, that we were to be transferred to another prison and assassinated on the way.

"I called Manscourt to tell him the news I had gathered; but we thought it a false rumour, and took no more notice of it.

"That very evening, towards eleven o'clock, when we were asleep, my door was suddenly opened with a great crash, and the marquis de la Squiave entered, accompanied by some fifty of his hirelings, and intimated to us that we were to set out at once for Brindisi. Immediately the warning I had received during the day came back to my mind; and, considering that the first part of this warning, as to taking us away, had come true, the second, concerning our intended assassination, might also be true, I thought we might just as well die at once; for it would be preferable to die resisting, to die fighting, to die in combat, than to die slowly, hour by hour, minute by minute. I therefore swore that I would not stir, that they must take me away by force, for I meant to resist to the very last.

"To this reply the marquis drew his sword and approached me.

"I had a stick at the head of my bed, with a heavy solid gold head, which they had left me, no doubt, because they took the head to be only copper. I seized hold of this stick and, leaping to the foot of my bed, I fell upon the marquis and all his rabble in such a furious fashion that the marquis dropped his sword and fled, and all his miserable rascals followed suit; throwing down their knives and poignards, shrieking with fear, and flying in such hot haste that in less than ten seconds my room was completely empty.

"I do not know at all how this act of rebellion would have ended for us, if the armistice concluded at Foligno had not come to put an end to our protracted sufferings: we must inevitably have succumbed to them in the long run. But, as the Neapolitan Government was bent on treating us shamefully to the last moment, they took great care not to tell us our captivity was at an end. On the contrary, with fresh menacings, with formidable preparations, and as though they meant to send us there so that we should all perish together, they transferred us all to Brindisi, although we were under French law at Taranto and in its environs.

"Not until the moment of going on board did we know that the armistice was concluded and the cartel of exchange arranged: we were free.

"Our term of liberty did not seem as though, in all probability, it would be of long duration.

"They embarked us at Brindisi for Ancona, and on a sea bristling with enemies. The English would no doubt inherit us next, and we should be only changing our old captivity for a new one.

"I laid all these facts before the marquis de la Squiave, and protested, on behalf of myself and all my companions, against this embarkation; but my protests were useless: they crowded us into a felucca, and made us set sail for Ancona.

"Before starting, I of course asked for all my papers, my arms, my horses, and, in short, for everything that had been stolen from me, above all for my sword, which I valued greatly, as it had been presented to me by Bonaparte at Alexandria. They tritely replied to all my demands that they would refer the matter to His Majesty.

"I have since learnt that they really did transmit the request to King Ferdinand; but as he used my rifles and my horses daily for hunting—as he found the guns carried well and the horses were excellent hunters—he kept both guns and horses.

"We reached Ancona, escaping the English and the Barbary-raiders by nothing short of a miracle.

"At Ancona we found General Watrin, who, seeing us stripped of our all (for we had sold everything we possessed for food), laid his purse at our disposal.

"This money enabled us in the first place to clothe ourselves, then to give a hundred piastres to the Neapolitan captain who had transported us, and who was not ashamed to come and demand this sum from us for his *buona mano*.

"Such is an exact account of those twenty months of captivity, during which three attempts to poison and one to assassinate me were made.

"And now, although I cannot live much longer, I thank Heaven that I have been spared till to-day.

"I am near death's door, but I still have strength enough to lay bare this infamous treatment, so that all the world may be made aware of it—a treatment such as the least civilised of peoples would blush to use towards their bitterest enemies.

"Written at the Headquarters of the Southern Army of Observation, Florence, the 15th Germinal, year IX of the Republic.

ALEX. DUMAS."

[1] This assertion would seem well-nigh incredible if it were not given in pretty nearly the same terms by the pen of General Coletta. "These impostors directed their steps towards the town of Taranto, but directly they reached it they saw a vessel coming into the harbour, and learnt that it contained the old princesses of France on their way from Naples to Sicily. Nothing daunted, the adventurers sent a messenger in advance of Corbara to inform the princesses of the marvellous credulity of the people; they then presented themselves before these ladies with regal pomp and with as much assurance as though of the blood royal. In spite of the inborn pride of the race of Bourbon, the princesses received the obscure adventurer as though he were their grandson; deeming, by so doing, that they were thus serving the king's cause; they addressed him by the title of 'your Highness,' and

lavished marks of respect and affection upon him" (*History of Naples from 1734 to 1825*, by Coletta).

[2] Dolomieu was taken to the prison of Naples, where he implored his gaoler to alleviate his hardships, but the gaoler refused the illustrious savant's request. "If you are not careful," Dolomieu said to him, "I shall die in a few days under such treatment."

"What does that matter to me?" replied the gaoler. "I am only responsible for your bones."

Dolomieu died two years after his release from prison.

CHAPTER VII

My father is exchanged for General Mack—Events during his captivity—He asks in vain for a share in the distribution of the 500,000 francs indemnity granted to the prisoners—The arrears of his pay also refused him—He is placed on the retired list, in spite of his energetic protests.

My father was exchanged for the famous general, Mack, whom the Austrian emperor had lent to the Neapolitans. This general was later captured at Ulm, for the third time, hence the following quatrain:—

"En loyauté comme en vaillance,
Mack est un homme singulier;
Retenu sur parole, il s'échappe de France;
Libre dans Ulm, il se rend prisonnier."

My father's imprisonment had lasted from the 27th Ventôse, year VII (17th March 1799) to the 15th Germinal, year IX (5th April 1801), during which period great events had taken place.

Bonaparte saw his gigantic designs upon the East miscarry before the successful resistance of a paltry seaport town like St. Jean-d'Acre. He had heard no news from Europe for ten months, when suddenly he learnt, through the medium of a stray Gazette that came in his way, of our reverses in Italy, of the re-capture of Mantua, the battle of Novi and the death of Joubert. He immediately left Egypt, reached Fréjus after a forty days' crossing on board *la Muiron*, and arrived in Paris on the 16th October 1799; a month later he overthrew the Directory on the famous 18th of Brumaire, and had himself appointed First Consul. He then married his sister Caroline to Murat, set out for Italy on May 6th, 1800, crossed the Saint Bernard with his army on the 19th and 20th, and defeated the Austrians at Marengo on June 14th, 1800—the same day that Kléber was assassinated at Cairo by Soliman.

On January 12, 1801, Murat left Milan to invade Naples and to deliver Rome.

On the 18th February the armistice to which we have referred, and to which my father owed his liberty, was concluded between France and the King of Naples.

And finally, as we have seen, my father reached the headquarters at Florence on the 5th April, from whence he hastened to despatch to the First Consul the report we have just read, which I have copied from the manuscript written and signed in his own handwriting.

When he landed at Ancona, on the 23rd Germinal, year IX, my father at once wrote the following letter to the Consuls:—

"CITIZEN CONSULS,—I have the honour to inform you that we arrived at this town yesterday, with ninety-four prisoners, the officers and non-commissioned officers among whom about equal the soldiers and marines, and most of them are blind or maimed. We will confine ourselves for the present to informing you that the treatment we experienced at the hands of the Government of Naples disgraces that State in the eyes of humanity and of all nations, for the most frightful means were employed to get rid of us, even poisoning being resorted to.

"I have the honour to send to you at the headquarters at Florence a detailed report of all the scandalous deeds which the Neapolitan Government committed with regard to us.

"Accept, Citizen Consuls, our respectful greetings."

In the following July he wrote to Murat:—

"MY DEAR MURAT,—If I have not been able to correspond with you sooner, you must put it down entirely to my wretched state of health, which, always uncertain and shaky, now forcibly reminds me, acutely and constantly, of the terrible treatment the King of Naples meted out to me.

"I want to know something definite, my dear Murat, about the 500,000 francs indemnity you tell me the Neapolitan Government was made to pay to such of the prisoners of war as survived the sojourn in their prison. I have spoken to many people upon this subject, but no one seems able to tell me exactly what the facts are with respect to this indemnity. You alone, my dear Murat, were probably entrusted to treat with the King of Naples, in which case I have not the slightest doubt you will remember me, on two counts: first, from the interest you have apparently taken in my misfortunes, and secondly, on account of the lasting friendship we mutually vowed long ago. I beg you not to forget to reclaim the things the king stole from me, and to remind him of the promises made by his agents at the time of my departure from Brindisi: these are among the documents I deposited with you. Urge them to send back all those things, if they are not already in your hands, and especially my two horses. You know how attached I am to the mare you gave me; I saved her out of my eleven horses, when nine had to be thrown overboard.

"I am told the First Consul was very indignant at the conduct of the King of Naples towards me. He promised to have all my things restored to me, particularly the sword he gave me at Alexandria, which is in the hands of that wretched successor of the Cæsars.

"I hope with all my heart you may be able to get the better of him.—Ever yours," etc.

But although my father's appeal might seem to the First Consul at first sight quite fair, it had to be followed up by others, as this letter addressed to Bonaparte himself will show:—

"General Lannes informs me that you cannot grant me any indemnity before you know whether General Murat really did exact this same indemnity from the Neapolitan Government. Nobody, however, knows better than you what sufferings I underwent, and how completely I have been robbed of my goods.

"General Murat writes me that the minister for foreign affairs is charged with the distribution of the sum of 500,000 francs which the Neapolitan Government has been compelled to pay over to the French victims of its barbarity. I will therefore content myself, citizen, by begging you to have the goodness to give orders that I may be included in the distribution of that sum.

"I trust you will do your best in the matter of this just demand in the case of a man to whom you have given so many verbal tokens, so many written testimonies, of your esteem and your friendship."

It is evident that those clouds of Egypt which, according to Bonaparte's prophecy, were only to last six hours, had crossed the Mediterranean, and had thickened over my poor father's head. He had, moreover, himself declared that he had not long to live, and should soon cease to embarrass Napoleon with the presence of one of the old Republican generals who had crossed Bonaparte's path.

Hoche had died of poison; Joubert had been killed at Novi; Kléber had been assassinated at Cairo; and my father was feeling the first symptoms of cancer in the stomach—the natural consequence of the arsenic that had been given him. I need hardly say he was not included among those who shared the distribution of this 500,000 francs indemnity granted to the prisoners.

My father then thought he might at least count on receiving the arrears of his pay during the two years of captivity.

He addressed himself on this subject to Bonaparte, and Bonaparte replied favourably; then my father learnt that this request, however just it might seem at first sight, was surrounded by considerable difficulties. On hearing this, my father addressed the following letter to Bonaparte, the last, I believe, he ever wrote him; it was sent a few days after my birth:—

"7 *Vendémiaire, Year X.*

"I believed, since you did me the honour to tell me that it would be so, that my arrears of salary from the 30th Pluviôse, year VII, would be made good. An examination of the accounts will show the deductions to be made from that which is due to me for this period. I was paid for the first three quarters of the year IX, but the minister of war tells me in his letter of the 29 Fructidor last, that I can only receive what is owing to me for a portion of the years VII and VIII in full, inasmuch as the order you have made in my favour says, in so many words, that I am only to receive what the law strictly grants me— that is to say, my salary for two months of active service.

"But, Consul-General, you know what misfortunes I have had, you know how small my fortune is! Remember how I gave up the treasure at Cairo!

"I hope I may rely sufficiently upon your friendship to believe that you will give orders that I may be paid for the remaining months of the years VII and VIII. It is the only thing I ask of you.

"The successive poisonings I underwent in the prisons of Naples have so much undermined my health, that already at the age of thirty-six I am the victim of infirmities which I should not naturally expect to feel until much later in life.

"I trust then, Consul-General, that you will not allow the man who shared your labours and your perils to languish in poverty when it lies in your power to place him above want. You will thus be the means of conveying to him evidence of the nation's generosity.

"I have another grievance, too, Consul-General, and one, I confess, that troubles me far more than those of which I have complained. The minister of war informed me in a letter of 29 Fructidor last, that during the year X I was put down on the list of generals no longer on active service. What! at my age and With my reputation! to be placed on the retired list! Surely my past services should have saved me from this....

"In 1793 I was chief commander of the Republican armies. I am the oldest general officer of my rank; feats of daring performed by me have greatly influenced the tide of affairs; I have always led the defenders of the country to victory. Tell me, then! who received more marks of your esteem? And yet I see officers of all grades, junior to me, unreservedly employed while I am left inactive!

"I appeal, Consul-General, to the goodness of your heart; allow me to lay bare my complaints and to place in your hands my vindication against my enemies."

A week previously my father had written to the minister of war:—

"I received your letter of the 29th of last month, which informed me that, as I was without fixed destination, I was placed upon the list of general officers on half pay; that I shall receive a salary of 7500 francs from the 1st Vendémiaire, year X.

"The services I have rendered to the nation readily lead me to believe that the Government will lose no time in employing me on the first opportunity that may offer, when you lay before them the details of those services.

"I will not speak of my recent misfortunes: I am a son of France, and bore them for my country's sake! But on that very ground, those afflictions should give me some claim upon the nation's gratitude.

"Furthermore, you are aware that I passed through every military grade, from ordinary soldier to general-in-chief; winning my promotion with my own sword, and not by private influence.

"Mont Cenis; Mont St. Bernard; the obstinate struggle before Mantua on the 27 Nivôse, year VII, where two horses were killed under me; the crossing of the Weiss, which was laid to the credit of Generals Baraguay-d'Hilliers and Delmas, but was really due to me; the act of Horatius Codes performed afresh in the Tyrol, which won me the honour of being introduced to the Executive Directory under that name by General Bonaparte, who thought of appointing me, at that time, commander-in-chief of the Army of the Tyrol; finally, the insurrection at Cairo, which I quelled in the absence of all; you are well aware, Citizen Minister, those are my inalienable claims in the eyes of my old comrades-in-arms, and deserving of the recognition of my country.

"From 1793, Citizen Minister, I was commander-in-chief of the Republican armies, and throughout these unfortunate and difficult times I was never beaten; on the contrary, my enterprises were invariably crowned with success.

"I am now the oldest general in my rank; I was the companion of the Consul-General in nearly all his Italian and Egyptian wars, and no one contributed more to his triumphs and to the glory of our arms than did I; his letters, which I have in my possession, testify no less to the respect in which he held me than to his friendship. You yourself lavished tokens of lively interest on me when I returned from the Neapolitan prisons, and now I am to be put aside on half pay!

"Citizen Minister, I cannot endure such an indignity; I beg you, therefore, to show this letter to the First Consul, and to tell him that I trust in his old friendship to obtain for me a place on the active list.

"Honour has always directed my conduct; sincerity and loyalty are the bases of my character; and injustice is the cruellest torture to me."

I have before me the register of all my father's correspondence; it stops short at this letter, and the rest of the pages are blank.

These two letters to the minister of war and to the First Consul were the last he wrote.

Doubtless they were never answered.

Despair beset him after this; he buried himself in the shadow of his enforced inactivity as those condemned to death await their doom in their cells before being taken to the scaffold: in a state of torpor, varied by fits of despair, he awaited that last supreme moment; most of his comrades-in-arms, more fortunate than he, had met it on the field of battle.

CHAPTER VIII

Letter from my father to General Brune on my birth—The postscript—My godfather and godmother—First recollections of infancy—Topography of the château des Fossés and sketches of some of its inhabitants—The snake and the frog—Why I asked Pierre if he could swim—Continuation of *Jocrisse*.

As I mentioned at the beginning of these Memoirs, I was born on the 5th Thermidor, year X (24th of July 1802), at 4.30 a.m.

I came on the scene with a great show of strength and vigour, judging from a letter my father wrote to his friend, General Brune, the day after my birth.

It is an odd letter, and possesses a *post scriptum* of a still more eccentric nature; but those who have had the patience to read these Memoirs so far will have become acquainted with some of my father's whimsical and vivacious characteristics, and should understand his nature. Others, who take no interest in any details such as those given by my father to Brune, can skip this letter, without reading either it or its postscript. However that may be, here it is:—

"*6th Thermidor, Year X.*

"MY DEAR BRUNE,—I am glad to tell you my wife gave birth yesterday morning to a fine boy, who weighs nine pounds and is eighteen inches long. So you will see that if he continues to increase in the outside world at the rate he has done inside, he bids fair to attain to a pretty fine stature.

"And another thing you should know too: I rely on you to be his godfather. My eldest daughter, who sends you a thousand kisses from the tips of her little black fingers, will be your fellow-godparent. Make haste and come, although the new arrival into this world does not seem to wish to leave it in a hurry; come soon, for it is long since I saw you, and I want to see you very much.—Your friend,

AL. DUMAS.

"*P.S.*—I open my letter to tell you that the young dog has just eased himself all over his head. That's a good sign, surely! Eh?"

We must make allowances for my dear father's pride; he had much wanted a boy all the ten years he had been married, and he fancied that the birth should be preceded, accompanied, and followed by auguries of great import to the world, as in the case of Augustus.

However, although these omens seemed so satisfactory to my father, Brune apparently was not so positive about them. This is what he wrote by return of post:—

"COUNCIL OF STATE, PARIS,

"10*th Thermidor, Year X of the French Republic.*

"To GENERAL DUMAS.

"MY DEAR GENERAL,—A superstition prevents my complying with your request. I have been godfather five times, and my five *godsons* have all *died*! When the last died I vowed I would never name another child. You will probably think my superstition fanciful, but it would make me wretched to change my mind. I am an old friend of your family, therefore I feel sure I can count on your indulgence. My resolution must indeed be firmly fixed to refuse to act with your charming daughter. Offer my sincerest regrets to her and to your charming wife, and accept the assurance of my sincere attachment.

"BRUNE.

"*P.S.*—I have despatched various parcels for the little godmother and her mamma."

Nevertheless, my father insisted, in spite of this refusal and the superstitious fears it implied. I never saw the second letter, but I presume the omens were even more propitious and more convincing than in the first instance, for, at my father's urgent entreaties, a *mezzo termine* (half-way house) was arranged, and Brune agreed to stand, but he was to have a proxy in the person of my father, who was to hold me at the font in his stead.

No change was made with regard to my godmamma, who had no feelings of repugnance whatever towards her part in the ceremony, since it had already brought her so many bonbons, and promised more. For her it was a fête.

Brune, by proxy, and Aimée-Alexandre Dumas, my sister, aged nine years, were, therefore, my godfather and godmother.

It will be remembered that just before the Egyptian campaign it had been settled that if my mother bore a son, the godparents of this said son were to be Bonaparte and Joséphine. But things had changed greatly since then, and my father had no inclination to remind the First Consul of the general-in-chief's promise.

Bonaparte cruelly proved to my mother that he was not a Louis XII., who forgave the injuries he had received when duc d'Orléans.

The first glimmering of recollection in the darkness of my infant life would be about the year 1805. I can faintly remember the arrangements of the small country house we lived in, which was called *les Fossés*.

My topographical recollections stop short at the kitchen and dining-room, the two parts of the house I doubtless frequented with most sympathy.

I have not seen this house since 1805, but I can still recollect that there was a step down into the kitchen and a big block opposite the door; that the kitchen table came directly behind it; and, in front of this kitchen table, to the left, was the chimneyplace. This chimneyplace was an immense one, and inside it nearly always lay my father's favourite gun, a silver-mounted one, with a pad of green morocco at the butt-end. I was forbidden ever to touch this gun, under penalty of the most severe punishment, but I was always touching it, and my mother, in spite of her fears, never carried her threats into execution. Then, farther on, beyond the chimneyplace, was the dining-room, up three steps: the floor was parqueted in deal, and the wooden wainscoting was painted grey.

Our household comprised, besides my father and mother, the following members, whom I will enumerate in the order of importance they filled in my own mind:—

1st. A large black dog called *Truffe*, who was privileged to be welcomed everywhere, because he allowed me to ride him regularly.

2nd. A gardener named Pierre, who used to provide me with frogs and grass snakes, reptiles I was extremely inquisitive about.

3rd. A negro, my father's valet, named Hippolyte, pretty much a black simpleton, whose queer sayings became family bywords, which my father treasured up, I believe, to use in a series of stories meant to rival the tomfooleries of Brunet.

4th. A guardsman called Mocquet, for whom I had a profound admiration, because every evening he would relate magnificent stories of his deeds of prowess, stories which were immediately interrupted if the general appeared on the scenes—the general not having such a great opinion of these deeds as the narrator had himself.

5th. A kitchen girl named Marie. This last creature is totally lost in the twilight mists of my memory. She is just a name which I heard given to some indistinct figure, now a mere blurred form in my memory; so far as I can remember, she was in nowise a sylph.

Truffe died of old age towards the end of 1805, and Mocquet and Pierre buried him in a corner of the garden. This was the first funeral I had seen, and I wept very bitterly over the old friend of my early days.

My next recollections are confused half flashes in the semidarkness of early memories, and quite dateless.

One day when I was playing in the garden Pierre called me, and I ran to him. Whenever Pierre called me it always meant that he had found something worthy of my notice. Indeed, he had just discovered a snake in a meadow by the roadside, and it had a great lump in its stomach. With one blow of his spade he cut the snake in half, and out of the reptile hopped a frog, a trifle dazed by the beginning of the digestive process of which it had been the victim. It soon revived, stretched out its legs one after the other, yawned prodigiously, and began to leap; slowly at first, then more quickly and, at last, as fast as though nothing whatever had happened to it.

This phenomenon, which I have never again seen, impressed me so much, and remains in my mind so vividly, that if I close my eyes I can see as I write these lines the two wriggling portions of the snake, the frog still motionless, and Pierre leaning upon his spade, smiling at my astonishment, just as clearly as though Pierre, the frog, and the snake were still before my eyes—only Pierre's features are almost effaced by time, like a badly-taken photograph.

I remember also that, about the middle of the year 1805, my father, who was suffering from very bad health, left our château des Fossés for a house or château at Antilly,—I have not a single recollection of that sojourn beyond being taken there on Pierre's back. It had rained a great deal for two nights previously, and I was filled with surprise to see Pierre walk unconcernedly through the puddles of water which intersected the road.

"Do you know how to swim, Pierre?" I asked him. The impression Pierre's courage in crossing these puddles made upon me must have been very strong, for these words are the first I remember speaking, and, like those of M. de Crac, which froze in winter and thawed in spring, I can hear them ringing in my ears with the distant and faint accents of my childish voice. The question, "Pierre, can you swim?" was suggested to me by an event that happened at our house which deeply impressed my youthful imagination. Three young men, one called Dupuis, whom I have since seen as a jeweller in Paris—all of Villers-Cotterets—came to the château des Fossés, which was surrounded by water, to ask permission to bathe in the kind of moat which ran round it. My father gave them leave, and asked them if they could swim; they replied in the negative, and he showed them a place where they could touch the bottom safely without running any risk of drowning. The bathers kept to this spot at first, but, little by little, they grew bolder; and all at once we heard loud cries from the moat and ran to see,—there were the three bathers all on the point of drowning.

Fortunately, Hippolyte was there, and he could swim like a fish. In an instant he was in the water, and when my father reached the edge of the moat he had already almost saved the first of the three. My father, who was a splendid swimmer, like most Colonials, threw himself into the water and saved the second; and Hippolyte saved the third.

They were all pulled out in less than five minutes' time, but one of the three bathers had already lost consciousness, and, seeing him lying with his eyes shut and not breathing, I thought he was dead. My mother, who knew he had only fainted, as she had been reassured by my father that he was in no danger, turned the occasion, which had impressed me profoundly, to good account by giving me an eloquent sermon on the dangers of playing on the banks of the stream. No sermon ever had a more attentive listener; nor preacher a more fervent convert!

From that moment no one could ever persuade me to gather a single flower from the sides of the stream, not had they bribed me with all the coveted treasures of childhood—with rocking-horses, bleating lambs, or barking dogs.

Yet another thing had struck me: my father's grand form (which looked as though it might have been made in the same mould as that which formed the statues of Hercules or Antinous) compared with Hippolyte's poor small limbs.

It was my father's naked form I saw, dripping with water; he smiled an almost unearthly smile, as a man may who has accomplished a god-like act, the saving of another man's life.

And that was why I asked Pierre if he could swim; I remembered the fainting youth on the grass by the stream, as I saw Pierre venturing through puddles of water two inches deep, and I realised that neither my father nor Hippolyte were near at hand to save us.

Hippolyte was an excellent swimmer, a clever runner, and quite a good horseman, but, as I have before implied, his intellectual faculties were far from corresponding to his physical abilities. Two instances will give an idea of the state of his intelligence.

One evening, my mother fearing a frost in the night, and wishing to shelter some beautiful autumn flowers which were under a little wall breast high, and which brightened our outlook from the dining-room windows, called Hippolyte.

Hippolyte ran up, and stood listening to her orders with his big eyes and thick lips wide open.

"Hippolyte," said my mother, "you must carry those pots into the house this evening and put them in the kitchen."

"Yes, madame," replied Hippolyte.

In the evening my mother indeed found the pots in the kitchen, but piled up one on top of the other, so as to take up as little room as possible in the domains of Marie the kitchenmaid.

A cold perspiration broke out on my poor mother's face, for too well did she understand what had happened. Hippolyte had obeyed her to the letter. He had emptied out the flowers and taken the pots inside.

Next morning my mother found the flowers broken, heaped on top of one another, glistening with frost, at the foot of the wall.

Pierre, the plant-doctor, was called in, and managed to save a few, but most of them were destroyed.

The second thing was more serious in its nature. I have offered it to Alcide Tousez to incorporate in his *Soeur de Jocrisse*; but he dared not use it.

I possessed a delightful little sparrow Pierre had caught for me. The poor little bird could scarcely fly, and had tried to go on a voyage of discovery after its father, like Icarus. It had passed from its nest into a cage, where it had grown and developed its wings properly.

Hippolyte had the special charge of feeding my sparrow and cleaning out its cage.

One day I found the cage open, and my sparrow had gone. Much weeping, lamentation, and woe followed, and finally maternal intervention.

"Who left the door open?" she asked Hippolyte.

"I did, madame," he replied, with as much glee as though he had done the cleverest thing imaginable.

"What did you do that for?"

"Oouf! the poor little beast's cage smelt as though it needed fresh air."

There was nothing to say in reply. Did not my mother herself open the doors and windows of rooms which needed fresh air, and order the servants always to do the same under similar circumstances?

They gave me another sparrow, and instructed Hippolyte to keep its cage cleaner, and so prevent any smell.

I do not remember if he obeyed properly; for another event took up the attention of our household.

CHAPTER IX

Mocquet's nightmare—His pipe—Mother Durand—Les bêtes *fausses* et le *pierge*—M. Collard—My father's remedy—Radical cure of Mocquet.

Mocquet had the nightmare.

Do you know what a nightmare is? I think you must have seen that huge-eyed monster, seated on the chest of a panting and sleeping man.

I do not know how to paint it in words, but I have seen it, even as you have.

Mocquet's nightmare was no monkey with big eyes, or fantastic monster of Hugo's imagination reproduced by the brush of Delacroix, by the pencil of Boulanger, or by the chisel of Feuchères; none of these, it was a little old woman, who lived in the village of Haramont, about a quarter of a league from our château des Fossés, whom Mocquet considered in the light of his personal enemy.

One morning very early Mocquet, came into my father's room before he was up and stood by the bedside.

"Well, Mocquet, what is the matter?" asked my father. "Why that melancholy face?"

"General, I have been *nightmared*," replied Mocquet solemnly. Mocquet, all unconsciously, had enriched the language with an active verb.

"Oh! you have been *nightmared*—have you?" exclaimed my father, as he raised himself on one elbow.

"Yes, General."

And Mocquet drew his cutty-pipe out of his mouth, a thing he rarely did, and only under very serious provocation.

Now this pipe was more than an accessary to Mocquet—it was an integral part of the man.

No one had ever seen Mocquet without his pipe. If, by chance, it was out of his mouth, he held it in his hand.

This pipe, intended to accompany Mocquet into the midst of the thickest forests, presented the least possible surface that could encounter destruction by contact with any solid body.

Now the destruction of a well seasoned cutty-pipe would, in Mocquet's eyes, mean a loss that only the work of years could repair.

The stem of this pipe of Mocquet's never projected more than half an inch.

This habit of never being without his pipe had filed a hollow between Mocquet's incisors and canine teeth: it had also led to another habit, that of speaking through his shut teeth, which gave a peculiarly impressive character to all he said; for nothing prevented his teeth from keeping tight shut.

"How long have you been *nightmared*, my poor Mocquet?" my father asked.

"For a whole week, General."

"By whom?"

"Oh! I know well enough who it is," he replied, shutting his teeth tighter than ever.

"Indeed, may I know who it is?"

"That old witch, mother Durand, General!"

"Mother Durand of Haramont?"

"Yes, hard enough."

"The deuce, Mocquet—we must look into this!"

"I'll see to it too; she shall pay me for this, the old mole!"

The old mole was an expression of hatred which Mocquet had borrowed from Pierre, who, having no greater enemies than moles, dubbed all he detested by that name.

"We must look into this, Mocquet," my father had said; not that he believed in Mocquet's nightmare, not even that, admitting the existence of the nightmare, he believed it was mother Durand who had *nightmared* his guardsman. Nothing of the kind; but my father knew the superstitious nature of our peasants; he knew that a belief in *spells* was still largely prevalent in the countryside. He had heard some terrible tales of vengeance taken by folk who thought themselves bewitched, who had sought to break the spell by killing the person or persons who had *bewitched* them. And when Mocquet denounced mother Durand to my father, there was such a threatening accent in his voice, and he had pressed the butt of his rifle with so much intention, that my father deemed it wise policy to appear to chime in with Mocquet's opinion in order to keep a hold on him, so that he should not do anything before first consulting him.

"But before punishing her, my good Mocquet," my father said to him, "we must do our best to see if we cannot cure you of your nightmare."

"You cannot, General."

"Why not?"

"No, I have done everything possible."

"What have you done?"

"First I drank a large bowl of warm wine before going to bed."

"Who recommended you to do that? Was it M. Lécosse?"

M. Lécosse was the leading doctor in Villers-Cotterets.

"M. Lécosse?" said Mocquet with scorn. "He? what does he know about spells? Goodness! No, it wasn't M. Lécosse."

"Who was it, then?"

"The shepherd at Longpré."

"A whole bowl of hot wine, you idiot! You would be dead drunk after you had taken it!"

"The shepherd drank half."

"Well, I understand the prescription; and the bowl of warm wine did no good?"

"General, she stamped on my chest all night, just as though I had taken absolutely nothing."

"And what did you do next?"

"I did what I always do when I want to catch a *false* beast (*une bête fausse.*)"

Mocquet had a vocabulary peculiar to himself. He could never be made to say a fallow deer (*une bête fauve.*) Each time my father said *une bête fauve* Mocquet took him up.

"Yes, General, a *false* beast—for, General, with all respect, you are wrong."

"How am I wrong?"

"It is not a fallow deer I mean, but a false beast."

"Why?"

"Because a fallow deer does not express what I mean."

"And what do you mean by a false beast?"

"I mean a beast that only walks by night, one that is deceitful—in short, a *false* beast."

It was such a logical definition that there was nothing further to be said; so my father did not answer, and Mocquet triumphantly continued to call fallow deer false beasts.

So to my father's question, "What did you do next?" Mocquet replied, "I did what I always do when I want to catch a false beast."

"What is that, Mocquet?"

"I set a trap *(piège)*."

Mocquet always pronounced *piège pierge*.

"You set a trap to catch mother Durand?"

Mocquet did not like to have his words said differently from his own pronunciation. He replied: "I set a *pierge* for mother Durand."

"And where did you put it? At your door?"

"At my door? Rather not! Do you think the old witch would go through my door? She would enter my bedroom in some unheard-of way."

"By the chimney, perhaps?"

"There isn't one. I never saw her until I felt her stamping on my chest: click, clack, click, clack!"

"Well, where did you put the snare?"

"The *pierge?* I put it on my stomach, to be sure."

"What sort of a snare did you use?"

"Oh! a famous *pierge*, with an iron chain, which I passed round my wrist. It weighed about ten pounds. Oh! yes, ten or twelve pounds, at least."

"And that night——?"

"Oh! She was much worse that night. She generally kneads my chest with her goloshes, but that night she had clogs on."

"And did she come like that?"

"Every living night the good Lord made. I get so thin with it that I am becoming quite consumptive: but this morning I have made up my mind."

"What have you decided to do, Mocquet?"

"I have made up my mind to give her the contents of my gun."

"That is a wise decision. When will you put it into execution?"

"Oh, either to-night or to-morrow, General."

"That's a nuisance, for I was just going to send you to Villers-Hellon."

"Oh, that doesn't matter, General. Is what I have to do urgent?"

"Very urgent."

"Well, I can go to Villers-Hellon,—it is only four leagues,—and be back by night. That will make eight leagues in the day. We have put many more behind us in hunting, General."

"True enough, Mocquet. I will give you a letter for M. Collard, and then you will set off."

"Yes, I will start at once, General."

My father got up and wrote to M. Collard. We will explain later who that gentleman was; in the meantime we will merely mention that he was one of my father's best friends.

The letter was as follows:—

"MY DEAR COLLARD,—I send herewith my idiot of a guardsman, whom you know. He fancies an old woman bewitches him every night, and, to put an end to his vampire, he proposes, quite nonchalantly, to kill her. But as the law looks askance on such rough-and-ready methods of cure for nightmare, I send him to you on a trivial pretext. Send him to Danré de Youty, who, on some other pretext, must send him to Dulauloy, who—with or without a pretext—can send him to the devil if he wishes.

"In short, his tour must be made to last a fortnight. During that time we shall have moved to Antilly, and then, as he will be no longer in the neighbourhood of Haramont, and as his nightmare will probably disappear during his journey, mother Durand may be able to sleep in peace—I should not advise her to do this while Mocquet lives in the district.

"He brings you a dozen snipe and a hare which we shot yesterday when hunting in the marsh of Walue.

"A thousand tender messages to your lovely Herminie, and a thousand kisses to your dear little Caroline.—Your friend,

"ALEX. DUMAS.

"*P.S.*—"We received yesterday news of your goddaughter Aimée, who is very well; as for Berlick, he grows an inch a month, and runs always on the tips of his toes,—his shoes make no difference."

Mocquet left an hour after the letter was written, and three weeks sped by before he rejoined us at Antilly.

"Well?" asked my father, seeing him look cheerful and the picture of health— "Well! what about mother Durand?"

"Why, General! the old mole has left me. It looks as though she had no power in this district."

And now the reader has the right to ask for an explanation of my father's postscript, and to be told who was this Berlick who grew an inch a month and who ran on tiptoe in spite of his shoes.

CHAPTER X

Who was Berlick?—The fête of Villers-Cotterets—Faust and Polichinelle—
The sabots—Journey to Paris—Dollé—Manette—Madame de Mauclerc's
pension—Madame de Montesson—*Paul and Virginia*—Madame de Saint-
Aubin.

I was Berlick: and this is how I obtained the charming nickname.

While my mother was *enceinte* the usual Whitsuntide fête took place at Villers-
Cotterets; a delightful fête it was, to which I shall again refer. It took place at
the time of the first spring foliage and amid the opening flowers, when
butterflies are dancing and linnets singing. In olden days this fête was famed
far and wide, and people attended it from twenty leagues round; like all other
fêtes, it began as a Corpus Christi festival, but now only exists in the calendar.

Well, to this well-attended fête came a man carrying a booth on his back, as
a snail carries its shell.

This booth contained the essentially national spectacle of Polichinelle, from
which Goethe borrowed the idea of his *Faust*.

Polichinelle is simply a worn-out, callous, crafty libertine, who abducts
women, and flouts brothers and husbands, who thrashes the officers of the
law, and ends up by being carried off by the devil. And what else was Faust?
A worn-out, callous libertine, not very cunning, it is true, who seduces
Marguerite, kills her brother, beats burgomasters and is carried off by
Mephistopheles in the end.

I will not venture to say that Polichinelle is more picturesque than Faust, but
I will go so far as to maintain that he is quite as philosophical and more
amusing.

Our friend with the booth had set up his show on the green, and gave daily
thirty or forty representations of that sublime comedy, which has made us all
laugh as children, and ponder over when grown men.

My mother was seven months gone in pregnancy when she went to see
Polichinelle. The showman was a man of some imagination, and instead of
simply calling his devil the devil, he gave him a name.

He called him Berlick.

The sight of Berlick impressed my mother terribly. Berlick was as black as a
devil. Berlick had a scarlet tongue and tail. Berlick spoke with a sort of growl,

like the noise made by a syphon of Seltzer water when the bottle is just running empty; an unknown sound in those days, before the invention of syphons, and therefore all the more awful.

My mother's mind was so taken up with this queer figure, that, on leaving the booth, she leant on a neighbour and exclaimed:

"Oh! my dear, it is all up with me. I shall give birth to a Berlick!"

Her neighbour, who was also in the same condition, was called Madame Duez. She replied:

"Then, my dear, if you give birth to a Berlick, I, who have been with you, shall give birth to a Berlock."

The two friends returned home laughing. But my mother's laugh was half-hearted, and she remained convinced that she would bring forth a black-faced child with a red tail and a tongue of flame.

The day of her confinement drew near, and, the nearer it came, the firmer grew my mother's belief. She imagined I leapt inside her womb as only a demon could, and when I kicked she could feel the claws with which my feet were furnished.

At length the 24th of July arrived. It struck half-past four in the morning, and I was born.

But in coming into the world it seems I turned and twisted in such a manner that the umbilical cord got round my neck, and I looked purple and half-strangled.

The woman who was with my mother uttered a cry, and my mother took it up.

"Oh, my God!" she murmured,—"it is black, is it not?"

The woman dared not answer her: there is so very little difference of colour between dark purple and black that it was not worth while to contradict.

The next moment I cried, as that creature destined to sorrow, whom we call man, generally does as he comes into the world.

The cord pressed round my neck so that I could only utter a kind of growl, similar in its nature to the noise that was always ringing in my mother's ears.

"Berlick! Berlick!" my mother cried out in despair.

Happily the doctor hastened to reassure her: he set my neck free, my face took its natural colour, and my cries were the wailings of an infant, and not the growls of a demon.

But I was none the less baptized with the name of Berlick, and it stuck to me ever after.

With regard to the second paragraph of the postscript, "He runs always on the tips of his toes,—his shoes make no difference," this second paragraph referred to a peculiarity of my construction. Until I was four years old I walked, or rather ran—for I never walked, and I always ran—I ran, I say, on the very tips of my toes. Ellsler, compared with me, would have appeared to be dancing on his heels. From the peculiar gait I indulged in, and in spite of the fact that I did not fall more often than other children, my mother was always possessed with a fear other mothers did not share, the fear of seeing me tumble down, and she was always asking people what she could do to make me walk in a more Christian fashion.

I think it was M. Collard who advised my mother to put me into sabots. These were a kind of shoe which made it almost impossible to walk, if I did not change my nature. I ran harder than ever, it would seem, by my father's letter, only I fell more often. That caused the sabots to be abandoned.

One fine day I gave up walking on tiptoe, and began to walk like everybody else. Of course I never explained why I gave up doing this, I never admitted whether it was from whim or a more justifiable cause. But there was great rejoicing throughout the household, and the happy news was spread abroad among friends and acquaintances. M. Collard was one of the first to be informed.

In the meantime my father's health had been growing worse. He was told of a doctor called Duval, who lived at Senlis, and who had a certain repute in these parts. So we went to Senlis.

That journey left no recollection on my mind, and the only trace of it I can find is in a letter of my mother, entrusting a deed to her lawyer during her absence.

It would seem that M. Duval recommended my father to go to Paris to consult Corvisart. My father had been meaning to go there for a long while. He longed to see Brune and Murat; he hoped to obtain through their advocacy the indemnity due to him as one of the prisoners of Brindisi, and still further he hoped to obtain payment of his arrears of salary left over from the years VII and VIII.

So we set out for Paris.

That journey was quite another thing, and I remember it perfectly; not exactly the time spent in the train, but the actual arrival in Paris. It was about August or September 1805. We alighted in the rue Thiroux, at the house of a friend of my father, called Dollé. He was a little old man, who wore a grey coat, velvet breeches, striped cotton stockings and buckled shoes; his hair was dressed *en ailes de pigeon*, the tail tied up with black ribbon and ending like a white paintbrush. His coat collar made this tail stick up towards the heavens in a most threatening manner.

His wife must once have been very pretty, and I suspect my father had been a friend of the wife before he became acquainted with the husband.

Her name was Manette.

I give all these details to show how accurate my memory is, and how thoroughly I can depend upon it.

Our first visit was to my sister, who was in an excellent boarding-school kept by a Madame de Mauclerc and a Miss Ryan, an English lady, who has since deprived us of the whole of a small fortune which we ought to have inherited. This boarding-school was situated in the rue de Harlay, au Marais.

The Abbé Conseil, a cousin of ours and an old tutor to Louis XVI.'s pages, had placed her at this school.

I shall have a word to say presently about our cousin the abbé, who left his whole fortune later to the Ryan girl.

I arrived in the play-hour, and all the young girls were out walking, chatting, playing in a large court. They had scarcely caught sight of me, with my long fair hair, which at that time curled instead of being wavy, before the whole school descended upon me like a flock of doves, learning that I was their friend's brother. Unluckily, the society of Pierre and Mocquet had taught me bad manners, and I had seen few people at Fossés and at Antilly. All these friendly but clamorous attentions did but double my habitual wildness, and, in exchange for the caresses with which all these charming sylphs embarrassed me, I dealt out kicks and cuffs to all who ventured to approach near me. The two who suffered most were Mademoiselle Pauline Masseron, who has since married Count d'Houdetot, a peer of France; and Mademoiselle Destillères, whose mansion, l'hôtel *d'Osmond*, is to-day the envy of everyone who passes along the boulevard des Capucines.

Perhaps my want of natural gallantry was still further increased by my knowledge that an operation, to my thinking most objectionable, awaited me when we left the school.

There was a great rage on just then for earrings, and they were going to take advantage of being in the boulevard to have each of my ears adorned with a little gold ring. When the operation was about to take place, I resisted with might and main; but an immense apricot, which my father went to buy for me, overcame all difficulties, and I set out for the rue Thiroux enriched with one more decoration.

About a third of the way down the rue du Mont-Blanc, my father separated from my mother, and took me with him to a grand house with men-servants in red livery. My father gave his name. We were kept waiting a moment; then they showed us through what seemed to me to be most sumptuously fitted rooms, till we reached a bedroom. Here we found an old lady lying on a couch, who held out her hand to my father with a most dignified gesture. My father kissed her hand respectfully, and seated himself near this lady.

Now how did it come about that I, who had just been so free with rude words and vulgar actions among all those charming young girls who wanted to kiss me, now, when this old lady called me to her, eagerly offered her both my cheeks to kiss? Because this old lady had something about her which both attracted and commanded at the same time.

My father remained nearly half an hour with this lady, during which time I kept quite still at her feet. Then we left her, and she would always remain convinced that I was the best behaved child imaginable.

My father stopped at the door and took me in his arms to bring me up to the level of his face; he always did so when he had something serious to tell me.

"My child," he said, "while I was in Florence I read the story of a sculptor, who relates that when he was just about your age, he showed his father a salamander which was sporting in the fire; his father slapped his face and said, 'My son, that slap was not meant to punish you, but to make you remember that you have seen not only what few men of our generation have seen, but also what few men of your generation will see, namely, a salamander.' Very well, then! I will do the same as the father of the Florentine sculptor; only instead of a slap I will give you this piece of gold, to make you remember that you have been kissed by one of the best and one of the greatest ladies who have ever lived, Madame la marquise de Montesson, the widow of Louis-Philippe d'Orléans, who died just twenty years ago."

I do not know what effect on my memory a slap on the face from my father's hand might have had, but I know that that gentle reminder coupled with the gold coin engraved this scene so deeply on my memory that I can still at this date see myself seated by the gracious old lady, who played gently with my hair all the while she was talking to my father.

Madame la marquise de Montesson died on February the 6th, and my father on February the 26th, 1806.

So it was that I, who pen these lines in 1850 (for nearly three years have flown by since I began these Memoirs, abandoned the idea, then resumed the work again) saw Charlotte-Jeanne Béraud de le Haie de Riou, marquise of Montesson, widow of the regent's grandson.

And my father knew M. de Richelieu, who was placed in the Bastille by Louis XIV. for being found concealed under the bed of madame la duchesse de Bourgogne.

If you thus unite the recollections of two generations, the events of a century will seem to have only happened but yesterday.

My father and mother went to the play at night, and took me with them. It was at the Opéra Comique, and *Paul and Virginia* was being played, the two leading parts being taken by Méhu and Madame de Saint-Aubin.

In later years I hunted up good little Madame de Saint-Aubin, who would be about thirty-eight when I first saw her, and therefore now would be between eighty-two and eighty-three years of age, and I retailed to her every detail of that evening in the August of 1805: one of them was a matter personal to herself: Virginia was far advanced in pregnancy.

Poor Saint-Aubin could not remember anything about it.

So vivid an impression did that night make on my memory that its events are perfectly present to me to-day: the changes of scene representing Madame Latour's house buried among orange-trees with their golden fruit, the angry sea and the lightning which struck and destroyed the *Saint-Géran*.

CHAPTER XI

Brune and Murat—The return to Villers-Cotterets—L'hôtel de l'Épée—
Princess Pauline—The chase—The chief forester's permission—My father
takes to his bed never to rise again—Delirium—The goldheaded cane—
Death.

He next day Murat and Brune lunched with us. Luncheon was served in a
room on the first floor; from the window of this room Montmartre could be
seen, and I remember that I was watching a huge kite floating gracefully in
the air above some windmills, when my father called me to him, put Brune's
sword between my legs, Murat's hat on my head, and made me gallop round
the table. "Do not ever forget, my child," he said to me, "how to-day you
have ridden round that table on Brune's sword, and had Murat's hat on your
head, also that you were kissed yesterday by Madame de Montesson, widow
of the duc d'Orléans, the regent's grandson."

See, my father, how well I have remembered all the incidents you bade me
recollect. And since I came to years of discretion my memories of you have
lived in me like a sacred lamp, illuminating everything and every person you
ever laid a finger on, although time has destroyed those things, and death has
taken away those persons.

Moreover, I paid my tribute of respect to the memory of both these men, to
the one at Avignon and to the other at Pizzo, when, ten years later, they were
both assassinated, within two months of each other.

Alas! who would have foretold that the child of three years old who capered
so gaily round them was one day to recount their death, to see the place
where they were killed, and to put his fingers in the very hole made by the
bullets which pierced their bodies and indented the wall behind?

What dark and bloody secrets the mysterious future hides from us! When
they are unfolded, may men realise that it is by the good providence of God
they were kept in ignorance of them until the appointed time!

One last word about that luncheon.... My father had consulted Corvisart,
and, although Corvisart did his best to reassure him, my father knew he was
a dying man. My father had tried to get an interview with the emperor,—for
Bonaparte, the general of the Army of the Interior, had become the Emperor
Napoleon,—and the emperor had declined to see my father. He had then
fallen back on his two friends, Brune and Murat, who had just become
marshals of the Empire. He found Brune as cordial as ever, but Murat very
cool towards him. This luncheon was for the purpose of commending my
mother and me to Brune and Murat; my mother, so soon to become a widow,

and I an orphan; for, when my father died, his allowance would die with him, and we should be left without means.

They both promised to do all they could, should this come about.

My father embraced Brune, shook Murat by the hand and left Paris the next day with death both in his body and in his heart.

We left Paris, but the return journey is no clearer to me than our going. Only a few things remain in my memory: they slumbered in my childhood and youth, and then burst forth into bright flame during manhood.

To what place we returned I cannot remember; I think, however, it must have been to Villers-Cotterets. I recollect that about the 3rd October we were staying in the famous hôtel de *l'Écu*, in the rue de Soissons, of which my grandfather was proprietor at the time of his daughter's marriage. As this crown was the crown of France, as the crown of France bore three *fleurs de lis* and as these flowers had ceased to be used since 1792, l'hôtel de *l'Écu* became l'hôtel de *l'Épée,* and was kept by a M. Picot, who was called Picot de l'Épée to distinguish him from two other Picots, one called Picot de None, and the other Picot the lawyer.

I shall have occasion to refer again to the latter two, who were closely connected with my early life.

I remember that towards the end of October a cab drew up at the main entrance, to take my father and me away.

I was always highly delighted when my father took me on his excursions.

On this occasion we crossed the park, and I remember that it was late October, because of the dead leaves which flew about like flocks of birds.

We reached a gate, and my father had forgotten the key. We were already three-quarters of a league from the house, and therefore too far away to go back for it; so my father got down, took *the gate* in his arms, shook it violently, and caused the stone in which the bolt of the lock was secured, to become detached from the post that held it.

We continued our drive, and in about half an hour's time we reached the château of Montgobert. The livery of the servants there was green, and not red, like that of Madame de Montesson. As at Madame de Montesson's mansion, we walked through a suite of rooms until we reached a boudoir hung with cashmere. A woman reclined on a sofa, a young and beautiful woman, very young and very beautiful; indeed, so beautiful that even I, a child, noticed it.

This lady was Pauline Bonaparte, who was born in Ajaccio in 1790, became the widow of General Leclerc in 1802, married Prince Aldobrandini Borghèse in 1803, and separated from her husband in 1804.

She appeared a delightful creature to my young imagination, so slight, so gracious, so pure; she wore tiny embroidered slippers, given her, no doubt, by Cinderella's fairy godmother. When my father entered the room she did not rise up, but only raised her head and held out her hand. My father wished to sit on a chair by her side, but she made him sit at her feet, which she rested on his knees, the toes of her slippers playing with his coat buttons. Her feet, her hands, her dainty slim figure, white and plump, and that Hercules of a mulatto, still handsome and powerful-looking in spite of his sufferings, made the most charming picture you could imagine.

I laughed as I looked at them, and the princess called me to her and gave me a tortoiseshell bonbon box, inlaid all over with gold.

I was greatly surprised to see her empty out the bonbons that were inside before she gave me the box. My father made some remark to her, and she bent down towards his ear, whispered a few words and they both began to laugh. As she bent down, the princess's white and pink cheek brushed against my father's dusky one, making his skin look darker and hers more white. They were both superb.

Perhaps childish eyes—full of astonishment at everything they see—lent a glamour to the scene, but I feel certain that, were I a painter, I could make a lovely picture of those two beings.

Suddenly we heard the sound of a horn out in the park.

"What is that?" asked my father.

"Oh!" the princess replied, "it is the people of Montbreton out hunting."

"Ah! see," said my father, "the hunt is coming near; the brute is running down this avenue, Princess, do come and look."

"Not I, my dear General," she said. "I am comfortable, and I do not want to disturb myself; it tires me to walk. You may carry me to the window, if you like."

My father picked her up in his arms, as a nurse takes up a baby, and carried her to the window.

He held her there quite ten minutes. The animal would not break cover. At last it passed down the avenue, with both hounds and men after it.

The princess waved her handkerchief to the hunters, and they responded by raising their hats.

Then my father laid her on the couch again, and resumed his seat by her side.

I do not know what happened behind me. I was completely taken up with watching the stag, which was escaping down the avenue from both hounds and hunters. That scene interested me far more than did the princess.

I remember no more of her beyond the waving of her white hand and her white handkerchief.

I have never seen her since, but she left so vivid an impression upon me that day that I can see her now.

I do not recollect in the least whether we remained on at Montgobert or returned the same day to Villers-Cotterets.

But I remember that my father soon after became weaker; he went out less often, he more rarely rode on horseback, he kept to his room for longer periods and he took me on his knees in a sadder mood. But these reminiscences only return to me in flashes, like objects seen by lightning on a dark night.

Some days before his death my father received permission to hunt. It came from Alexandre Berthier, marshal of the Empire, master of hounds to the Crown. Alexandre Berthier was an old enemy of my father. I quite believe it was he who had reported him as standing looking on at the siege of Mantua. Moreover, he had been a precious time in granting this permission, which was available from Vendémiaire the 1st to the 15th of Ventôse—in other words, from the 23rd of September to the 6th March. My father received it on the 24th February, and he died on the 26th.

This is a copy of the letter of leave from M. Deviolaine, Inspector of Forests:—

"Just as I am starting for the forest I have received an order from M. Collard to permit General Dumas to hunt and shoot. I hasten to send it to him with all good wishes, and my sincere hopes that his state of health will permit him to make use of it.

"Our sincere regards to Madame Dumas.

DEVIOLAINE.

"*Feb.* 24, 1806."

Even supposing my father had been well, the matter had been so arranged that he only received on February 24th a leave which expired on the 6th March. Thus, a dozen days of hunting were granted him.

My father flung both letter and order down on the table. My mother put them into her portfolio, where, forty-four years later, I came across them, enclosed one within the other.

The same evening my father tried to forget his sufferings by a ride on horseback; but the conqueror was vanquished at last, and he was obliged to return in half an hour's time. He went at once to bed, never again to rise from it.

My mother went for the doctor, leaving my father alone under a neighbour's care—a most excellent woman—Madame Darcourt, of whom 1 shall have occasion to speak. My father fell into a short access of delirium and despair.

"Oh!" he exclaimed, "Oh, my God, my God, must a general, who at thirty-five years of age was at the head of three armies, die in his bed, like a coward, at forty! What have I done that Thou shouldst condemn one so young to leave wife and children?"

Then, after a few minutes of quietness, he began:

"See, dear Madame Darcourt, this cane saved my life in the prisons of Brindisi, when those Neapolitan ruffians tried to assassinate me. Look to it that it never leaves me, let it be buried with me! My boy will not know the price I set on it, and it would only be lost before he is old enough to use it."

And Madame Darcourt, who saw that he was still somewhat delirious, replied, in order to soothe him, that it should be done as he wished.

"See," my father said,—"the head is gold."

"Certainly it is," she replied.

"Well, then, as I cannot leave my children sufficiently well off to deprive them of the money that knob might fetch—little though it may be—take the cane to Duguet's, the goldsmith's opposite, who will melt it down into a nugget,—then let him bring the nugget to me directly he has done it."

Madame Darcourt was about to venture a remark, but he entreated her so insistently to do what he asked, that she consented, and took the cane to Duguet.

She returned immediately, as she only had to run across the street.

"Well?" my father asked.

"All right, you shall have your nugget at six o'clock to-morrow evening, General."

"To-morrow at six in the evening," repeated my father. "That will do; it is probable I shall not be dead by then."

Next day Duguet brought the nugget over, and the dying man gave it to my mother: he was exceedingly weak by then, but his mind was perfectly clear, and he was able to hear what was said to him and to talk.

At ten at night, feeling death near at hand, he asked for Abbé Grégoire.

Abbé Grégoire was not only a good priest, he was an excellent friend of my father.

It was not a confession that the dying man wanted to make, for in all his life my father had not done a single bad action with which he could reproach himself; maybe in the depths of his heart he harboured feelings of hatred towards Berthier and Napoleon. But how could the last hours of a dying man concern these men at the pinnacle of fame and fortune? Moreover, all feelings of hatred were forgotten in the two hours before his death, which were spent in trying to comfort those he was to leave alone in the world, when he had departed from it.

Once, he asked to see me; but, as they were preparing to fetch me from my cousin's, where I had been sent, he forbade them. "No," he said,—"poor child, he is asleep, do not disturb him."

Finally, after bidding farewell to Madame Darcourt and the abbé, he turned towards my mother and, keeping his last breath for her, he died in her arms as midnight struck.

CHAPTER XII

My love for my father—His love for me—I am taken away to my cousin Marianne's—Plan of the house—The forge—The apparition—I learn the death of my father—I wish to go to heaven to kill God—Our situation at the death of my father—Hatred of Bonaparte.

The night my father died I had been carried out of the house by Maman Zine and deposited with my other cousin, Marianne, who lived with her father in the rue de Soissons.

They did not want me to be acquainted with death at my early age, and foreseeing its near approach and dreading the disturbance I should be sure to make, they took the precaution of taking me away at five o'clock in the afternoon. Maman Zine returned to the house after leaving me, as my poor mother needed help during the coming night.

I worshipped my father. Maybe, at so early an age, the feeling which now I should call love was nothing but an innocent and wondering admiration for the herculean stature and giant strength which I had seen my father exercise on various occasions. Perhaps it was only a childish pride in his braided coat, his tricoloured cockade, and his big sword, which I could scarcely lift. But, whatever it may have been, the recollection of my father, in every detail of his figure, in every feature of his face, is as present with me as though I had but lost him yesterday. No matter from what reasons, I love him still with as tender and deep and true a love as though he had watched over my youth and I had had the blessing of leaning on his strong arm throughout my childhood and early manhood.

On his side, too, my father worshipped me. I have said it, and I cannot repeat the fact too often, especially if the dead hear what is said of them; and, although during the last period of his life his great sufferings had got on his nerves to such an extent that he could not bear any noise or movement in his room, he made an exception for me.

I do not remember whether they took me to kiss my father before I was taken away; what happened during the night the events of which I am about to relate, whether or not it be put down to my youthful imagination, makes me think that they had forgotten that pious care. As I have said, my only notions of death were taken from the death of my big black dog and the fainting bather. It would, besides, have been extremely difficult for me to realise the death of my father, whom I had seen on his horse only three days previously. So I did not approve of being taken from home, and, once away, I was ignorant as to whether my father spoke of me or asked for me. A veil is drawn over my eyes in connection with that last day of his life. I only remember the following incident I am about to relate, the details of which are perfectly clear to my mind.

They had taken me to my uncle's house.

This worthy individual was a locksmith, named Fortier; and he had a brother who was a village priest. I shall speak of this brother later, for he was a very curious type of person.

I remained, therefore, under the care of my cousin Marianne.

Allow me to give an exact plan of the house, in order to make the situation clear. It is forty years or more since I entered the house and yet I can see it as though I had just left it.

As can be seen, the house was in reality one long passage, composed of the forge, which opened upon the rue de Soissons; an inner court just behind the forge; the dwelling-house, consisting of a bedroom furnished in the usual style, with a great walnut chest of drawers, a large four-post bed with green serge hangings, a table and several chairs, and, in addition, a little bed that had been improvised for me, on two chairs, for that night, which they had put opposite the big bed. Next after this bedroom came the kitchen, the accustomed home of a big cat called the *Doctor,* by whose claws I one day nearly lost the sight of one of my eyes. Then after the kitchen was a little garden shaded by some trees and littered with many stones, a garden which never grew anything but nettles, as no one seemed ever to have thought of putting anything else in it—this looked out on the place du Château. It will be seen that the dwelling-house was shut off completely from the rest of the world when the door of the forge, opening on the rue de Soissons and the garden gate, leading into the place du Château were closed; unless, indeed, the walls of the garden were scaled.

I stayed then with my cousin Marianne without raising any objection to doing so. I loved going to the forge, where a lad named Picard was very partial to me. I used to make fireworks there with iron filings, and the workmen, Picard in particular, would tell me thrilling stories.

I stayed in the forge till quite late in the evening; the forge gave me infinite delight that night, with its fantastic reflections and dancing play of light and shadow. About eight o'clock my cousin Marianne fetched me away and put me to bed in the little bed opposite the large one; and I slept the sound sleep that God gives to little children as He gives refreshing dew in spring-tide.

At midnight I was waked up, or rather we were waked up, my cousin and I, by a loud knocking at our door. A night lamp glimmered on a table near the bedside, and by the light of this lamp I could see my cousin sitting up in bed, silent, terrified.

Nobody could knock at that inner door, as the two other doors were shut.

But I, who to-day almost shudder with fear as I write these lines, I, on the contrary, felt no fear: I got out of my cot and approached the door.

"Where are you going, Alexandre?" cried my cousin. "Where are you going, child?"

"You will soon see," I calmly replied. "I am going to open the door for papa, who has come to say good-bye to us."

Window

Door leading to street

Bench

Bench

Anvil

Forge

Door

Inner Court

Window

Door

Chest of Drawers

Bedroom

Improvised Bed

Bed

Door

Kitchen

Fireplace

Door

· · · · ·
· · · ·
· · ·
· ·
·

Small garden littered with stones, where grew a few trees and much grass

Door

PLACE DU CHÂTEAU

Plan of House

The poor girl leapt from her bed, terrified, seized hold of me just as I was putting my hand on the lock, and forced me back into bed.

I struggled in her arms, crying out with all my might: "Good-bye, papa! Good-bye, papa!"

Something like a dying breath passed over my face and quietened me. But I fell asleep sobbing, with tears on my cheeks.

Next day they woke us at dawn, my father had died precisely at the time we heard the knocking at the door! Then it was that I heard these words, but without taking in their significance: "*My poor child, the papa who loved you so much is dead!*"

I cannot tell what lips uttered those words over me, the little orphan of three and a half years, nor who it was that announced the greatest misfortune of my life.

"My father is dead?" said I. "What does that mean?"

"It means that you will never see him again."

"What! I shall never see my papa again?"

"No."

"Why shall I not see him?"

"Because the good God has taken him from you."

"For ever?"

"For ever."

"And you say I shall never see him any more?"

"Never again."

"Never, never at all?"

"Nevermore!"

"Where does the good God live?"

"He lives in heaven."

I remained in thought for a moment; unreasoning baby though I was, I quite understood that something dreadful had happened in my life. Then I took advantage of the first moment when attention was diverted from me to escape from my uncle's house and run straight home to my mother.

All the doors were open, and everybody looked scared; one could tell that death was in the house.

I got in without being noticed at all, and reached a little room where arms were kept; I took up one of my father's single-barrelled guns, which he had often promised to give me when I should be grown up.

Then, armed with this gun, I climbed the stairs.

I met my mother on the first landing; she was coming out of the death-chamber, weeping bitterly.

"Where are you going?" she asked, surprised to see me there, when she thought I was at my uncle's.

"I am going to heaven," I replied.

"What! you are going to heaven?"

"Yes, let me go."

"What are you going to do in heaven, my poor child?"

"I am going to kill the good God for killing papa."

My mother seized me in her arms and pressed me closely to her.

"Oh! my child," she cried, "do not say such things; we are quite unhappy enough already."

Indeed, the death of my father, who had only received a retiring salary of 4000 francs, left us with no other fortune than about 30 roods of land in the village of Soucy, which had belonged to my maternal grandfather, who was still living at that time. There were arrears of salary due to my father, as I have said, arrears of 28,500 francs, for the years VII and VIII, but since our journey to Paris a law had been passed which declared that no arrears before the year IX should be paid.

As for the indemnity of 500,000 francs, due from the King of Naples for the French prisoners, which Bonaparte had exacted, nothing was heard of it, and it was for this reason, no doubt, that the French seized the kingdom of Naples.

It is true that some day a house and a fine garden, situated in the place de la Fontaine, would revert to us; but in the meantime the rent of it went to a certain M. Harlay, who had already been in receipt of it for twenty years. That good man, in fact, exemplified the truth of the proverb that a life interest is a certificate of long life for the payee: he died in 1817, at the age of ninety-two or ninety-three, and by that time we had paid the value of the house and garden nearly four times over. Thus, besides the irreparable loss of father and husband, my mother and I were losing also, she her whole income and I that future benefit which only the presence of a father can give to a son.

Murat and Brune then tried—Brune zealously, Murat half-heartedly—to keep the promise they had made to my father on our behalf. But it was quite useless. Napoleon never forgot the meeting held in my father's tent during the third day of the march between Alexandria and Cairo, and my mother, the innocent victim of my father's Republican sentiments, could not obtain from the man who had offered to stand godfather to me before my birth the very smallest pension, although she was the widow of a general officer who had been chief-in-command of three armies.

Nor was this all. Napoleon's hatred, not content with wreaking itself on my father's fortune, aimed at his reputation too. A painting had been ordered, representing my father's entry into the Grand Mosque, the day of the insurrection at Cairo, during the revolt which he had quelled "*in the absence of everyone else*," as Bonaparte had himself expressed it. They substituted a tall fair hussar for my father, the portrait of no one in particular, thus causing the picture to be devoid of meaning alike to contemporaries and to posterity.

We shall see later how this hatred extended even to me, for in spite of the applications which were made on my behalf by my father's old comrades, I could never obtain entrance to any military school or civil college.

Finally, my father died without even having been made a Chevalier of the Légion d'Honneur—he who had been the hero of the day at Maulde, at la Madeleine, at Mont Cenis, at the siege of Mantua, at the bridge of Brixen, at the revolt of Cairo, the man whom Bonaparte had made governor of the Trévisan, and whom he presented to the Directory as the Horatius Codes of the Tyrol.

Small wonder then if the spirit of my father, on its way heavenwards, hovered for a moment over his poor child, whom he was leaving so destitute of all hope on earth.

What did I divine of it all in the midst of the storm of grief which raged around me? What part I played at this time, my young life just beginning, his ended, I have not the faintest remembrance; I recollect nothing after my mother took me in her arms, as I have related, and carried me away.

A letter from M. Deviolaine announcing my father's death to his friend, General Pille, is my sole guide in this darkness: it informs me that we took shelter at Antilly.

This is the letter:—

"VILLERS-COTTERETS,

"*27th February 1806.*

"MY DEAR COUSIN,—I little thought I should so soon have to inform you of the death of our brave and unfortunate General Dumas. He finished his course at eleven o'clock last night, at Villers-Cotterets, where he had returned to carry out his doctor's orders. The malady of which he died was the result of the shocking treatment he experienced at Naples, on his return from Egypt. He had the consolation of learning, on the very day of his death, that that country was conquered by the French; but this satisfaction did not at all comfort him for the privation of not being able to end his days on the field of battle. Ever since his retirement from active service—all through his illness—he never ceased offering prayers for the success of the French arms. It was most touching to hear him say, only a few hours before his death, that, for his wife and children's sake, he would like to be buried on the field of Austerlitz.

"As a matter of fact, my dear cousin, he has left them without any means of existence; his illness consumed his small remaining capital.

"My wife is going to take Madame Dumas—her relative—to Antilly, where she will remain a few days, whilst we do all we possibly can to give the general the funeral honours to which his rank, his brave deeds, and the love of his citizens entitle him.

"In charging myself with conveying to you this melancholy and distressing news I told Madame Dumas that I would invite you to join her husband's comrades-in-arms; their share in this melancholy affair will soften in some small degree the bitterness of her sorrows.

"I thank you, my dear cousin, for the certificate of death in the case of Lasne, *maréchal des logis*. If it is not quite in form, I will inform you.

"Believe me, my dear cousin, your attached friend,

"DEVIOLAINE."

M. Deviolaine had not at all exaggerated our state of distress. My father's only income had been his half-pay pension of 4000 francs; my sister's boarding-school expenses took about 1200 francs of this, so there only remained 2800 francs to provide for the expenses of illness, for the constant changes of place which the restlessness of a dying man craved, and for our usual wants; it was very little, as the reader can see for himself.

Accordingly, my poor mother asked all my father's old friends, Brune, Murat, Augereau, Lannes, Jourdan, to endeavour to obtain a pension from the emperor. It was all in vain. The most urgent entreaties were of no avail against that extraordinary hatred, and, tired of hearing a name repeated so often which was already merely a dim recollection in his career, Napoleon angrily exclaimed to Brune, our warmest partisan:

"I forbid you ever to mention that fellow to me again."

My mother could not believe that the widow of a man who had been chief commander of three armies, and had served under his country's flag for twenty years, whose various campaigns were equivalent to forty-four years of service, although he was only forty-one years of age, had not the right to beg a pension from France, some little help, a morsel of bread. A letter from Jourdan came to destroy her last hope and to teach her that she must depend on God alone for help.

Here is the letter. No one would believe me if I simply related its contents, no one would believe that, at this period of supreme triumph, Napoleon, installed in the palace of the kings of France, handling more millions than Louis XIV. ever touched, regarded as the conqueror, victor, Cæsar, *Augustus,* who had placed his foot on the neck of Europe and had stretched out his hands over the whole world, would knowingly refuse to save from starvation the wife and children of him who had taken Mont Cenis, reduced Mantua to capitulation, forced the passes of the Tyrol, and quelled the insurrection of Cairo.

But, sire, as it is right that people should believe these things, I will quote Jourdan's letter, even though it cast a stain on your Majesty's imperial robes.

"NAPLES, 28*th April 1806.*

"MADAME,—I have the honour to inform you that I have just received from His Excellency the Minister of War an answer to the letter I wrote him on your behalf. He regrets to inform me that you cannot obtain any pension, as the law of 8 Floréal, year XI, only allows pensions to be granted to the widows of soldiers killed on the field of battle, or of those who die of their wounds within six months after receiving them; and as General Dumas was not in active service when he died, there remains, madame, but one other means of hope, namely, for you to go personally to His Majesty the Emperor, and throw yourself upon his generosity.

"I have the honour to remain, madame, your most obedient servant,

JOURDAN (Marshal)."

There was thus one hope still left. My mother went to Paris in order to present herself to His Majesty the Emperor, to beg him for help. But His Majesty the Emperor declined the audience she craved, and she returned to Villers-Cotterets the poorer by the money she had spent on her journey.

Sire, you may be a Hannibal, you may be a Cæsar, you may be an Octavius, posterity may not yet have had time to decide this question, or maybe the question is already settled; but I am very sure you are no Augustus! Augustus pleaded in person for the old soldier who had served under him at Actium;

while you, you condemn to misery the widow of the man who served not only under you, but with you!

I have said, sire, that if you failed us, there remained but God to help us. We will see what God did for this poor forsaken family.

BOOK III

CHAPTER I

My mother and I take refuge with my grandfather—Madame Darcourt's house—My first books and my first terrors—The park at Villers-Cotterets—M. Deviolaine and his family—The swarm of bees—The old cloister.

We all went to live with my grandfather and grandmother, who were still alive. They enlarged their hearth for us, and took in my mother, my sister, and me.

My grandfather reserved rooms at the hôtel de *l'Épée*, where my father had died. We took possession of his chamber of death, and lived in it surrounded by all his belongings.

Now, in the midst of the obscurity in which my earliest years float, like half-forgotten dreams, the recollection of the three principal houses in which all my childhood was spent stand sharply defined.

These three houses were those of Madame Darcourt, M. Deviolaine, and M. Collard. It will be remembered that I have already had occasion to speak of these three persons, and I may be permitted to say a little about them, were it only to discharge the debt of gratitude we owe them. Moreover, pictures of the kind I am about to draw are nothing without their accessary details.

Madame Darcourt was our neighbour; she resided on the ground floor of the house adjoining the one in which my father died. She was the widow of a distinguished military surgeon. She had two children, a son and a daughter. The son might have been twenty-eight, and his name was Antoine. The daughter was perhaps twenty-four or twenty-five, and was called Éléonore.

God granted the mother a long and happy life—she lived to eighty years of age.

I hardly knew Antoine, but I was almost brought up by Éléonore.

The great attraction to me about this house, besides their kindness to me, was a splendid edition of Buffon with coloured pictures.

Every evening, after my mother had made her visit to the cemetery,—a religious office she never missed one single day,—whilst she sat absorbed in her grief in a corner by the fireplace, whilst Madame Darcourt and her daughter sewed, they would put a volume of Buffon in my hands, and were then relieved of any further trouble on my account throughout the evening.

In consequence I learnt to read—and though I do not know *how*, I can say *why*: I wanted to read about the history, the habits, the instincts of the animals whose portraits I looked at. The result of this interest of mine in batrachians, and especially in ophidians, was such that, at the age when children are still spelling, I had already read all the books other which form a child's library.

While at Madame Darcourt's house I experienced the sensation of fear for the first time—a feeling hitherto totally unknown to me.

My mania for reading extended in every direction, even to newspapers—in later years so little read by me.

One day I came upon the *Journal de l'Empire*, and I read in it a short article relating how a prisoner, entombed in the dungeons of Amiens, had been devoured there by a snake.

I had hitherto looked upon snakes as monsters, if not altogether mythical yet belonging to quite another part of the globe than ours.

In Buffon, or rather in Daudin's continuation of him, snakes had been a constant source of curiosity to me; after reading the *Journal de l'Empire*, they inspired me with the greatest terror.

The evening I read that fatal article I pretended to be absorbed in reading *Robinson Crusoe*, and I asked to be allowed to sit up as late as possible, meaning until my mother should herself go to bed.

The favour was readily granted me; but when the same excuse was renewed the next day, the day after that and several nights running, I was compelled to give an explanation.

I recounted the story of the prisoner of Amiens, and I confessed that if I went to bed by myself I should be afraid of being eaten up by a snake.

My mother was greatly surprised at this confession, for I had been so brave hitherto. She did her utmost to reason away my fears, but reason failed in the face of instinct, and time alone softened although it did not altogether efface the recollection of that awful picture.

Next to Madame Darcourt's house—to which I shall again have occasion to refer—were the other two households who were so hospitable to us in our misfortunes, those of M. Deviolaine and M. Collard.

M. Deviolaine was our cousin by marriage; he had married a niece of my grandfather, who, as she was an orphan, had been brought up with my mother in our family circle; furthermore, he had been my father's intimate friend.

M. Deviolaine was Inspector of Forests for the district of Villers-Cotterets, which gave him a leading position in our little town; and quite naturally, too, since there were only 2400 inhabitants in the town, whereas the forest covered 50,000 acres.

M. Deviolaine was a great dignitary in my eyes, not so much because of the above-mentioned reason, but because, in virtue of the position he held, he could grant leave to shoot in the forest, and to go hunting freely some day in that forest was one of the ambitions of my childhood.

This ambition, among several others, has since been realised; and I should add that it has been one that has yielded the least disappointment in the fulfilment.

In comparison with the small rooms to which we had been confined since my father's death, M. Deviolaine's house seemed a palace; and I, poor child, greatly appreciated the change, for, brought up as I had been at the châteaux of Fossés and of Antilly, and running wild in the walks and over the lawns, I seemed to live on air and sunshine. M. Deviolaine's house contained first and foremost a suite of rooms covering a considerable area, stables and coach-houses, yards and a charming garden, partly English, partly French, partly picturesque, partly kitchen garden. The English garden contained waterfalls, pools, and weeping-willow trees; the fruit garden was full of pears, peaches, greengages, artichokes, and melons, and then it opened upon a fine park, which you could see through the railings, and which you could walk into through a gateway.

This park, planted by François I., was cut down by Louis-Philippe.

Grand trees they were! Under their shade François I. had lain by the side of Madame d'Étampes, Henri II. with his Diane de Poitiers, Henri IV. with Gabrielle: it was natural to expect that a Bourbon would have reverenced these trees, and permitted the long life of beeches and oaks; that birds would have sung on their dead and leafless boughs as they sang on them when green and in full leaf! Unluckily, there is a material value attached to them, besides the inestimable one of poetry and memories. You glorious beeches, with your polished, silvery trunks, you fine oaks with your dark and rugged bark—you were worth 100,000 crowns! The King of France, who thought himself too poor to keep you standing, and had his twelve millions from the civil list besides his private fortune of six millions, must needs sell you! Had you been my sole means of fortune, I would have kept you; for, being a poet, I love the murmur of the wind through your leaves above all the gold earth can give; the shadows that flicker under my tread; the delicious visions, the lovely phantoms, which, at eventide, between day and night, in the dubious hour of twilight, glide in and out between your venerable trunks, as flit the shades of the ancient race of Abencérage between the myriad columns of Cordova's royal mosque.

There was not the least idea of this in the mind of that other poet, Demoustier, when he wrote on the bark of one of these trees the following verse: with the trees has it also disappeared, and perhaps I alone remember it:—

"Ce bois fut l'asile chéri
De l'amour autrefois fidèle;
Tout l'y rappelle encore, et le coeur attendri
Soupire en se disant: C'est ici que Henri
Soupirait près de Gabrielle."

And notwithstanding all this the king destroyed the forest, the man who believed himself more firmly fixed to the throne than the trees were to the earth. Nothing did he understand of the really great; everything was stripped of the glamour of imagination, and only its material value did he appraise. He said to himself, "Every man can be bought, just as every tree can be sold. I possess vast forests, I will sell the trees, and I will purchase men."

Sire, you were self-deceived. There are other things in life than algebra and mathematics: there is faith, there is belief; you put no faith in others, and others therefore put no faith in you; you breathed scorn on the past, and now the past scorns you.

What a long way we have travelled, though, from the home of M. Deviolaine—which to me seemed such a palace!

Glorious trees, you are more than a palace—you are like a temple! a temple wherein the Lord reveals Himself to me, as I lie at your feet, and try to study the stars, in utter ignorance of their names, through the moving canopy of your foliage, on the fine nights of summer. How many times, when the laughing, restless spirit of childhood begins to yield to the dreams of early manhood; how many times, kissed by the wind-bent grass under me, have I stretched two eager hands towards some star more brilliant than others, and tried to seize a ray of moonlight as it played upon my face! And I have prayed: "Saviour, who art in heaven! Saviour, who art on earth! Saviour, who art everywhere! O Saviour, take me in Thy mighty arms and make me an instrument to glorify and bless Thy power; a harp to sing to Thee, a lyre to praise Thee, a voice to pray to Thee! Make me grow great, O Lord, so that I may be nearer to Thee! and the greater I am the more humbly will I acknowledge Thy name, Thy splendour, Thy majesty!

"It is Thou, O God! who makest the forests to grow which kings sell; Thou who createst the little birds that sing among their branches; Thou who caressest them with the breeze which is Thy smile, and refreshest them with sunshine, which is Thy face, and tearest them up in the storm, which is Thy anger!

"Lord, Thou alone art great, Thou alone art eternal!"

But to return to M. Deviolaine and his house.

Although it was large, its accommodation was far from being superfluous. M. Deviolaine had veritably the family of a patriarch. He had one son and two daughters by his first marriage, and a son and two more daughters by his second.

The latter were our relatives, our cousin being his second wife.

As the name of M. Deviolaine and those of his children are constantly recurring in the relation of the first portion of my life, I must dwell for a moment on this ample family.

The names of the three children by the first marriage were Victor, Léontine, and Léonore; those of the three children of the second were, Félix, Cécile, and Augustine.

Seven or eight years later, a third daughter arrived, but I shall speak of her birth in the proper order of time.

Victor, Léontine, and Léonore were much older than I, and more naturally became my sister's companions, who was nine years my senior. Cécile, the oldest of the second set of children, whose age was nearer my sister's than mine, joined their ranks.

This left me for my playfellows, Augustine, a year older than I, and Félix, two years younger.

M, Deviolaine, the head of the family, was an excellent man at heart,—I say at heart, for on the surface nature had endowed him with a tough skin, which for roughness might have vied with the most rugged oak trees in his forest.

He was five feet seven inches in height, and had small black eyes, shaded by enormous eyebrows; his lips were thick and protruding, his frame was that of a Hercules, he was clothed with hair like a wild boar and he was hardly as sociable as the animal with which we have taken the liberty of comparing him. His paroxysms of rage—and every day was an April day with him— were the terror of his family. When he came down from his study, which was isolated from the rest of the house, with his face portending storms to come, women, children, and servants fled from his presence, terrified, with their heads down, as shepherd, dogs, and flocks flee before a coming storm.

Never but once did I see him with a gracious countenance.

Never but once did I hear him speak without swearing.

This moral and physical change had been wrought in him by his attempt to gather in a swarm of bees, which he feared would fly away out of his reach.

It was summer, and he wore his shirt open. He had rashly shaken the tree in which the swarm was grouped, and half the swarm—that is to say, about ten thousand bees—tumbled on his open breast.

This accident took place at the bottom of the garden; we were all gathered round the kitchen door, waiting to see the result of the operation, when all at once we caught sight of him at the end of a path, coming towards the house with measured steps, smiling, holding out his shirt with both his hands and saying in the gentlest tones:

"There, my little ones—there—"

And we gazed at him from afar, marvelling to see him walk with such an unaccustomed gait, smiling such an unusual smile, talking with that incomprehensible urbanity. Everyone asked himself to whom M. Deviolaine was talking and smiling thus.

M. Deviolaine was talking and smiling to the bees.

His mild tones succeeded, and they all flew off him, every single bee, not one of them stinging him; but when the last had flown away, and he raised his eyes, and discovered his wife, his children, and his servants all perched on the kitchen steps looking at him, there was such an outburst of "*mille tonnerres*" and other oaths that the household did not recover for a week after!

As for us, we disappeared like magic; one would have thought the ground had opened beneath our feet and swallowed us up.

The remarkable fact about all these tempests was, that they ended in nothing worse than clouds and lightning, without any hailstones or thunderbolts. No one ever remembered seeing M. Deviolaine even kick out at his dog—unless the beast were well outside the reach of his foot.

M. Deviolaine possessed another house besides this one; it was called St. Remy, and stood in the middle of a charming little plateau, surrounded on all sides by the forest.

St. Remy specially deserves a few words; the days we went there were fête days indeed!

St. Remy had once been a nunnery, but I do not know to what order it had belonged. I only remember the portrait of the abbess, in a frame above the chimney-piece in the large hall. She was a beautiful woman, clothed entirely in black, with a blue cord round her to which was attached a cross; she was round and plump, stout with the corpulence only to be found among buxom saints. She bore some titled name known in those parts, which I forget.

The convent had been in use until 1791 or 1792; then the laws came into force which destroyed cloistered life, and all these doves of the Lord had to flee: I believe M. Deviolaine bought the convent as ecclesiastical property.

There was an immense cloister attached to this convent—though not so large perhaps in reality as in my remembrance of it: children's eyes see strange hallucinations in the region of memory—space, to their minds, is infinite.

Outside this cloister were great staircases, with iron bannisters, leading to the former apartments of the abbess. Only a portion of these had been fitted up, the rest belonged to rats and cats, which appeared to have settled a truce, for they lived together on a pretty good understanding.

A dozen acres of meadow-land, little woods, and walled-in gardens enclosed this old cloistered building, which was shaded with trees as old as itself.

To-day, trees and cloister have fallen down: nothing really remains on the earth's surface; everything springs up only to decay: the lives of monuments, of trees, and of men, are all but a question of durability; stone and wood decay just as do flesh and bones.

But at that time all was still standing, like the hopes of our young lives; the cloister knew not of black bands or the trees of speculators. It was all sold together, felled timber and ruins, and from the débris of the immense building and the trunks of the oak trees there was left sufficient material to build a pretty little house, of the kind built nowadays, containing one sitting-room four mètres square, and several rooms about twelve feet long by eight feet wide; regular Socrates' houses, empty, small though they be, for want of friends to fill them!

Oh! that great cloister, how full it was on Sundays with the sound of joyous shouting and mad races! How happy were all children who loved adventure beyond the borders of their native town, far from the watchful eye of family and townsfolk, how grateful to the unknown founder of that great nest, once melancholy, but to-day peopled by gay singing birds! How this noise from the living world must have made the nuns tremble in their graves—those black shades that had been women, with bodies containing souls, those skeletons which had once possessed hearts, and had come to bury the passions of their hearts, and the hopes of their souls, and the beauty of their faces in the obscurity of the cloister, in the night of penitence, and in the mysteries of the ascetic life!

We laughed where, mayhap, many had wept bitter tears; we leaped and bounded in our joyous childhood, where probably many had paced towards death with slow, sad, hopeless steps.

But what cared we, children born but yesterday? Did a past exist in our thoughts? Why, we could scarcely remember last autumn's yellow leaves, scarcely recall last spring's emerald leaves: our memories only went as far back as yesterday's sunshine; our hopes were centred only on to-morrow's sunshine; our future was twenty-four hours; to us, a month was eternity!

Oh! what recollections of my childhood, hitherto forgotten, are stored in the pathways of that cloistered domain! When I retrace my steps to-day, at every footfall they arise, as precious as those flowers of diamonds, rubies, and sapphires, gathered in the gardens of the *Thousand and one Nights*, which never faded!

CHAPTER II

The two snakes—M. de Valence and Madame de Montesson—Who little Hermine was—Garnier the wheelwright and Madame de Valence—Madame Lafarge—Fantastic apparition of Madame de Genlis.

I had a great fright one day in that beautiful garden. At one corner stood a kind of ruined and roofless tower; in August, the sun's rays concentrated inside this tower and made it as hot as a furnace. It was a curious sight then to watch the flies buzzing there, and the butterflies dancing, the beautiful grey and green lizards gliding along its walls. One day when I was playing near the tower, I heard a sharp hissing noise, and, on going to look what it was, I saw through the opening which had once been a door, two long snakes sitting on their tails, with their bodies coiled round in spirals, darting out their long black tongues at one another, and hissing either with love or rage. Such as these must have been the two serpents to whom Mercury threw his wand, for they looked just like the two that have for ever coiled round that rod.

But I was not Mercury, I had not the magic wand that pacified the bitterest hatreds; I took to flight, as Laocoon would have done if he had seen the two serpents of Tenedos rolling in with the tide of the Dardanelles, had he known they had left their island on purpose to strangle himself and his children.

As I fled I met M. Deviolaine, who, seeing me in such a fright, asked me what was the matter: I told him, and to my great amazement he did not in the least share my fears; he merely tore up from the ground a pole which propped up a young tree and walked towards the tower, whence, after five minutes' fight, he came out, having conquered the two hydras.

From that moment I looked upon M. Deviolaine as a Hercules, the tamer of monsters.

I shall often return to M. Deviolaine, for he had great influence over my life; I was more afraid of him than of any man, but at the same time I loved him next after my father.

We will now proceed to M. Collard.

M. Collard was as good-natured as M. Deviolaine, his most intimate friend, was ill-tempered: his smiling face was as great a contrast to his friend's forbidding aspect. M. Collard was the head of a family to which the terrible and mysterious Glandier law-suit has since given such a sinister notoriety.

M. Collard, who occupied the delightful little château of Villers-Hellon, about three leagues from Villers-Cotterets, was of aristocratic descent; but he had dropped the name of Montjouy and simply kept that of Collard, to give less offence to democratic ears. He had formerly been acquainted with M. de Talleyrand in the Legislative Assembly, and, in 1795 or 1796, he had married a young girl named Hermine, who lived with Madame de Valence.

One day the duc d'Orléans unexpectedly called on Madame de Montesson, who was then his wife, and found M. de Valence at her feet, with his head on her lap. The situation was embarrassing, but Madame de Montesson was a great lady not easily put to confusion: she turned laughingly to her husband, who stood petrified in the doorway, and she said to him:

"Come and help me, my dear duke, to get rid of Valence: he has fallen in love with Pulchérie, and insists on marrying her."

Pulchérie was Madame de Genlis's second daughter; the first was called Caroline, and had married M. de Lawoestine.

After the fright he had just had, the duke was ready enough to give Pulchérie to M. de Valence. He settled 600,000 francs on the bride, and they were married. Now how came little Hermine to the house of Madame de Valence, and who was she? I am going to explain.

Madame de Montesson was aunt to Madame de Genlis. Madame de Genlis had been placed with the duchesse d'Orléans (Mademoiselle de Penthièvre) by Madame de Montesson, in the position of maid of honour. While with the duchess, Philippe-Joseph (since Philippe-Égalité) had met her, fallen in love, made her his mistress, and had had a daughter by her.

That daughter was little Hermine.

She was brought up in England, and when Madame Adélaïde, sister to King Louis-Philippe, was seven or eight years old, they wished to give her a young English companion, with whom she could do her lessons and learn to talk English. Here was an opportunity to bring Hermine near her parents. She therefore left London and came to Paris.

After the emigration of the duc de Chartres, of MM. de Beaujolais, de Montpensier, and the Princess Adélaïde, Hermine, then about fourteen or fifteen years of age, took refuge with her sister, Madame de Valence; but Madame de Valence herself was soon arrested and thrown into prison, and Philippe-Égalité lost his head on the scaffold.

So Hermine then lived with the children of Madame de Valence; Félicie, who married M. de Celles, and Rosamonde, wife of Marshal Gérard.

These poor children were only saved by a miracle from becoming orphans.

A wheelwright named Garnier living in the rue Neuve-des-Mathurins was in love with her; he was a member of the Town Council, and at the peril of his life he twice burnt the despatches sent by the governor of the prison to the

Revolutionary Tribunal, in which Madame de Valence was denounced as the most aristocratic prisoner there. This devoted act saved Madame de Valence, for it tided her over till the 9th Thermidor.

Every New Year's Day for years after the wheelwright Garnier paid a visit to Madame de Valence. It should be borne in mind that she owed her precious life to him, and the whole family welcomed him as he deserved to be welcomed for his heroism.

On the death of my father, M. Collard had been appointed my guardian; and I therefore saw Madame Collard when she was still young, not more than thirty or thirty-two. It would have been difficult to find more perfectly distinguished manners, with such dignity of movement and actions, or more graceful hospitality, than were blended in Madame Collard's character.

She had one son and three daughters: Maurice, who became a country squire; Caroline, who married Baron Capelle, whose daughter Marie, under the name of Madame Lafarge, was the heroine in one of the most touching dramas that ever was played before a Court of Assize; Hermine, who married the baron de Martens, the Prussian ambassador in Portugal,—she inherited her mother's wit, aristocratic bearing, and never-failing youthfulness of spirits; lastly, Louise, who married Garat, whose commercial signature carries more weight than that of any other man. Louise was, and is still, one of the prettiest women in Paris.

I have spoken of M. Deviolaine's town and country gardens; but they were nothing when compared with those near the park of Villers-Hellon, with their grand trees, their fine groves, and the little stream of green water winding through the gardens like a necklace of emeralds. And therefore, with the selfishness of childhood, of the three houses I preferred M. Collard's. The Darcourts' house contained a most beautiful copy of Buffon, but it had nothing of a garden. The Deviolaine house had a fine situation, and even two very beautiful gardens; but M. Deviolaine had a scowling face, whilst M. Collard had a fine garden, a kind face, and, furthermore, a splendid Bible.

From that Bible I learnt my sacred history so thoroughly that I have never needed to study it since.

I have spoken of two great alarms I had already experienced in my life—the third happened at Villers-Hellon.

One evening, when I was as usual busy turning over the pictures in my fine Bible (I was between four and five years old at the time), we heard a carriage draw up in front of the porch, then loud shrieks in the dining-room. Everyone rushed towards the door, and when it opened it gave entrance to the strangest Meg Merrilies that the imagination of any Walter Scott could ever conceive. This witch—and at first sight her appearance was such as to justify one in calling her so—was dressed in black, and, as she had lost her bonnet, her mass of false hair had taken advantage of its freedom from restraint to fly in all directions, so that her own grey hairs fell down on each side of her face and floated over her shoulders.

The vision was entirely different from the famous snake of Amiens and the two serpents at St. Remy; moreover, the Amiens snake I had only seen in imagination, and the two serpents of St. Remy I had had time to escape from; but this sorceress I beheld with my very eyes, and we met in the same room.

I threw down my Bible, and, under cover of the tumult occasioned by this apparition, I fled to my room, hid in my bed, dressed as I was, and drew the bed-clothes well over my head.

Next day I learnt that the cause of my fright was the illustrious Madame de Genlis, who, coming to visit her daughter, Madame Collard, had lost her way in the forest of Villers-Cotterets through the fault of her coachman, and had given way to panic, being in profound dread of ghosts: she had not even then recovered from her fright, although she had communicated the greater part of it to me.

It was in these three houses that the first portion of my childhood was passed,—those early years studded with sunny memories as soft and as fresh as the dawn; for, indeed, with the exception of M. Deviolaine's surly countenance, and the grotesque apparition of Madame de Genlis, everything connected with those two houses was sunny. The gardens were full of green trees and brilliantly-coloured flowers; the walks were peopled by fair and dark young girls, with rosy, smiling faces—nearly all rosy and sweet, even when they were not pretty.

Then, from time to time, some woman noted for her beauty in the days of the century about to close would appear in the midst of this laughing, younger generation; some woman who, having retained somewhat of the fashions of the days of the Directory, looked like a glorious statue of Summer amidst that budding Spring.

These ladies were Madame de Valence, Madame Menin, or Madame Dusauloy.

I have already spoken of the Princess Pauline Borghèse and the impression she left on my mind. And now we must return to my own story.

CHAPTER III

Mademoiselle Pivert—I make her read the *Thousand and One Nights*, or, rather, one story in that collection—Old Hiraux, my music-master—The little worries of his life—He takes his revenge on his persecutors after the fashion of the Maréchal de Montluc—He is condemned to be flogged, and nearly loses the sight of his eyes—What happened on Easter Day in the organ-loft at the monastery—He becomes a grocer's lad—His vocation leads him to the study of music—I have little aptitude for the violin.

I had learnt to read at a very early age, as I have said, thanks to Madame Darcourt's Buffon, M. Collard's Bible and, above all, to my mother's kindly pains. My sister too, who was at a boarding-school in Paris, during her six weeks' vacations, which were spent with us, completed my early education by teaching me to write.

So at five or six years of age I was very well up in these two accomplishments, and extraordinarily conceited about them. I can still see myself, about the height of a jack-boot, in a little cotton jacket (for, like the Romans, I did not leave off the *toga praetexta* till I was fifteen),—I can still see myself, pedantically joining in the conversation of grown-up people, contributing items of sacred or profane learning which I had derived from the Bible or mythology, theories of natural history cribbed from M. de Buffon and M. Daudin, geographical information borrowed from *Robinson Crusoe*, and social and political ideas culled from the sage Idomeneus, founder of Salentum.

But mythology was my strong point. Besides the *Lettres à Emilie sur la Mythologie* of my compatriot Demoustier, which I knew by heart, I possessed a *Mythologie de la Jeunesse*, illustrated with pictures and interspersed with verses from Racine and Saint-Ange, which I was everlastingly devouring. Not a god or goddess or demi-god, not a single faun or dryad, not a hero was there whose attributes I did not know. Hercules and his twelve labours, Jupiter and his twenty transformations, Vulcan and his thirty-six misfortunes, I knew them all at my fingers' ends, and, what is still more extraordinary, I know them still.

One day (it was at M. Deviolaine's house, in 1809, at a time when each morning's paper contained bulletins of deeds which, for ten years, made our history seem like one of the heroic fables of old) I remember some of the guests asked, just after luncheon, what the news of the day was; but as it was still early no one had read the papers, and consequently no one could satisfy the general curiosity.

M. Deviolaine rang the bell, and the servant appeared.

"Mas," he said (the name of the servant), "get a *Gazette* and bring it us."

"Oh! there is no need for that, cousin," I said, crossing my hands behind my back; "I have read the paper and there is nothing of importance in it—only a sitting of the *Corps Législatif*."

I have said that M. Deviolaine often shot out his foot when angry, but never kicked anything; I was wrong; he did kick something that time!

I left the room furious, and for three months after I would not enter the house where I had received such a humiliation.

How came it about that I knew anything concerning the *Corps Législatif*?

It was in this wise.

One day I had seen M. Collard in a blue coat braided with gold.

"You are a general, then, like my papa?" I asked him roguishly.

"No, my little friend," he answered, "I am a member of the *Corps Législatif*."

And from that time I used to read the proceedings of the *Corps Législatif* to find out what M. Collard said there.

But my curiosity was never gratified.

However, everybody was not so contemptuous about my learning as M. Deviolaine had shown himself to be. Among others, there were three or four elderly devotees—one of them a certain damsel of sixty-five or sixty-six called Pivert—who appreciated and praised my knowledge. There was no kind of story, whether sacred or profane, that they did not make me relate; and Mademoiselle Pivert in particular, not contented with my recitals, had recourse to my library, in order to get at the source of my information.

Well, I gave her an imperfect copy of the *Thousand and One Nights*, which I possessed; it contained only the *Wonderful Lamp*, nothing else. She would be absorbed in the reading of this for a whole week, then she would return me the volume and ask for the next, which I would promise to give her on the morrow; I lent her the same again, which she always conscientiously re-read, and, I must add, with renewed delight.

This lasted quite a year, during which time she re-read the same volume fifty-two times.

"Well, Mademoiselle Pivert," I asked her at the end of the year, "does the *Thousand and One Nights* still entertain you?"

"Immensely, my little friend," she replied; "but one thing puzzles me; you may be able to explain it, as you are so learned."

"What is it, Mademoiselle Pivert?"

"Why are they all called Aladdin?"

Now, clever though I was, I could not answer Mademoiselle Pivert without confessing the truth, therefore I declared my ignorance, while she regarded it as an unpardonable fault in the unknown poet-author of the *Thousand and One Nights* to have labelled all his characters *Aladdin*.

Notwithstanding all this, the prodigious stock of learning, which was my pride and Mademoiselle Pivert's admiration, was still considered incomplete by my dear mother.

My sister was quite a good musician, and sang prettily; and my mother reproached herself, in spite of our poverty, for not giving equal advantages to both her children; so she decided that I also should learn music. But as it had already been discovered that good Mother Nature, so bountiful towards me in other respects, had endowed me with the most discordant of voices imaginable; and as it had been noticed that I had very nimble fingers and was clever with my hands; they elected to make me an instrumentalist only, and chose the violin,—the instrument which a musician does not use to accompany his voice, unless he is afflicted with blindness.

As the town of Villers-Cotterets only possessed one teacher there was no difficulty in choosing a professor.

This professor's name was Hiraux.

Hiraux really deserves a chapter to himself—or rather two.

Hiraux—or Old Hiraux, as he was familiarly called by the town—was for all the world a second Hoffmann; with his long, slender figure, his maroon-coloured coat, and his wig, which had a way of always accompanying his hat with each salutation he made. Because of this, in order to avoid such an inconvenience, Hiraux decided not to wear his wig save on Sundays and on great fête days. On ordinary days, the wig was replaced by a black silk cap, which he would pull down violently over his ears whenever his pupils played a wrong note.

Now, after considerable reflection upon the matter, and in view of all I saw and heard, I came to the conclusion that Hiraux gave up wearing his wig daily because of the difficulty of applying it to the same purpose as the cap.

Consequently, except on fête days and Sundays, he only half saluted anyone; if by salutation it is understood that I mean he uncovered his head, because, when he took off his hat, he still kept on his black silk cap.

Moreover, his black silk cap had become an integral part of his person. A score of times did I touch it, as the inhabitants of Lilliput fingered Gulliver's clothes,—to make sure that this adornment was not his own skin,—Hiraux was so good-natured that he permitted me to make this investigation.

Under that cap, Hiraux had one of the most emaciated and parchment-like faces I have ever seen—the cleverest and the most mobile, owing to the play of every muscle on it, which seemed to vibrate in unison with his thoughts, even as the strings of his violin or the keys of his pianoforte vibrated under his long, thin, flexible fingers, fingers like those of Paganini.

Hiraux had had an adventurous youth; he had been a choir-boy, an organ-blower in a monastery of Piedmontese monks, then a grocer's lad, then a fiddler, then a music-teacher, and finally an organist.

It would puzzle me to tell you how his steps were first directed to the precincts of the Church of Bourg-Fontaine (the convent where Hiraux was brought up); but at times he would relate, among his early recollections, as I am doing in these Memoirs, some good stories of the monks similar to those of Rabelais and la Fontaine.

Hiraux was a living chronicle of those old claustral traditions, already so remote from the ideas of men of to-day, forty years later, that they are lost like phantasms of another world, behind the early recollections of our youth, and lost so effectually that in the generation to come after ours there will be no trace left of them at all.

The monks were driven from France, then from Spain, then from Italy, till they ended by existing only in the paintings of Dominiquin, Zurbaran, and Lesueur.

I do not know whether society has been the gainer, but, very certainly, art and romance have lost considerably by their disappearance. I have seen the Escurial without its monks, and it looked like a tomb.

When I go to see Rome I cannot tell what effect it will produce upon me.

I have stated that I could not say in what way Hiraux entered the monastery of Bourg-Fontaine, but I know well enough how he left it.

Hiraux was a coward; he cannot he blamed for this; it was characteristic of him. As a matter of fact, he had the quick wittedness to boast about it, just as another man might have bragged about his courage.

Now, he still lived in the happy days when *farces* were all the rage, and all his life he had been the object of more or less comic practical jokes, several of which were nearly the death of him.

As we have said before, or as we say now if we forgot to mention it previously, Hiraux combined the two offices of choir-boy and organ-blower in the monastery of Bourg-Fontaine. In virtue of this double qualification he slept in the sacristy of the monastery, and every night he had to go through the church to get to his bedroom.

It was a nightly terror to him to have to walk down that vast arched nave (I have only seen the ruins of it, wherein Hiraux's son and I used to rob crows' nests): the great windows with their carved traceries through which the pallid and flickering moonlight shone upon the tombstones in the floor; the mysterious vistas where darkness reigned even in daytime; all these together, especially on a winter's night when the north wind whistled through the great gaunt trees whose dry branches rubbed against one another like the bones of a skeleton, and the wind made long-drawn moanings down the abbey corridors; all these, I say, combined to make such a funereal and gloomy effect that poor Hiraux's blood ran cold in his veins, accustomed as he was to witness the malice of men so constantly intermingle with the awe-inspiring majesty of the place.

The monks were not the people who plagued him; nor the prior, who loved Hiraux like a son; but it was that semi-religious, semi-secular race which forms a connecting link between the men of heaven and the men of this world, and which swarms in every monastery.

Hiraux's most relentless persecutors were the brothers who served as scullions.

One November day—All Souls Day it was—when the customary empty coffin had been exposed all day covered with a black-and-silver cloth surrounded by a forest of candles, which remained lighted all the night, Hiraux entered the church, still more afraid of the light on this night than he was ordinarily of the darkness.

After closing the door of the church as gently as possible behind him, walking on tiptoe, brushing against the wall so as to keep as far away as possible from the centre of the church, so funereally lighted up as we have explained, he reached the sacristy.

Suddenly Hiraux stood still, glued to the wall, with his limbs rigid, his mouth open, his hair on end, the perspiration coming out on his forehead, as motionless as the stone statues of the priors in their tombs in the Abbey.

The catafalque had moved.

At first Hiraux thought he must have been mistaken, and tried to reason away his fears; but what good was reason against the actual fact? For the catafalque had not only moved, but it began to come straight towards him! Hiraux tried to shriek out, but, like the voices of Virgil's heroes, the sound stuck in his throat; and, seeing that the catafalque continued to make straight for him, his legs failed him, he leant helpless against the wall, and fell in a faint.

At three o'clock in the morning, the church opened for matins; Hiraux was still in the same place, as still as though he were dead. He had come to his senses; but, although he found the catafalque in its place, he dared not stir for fear it would move again.

The sacristan brother hearing himself called in a stifled voice, turned to see where it came from, and found Hiraux with his face to the ground, icily cold and bathed in perspiration at the same time.

But he found something else on the floor, too, as he went to Hiraux.

He found a cotton cap.

Now, while Hiraux was telling the sacristan of the horrible apparition he had seen in the night, his eyes fixed on the cotton cap, which the sacristan held in his hand, and, thanks to that tell-tale cap, light rapidly dawned on his mind and dissipated the panic terror that had overwhelmed him.

So, as Hiraux continued his narrative, the supernatural phenomenon gave place to natural causes, and, while going over his nocturnal experiences with his friend, the sacristan, guided by the clue of the cotton cap, he became convinced that, if the catafalque had moved, and had walked towards him, it was the brother who cooked for the monks, with perhaps two or three of his scullion knaves, who had got underneath and carried it along.

People are not brought up in convents without acquiring a certain amount of the spirit of revenge. Hiraux kept his own counsel, and did not speak of his suspicions to a soul; he let them laugh at his fright, he let them circulate the story all through the monastery, and even outside, internally vowing vengeance.

The reader may recall the story of Marshal Montluc, and the famous hanging of Huguenots he ordered as he passed through some town whose name I do not remember. I am going to repeat it in case it has been forgotten.

Marshal de Montluc, then, was passing through a certain town, and thought he had a grievance against some judges who, in virtue of the axiom *Cedant arma togo*, had neglected to pay him the respect he thought was his due.

He set to work to make these judges repent their impertinent conduct. He found out what they were busy over, and learnt that they were looking forward with great pleasure to judging a dozen Huguenots on the morrow, who had been taken captive for carrying arms, and were awaiting their sentence in the town prisons.

So the marshal de Montluc went to the prisons, under a strong escort, had them opened, had a dozen nails driven into the beams, attached a dozen ropes thereto, and, from these twelve ropes, hung the twelve Huguenots. "And the judges were well taken in the next day," says the marshal in his Memoirs, "when they found nobody left to try."

Hiraux punished the scullions in pretty much the same way as the marshal de Montluc punished the judges. He stole into the monastic dispensary, seized upon a copious dose of jalap and mixed it with the kitchen sauces.

Had Hiraux written his Memoirs he would, no doubt, have written, after the fashion of the marshal de Montluc: "Next day, the scullions were well taken aback at seeing their monks purged inside out; just as though they had swallowed a triple dose of Doctor Leroy's physic."

This happened at Epiphany.

There was a great commotion in the Abbey, as may well be imagined. A whole monastery—from prior to sacristan—is not purged at Epiphany without religious duties suffering considerably.

Hiraux, the choir-boy, was the only one who kept his post. And it was that very attitude, the calmness of one who stands steadfast while the heavens are falling round him, that ruined Hiraux. Proserpina found an Æsculapius who declared that he had seen her eat seven pomegranate seeds. Hiraux had his Æsculapius who declared that he had seen him stealing at nightfall on tiptoe from the dispensary.

The monastery organist was his accuser.

The denunciation was credited, and when the evidence was put together everybody held Hiraux to be the true culprit. One is not brought up in a monastery, moreover, without learning to lie on occasion. Hiraux denied, protested, swore; but this only made things worse, whereas an honest confession might perhaps have smoothed matters.

Hiraux was therefore given over by the prior to the cook, that is to say, religious justice handed him over to the secular arm.

The cook condemned him to twenty-four hours' solitary confinement, accompanied by bread and water, and, to make sure that the punishment should not be mitigated by any friend of the criminal, he shut him up in the monastery cellar.

But the cook had forgotten that the cellar was well filled with wines, cider, oil, vinegar, brandy, rum, etc., etc.

All these liquids were arranged symmetrically in barrels, as becometh honest barrels, in a well-regulated cellar belonging to a Premonstratensian Monastery.

Hiraux went to all the casks and turned on all the taps, one after the other, saying at each turn of the keys: That's the wine running out, that's the cider running out, that's the oil running out, that's the vinegar running out, that's the brandy running out, that's the rum running out, etc., etc.

The operation took some time, and as Hiraux pronounced his remarks in a loud voice those in the kitchens heard sounds like distant chanting, but could catch no words. But, as the murmur continued, the cook became uneasy and went to listen at the door. He heard Hiraux's litany; he fearfully comprehended what it meant. In a second he had lit a lamp, the cellar door was opened, and the anticipated spectacle was revealed in all its heinousness.

Every cask had its tap at full cock, and was emptying itself of its contents; the mixture of all the liquids had already created a flood six inches deep, which was increasing fast.

Hiraux was seated astride a big barrel, as composed as an Indian Bacchus, philosophically waiting till the lake reached him.

The crime was so patent this time that, instead of the culprit denying it, he boasted of it so impudently that the cook did not stop to refer the matter to the prior, but decided to take the law into his own hands.

But the first and most urgent thing to do was to shut off the taps.

Then they seized upon Hiraux, who made no attempt to escape. Next they called a court of justice, comprised of the cook and his scullions.

It was decided unanimously that Hiraux should be birched.

The sentence admitted of no appeal, and it was instantly put into execution. Furthermore, it was carried out vigorously, lasting for ten minutes, in spite of the victim's cries. At the conclusion, the brother cook took a handful of pepper and rubbed it on the injured part to soothe his pains and to efface the bleeding traces the infliction had left.

Hiraux nearly lost the sight of his eyes in consequence.

This may seem odd at first, and it may be thought I have used the wrong phrase: but not at all.

Hiraux wept, Hiraux bled; his eyes and his flanks were almost equally sore. He alternately rubbed his eyes and his flanks, carrying, by this double exercise, the pepper from behind to his eyes. Consequently inflammation gained rapidly, and the more Hiraux rubbed, the worse it became, until his eyes had swollen to the size of eggs, when a sympathetic person advised him to go and allay his pain in the lavatory of the monastery. He comprehended the sense of that advice, immediately rushed off there, and, thanks to a prolonged bath, the burning sensations which tortured him were in a measure allayed.

But he could not extinguish a burning fever which kept him to his bed for a week.

When the prior heard of his illness he inquired into its causes, and punished the cook and his scullions.

Hiraux was revenged upon them, but the real culprit, in the sufferer's eyes, had escaped the prior's sentence of justice; the true culprit was the organist who had given him away—thus betraying the sacred brotherhood of musicians; for Hiraux, in his capacity of organ-blower, looked upon himself as already a musician.

He therefore made up his mind to pay the organist out.

Hiraux could be as deep and unfathomable as the corridors of his cloisters; he locked up his revengeful determination in his breast and decided to wait until Easter Day should come.

Easter Day is a high festival throughout all Christendom. All the peasantry from the outlying districts came to hear Mass at the monastery of Bourg-Fontaine on that day. It was a day of rejoicing for everybody—from the prior, who said Mass, the monks who chanted it, the choir-boys who served it, to the organist who accompanied it, and even to Hiraux who blew the organ.

The day before Easter, Hiraux ascended to the organ-loft, feather-broom in hand, and spent the day cleaning the organ with the most praiseworthy carefulness.

But next morning, contrary to all expectation, and in spite of the efforts of the blower, in spite of the dexterity of the player, the organ would produce nothing but muffled and doleful sounds, which confused the choir instead of aiding their chants. No matter how hard the organist tried or pulled out the various stops, the oboe was mute, the trumpet was hoarse and the vox humana had lost its voice.

Whilst the unlucky musician, wondering what to be at, was groaning and swearing and striking the keyboard, with fingers, fists, and elbows, Hiraux went on blowing as solemn as Oculi.

Oculi, of course, was the son of St. Éloi, and blew the bellows whilst St. Éloi forged. There is a song about it somewhere.

Mass was not over before Hiraux was suspected of being the cause of this novel entertainment, in spite of the pains he had taken and in spite of his grave demeanour.

So whilst he was applying himself with greater vigour than ever to the bellows handle, now quite useless, the organist left his place, and going to the door of the organ-loft, he closed it, double-locked it and put the key in his pocket.

Hiraux instantly perceived what was going to happen, and exclaimed: "I didn't do it, sir!" leaving hold of his handle for the first time; "it wasn't me!"

"We shall see about that," replied the enraged organist, as he began to take the organ to pieces. "Ho, ho!" the said, "the vox humana has something wrong with its throat to-day!"

The organist did not need to go further afield, for he had discovered the mystery of the crime. Hiraux, out of revenge, had disabled the three vox humana, the trumpet and hautbois, and there is good reason to believe that if he had only directed his energies towards those three pipes, it was because he had not been able to do worse damage.

Hiraux had counted upon flying from the monastery directly after Mass, only he had not reckoned on being found out so soon. Now, the discovery was made, and as he could not escape because the door was locked, he flung himself on his knees and begged for mercy.

The organist could dissimulate as well as Hiraux. He made a pretence of forgiving him on condition that Hiraux should put things to rights as he had found them, as they say in leases.

Hiraux was only too glad to get off so easily, and he accepted the terms.

When Mass was finished, the organist left, promising Hiraux not to tell the prior of his latest prank. Hiraux knew that this one surpassed all his others, and bordered on sacrilege; so when left to himself, he did his very best to fulfil the task allotted to him; a task that Fourier, in his distribution of the passions, reserved for children who, in his opinion, should do their work ardently.

We shall see whether Fourier is right or wrong when Considérant has erected his phalanstery.

Whether Hiraux did his task heartily or indifferently, it was done when the organist returned—he might really have been on the watch for that moment—followed by the brother cook and his scullions.

He had been to fetch his own allies,—Hiraux's born foes.

Hostilities began immediately the door of the organ-loft was shut. Hiraux expected he would be flogged again as before. But they could not repeat that punishment for want of rods. Still, a presentiment warned him to be more alarmed on account of the absence of rods than he would have been by their presence.

For as a matter of fact they did not intend to birch him, but to inflate him, and the operation was accomplished with the aid of the organ bellows.

This time Hiraux was not-blinded, but they very nearly killed him. They let him go when the operation was over, and he fled as far as he could from the accursed monastery, feeling more like an inflated balloon than a human being, till finally he fell, or rather he rolled, down at the foot of a tree.

It was more than a fortnight before he was completely disinflated.

In consequence of this little episode Hiraux became a grocer's lad; but no one can avoid his fate.

Hiraux was heart and soul a musician. He got hold of an old violin, and perseveringly scraped away in his odd moments.

The grocer's wife was young, and she was unappreciated by her husband— in all times there have been unappreciated wives;—she played the spinet, and at night she and Hiraux gave concerts which so enchanted the grocer that Hiraux, exalted by his domestic achievements, determined to abandon the grocery trade, and to devote himself entirely to instrumental music.

His talents were genuine enough, and almost entirely self-taught; he attained to such skill on the spinet and on the violin that the town of Villers-Cotterets appointed him organist at a salary of 800 livres per annum.

Hiraux made a little more by giving violin and pianoforte lessons. But all his pupils did not pay him in money; he received some of his fees in kind. The timber merchant would pay him in wood and shavings; the grocer in sugar, in prunes and in jam; the tailor in coats, in trousers and in waistcoats. So, what with his 1600 francs in money, and his income in goods, Hiraux had not only enough to live on but sufficient to enjoy a certain independence, which enabled him to send away pupils who did not satisfy him or who had no taste for music.

My mother, therefore, asked Hiraux to undertake my musical education— and he accepted the office with alacrity, while I, on my side, viewed the arrangement not wholly with repugnance. Hiraux was at that time already sixty years old, but so gay and jolly, so witty, so full of funny stories, possessing such an inexhaustible flow of spirits that he was beloved both by young and old alike. I had known Hiraux as long as I could remember anyone; he had been my sister's first music teacher, before she went to Paris, and he remained her private teacher during her vacations.

During the latter days of my father's illness, who, as I have said, suffered a great deal, and knew he was dying in the heyday of his life, Hiraux used to be invited to come and see us at the château des Fossés; and, as Villers-Cotterets was only a league from Fossés, Hiraux would come and return on foot, sleeping at Villers-Cotterets.

That is to say, to make ourselves quite understood, Hiraux, being always a coward, began by sleeping at Fossés: but it was decreed that persecution should follow this poor man all his life long. The stories of his youth were known by everybody: I have only related a twentieth part of these anecdotes in order to enable everyone else to add another fresh story about his most eventful life.

Now, to our house came secretaries and aides-de-camp,—people as lively and as ingenious at practical jokes as any monks of forty or fifty years back.

The invariable result was that, on going to his room at night, a pot of water placed above the door would fall on Hiraux, or he would find a needle in his bed, or a cock in his wardrobe, until at last he gave up sleeping at Fossés, and would return to Villers-Cotterets no matter what the hour or the weather.

This resolution taken, Hiraux usually came to our house armed with a long sword-stick, enclosed in a leather sheath, to give him courage during his nocturnal walk back.

In spite of this stick—or rather because of it—two young men, who had been dining at the house with Hiraux, invented a fresh trick for him. It needed some imagination to do this, for poor Hiraux, ever since the year of grace 1750, had been the victim of so many different pleasantries, that he believed himself proof, not against any prank, but at any rate against any fresh prank.

They took the sword-blade out of the scabbard, relieving Hiraux of that which constituted his protection, and fastened a long peacock's-feather in the handle in its place.

That night Hiraux, ever cautious, wished to leave early; but the young men held him back and would not let him go, promising to accompany him home. This promise put Hiraux's mind at rest. Sure of an escort home, he gave free vent to his merry wit, made more talkative perhaps than usual that evening by generous libations of champagne.

When ten o'clock struck, he began to say it was time they made a move for the town; but the young men protested that they were too comfortable to leave the castle, and that as the general had kindly offered to put them up for the night they would accept, suggesting that Hiraux should do the same.

But he took care not to accept; he suspected the visitors of being capable of any amount of tricks.

He declared that his intention of beating a retreat was immovable, and, taking up his stick and his hat, he said his adieus and departed.

The young men impatiently awaited his departure, and the great door of the château was scarcely shut behind the nocturnal traveller when they left the house by the smaller door, outran him by means of a cross-cut, and hid themselves in a corner of the forest.

The moon was shining brilliantly. Hiraux sang as people do who are frightened; but, to reassure anyone who heard him of his peaceful habits, he sang Gregorian chants, instead of singing a merry song or a lusty battle-hymn.

Suddenly, two masked men rushed out of the wood, sprang on him and demanded his money or his life.

They say no one is more dangerous than a terrified coward; Hiraux, it seemed, had something in his purse and valued his life, for he replied merely by stepping back and drawing his sword.

The sword, as we have said, had been transformed into a peacock's feather.

There was that in the scabbard which would have baffled Roland and the eleven peers of Charlemagne. Hiraux found therein what certainly neither the one nor the other of those valiant chevaliers did.

"You can see for yourselves, my friends," he said, as he showed the peacock's feather to his assailants, "you can see for yourselves I do not want to harm you."

No one could have resisted such artlessness. Threats gave way to shouts of laughter, masks fell off, and, when they had given Hiraux's legs time to recover their stability, all three returned amicably to the town.

Hiraux added one more adventure to his record.

Hiraux made me laugh so much in my childhood, and I loved him so dearly, that my sympathy for the musician overcame my antipathy to music and I agreed to take violin lessons.

But I insisted that they should buy me a violin in Paris, and not one of those for sale in the old curiosity shops of Villers-Cotterets, which did not satisfy my pride as good enough.

My mother always let me go my own way; so it was decided that Hiraux should buy me a violin the next time he went to Paris, and that my musical education should begin on his return.

Only, when would that journey be likely to take place? It looked at first as though I had counted on a postponement to the Greek Kalends. But such was not to be: chance, or rather a new joke, of which Hiraux was the victim, decreed otherwise.

The journey to Paris was arranged at the close of a dinner, at which Hiraux and some friends of his were present—among others were his two intimate friends, Mussart and Duez, whose names we mention now as we shall hear of them again presently.

It was settled under the drollest of conditions.

They were dining at the house of a man named Hutin, where all the diligences stop on their way between Laon and Paris. They made Hiraux so tipsy that he neither knew what he was doing, nor what was done to him. They undressed him and, with only his drawers and shirt on, they bundled him under the box of the diligence, among the trunks, portmanteaus and hat-boxes.

Of course they did not leave a single farthing on him—where would the fun have been if Hiraux had had money?

Hiraux came to his senses in Paris. The conductor was completely ignorant of the joke, and was therefore quite as astonished to find Hiraux there as Hiraux was himself. Hiraux was greatly embarrassed at first at finding himself dressed only in his shirt and pants, in the courtyard among all the diligences; but, being a man of resource, he bethought him of a nephew, named Camusat,—a good, excellent fellow, who has since been and still is my friend. He called a cab, got in, and cried out through the top:—

"To M. Camusat at the Rapée!" Hiraux remembered his nephew's address, so he was able to drive straight there: I am sure I should have been too much embarrassed to have remembered it, in like circumstances.

Camusat was long and thin like his uncle; he provided him with coat, trousers and waistcoat; then he lent him twenty francs to buy me a violin and fifteen francs for the return journey.

With the fifteen francs Hiraux brought me back a violin rather worn at the neck, but quite sound in all its essential organs.

I could make a book out of Hiraux's adventures, if I liked, and quite as entertaining as many books I know. But I will restrict myself to one last instance, the saddest of them all.

At the end of three years' lessons under Hiraux, I could not even tune my violin!

He was obliged to recognise my phenomenal dislike to music, and to tell my poor disappointed mother that it was simply stealing her money to attempt any longer to make a musician of me.

So I gave up the violin.

Poor Hiraux! After his stirring life he now sleeps the peaceful sleep of death in the pretty cemetery of Villers-Cotterets, surrounded by green weeping willows and flowers in full bloom; and, in thinking of that excellent man, gay, sharp-witted, quaint, I am inevitably reminded of Shakespeare's lines wherein Hamlet apostrophises the skull of his father's former fool:—

"Alas, poor Yorick! I knew him, Horatio: a fellow of infinite jest, of most excellent fancy: he hath borne me on his back a thousand times; and now, how abhorred in my imagination it is! my gorge rises at it. Here hung those lips that I have kissed I know not how oft. Where be your gibes now? your gambols? your songs? your flashes of merriment, that were wont to set the table on a roar? Not one now, to mock your own grinning; quite chap-fallen? Now get you to my lady's chamber, and tell her, let her paint an inch thick, to this favour she must come; make her laugh at that."

CHAPTER IV

The dog lantern-bearer—Demoustier's epitaph—My first fencing-master—
"The king drinks"—The fourth tenor of my life—The tub of honey.

While all these things that we have related were happening, my mother
experienced two fresh sorrows, quite as great as her first: she lost both her
father and her mother.

I can scarcely recall my grandmother Labouret; neither do I remember any
particulars relative to her life or her death. She was a worthy soul, who lived
and died blamelessly.

But I remember my grandfather quite distinctly, with a pipe in his mouth and
his solemn walk, which he had acquired when he was *maître d'hôtel*. He died
of a liver complaint, in 1808.

He was a great domino-player, and was renowned for his very great skill at
that game. Every evening he went to play in a café where a good portion of
my infancy was spent. This café was kept, I remember, by two people of
opposite sex, who were both devoted to me; one was Mademoiselle Wafflart
and the other M. Camberlin.

As my grandfather spent all his evenings there I often joined him. I used to
watch billiards being played, a game I was passionately attracted to, and one
for which I possessed the greatest possible aptitude. Unluckily, billiards, no
matter whether played by day or by night, was quite beyond my means; so I
was compelled to look on at the play of others and to count the points;—
but nothing further.

Every night at ten o'clock a scratch was heard at the door; it was my
grandfather's dog come to fetch him home,—her jaws empty on moonlit
nights, but filled by a stick bearing a lantern at each end when there was no
moon. Her name was *Charmante*, and she was indeed charmingly intelligent.
For eight or ten years, until her death, she performed this trick, and she was
never known to have scratched at the door either ten minutes too soon or
ten minutes too late, or to have taken the longest way instead of the shortest,
or to have broken a single lantern.

One day my grandfather complained of violent pains in his side, took to his
room and then to his bed. Finally, one evening, they sent me away from the
house as they had done when my father died. They took me to the house of
one of our neighbours, named Lepage, who was a glazier. There I spent the
night, and on the morrow my grandfather died.

My mother inherited the famous thirty acres of land I have already spoken of, and the house for which we paid the life-annuity. But it was the obligation to pay the annuity, that she inherited really, and not the house.

Had my mother only given up all hope of obtaining a pension, and of being paid the arrears of 28,500 francs due to my father, she would have sold the thirty acres of ground for the 30,000 or 35,000 francs which it was worth, she would have waived her rights to M. Harlay's house for 5000 or 6000 francs, and, with these 40,000 francs she would have had 2000 livres income, on which with care we could have lived perfectly well.

On the contrary, however, she began borrowing on the land by mortgaging it, ever hoping to repay herself by the unlucky arrears.

It was quite out of the question to live out of the revenue from the land; it scarcely paid two per cent.

I do not know whether we had moved before or after my grandfather's death: I think, however, it must have been before.

We lived then in the rue de Lormet, quite close to the house where I was born.

Shortly after this time we lost in this house the cousin whom I used to call Mamma Zine.

So death had fallen heavily on our family circle; in four years four relatives had gone to eternity, one after the other, and were laid in the little cemetery of which I have already spoken.

But, with the exception of my father's, none of the other deaths made any lasting impression on my mind. They only meant a daily walk to the cemetery, and one more mound added to the rest, which my mother called her garden; a fresh cypress was planted near the old cypresses; new roses blossomed by the old rose; my mother shed more tears; and that was all.

Our graves were near that of Demoustier; and his epitaph was the first memorial inscription I had deciphered; it had been composed by Legouvé, and ran thus:—

"Beneath this stone rests, in the sleep of the just,

"CHARLES-ALBERT DEMOUSTIER,

"Associated Member of the National Institute, who was born at Villers-Cotterets, March 31st 1760, and whose peaceful spirit entered upon its immortal rest, on the 11th Ventôse, year IX of the Republic.

(2 March 1801)

"En ces mots l'amitié consacra son histoire;
Il montra les talents, aux vertus réunis;
Son esprit lui donna la gloire.
Et sa belle âme des amis.

"Rest in peace, beloved one!"

And indeed if any soul should rest in peace it ought indeed to be that of the good and religious-minded Demoustier, whose memory was venerated by all Villers-Cotterets. My mother often used to tell me that a gentler, more sympathetic, more delightful man never breathed. He died at the same age as my father—forty-one—and faced his end with the gentle and pious resignation of all good souls. The day before his death, my mother sat beside his bedside and, though hopeless herself, she tried to instil hope into him. He smiled sweetly at her, and looked out upon a gleam of beautiful spring sunshine, the sunshine that comes more like nature's first smile than the sun of summer.

Demoustier laid his hand on hers and, looking at her, he said:—

"Dear Madame Dumas, we must not delude ourselves: I can no longer take broth or milk or water, so I must die."

And he died next day with a smile upon his lips.

Alas! it was my mother's ambition to erect just such a stone as was put over Demoustier's resting-place; but she could not afford to consecrate the dead at the cost of the living.

I fancy I must have acquired my partiality for cemeteries, that is to say village cemeteries, from my frequent walks with my mother to the Villers-Cotterets cemetery: nothing impresses me so much even now—their churches, their tall weeping willows, their broken-off columns, and their crosses painted black, with a simple white inscription stating the name and the age of the deceased.

Alas! if I were now to return to our cemetery how many graves of friends I should find there, besides my mother's! Nearly all whom I knew in my childhood lie there, and, with Christ in the early days of Christian Rome, I could exclaim: "I have more friends under the earth than on it."

Let those who take the trouble of studying small details study the different localties where my childhood was passed: les Fossés, Antilly, the confined room at the hôtel de *l'Epée*, the ruined castle of Villers-Cotterets, the house and the town garden of M. Deviolaine, the cloister at Saint-Remy, the château of Villers-Hellon, the grand park of François I., of Henri II. and of Henri

IV., and the little cemetery of Pieux,—the name of the place where the Villers-Cotterets cemetery was situated,—and they may find the origins of many qualities in my books, of many traits in my character.

To all these my early impressions I owe my deep respect for all holy things, my deep faith in Providence and my great love of God. Never, throughout my long life, have I had one moment of despair, one minute of doubt, not even in the darkest hours of life; I dare not say I am certain of the immortality of my soul, but I can go as far as to say I hope in it. I believe that death is a forgetting of the past without being a renunciation of the future. If science succeeds in endowing spirits with memory it will have solved the great mystery, of which God has hitherto kept the key; souls will then remember, and immortality be laid bare to us.

But to conclude. In the midst of these walks and games and early schooling, I was growing up, I could play the *Marche des Samnites* and the Overture to *Lodoïska*, upon my violin, and Hiraux, with his black cap pulled down over his ears, was confessing to my mother that he was too honest to steal from her any longer the ten francs per month which she gave him to make a musician of me.

I was very ready to give up these lessons, and I should have done so long before, had my attraction for Hiraux not surmounted my dislike of the solfeggio. I renounced them, too, the more eagerly as I had now begun taking lessons far more seductive to my mind—namely, lessons in fencing.

The Republic had turned the fine castle and ancient pleasure-house of the dukes of Orléans into barracks, and the Empire into a workhouse. Here I had discovered an old fencing master. He had been injured once when giving a lesson without a mask: the foil of one of his pupils had pierced his mouth and destroyed his uvula. This accident, by making him almost dumb, or rather by reducing him to an almost unintelligible gibberer, had made teaching almost an impossibility—this accident, I say, together with a great love for the bottle, had brought our old St. Georges to the royal dwelling-place of François I., then an auxiliary to the Workhouse of the Seine.

This man was called old Mounier, and, though I must ask pardon of my later master Grisier, I beg to state I received my first lessons in fencing from Mounier when I was ten years old.

For I was about ten years old when I began to show such disinclination towards music and such intense enthusiasm for physical exercises.

While all this was going on, and while I was dreaming of nothing but swords and sabres, pistols and guns, I remained very cowardly on one single point.

Like nature, I abhorred a vacuum. So soon as I felt myself suspended a certain distance above the earth, like Antæus, my head began to whirl, and I lost all my wits. I dared not even go down steps if they were somewhat steep, and I had never ventured to climb trees after birds' nests with my young playfellows.

This cowardliness brought all kinds of tricks down upon me from my cousins Deviolaine, their brother Félix and my oldest sister. They delighted to lead me up into hay-lofts, under the pretext of playing hide-and-seek, or some other game: then, when the door was shut, the only way to descend was by a ladder. I used to beg and implore the other children, to their great amusement, to open the door for me; then, when they took no notice of my entreaties, I would at last make up my mind to come down by the ladder, and my descent was most clumsily performed before the eyes of my jeering play-fellows.

I was very nearly killed one day by stopping below while the other children had gone aloft. They had all climbed up a rick of straw at the foot of which I was sitting. My cousin Cécile was a real tomboy in her ways, and seemed to think, with the Princess Palatine, that she could change her sex if she went on leaping and jumping. She had reached the top first, and was bending over to look down at and tease me, when her foot slipped, and she rolled down the steep side of the rick alighting astride on my shoulders, nearly breaking my neck.

I displayed one proof of coolness in great danger which reinstated me in my young friends' good opinion. It was Twelfth-Day, and we had been dining with M. Deviolaine. The Twelfth-Day Bean, constituting me King of the Day, had fallen to my share, so after dinner I hastened to transfer the seat of my empire to the garden. While thrusting a paper-boat out into the pond in the middle of the lawn, I apparently leant a little too far over; I lost my balance, and head foremost I went into the icy cold water, which was four feet deep, with a tremendous plunge, to the great alarm of the spectators, who threw up their arms and began shouting at the top of their voices, "Help, help, Dumas is drowning!" ... Luckily, I did not lose my head, I caught hold of the plants which hung over the edge of the pool, and, thanks to that support, I reappeared on the surface of the water, streaming like the river Scamander. Then it only needed Victor's hand to haul me back to my own element on mother-earth.

This done, I turned towards the terrified company with a judicial and serious air, and I said to them:—

"Idiots, you should not have said, 'Dumas is drowning,' you should have said, 'The king drinks!'"

This charmed everybody; and, as I was then only seven years of age, and it was my first clever saying, I crave the indulgence of the public for mentioning it.

It did not, however, prevent my cousin Cécile from declaring, when she was performing some of her common tomboy tricks, that I neither was nor ever would be fit to be anything but a Seminarist.

We shall soon see how very nearly her prediction came to being fulfilled.

I believe I had five great frights in my life, and, happily, all came in my early childhood. I have mentioned the first three; the Amiens snake, the two adders at Saint Remy and Madame de Genlis.

We will now proceed to the fourth.

I was playing at marbles at the door of a grocer called Lebègue, who was scraping and spreading out chocolate on a marble slab with a long, flexible knife that I believe they call a spatula. I began a dispute with my companion, and we fell to pummelling one another. Please take note that when it was a question of fists I was never a coward. He was stronger than I, he pushed me roughly back and I fell over backwards into a tub of honey.

I at once saw the consequences of my accident, I uttered a cry which made the grocer look up, and he soon saw what had happened, namely, that, as I have said, I was seated in a tub of honey. I sprang up as though springs were attached to my legs, in spite of the resistance of the substance to which I was glued: and I fled incontinently.

My prudent and rapid flight was due to a view of the grocer dashing out knife in hand at the same time.

I naturally ran in the direction of my home, but it was in the centre of the rue de Lormet, and a good way off the scene of the accident. I ran with all my might, but the grocer's legs were double the length of mine; I was driven by terror, but he was moved by greed. I turned to look behind me as I ran, and saw that awful tradesman, with fiery eyes and open lips and frowning brow, knife in hand, gaining upon me every minute. At last, weltering with heat, panting, speechless, and on the point of a collapse, I flung myself on the pavement ten paces from our door, convinced that it was all over with me, and that Lebègue was pursuing me for no other purpose than to cut my throat.

Nothing of the kind happened. After a struggle, in which I resisted him tooth and nail, he laid me face down on his knees, and scraped the seat of my trousers with his spatula, set me on my feet, and returned perfectly content to his shop.

But in spite of this forbearance on the part of M. Lebègue it was more than a year before I ventured to pass by on the same side of the street as his grocer's shop.

CHAPTER V

My horror of great heights—The Abbé Conseil—My opening at the Seminary—My mother, much pressed, decides to enter me there—The horn inkstand—Cécile at the grocer's—My flight.

But I was now ten years old, and it was time to take my mental education seriously in hand. My physical training was proceeding fast enough. I could throw stones like David, I could draw a bow like a Balearic archer, I could ride like a Numidian; but I could not climb trees or steeples.

I have travelled much, and, whether in the Alps or in Sicily, in Calabria, or in Spain or in Africa, I have gone over difficult enough places; but I only crossed them because I was obliged to; and no one but myself will ever now know what I endured in the process. My terror is purely nervous, and therefore incurable; it is so great that, if I were given the choice, I would rather fight a duel than climb to the top of the column in the place Vendôme.

I went up to the top of the towers of Nôtre Dame once with Hugo, and I do not like to think what it cost me in perspirations and cold shivers.

But we must return to the question of my mental training, for it was high time it was begun in earnest. They had tried to get me entered free at all the colleges endowed for the education of sons of superior officers. But, in spite of the most urgent representations, they could neither obtain for me admission to the Prytanée nor a bursary in any Imperial lycée.

Had I been of sufficient age to be of any importance at that time I should have flattered myself that Bonaparte's hatred for my father was being continued towards me.

None of the applications on my behalf, then, had been successful, when one of my cousins died, of whom I have already spoken,—the Abbé Conseil.

He had been tutor to the royal pages, he had received all sorts of benefices from Louis XV. and Louis XVI., and he was accordingly wealthy. He owned a charming house in the village of Largny, within a league of Villers-Cotterets, and a most picturesque garden, both in the centre of a valley; I have not referred to all this before because our cousin Conseil showed us but scant hospitality.

He also had a house at Villers-Cotterets—number 3 or 5, I think, in the rue de Lormet, just opposite the house where Demoustier died.

I paid two visits a year to this cousin Conseil, one on New Year's Day, the other on his birthday. He would give me a kiss on one cheek and a slap on the other, and there ended his generosity.

Once he gave me half a crown. But my mother and I never went again, and he died the same year. He left an income of something like 12,000 livres behind him, to a certain Miss Ryan, before mentioned.

My mother received a legacy of 1500 francs, and to one of his relatives he bequeathed a bursary at the Seminary of Soissons.

My destiny was clear, and Cécile's prophecy was to be realised: I was to be the future Seminarist.

But the question remained how to get me there,—not an easy matter. I had an unreasoning aversion to priests, and Cécile's prediction had sown in my heart the seeds of revolt against its coming true.

My mother's mind was not made up. She, poor woman, was incapable of insisting on anything that she saw was the least distasteful to me; but she desired to give me as good an education as possible. The thought of making a priest of me had, however, never entered her head. I believe, indeed, if she had thought such a thing were likely to come of it she would have been the first to oppose the plan, which she now put before me in the most glowing colours.

Two or three months passed, I resisting and my mother begging and praying me to go.

Finally, one fine day when she had used every inducement she could think of to make me go, promising solemnly, on her word of honour, that I should always be free to come home if I did not like the rules of the Seminary, I let fall the fatal *yes*, and I consented to all her wishes.

There was a week granted me to make my preparations for departure. It was a great separation, and it cost my mother as much as it did me; but she tried to hide her tears, till I unjustly imagined she was quite pleased to get rid of me.

The day before that on which I was to travel in the coach which plied twice a week between Villers-Cotterets and Soissons, as I was collecting all my little wants for my school life, I discovered I hadn't an inkstand. I told my mother of this, and she, recognising the justice of my request, asked me what sort I would like.

I had luxurious ideas concerning that inkstand. I wished a horn inkstand with a place for pens. But, as my mother did not clearly understand my explanations, she gave me twelve sous, and told me to go and buy the inkstand myself.

Please pay great attention to this little matter; for, puerile though it may seem, it changed the whole course of my life.

I hurried off to a grocer named Devaux. I took good care not to go to Lebègue's: the reader knows why.

The grocer had not the kind of inkpot I wanted; but he promised to get me one by evening.

When evening came, I returned, and he had the inkpot ready for me; but as luck would have it I found my cousin Cécile in the shop.

She was very glad to see me, she took the opportunity to wish me all possible success in the career I had chosen and she promised that, as soon as I was ordained, she would ask me to become her spiritual director.

I cannot say whether it was that her sarcasm galled me past bearing, or whether the responsibility of the suggested office seemed too heavy, but I flung the inkpot in the grocer's face. I pocketed my twelve sous, and I rushed out of the shop crying—"Very well; I don't care. I will not go to the Seminary!"

Like Cæsar I had crossed my Rubicon: but the next step was to try and escape my mother's urgent entreaties, which I might not perhaps have been able to withstand.

I ventured on my first wilful act. I bought a loaf and a sausage with my twelve sous, food to last me two or three days, in fact, and then I went to find Boudoux.

I must explain who he was.

Boudoux was a character. Had not the disease termed *bulimia* already received its name at that epoch it would certainly have been christened after him.

I have never seen such a voracious eater as was Boudoux.

One day he came to our house, and a calf had just been killed; he gazed at it with longing eyes, and my father said to him—

"Do you want to eat the whole of it? You can have it."

"Oh! general, you are joking!" was Boudoux's reply.

"Upon my word I am not."

"Indeed I should love it, general."

They put the whole calf in the oven, and when it was cooked Boudoux ate it all.

When he had picked the last bone, my father complimented him on his performance.

"I hope your hunger is satisfied now, Boudoux?" he said.

"Put the mother on the spit, general," replied Boudoux, "and you will see."

My father drew back, for he was fond of his cow, and Boudoux was likely to leave nothing of her but her horns.

I could cite other instances than this; but they would pale before the one I have just given.

One day at the opening of the hunting season M. Danré, of Vouty, had two dozen chickens on the spit. Boudoux looked at them as he had looked at my father's veal; and M. Danré was unwise enough to make a proposal to him similar to the one which had been made at our house.

Boudoux made twenty-four mouthfuls of the twenty-four chickens.

Later (I must not stop much longer over Boudoux's appetite), after the Restoration, when the prince de Condé came to hunt at Villers-Cotterets, he brought a pack of a hundred and twenty hounds.

Boudoux obtained the post of kennelman to the huntsmen, and it was therefore his business to distribute food to the princely Roquadors and Barbaros.

It was soon discovered that although the purchase of bread and meat was the same as always, the poor beasts grew thin and languid and unsteady on their legs.

Suspicions were aroused, and Boudoux was watched.

It was found out that he himself had eaten the portions of forty dogs—one-third, that was, of the whole food supply.

The prince ordered that Boudoux's portion of food should be served separately to him each day, and that this portion should be as much as for forty dogs.

So much, then, for Boudoux's appetite. We will next speak of his physical attainments, and lastly of his moral qualities.

Physically, Boudoux seemed as though he were of the refuse of creation; Quasimodo would have appeared almost beautiful beside him. Boudoux's face was not merely pitted, it was scarred, furrowed and almost eaten away by smallpox; his eyes, drawn out of their sockets by the hollowness of his eyelids, seemed to hang over his cheeks, watery and bloodshot; his nose was depressed instead of being raised, and flattened down on his upper lip; from his lips flowed a constant trickle of saliva blackened by the quids of tobacco he chewed; the upper lip curved like a serpent's, almost round to his ears, and gave his mouth the appearance of being able to accommodate a whole leg of mutton at once; the picture was completed by hair that Polyphemus himself might have envied; his beard was scanty, red and coarse, and only grew out of the rare spaces not covered with pox marks.

His head was supported by a body five feet nine inches in height, but that height was never realised on account of a defect in one leg, which doubled and yielded under him to such an extent; with every step he took, that the lower part of his leg and the top of his thigh looked like the two pointers of a compass opened triangle-fashion.

For all that, Boudoux had almost superhuman strength. During a house-move he was worth his weight in gold: he would carry trunks, sideboards, bedsteads, tables, on his head, and, as his limping stride measured over a yard and a half at each step he took, he could move the entire furniture of one house to another in a trice.

Furthermore, Boudoux, who could have taken up a horse by its hind hoofs and torn off its shoes like Alcidamas; or, like Samson, have taken the gates of Gaza from their hinges and carried them on his back; or like Milo of Crotona, have gone round the circus with an ox on his shoulders, and then felled it and eaten it; Boudoux, I say, with the strength of an elephant, was as gentle as a lamb.

And now as to his character.

Although ugly, repulsive, hideous to look at, everybody liked Boudoux. He lodged with his aunt, Mademoiselle Chapuis, the postmistress, but he had his meals everywhere. Three times a day he went the round of the town and, like the begging Friars of the ancient monasteries, he collected enough to feed a convent; only, as he had no monks to feed, he ate the whole supply himself.

It was not enough to satisfy him, but it just kept him going.

Boudoux had a calling, or rather two callings, for he worked *à la marette* and *à la pipée*.

We must explain to Parisians; who will probably not know what are the two trades we have referred to under the names of *marette* and *pipée*. We will take *marette* first.

There are very few forests, woods, or covers that do not contain some pools of water, commonly called *mares*; for instance, the *mare* d'Auteuil, which has been noted as long as I can remember. At these pools in the woods, forests, and covers, birds are accustomed to drink at certain times of day. Here the bird-catcher drives small birch twigs coated with bird-lime into the soft, muddy soil along the edges of the pools, and when the birds come to drink they are caught on these limed twigs.

This is called snaring a *mare*, and in the clever setting of these traps consists the whole success and art of the hunter.

And as, to explain everything fully, there are more small *mares* than large ones, and as the smaller *mares* are better than the large, because they need less bird-lime, and consequently are less expensive, these small *mares* are called "*marelles*," and in the language of the snarers of small birds, the phrase to work *à la marette* indicates the nature of their calling.

La pipée is worked in the same way, but with differences of detail. A tree high enough to out-top the rest of the coppice is chosen; it is stripped of its smaller branches, and these are replaced by lime-twigs fitted into notches made by a bill-hook; the bird-catchers then take their place inside a hut made of foliage constructed round the trunk of the tree, and they attract all the birds in the district by three methods.

The first is to attach an owl to the centre of the tree.

The owl, with his buff plumage and great round eyes, plays in the forest the part that Jean Jacques Rousseau played in the streets of Paris when he went forth dressed as an Armenian.

All the street arabs ran after the Genevan philosopher.

All the birds chase the owl.

But a fate awaits these poor creatures that did not overtake the hooligans: when they fly against the tree, in attacking the owl which is fastened to the tree, each bird that settles on a lime-twig is lost; he falls from bough to bough, and passes from freedom to a cage, lucky if he does not go from his cage to the spit.

The second method of attraction is to take a jay.

Out of a hare one can only make jugged hare, but in the case of a jay something else can be constructed.

It must, however, be a living jay, that is a condition *sine quâ non*.

The jay has a shocking reputation in the bird world.

It is accused by la Fontaine of stealing peacock's feathers; and, like all reputations made by man, this one, perhaps, is least deserved; another accusation brought against it—and a far more serious charge in the eyes of the birds—is that it eats the eggs of its smaller and weaker brethren. So the hatred in which birds hold this glutton is in proportion to the number of eggs they lay; the titmouse, for instance, which sometimes lays as many as twenty to twenty-five tiny eggs, is the most relentless against this robber; next come *fourgons*, which lay fifteen; chaffinches, which lay five or six; and last, redbreasts and warblers, which lay three or four. So they take a live jay, stretch out his wings and pull the feathers from it.

It is not a very humane process, but it is very efficacious.

The cry of the jay is a frightful noise: as each feather is pulled out, the jay utters that cry, and at each cry flocks of chaffinches, titmice, *fourgons*, warblers, and robins come flying down to enjoy their enemy's discomfort; for they are not deceived, they recognise his cry as one of pain.

But this time they are punished for their want of forgiveness towards their enemy, and the lime-twigs execute justice on their hard hearts.

The success of the third means depends entirely on the degree of skill with which the bird-catcher has been naturally endowed, in producing sounds to imitate the songs of birds, by the aid of blades of couch-grass or a piece of glossy silk. The musician who can imitate birds' notes requires no jay or owl to help him; he retires into his hut, counterfeits cries of distress of the different birds he wants to catch, and all the birds of the same species that are in the district flock to the call.

I must say, however, that I have met few *pipurs* (and I have known a great number) who have reached such a pitch of perfection.

But Boudoux, who spoke no dead language, and could only talk his own among living ones, and that very imperfectly, took, in the matter of birds, the first rank as a philologist, and not merely in the forest of Villers-Cotterets, but, I dare venture to assert, in any forest of the world.

There was not an ornithological language or jargon or patois that he could not talk, from the language of the crow to that of the wren.

He held those of his confrères in contempt who made use of grass and silk, for he could imitate the cry of an owl so perfectly that I have seen one come and perch on his hat as on the helmet of Minerva.

I went to find Boudoux. I unburdened my heart to him, and I asked him to hide me for two or three days in one of his huts.

Of course he granted my request.

His only condition was that, as it was autumn, I ought to take a blanket with me, as the nights were not so warm as they had been.

I returned home, slipped into my room, took a blanket off my bed, and wrote on a bit of paper:—

"Do not be anxious about me, mother dear; I have run away, because I do not want to be a priest."

Then I rejoined Boudoux, who had collected his evening food and was waiting for me at the entrance to the park.

Boudoux had two snaring pools, one on the road to Vivières, and the other on the road to Compiègne. Near the pool on the road to Compiègne he had a hut, and it was in this hut that I asked shelter from the Seminary of Soissons.

I spent three days and three nights in the forest. At night, I rolled myself in my blanket, and I must own that I slept without any feeling of remorse; by day I wandered from one *mare* to another, collecting the snared birds. We took an incalculable number of birds during those three days; by the third day, the two *mares* were completely *ruined* until the next breeding season. I emphasise the word *ruined*, because that is the technical term for it.

Those three days increased my antipathy towards the Seminary, but at the same time it gave me a keen taste for *la marette*.

At the end of these three days I returned, but I did not dare to go straight to the house. I went to find my good friend Madame Darcourt, and I begged her to announce to my mother the return of her prodigal son, and to smooth the way for my re-entry under the maternal roof.

Alas! the more prodigal the children, the warmer their reception! When the original prodigal son returned home to his father after three years' absence, they killed a calf; if he had not returned until after an absence of six years, they would have killed an ox.

My mother hugged me to her and called me a bad boy. She promised me that there should be no more talk between us of my going to the Seminary, delighted to think that I should not leave her. She reserved all her wrath for Boudoux, and, the first time she saw him, poor as we were, she gave him five francs.

Just think what a trivial circumstance decided the course of my life. If the grocer had had the inkstand I wanted that morning, I should not have returned to his shop in the evening; I should not have met Cécile there; she would not have made that joke which exasperated me; I should not have placed myself under Boudoux's care; and the next day I should have gone to Soissons and entered the Seminary. When at the Seminary my latent inclinations for a religious life would have developed, and I might have become a great preacher instead of what I am—namely, a poor poet. I wonder whether that would have been better or worse?

What God does is well done. This was not the only danger I escaped; we shall see later how I nearly became something much worse than a Seminarist or a priest.

We shall see that I just missed being a tax-gatherer!

CHAPTER VI

The Abbé Grégoire's College—The reception I got there—The fountains play to celebrate my arrival—The conspiracy against me—Bligny challenges me to single combat—I win.

It was arranged that I should go to the Abbé Grégoire's college in Villers-Cotterets instead of to the Seminary. They styled the Abbé Grégoire's school a *College*, just as in England the illegitimate sons of noblemen are called "lords."

It is a matter of courtesy.

However that may be, it was decided that I should go to the Abbé Grégoire's college.

Oh! if I begin to talk of the Abbé Grégoire, I shall go on indefinitely,—for he was an upright, worthy, and saintly man.

He was not a genius, he was something better than that—he was a thoroughly good man; during the years he governed the school two hundred scholars passed through his hands, and I do not know of a single one who has turned out badly.

During the forty years he served the church at Villers-Cotterets, not a single petty scandal which could make the irreligious or the libertine smile had ever been brought against him. Mothers who had confessed to him in their girlhood and during his youth took their daughters to him in full confidence, for they knew that then, as in their own time, only good and fatherly advice would be given through the confessional grating.

He never had a servant or a housekeeper; he lived with his sister, a little wizened old lady, rather hunch-backed, rather inclined to be shrewish, who adored—nay, who worshipped her brother.

Poor dear abbé, what a life we led him! How we enraged him, how he scolded us, and how much he loved us!

It was the same with him as with Hiraux; I loved him so warmly before there was any thought of being his pupil, that I submitted to the great change in my life without the least dread. Besides, what was it, compared with the Seminary?

His classes began at half-past eight in the morning, directly after mass, and closed at noon. We all went home to our dinner for an hour, then returned at one o'clock; at five minutes past one, school began again, and went on until four.

Add to this Sundays, saints'-days, greater feasts and lesser feasts, and you can see my life was not a very hard one.

As a whole, I was not very much liked by the other children of the town at that age; I was vain and impudent and overbearing, and filled with self-confidence and admiration for my small person; yet, notwithstanding all this, I was capable of good feeling, when heart, rather than intellect or self-love, was called into play.

As far as physical qualities went, I was quite a pretty child: I had long, fair, curly hair, which fell on my shoulders, and which did not turn crisp until my fifteenth year; large blue eyes, which even until now have retained somewhat of their early freshness; a straight nose, small and well shaped; thick red sensitive lips; white but uneven teeth. In addition to this, my complexion was dazzlingly white, due, so my mother believed, to the brandy my father had made her drink during her pregnancy; it turned darker when my hair became crisp.

I was in figure as long and thin as a lath.

The school accommodation was not large: twenty-five or thirty pupils were enough to fill it, and it was quite an event when a fresh pupil arrived in the midst of the small circle.

It was a great event on my side too. I was dressed in a suit the whole of which was made out of a coat that had been my grandfather's. It was the colour of *café au lait*, deepened in tone, spotted all over with black points. I felt very proud of it, and I thought it would create quite a sensation among my comrades.

At eight o'clock one Monday morning, in the autumn, I took my way to the source whence I was to drink deep of the water of knowledge. I walked solemnly along, with my nose held proudly up, carrying my library of grammars, the *Epitome historiæ sacræ*, dictionaries and other aids under my arm, all of them as new as my clothes, and I enjoyed in anticipation the effect my appearance would produce upon the communion of martyrs.

The entrance to the courtyard at the Abbé Grégoire's was through a great door, which seemed like the entrance to a deep vault, and opened on the rue de Soissons. This door was wide open, and I looked through into the courtyard: it was empty.

I guessed at first that I was late and everyone was already in school. I quickly stepped across the threshold; as soon as the door closed behind me I heard loud shouts of glee, and a dewiness, which strongly resembled a shower, descended upon me from the top of a double amphitheatre of barrels.

I raised my eyes, and beheld each pupil perched on a barrel, in the same attitude and performing the same action, as the *Manneken-Pis* fountain of Brussels. The fountains were playing in honour of my arrival.

Such a manner of reception displeased me greatly. I took to my heels, in order to protect myself from this novel kind of shower-bath; but I had stood for a moment in hesitation and astonishment; then, when my mind was made up, I had had five or six paces to go before I was free; so, when I came out of the vault-like passage, I was streaming all over.

I was by nature very tearful. Often, as a child, I would sit down in a corner and cry without any reason. Then, as I always spoke of myself, like Cæsar, in the third person, and as they had adopted this manner of addressing me, for the fun of it, my mother would come to me and ask:

"Why is Dumas crying?"

"Dumas cries," I would reply, "because Dumas has tears."

This answer relieved her of all uneasiness, and nearly always satisfied my mother, who would go away laughing, leaving me to cry on at my leisure.

If I cried without any motive, the reader will readily understand that, when there was a strong incentive, there was all the more reason why I should give way to torrents of tears.

What more justifiable excuse could I have had than the humiliation to which I had just been subjected and the injury it had just done my new suit?

Therefore, when the Abbé Grégoire came by to say mass, he found me on the steps, in floods of water, like the Biblis of M. Dupaty.

The abbé had scarcely come in view when my schoolfellows came up to me, surrounded me in rings on the staircase, and, with every appearance of deep interest, asked each other why I was crying. The Abbé Grégoire broke through the hypocritical circle, ascended two or three steps, and, putting up his eyeglass, for he was as blind as a mole, looked at me and asked me what was the matter.

I was about to reply when I saw twenty shut fists behind the abbé, and twenty threatening faces making significant gestures at me. I uttered a howl, at which the abbé turned round: immediately all the faces smiled, all the hands were returned to their pockets.

"But what is the matter with him?" asked the abbé.

"We don't know," replied the hypocrites; "he has been going on like that ever since he came."

"What! he has cried ever since he came?"

"Yes, indeed he has. Hasn't he? hasn't he? hasn't he?"

"Yes! yes! yes!" all the voices responded. "Dumas is crying."

"Come, what are you crying for, Dumas?"

"Oh!" replied one of them who knew the tradition, "Dumas is probably crying because 'Dumas has tears'—"

This mocking remark infuriated me.

"No!" I cried, "no, I am not crying because I have tears; I am crying because—because—because they have made water on my head, there!"

The crime was so unusual, the idea so whimsical, that the abbé made me repeat the accusation twice over; then, turning to his pupils, he said:

"Go upstairs, gentlemen; we will go into this matter there."

"Ah! you brat! ah! you tell-tale! ah! you traitor!" a dozen lads whispered to me; "you wait a bit,—we'll see when school is over—!"

The abbé turned round.

All were silent, and they entered the classroom.

Each boy took his place, but I, who had not one, remained standing.

"Come here, my young friend," said the abbé.

"Here I am, M. l'abbé," I said, whimpering.

He felt me.

"The child is soaked through—!"

My lamentations broke forth afresh.

"Of course he is wet," said a big boy; "think of the time he has been crying."

"What!" cried the abbé, "you dare to suggest that his own tears have soaked him like this?"

"Certainly!"

"But, M. l'abbé," I exclaimed, "I could not cry down my back, and I am as wet behind as in front."

The abbé verified my statement.

"You are right," he said. "No recreation at midday; bring me the cane at once; and you boys must do three hundred lines by to-morrow morning."

Then arose a chorus of complaints and groans equal to those Dante heard in the first circle of the Inferno.

With these groans and complaints fierce threats were mingled which made my flesh creep.

Nevertheless, they had to submit: the abbé kept up the ancient scholastic traditions; he had a deaf ear and a vigorous hand; and a thrashing all round with the cane increased the groans, the complaints, and the threats.

I realised that I was collecting a storm over my head which would result later in a hail of fisticuffs.

The caning had this much good, that it did away with work during all that class; not a line was written from nine o'clock to midday, under pretext that the abbé had hit so hard that their hands were numbed.

The abbé accepted the excuse.

At noon, each boy tried to find some excuse to escape retention. It was incredible the things they had to do and what importance their going out was that day.

I remember three of the excuses given: Saunier had to take his clarionet lesson; Ronet had to take a dose of oil; Leloir ought to be drawing for conscription!

These three pretexts were handed in by the three scholars named Saunier, Ronet and Leloir.

Needless to relate, the clarionet lesson, castor oil, and drawing for conscription had to wait till the next day, and at midday I went out of college absolutely alone.

Oh! what profound reflections I made as I returned home! How well I realised that it would have been far better to laugh at the joke, no matter how grim it was, than to cry as I had done! I placed Heraclitus a thousand times higher than Democritus!

My mother was much struck by my sadness, and she questioned me closely upon the causes of my melancholy, but I had been too ready to tell tales, and I preserved profound silence.

At one o'clock I returned to the college: all the lads had had their dinner sent in to them from their homes; the greater number of these dinners, let it be said, to the parents' honour, consisted of a simple slice of dry bread.

The complaints and groans had stopped, but the threatenings had increased, the clouds were lowering and full of lightnings. I could not raise my nose from the paper upon which I was declining *rosa* but I caught sight of a fist which had nothing in common with the declension I was writing out.

I realised that, when I went out, I was going to be beaten to pulp. The bigger boys were too conscious of their superior strength to threaten the most, for they felt they could not take revenge on a child: the worst were those of about my own age, specially a lad called Bligny, the son of a draper, living in the place de la Fontaine, who was so angry with me that by common consent the task of taking a general vengeance on me was consigned to him. Bligny was two years older than I, so that I had been used to look upon him as a big lad, although I was really as tall as he.

I was therefore not too well at ease at the prospect of a duel with him.

Still, I had so often heard the story of the three duels my father had fought when he first entered the army, on behalf of the honour of the king and the queen, that I knew I must not shirk my first fight.

I was so preoccupied that I made quite a dozen mistakes in the three or four declensions I had to do during school hours.

I do not know how long the time may have seemed to my companions, but I know that never before had it seemed to me to fly so fast. Four o'clock struck, and the Abbé Grégoire said his prayer before I thought half the class was over.

There was nothing to be done but to leave, and I decided upon my line of action. I tied up my books in as leisurely a fashion as possible, hoping that, if I went down the staircase last, the torrent would have flown by and I should find a free passage; yet I knew in my inmost heart that I had brought too great a punishment down on my head by my denunciation to get off so cheaply.

I could have spoken to the Abbé Grégoire, and he would himself have taken me home or sent his sister Alexandrine with me; but I felt that that would be cowardly, and would only defer matters. M. Grégoire or his sister could not always conduct me home; there would come a day when I should be obliged to go by myself, and then I should be certain to have a brush with one or other of my schoolfellows.

I resolved, therefore, to face the danger and to take the bull by the horns.

Remember, all these thoughts were whirling in the head of a lad only ten years old.

I took my stand, I said good-bye to the Abbé Grégoire, I heaved a big sigh, and then I went downstairs.

I was not mistaken: the whole school was seated in a semi circle, like Roman spectators, on the raised seats of their amphitheatre; and, standing at the bottom of the stairs, with his coat off and his shirt sleeves tucked up, Bligny awaited me.

Ah! I confess that when I reached the turn of the stair case and saw all these preparations taken for the inevitable battle, my heart failed me, and I nearly ran up again; but although I had tried to repress my momentary hesitation it had not escaped my comrades; there was a general outcry and the most scurrilous epithets were yelled at me from the courtyard below. I felt myself turn pale and tremble all over, and a cold sweat broke out on my forehead. I took measure of the two extremities to which I was reduced,—either to receive a few blows in the eye or on the teeth and all would be settled, or ever afterwards to be the sport of my schoolfellows and to have to go through it afresh each day. I gripped hold of my courage, which was fast ebbing away; I pulled myself together by an act of the will, till I felt myself completely master of the situation. There was a brief struggle, at the end of which I felt my moral courage getting the better of my physical; reason conquered instinct.

All the same, I felt that I wanted an incentive to goad me forward, that that goad was within my own control, and that, if I would use it, I must stimulate my courage with lashing words.

"Ah!" I said, looking at Bligny—"Ah! is this the game?"

"Yes, this is the game," he replied.

"You want to fight, then, do you?"

"Yes, rather."

"Ah! you are longing for it?"

"Yes."

"Ah! really?"

"Yes."

"Well, then, come on!"

I had now goaded myself to action; I put my books on the ground, I threw off my jacket, and I hurled myself upon my antagonist, shouting:

"Ah! you want to fight!... ah! you want to fight!... take that! and that! and that!"

Marshal de Saxe, that great military philosopher, said very truly that the whole art of war consists in pretending not to be afraid and in inspiring fear in the enemy.

I appeared quite fearless, and Bligny was beaten.

I do not wish to imply he was beaten without a contest, not so; but it would have been better for him if he had not fought: he received a blow in the eye, another blow on his mouth, and made a hasty retreat after this double attack, which he only opposed by a feeble hit at my nose. The whole affair was over in less than a minute, and the victory was mine.

I ought to do my comrades the justice of saying that this victory was followed by unanimous applause.

I then put my jacket on again, and collected my books, murmuring:

"You see! you see! you see!" which seemed to mean, "Look at me, see what I am! a coward at bottom, but when driven to desperation, an Alexander, a Hannibal, or a Cæsar; you see!"

This seemed also to be the opinion of the spectators, for they opened their ranks to let me pass through, and I went out through the great porch, recently the scene of my humiliation and now my triumphal arch. I found a book which had dropped out of Bligny's waistcoat when he staggered from my blow; and, as I considered that the spoils of the conquered belonged by right to the conqueror, I picked it up and carried it off.

I opened it as I took it away, and saw it was M. Tissot's well-known work.

I did not know what the title meant, and I allowed my mother to take the book away from me and to hide it.

Two years afterwards I discovered it and read it.

Had I read it the day of my victory it would have been fruitless, because I should not have understood it.

Two years later it was providential.

CHAPTER VII

The Abbé Fortier—The jealous husband and the viaticum—A pleasant visit—Victor Letellier—The pocket-pistol—I terrify the population—Tournemolle is requisitioned—He disarms me.

School life is not remarkable for variety of incident; a country school certainly is not, and ours was no exception to the rule! I have recounted my entry because of this trait in my character that was developed thereby, but if it were to describe that life in all its details I should have nothing to relate beyond a few childish naughtinesses, followed by penitence and impositions, not even worth putting into M. Bouilly's *Jeunes Écoliers*.

A terrible accident happened to the Seminary at Soissons My mother was already reconciled to my conduct in refusing to go there, and this accident made her thank God afresh that I had not entered.

The powder-store of the town, which was situated about fifty mètres from the Seminary, blew up; the college was completely ruined, and eight or ten seminarists were, killed or wounded.

Meanwhile, another of our relatives died: the one who tool me in the night I lost my father. Her daughter Marianne my sister's cousin and mine then left Villers-Cotterets to go and live near her uncle, the Abbé Fortier, who was priest at the little village of Béthisy, five leagues from us and three leagues from Compiègne.

This abbé was supposed to be very rich, and it looked a good thing for my cousin to become his housekeeper; but he was rather a troublesome character.

Had the word been in use at that time, we should have said he was eccentric.

I cannot say what deviation from the path every man ought to follow in deciding upon his vocation had driven the Abbé Fortier into the Church. He was born to make a first-rate captain of dragoons, whilst as it was he made a somewhat odd priest. God forbid I should say he made a bad one!

He was a man of five feet eight inches, built like a Hercules, with an erect carriage, his head held high, and he stepped right foot foremost at each stride like a fencing-master in a fencing school; he was, too, one of the finest billiard players, one of the best huntsmen, and one of the greatest eaters I ever saw.

I do not, of course, even dream of comparing the Abbé Fortier with Boudoux in this last respect. The abbé could eat for a long time and a considerable quantity at once: Boudoux's desire to be always eating was a disease.

One day the Abbé Fortier bet a curé of the neighbourhood that he would eat a hundred eggs at his dinner. The hundred eggs were served up according to recipes in the *Cuisinière bourgeoise*, in twenty different ways.

When they were eaten, he said:

"Good, one ought to play fair and give four extra to the hundred: boil four more eggs—hard."

And he ate the four hard-boiled eggs, after having eaten a hundred cooked in all kinds of ways.

A very curious story is told of his early days. He would be thirty at the time I am referring to, and, as he was sixty-two at the time I am writing about, it must have happened thirty-two years before. He was then only a curate, and one evening he was taking the viaticum to a dying person in the next village.

A certain husband had conceived violent jealousy against him, doubtless without cause, and waited for him in a deep lane down which he was obliged to go from Béthisy in order to reach the village where he was wanted.

When the Abbé Fortier saw this man standing in the middle of the road, with his face drawn with anger and his first clenched, he quickly guessed what was going to happen; but, being a minister of the God of peace and averse to all scandal, he begged him as politely as possible to allow him to pass.

"Oh yes, let you pass, M. le vicaire," said the man in the jeering tones peculiar to our peasants; "you'll not get by so easily!"

"Why should I not pass?" asked the curate.

"Because you have a little account to settle with this poor Bastien."

"I owe you nothing," said the abbé; "allow me to pass; you know well I am being waited for and by one who has not time to wait long."

"He will just have to wait, then," said Bastien, throwing off his jacket and spitting on his hands; "he will just have to wait: if he is in too great a hurry, he must go before."

"Why must he wait?" the abbé demanded, now getting vexed.

"Because I have to give you a drubbing, M. le vicaire."

"Ah! that is it! Is that why you came here, Bastien?"

"Rather."

"It would not take much trouble to remove you, my friend."

"Do you think so?"

"I am certain of it."

The abbé put the viaticum down on the edge of a ditch and said in very reverent accents, "O Lord, O Lord, take neither side, and Thou shalt see a rogue well thrashed."

The abbé kept his word, and the good Lord saw what had been promised.

Then he picked up the viaticum, continued his walk, administered to the sick man and returned quietly home again.

Both Bastien and the abbé were interested in keeping the matter to themselves, and they did so, but a choir-boy had seen the fight, and it became known.

Let it be said to the honour of the abbé that nobody was surprised at the affair.

One day he intended to shoot at Lamotte, but, before beginning his sporting expedition, he had to say mass in the château chapel; he had taken with him his dog Finaud and his choir-boy *quiot* Pierre (which means *little* Pierre), to assist him in his operations.

The church was on the borders of the warren on which they were going to begin.

Now Finaud was a splendid retriever, and the Abbé Fortier, who never cared to shoot without him, had told the servants to shut him up carefully.

After the Gospel the abbé stopped and listened as he heard a well-known bark in the warren.

He listened for a minute; then he turned, and saw that the choir-boy was also listening, with a smile on his lips.

"Tell me, quiot Pierre," said the abbé, "isn't that Finaud's bark I hear over there?"

"Yes, M. l'abbé; they have let him loose, and he is after a rabbit."

"Ah! well!" replied the abbé, "the rabbit can be quite easy; we shall get him in any case."

And he went on saying mass.

Mass over, Finaud led the way.

The abbé took his gun, followed the trail and killed the rabbit.

This was the same choir-boy who told the story about Bastien. He told the second, as he had told the first, and there were many more, but some of them would not even bear relating by a choir-boy.

So Marianne went to live with her uncle Fortier, who, at the age of sixty-two, was reputed to be simply a great sportsman and a great eater; maybe this opinion of him was not quite right.

He gave her a wonderfully good reception, installed her at the parsonage, and, as my cousin Marianne was very fond of me, he allowed her to bring me back with her the next visit she paid to Villers-Cotterets, which was during my holidays in 1812.

When the holidays began, my cousin and I both perched on the back of one donkey. Picard, the fellow who used to tell me such fine stories at the forge, took a stick to beat the ass with, and we set off.

This journey, like all childish journeyings, was full of surprises for me. I remember seeing for a long time on our left a mountain with a ruin on the top of it, which seemed to me like an Alp or one of the Cordilleras; I have seen it since, and it did not look any higher than Montmartre.

I remember also seeing a tower on my right, which seemed so high to me that I asked if it were not the tower of Babel.

The mountain was the knoll of Montigny.

The tower was the tower of Vez.

We reached our destination after a journey that had seemed to me inordinately long, but had only lasted seven or eight hours; we went at the pace of Joseph and the Virgin Mary on their flight into Egypt.

However, we arrived at last. It was the right season to stop with Uncle Fortier, for it was early in September, and there was a splendid arbour of vines, from which hung bunches of grapes rivalling those of the Promised Land. There was also a wild plum tree laden with plums in a small courtyard; and, finally, an immense garden full of peaches, apricots and pears.

Moreover, shooting was just about to begin.

The Abbé Fortier gave me a very kind welcome, although he uttered several grunts which showed I was not in every respect satisfactory to him.

The abbé was a very learned man; he had Greek and Latin at his finger ends; he greeted me in the tongue of Cicero; I attempted to reply, and made three errors in five words.

He was transfixed.

That was my first intellectual humiliation. I will give the second in its right place.

I tried to recover my ground in natural history and mythology, but the abbé was proficient in both, and I sighed, crestfallen.

I was vanquished.

Directly I was beaten and avowed my error like Porus, the victor became as clement as Alexander.

The abbé began his fascination over me by the excellence of his dinner. If he ate well, he drank still better.

I was lost in admiration before this man—I had never imagined such curés: the Abbé Fortier came near to reconciling me to the Seminary.

Next day after mass the Abbé Fortier began his first day's shooting. Mass was not over before half-past eight; but not a soul was allowed to shoot a partridge upon the preserves until the Abbé Fortier had been seen to go by, his cassock tucked up, the game-bag on his back, a gun on shoulder, preceded by Finaud and followed by Diane.

He had a third acolyte this time, for I was with him. My recollections of hunting were lost in the obscurity of my early infancy; they went back to the days of my father and Mocquet. As in Racine's tragedies, all that happened to me at that period of my existence consisted of the hunting stories that were told me.

This time, I took some part in the action.

The abbé was an excellent shot, and there was abundance of game: he killed a dozen partridges and two or three hares.

I covered as much ground as Diane, and as each head of game fell, I rushed to pick it up, in emulation of the dogs.

No one shoots without swearing a bit at his dogs; the Abbé Fortier swore a good deal; and all these characteristics made up an entirely different picture of an abbé in my mind: he had nothing in common with the Abbé Grégoire.

From that day I was convinced there were two kinds of priests.

Since I have lived in Italy, and, above all, in Rome, I have discovered a third.

Oh! what a happy day that opening day of the shooting season was! How well I remember it! It made me the indefatigable sportsman I have since been, the despair of gamekeepers!

The abbé, on his side, was well pleased with my power of walking, which he found greatly superior to my brains; he made me some jeering compliments upon it, and I felt the full value of them; but he had given me so much pleasure that I had not the courage to be angry with him.

I remained a fortnight with the Abbé Fortier, and I would fain have stayed with him all my life; but my mother wanted me home: it was my first long absence. And she, poor woman, had wanted to send me to a Seminary! She wrote that she should die of ennui if they did not send me back soon.

The abbé shrugged his shoulders and said:

"Very well, let him be sent back!"

Sensitiveness was not a weakness the abbé suffered from.

They put me on a donkey and took me to Crépy, where, twice a week, there was a connection with Villers-Cotterets by means of an old woman, called mother Sabot, and her ass.

I passed from my ass to mother Sabot's, and the same evening I was back at Villers-Cotterets.

I found a fresh person installed at home—my future brother-in-law.

He was a young man of about twenty-six or twenty-seven, who, although not good-looking, had such a refined and intellectual type of face, it might easily have been taken for beauty. He was, besides, remarkably skilful at all physical exercises, clever at fencing, able to hit a cork out of a bottle with a bullet from his pistol at twenty-five paces off, without touching the bottle, a perfect horseman and, although not in the front rank as a sportsman, was considered a good shot.

He had been to our house already several times before I went away, and I was great chums with his dog, Figaro, whose reputation for cleverness was as great among dogs as his master's was among men.

I had the warmest of welcomes from everybody, and specially from this young man, whose name was Victor Letellier. He was very much in love with my sister, and wanted to make allies of all who surrounded her, even of me.

"My dear Alexandre," he said, when he caught sight of me, "something has been lying on my chimney-piece for you for a fortnight. I do not want to tell you what it is—go and fetch it for yourself."

I rushed off at full speed, Victor lived with M. Picot at l'Épée, the house wherein my father had died.

"Open M. Letellier's door for me," I cried, as I ran into the kitchen; "he has sent me to fetch something he has left on the mantelshelf."

They opened the door. I ran to the chimney-piece, and there, in the middle of two or three piles of money, spurs, riding-whips, bootjacks, and other objects, I saw a small pocket-pistol, quite a tiny one, upon which I pounced unhesitatingly, for I knew it was the thing intended for me.

That present was one of the first I ever received, and it gave me great joy.

But it was not enough to have the pistol, I must also have the means wherewith to enjoy it. I looked all round me: it was not difficult to find what I wanted in a sportsman's room: I was hunting for powder. I found a powder-horn, and poured half its contents into another horn; then I bolted off to a part of the park which was called the "parterre," that is to say, a stretch before the forest began.

Then began a fusillade which only ended with my last grain of powder, and which collected all the street urchins of the town. At the end of half an hour my mother was warned that I was devoting myself to a most terrific fire practice.

My mother always feared some accident would happen to me, for she loved me much. Once, one of our friends, whose name, M. Danré de Vouty, I have already mentioned, came to our house pale and bleeding. He had been shooting near Villers-Cotterets; it was winter, and in jumping over a ditch some snow got down his gun-barrel; the gun had burst, and the explosion had carried off part of his left hand.

Doctor Lécosse was called in, and at once amputated the thumb. M. Danré recovered, after a fearful attack of fever, but he was maimed for life.

Thus, every time the question of guns or pistols or any sort of firearms was brought up, my mother pictured me being brought home pale and bleeding like M. Danré de Vouty; she was so frightened that I took pity on her, and nearly gave up the idea of ever becoming a Hippolytus or a Nimrod.

Then I would return to my bow and arrows, but here was a fresh subject of alarm for my mother. One of our neighbours, a man called Bruyant (please remember this name, for we shall come across it again in an important event), had had, like Philip of Macedon, his right eye destroyed by an arrow.

My mother's terror, therefore, was great when she learnt that I had been supplied with a pistol and that I had munitions wherewith to practise; but it was very hard work to run after me, for my legs had grown since the adventure of Lebègue; moreover, the forest was my friend; as Bas-de-Cuir knew every nook and corner of his woods, so did I know all the turns and by-ways in ours. I could have hidden there three days without returning. Therefore, they decided to make use of the law.

There lived at the town hall a sort of deputy police agent, who almost fulfilled the office of a commissary: he cried the news of the day to the beating of a drum, as is still done in some country places; in summer, he killed stray dogs, not by shooting, but with a great hunting-knife; in winter, he broke the ice off the streams, and swept the snow from our doors.

His name was Tournemolle.

They told him, and he lay in wait for my return to my mother; then he appeared behind me.

When I saw Tournemolle, I foresaw something dreadful was going to happen.

He had come, in the name of all the inhabitants, who were disturbed by the noise of the pistol-shots, to ask, nay, if needs be to insist on, the disarmament of the culprit.

There was a struggle; but strength was on the side of authority, and the culprit was disarmed.

My joy was, therefore, short-lived; it had not even lasted as long as do the roses. Within the space of one hour, I had become the happy owner of a pistol, I had used up my powder, I had returned home and I had been disarmed by Tournemolle.

That disarmament was a terrible disgrace for me, such an ignominy that not even the grave news which reached us next day was able to cause me to forget it.

The next day was the 23rd of September 1812, when Paris saw the conspiracy of Mallet, whilst Napoleon from Moscow was dating his decree upon the Constitution of the Théâtre-Français, and upon the good men of Cambrai.

God had begun to withdraw His hand from this man. He had forced the battle of Moskova in the teeth of a weakened army and increasing distrust in his ability; he had left eleven of his generals dead on the field; he wrote to the bishops to sing *Te Deums*, for it was necessary to reassure Paris and to reassure himself; then he entered Moscow, believing that it was like any other capital, and that evening Moscow revealed itself by its first conflagrations.

Then, instead of taking a decisive course of action, such as to march on St. Petersburg or to return to Paris; instead of establishing his winter quarters in the heart of Russia, as Cæsar did in the heart of Gaul, he hesitated, he became worried, he felt he had adventured too far, and was, maybe, lost.

By a strange coincidence it was at this moment that, at Paris, before even present embarrassment and reverses to come had made themselves felt, Mallet's conspiracy burst out, seized hold of the Colossus in the full tide of his power, bound him, shook him to his foundations, and if it did not overthrow him, at any rate proved he could be overthrown.

On the 29th, Mallet, Lahorie, and Guidai were shot on the plain of Grenelle.

At length Napoleon made up his mind. For the first time he had taken a capital to no purpose; for the first time he beat a retreat after victories. The snow which fell on the 13th October settled the conqueror's vacillations, and the Almighty saved his pride by allowing him one last consolation—he could say he had been beaten by climate and not by man.

On the 19th of October Napoleon left Moscow, deputing the duc de Treviso to seize the Kremlin and to carry off the cross of the great Ivan, which he intended for the dome of the Invalides, and which he had to leave behind on his journey, lacking arms to carry it farther.

At last, on November the 18th, Napoleon reached the Tuileries at eleven o'clock at night, went close to a large fire, warmed himself, rubbed his hands, and said: "Decidedly it is better here than at Moscow."

That was the funeral oration over the finest army ever raised!

O Varus!... Varus!...

CHAPTER VIII

A political chronology—Trouble follows trouble—The fire at the farm at Noue—Death of Stanislas Picot—The hiding-place for the louis d'or—The Cossacks—The haricot mutton.

It would be indeed too preposterous of me to take up public attention with the feats and performances of an urchin of twelve, when, for two years, we were to pass through such grave events.

The decline of the Man of Destiny was rapid: he was sustained for a brief while by the victories of Lutzen, Bautzen, and Wurschen, but he left behind him two of his most faithful lieutenants—the dukes of Istria and Duroc. There was no danger of bullets striking down those who intended to betray him.

He was doomed—England had bought his ruin.

Will you learn at what price? On 14th June, 1813, she paid Prussia 660,660 livres sterling; on the 15th, 1,333,334 livres sterling to Russia; and finally, on 12th August, 500,000 livres sterling to Austria.

We see how scrupulous in this matter was his father-in-law, François; he refrained from selling his son-in-law until two months after the others, and for 160,000 livres sterling less than Prussia.

But what did that matter? Bonaparte could note down in his red-letter book that he became the son-in-law of a Cæsar and the nephew of King Louis XVI.

That was the height of his ambition. What was there to be sorry for when that ambition was once satisfied?

On the 16th and 18th of October, 117,000 rounds of cannon were fired off at Leipzig, 111,000 more at Malplaquet.

Each round cost two louis.

They celebrated the death service of the Empire in right regal style!

It was in this way that Napoleon lost another of his faithful followers, Poniatowski, who had been made a marshal on the 16th and who was drowned on the 19th, in the river Elster.

On the 1st of November the emperor sent twenty standards to Paris.

On the 8th the battle of Mochest took place, the last of the campaign.

On the 9th the emperor returned to Saint-Cloud.

On the 12th the allied armies entered Dusseldorf.

On the 13th the kings of Prussia and of Bavaria reached Frankfort.

On the 15th, 300,000 conscripts were mobilised.

On the 16th the emperor went hunting on foot on the plains of Satory.

On the 22nd he was present at a representation at the Opera, while the Russians were entering Amsterdam.

On the 2nd December the emperor witnessed a performance at the Odéon, while the allied armies were crossing the Rhine at Dusseldorf.

On the 6th the Prince of Orange, who had landed in Holland on the 30th November, issued a proclamation to the Dutch.

On the 17th the Allies crossed the Rhine at different points in Alsace.

On the 23rd they occupied Neuchâtel.

On the 31st they entered Geneva.

And with this news closed the year 1813.

The year 1814 was to see a continuation of these reverses and the beginning of defections.

On the 3rd January the Allies took Colmar.

On the 6th they invested Besançon; and Murat, who had re-conquered Naples, signed an armistice with England.

On the 7 h the Allies entered Dôle.

On the 8th Murat concluded a treaty of alliance with Austria.

On the 10th the Allies invested Landau and took Forbach.

On the 12th Murat signed a treaty of alliance with England.

On the 16th the Allies seized Langres.

On the 17th Murat declared war against France.

On the 21st the Allies took Châlons-sur-Saône.

On the 22nd Murat entered Rome.

Finally, on the 24th, the emperor left Paris to return to his army, on the 27th he took up the offensive again, and began that wonderful campaign of 1814, which lasted sixty-seven days, and during which, the end being the abdication at Fontainebleau, he showed his marvellous genius to greater effect than in taking Milan or Cairo, Berlin, Vienna, or Moscow.

None the less his hour had come; in vain had the Titan heaped Pelion upon Ossa, Champaubert on Montmirail—his hour had come, and he was to fall overwhelmed....

The sound of cannon boomed in my hearing for the first time.

I heard it in the foldyard of a farm belonging to M. Picot of Noue—a quarter of a league off Villers-Cotterets.

"Misfortunes come in flocks," says a Russian proverb; and a host of misfortunes had flown over and beaten against the head of that good man. The farm at Noue had been one of the finest in Villers-Cotterets, and M. Picot one of the most prosperous farmers.

But in 1812, I think it was, they stacked a damp crop in his barns, and one night the straw kindled, and we were awakened by the tocsin and by cries of "Fire!"

Everybody realises the dreadfulness of that cry in the middle of the night and in a little town: all Villers-Cotterets got up instantly and rushed to the burning farm.

I do not know a more splendid sight than a tremendous fire, such as that one. The farm blazed the whole length of its barns and stables, presenting a curtain three or four hundred paces in extent, from behind which came the lowing of cattle, the whinnying of horses, the bleating of sheep.

Everything was burnt, buildings and live-stock; for animals will not stir when they smell fire.

That fire was the first serious catastrophe I was ever present at, and it left a deep impression on my memory.

They did not get the mastery over the fire till next day, and the loss was enormous. Fortunately, as we have said, M. Picot was very rich.

The following year came another misfortune. M. Picot had two sons and a daughter. The eldest of his sons was eight or ten years, the younger only two or three, my senior.

Consequently I had scarcely anything to do with the eldest, who treated me like a little boy, but I was extremely friendly with the younger, whose name was Stanislas.

One day, my mother came into my room, in a great state of mind.

"There, now," she said, "never ask me to let you play with firearms again."

"Why not, mother?"

"Stanislas has just wounded himself, perhaps mortally."

"Oh! my goodness, where is he?"

"At his father's. Go and see him."

I set off running, and covered the quarter of a league in six or seven minutes. When I reached the farm, I saw a long trail of blood.

Everybody was in such a state of consternation that no one asked me where I was going. I crossed the yards, I went through the kitchen and I slipped into the room where Stanislas was. They were just putting the first bandage on the wound; the surgeon was there, with his surgical case open, his hands covered with blood. The poor sufferer was leaning back, clasping his mother's neck with both his arms as she bent over him.

They saw me, and told me to approach the bed. Stanislas kissed me, and thanked me for coming to see him. He was horribly pale.

He was ordered quiet before everything, so everybody, myself among the number, was told to go away.

This is how the accident happened: Stanislas was out shooting with his father, and had nearly done; he was nearing the farm, which he was just going to enter, when he heard a gun-shot.

The better to see who had fired it, and whether the shooter had killed anything, Stanislas climbed a post at the corner of a wall; but he forgot to unload his gun first, and unconsciously he leant his thigh against the barrel. His dog seeing him on the post, tried to reach him, standing on his hind legs, and with his fore paws leant on the gun-lock. The gun went off, and Stanislas received the full charge of partridge-shot in the neck of the femur.

It was this ghastly wound which the surgeon had just dressed when I arrived. For two days they were hopeful, but lockjaw set in on the third day, and Stanislas died.

The manner in which he met his death was an unending source of exhortation on my mother's part: she declared she should never be easy until I gave up hunting altogether. But, in spite of the impression which this death made upon me, I would not give up anything.

Whenever I met Madame Picot, after the death of Stanislas, she showed great kindness to me, no doubt on account of my boyish friendship with her son.

Her daughter, too, who was very friendly with my sister, was most cordial to me, and was the only one among grown-up people who never made fun of my absurdities.

This excellent and good-looking lady was called Éléonore Picot, or, more often, *Picote*.

Now to return to account for my being in the farmyard at Noue when I heard the firing of cannon for the first time. I have been sent far afield in what I have just related, and I must return.

Since the battle of Leipzig, one idea had been in everybody's mind, namely, that what had not happened in 1792 or in 1793 was now about to take place—there would be an invasion of France.

Those who did not live through that period can have no idea to what a pitch of execration the name of Napoleon had reached in the hearts of the mothers of France.

During 1813 and 1814 the old enthusiasm died down; for it was not for the sake of France, our common mother, nor for Liberty, the goddess of us all, that the mothers were sacrificing their children: it was to the ambition, the selfishness, the pride of one man.

Thanks to the successive levies, made in 1811 to 1814, thanks to the million of men squandered in the valleys and on the mountains of Spain, in the snows and in the rivers of Russia, in the swamps of Saxony and on the sands of Poland, the generation of men between twenty and twenty-two years of age had disappeared.

The very wealthiest people had fruitlessly purchased one, two, or even three substitutes, for which they had paid as much as 10,000, 12,000, or 15,000 francs. But Napoleon had invented his Guard of Honour, a relentless and fatal organisation for recruiting his army, which allowed of no substitutes, so that the wealthiest and therefore the most privileged classes were compelled to go to war with the rest.

Conscription began at sixteen, and men remained liable to service to the age of forty.

Mothers counted up the ages of their boys with alarm, and most gladly would they have wrestled with time to stop the days which were flying by all too quickly for them.

More than once my mother pressed me to her breast suddenly, with a suppressed sigh, and tears came into her eyes.

"What is the matter, mother?" I would ask.

"Oh! when I think," she exclaimed, "that in four years you will have to be a soldier, that that man will snatch you from me, he who has always taken away and never given anything in return, and that he will send you to be killed on a field of battle like Moskova or Leipzig!... Oh, my child! my poor child!"

My mother only expressed a general feeling, but the hatred of her fellows was expressed in different ways, according to their different temperaments and characters; with my mother, as we have seen, it was in sighs and tears; with other mothers, it would be in fierce threats; with others, insulting epithets.

I remember, there lived on the place de la Fontaine the wife of a gunsmith, whose son was at the Abbé Grégoire's school with me; her name was Madame Montagnon. During the heat of summer afternoons, when the greatest heat of the day had declined, she sat at her threshold with her spinning-wheel, and all the time she was spinning she sang a song against Bonaparte.

I only remember the first four lines of it, which begun thus:—

"Le Corse de Madame Ango
N'est pas le Corse de la Corse,
Car le Corse de Marengo
Est d'une bien plus dure écorce."

And—as Mademoiselle Pivert re-read the famous volume of *The Thousand and One Nights*, which contained the story of *The Wonderful Lamp*, every day in the week—so Madame Montagnon had scarcely finished the last couplet against the Corsican of Marengo when she began the first over again.

Now it will be readily understood that this hatred, which began to show itself after the Russian disasters, was aggravated by terror in proportion as the enemy drew nearer, step by step, town by town, narrowing the circle being drawn round France.

Finally, at the beginning of 1814, it suddenly became known that the enemy had set foot on French soil.

By that time all confidence in Napoleon's genius had disappeared. That stupendous adventurer's genius was his good fortune.

Now, God, in His inscrutable purposes, had designed his fall and had deserted him.

People not merely ceased to believe in him, but they ceased to hope.

Those who had anything to fear or to expect from a political movement, all those skin-changing serpents that live on different Governments as they come and go, already began to lay their plans—some to lessen their fears, others to augment their expectations. They began to feel, moreover, that Napoleon was not France; but that they had, so to speak, taken the heroic tenant on a lease, and the lease was up—France was prepared to bear the damages, but not to renew the lease.

You could still hear people saying: "Napoleon has beaten the enemy at Brienne; the Prussians are retreating to Bar"—but at the same time they said: "The Russians are marching on Troyes." We certainly read in the *Moniteur* that we had beaten them at Rosnay and on the road to Vitry; but at the same time that this bulletin was published appeared the first Royalist manifesto. We were routing the Allies at Champaubert and at Montmirail, but the duc d'Angoulême was issuing a proclamation dated from Saint Jean-de-Luz.

At each victory, Napoleon was using up his men, and losing ten leagues of ground. Wherever he fought personally, the enemy was beaten, but he could not be in every place at once.

Every moment was bringing the roar of cannons nearer to us, though we had not actually heard them yet.

There had been fighting at Château-Thierry; and at Nogent; and Laon was occupied.

Everyone began hiding his valuables, burying what he considered most precious.

We had a cellar which was reached through a trap-door; my mother filled it with linen, furniture, mattresses, she had the trap-door taken away and the whole room re-floored; so no treasure-seekers could see the exact spot to fasten upon.

Then she put thirty old louis in a box, she put this box in a small leather bag, she drove a stake in the garden and in the hole made by the stake she slipped the box.

Who on earth would find a box planted vertically in the very middle of a garden? It would have required a wizard to find it there.

We could not have found it again ourselves if I had not made a guiding mark on the wall.

One fine day we saw some soldiers come past, flying at full speed. Soissons had just been taken; they had leapt their horses over the ramparts, and six or eight had been killed or badly injured; three or four had escaped.

My poor mother began now to be frightened in real earnest, and her fear took the form of cooking an enormous haricot of mutton. The reader may well ask why her fear took that peculiar form.

Fearful pictures had been spread over the country of Cossacks from the Don, the Volga and the Borysthenes: making them look as hideous as possible. They were depicted mounted on hideous scarecrows, wearing caps made of wild beasts' skins, armed with lances, bows and arrows. A combination of utter impossibilities, one would have said.

Yet there were optimists who, in spite of these awful pictures, said that the Cossacks were brave men at heart, much less wicked than they looked to be, and that, provided we fed them well enough and gave them plenty to drink, they would do us no manner of harm.

Hence my mother's huge stew of mutton—it was for them to eat.

In the matter of drink, we did not give them our cellar (for we have seen to what use my mother had put it), but we set them aside our wine-bin, and they could then draw what Soissons' wine they liked.

Then, finally, if, in spite of the haricot mutton and the Soissons' wine, they still proved too objectionable, we were to escape by way of the quarry.

We will now describe what this was.

CHAPTER IX

The quarry—Frenchmen eat the haricot cooked for the Cossacks—The Duc de Treviso—He allows himself to be surprised—Ducoudray the hosier—Terrors.

Five or six hundred steps from the farmhouse at home, in the middle of open country, scattered over with dwarf juniper trees, where the rocks jutted out of the earth all round, as the bones of a consumptive patient stick out through his skin, an excavation suddenly opens similar to those one meets at every turn in the Campagna of Rome. This excavation looks like a cave of Cumæ or an air-hole of Avernus. When you bend over its opening you can hear the roar which astonishes one on holding a shell to the ear—only this roar is on a greater and more frightful and more gigantic scale; then, if you try for a moment to pierce through the darkness, which increases as the cavern deepens, you can make out a rock, sticking up perpendicularly, about twenty-five or thirty feet below you, and burying its base in the bowels of the earth at a steep angle.

This is the entrance to the quarry.

You ask to what quarry?

To *the* quarry, doubtless, since it was always called "The Quarry"—just as Rome was called *The City—Urbs*.

When, by the help of a ladder, you descend the twenty-five or thirty feet, you reach a platform from which you slide down the steep slope for five or six feet, and then you find yourself at the entrance of an immense labyrinth—compared with which that of the Cretan Dædalus was but a child's garden in a toy box.

Who had hewn out these great catacombs? What town had being in these unknown depths? It would indeed be difficult to tell.

Its subterranean passages had certainly communicated with some larger opening pointing to further undermining. The opening by which one entered was, as we have said, merely a crack, too narrow to have ever disgorged the quantity of stones missing from the bare sides of the mountain.

It was in this quarry, then, that half the people of Villers-Cotterets had taken refuge under stress of terror.

A large encampment had been set up; a regular village, inhabited by five or six hundred people, in the midst of the square hall of granite, under a granite vault upheld by granite pillars; nearly a quarter of a league from the opening, at a depth of a hundred or a hundred and fifty feet.

My mother was one of the first who had chosen and secured and marked out her allotment in it; and there we carried mattresses, blankets, a table and some books.

So, when the first alarm came, we had but to leave Villers-Cotterets and to hide in the quarry.

Before resorting to this extremity, my mother meant to try every means of conciliation, and one of her means of conciliation, the one she set most store by, was her haricot mutton and her Soissons wines.

But man proposes and God disposes. After three days of hanging over the fire, after three days of lying in the cellar, the haricot mutton was eaten and the wine was drunk by Frenchmen.

Marshal Mortier's Corps, with the remnant of the Young Guard, and a dozen of cannon, came; they were commissioned to defend the entrance to the forest.

Great was our joy! It was glorious to see these fine young fellows, full of hope and courage, instead of the hideous-looking Cossacks we had been expecting.

Youth never despairs, for it is still in harmony with the divine. It was not so with the old generals, above all with the duc de Treviso.

There was a strange lassitude in all the men who had followed the fortunes of the emperor. Their worldly position was secured; they had reached the zenith of their fortunes by becoming marshals; while Napoleon—that hankerer after the unattainable—still went on coveting something more!

Therefore, those who were not left sleeping dead and bleeding on the battle-fields, stopped, harassed, upon the road of his retreat; shaking their heads at his never-resting, feverish course; and saying: "It is right enough for that man of iron, but we—we are not able to follow him any further."

Villers-Cotterets was one of these halting-places where the duc de Treviso stopped, overpowered by fatigue. We saw him pass by on horseback in the morning and reconnoitre the forest, guided by the inspector, M. Deviolaine.

My mother took the old tricoloured cockade out of my father's hat, which had remained there since the Egyptian Campaign, and carried it to M. Deviolaine, with a blunderbuss.

M. Deviolaine put the cockade in his hat, and the blunderbuss at his saddle-bow.

I can still remember the marshal, that veteran of our earliest battles, who escaped, throughout all our wars, the grapeshot of Prussia, of England, of Russia and of Austria, only to fall at last on the boulevard du Temple by Fieschi's infernal machine.

The giant passed by, doubled up on his horse; one would have said then that a child would have been strong enough to defeat that invincible warrior.

So long as Hercules crowned carried the world on his own shoulders, all went well; but, when he shifted the least portion upon the shoulders of his lieutenants, they gave way beneath the weight.

When evening came there was a grand dinner-party at M. Deviolaine's, to which I was taken; and the marshal took me up on his knees and fondled me: for he had known my father.

I asked him for news of my godfather Brune; he was in disgrace, or on the verge of it.

The dinner was a sad affair, the evening depressing. The marshal retired early, went to bed and slept. We were awakened at midnight by the sound of firing. Fighting was going on in the parterre. The marshal had been careless about his sentries; the enemy had seized his park, and he only saved himself by escaping, half-dressed, by a back-door, from M. Deviolaine's house.

In the morning the enemy had disappeared, taking away our dozen pieces of artillery.

The same day the marshal retired, I think, to Compiègne, and the town was deserted.

The enemy would surely not be long in appearing after this; so my mother set to work on a second haricot mutton.

Our days passed in constant alarms. When a couple of horsemen were seen on the highroad, the cry would go forth, "The Cossacks! the Cossacks!" Then a great crowd of people would run along the streets, children crying, shutters and doors banging as they fled, and the town would assume the funereal aspect of a city of the dead.

In spite of my mother's haricot mutton, which boiled unceasingly in the copper, and her Soissonais wine, ready for the corkscrew, she grew frightened with the rest, shut our door, and, pressing me to her breast, agitated and trembling, she would retire into a far corner.

Of course there were no more classes amid all these alarms; no more college; no more Abbé Grégoire.

I am wrong: the Abbé Grégoire was, on the contrary, more than ever present.

The Abbé Grégoire was calmness itself, and accordingly a great comfort all round. He went from house to house reassuring everybody, pointing out that evil comes from evil, and that if no ill was done to these much dreaded Cossacks, they, on their side, would do none to us.

Moreover, it would be to their interest not to behave too outrageously. When at Villers-Cotterets, they would find themselves in the midst of a vast forest, occupied by thirty or forty foresters, who knew every turning and winding better than Osman knew those of the Seraglio, and who were all of them more or less capable of putting a bullet into a crown-piece at a hundred paces distance. These were considerations which even Cossacks could appreciate highly.

Meanwhile, time was passing by; there was fighting at Mormant, at Montmirail, at Montereau. We were assured that at this latter battle Bonaparte (to use his own expression), by turning back into an artillery-man, had saved Napoleon.

We had retaken Soissons on the 19th February, and the haricot had been on the fire for five days. No one expected any more Cossacks to come, at least for some time, so we ate the haricot mutton. We received more reassuring news; and there was even talk of an armistice to be concluded with the Emperor of Austria, through the intervention of the Prince of Lichtenstein. Napoleon had re-entered Troyes on the 24th, and had dismissed the prefect; finally, conferences had taken place at Largny for suspension of hostilities.

But soon the fire burst out again, rekindled by some spark or other, and we learnt, in quick succession, of fighting at Bar-sur-Aube, at Meaux, and of the surrender of la Fère.

The enemy was coming nearer and nearer to us.

My mother set to work on a third haricot mutton.

Suddenly, in the middle of a foggy February morning, again the cry of "The Cossacks!" sounded, we heard the galloping of several horses, and we saw about fifteen long-bearded cavaliers, with tall lances, ride through the rue de Soissons; they seemed, indeed, to be more like desperate runaways than threatening conquerors.

As they advanced, doors and windows were shut. Their horses, urged at full gallop, traversed the whole length of the rue de Largny; then they retraced their steps, galloping still, and plunged again into the rue de Soissons, whence they departed, disappearing like a misty and hideous dream.

They were scarcely out of sight before firing was heard.

The sound made my mother tremble; but powder had its usual effect on me; I slipped out of her hands, I escaped from her and ran off to the beginning of the rue de Soissons in spite of her cries. The Cossacks had entirely disappeared.

A woman stood on the threshold of an open door wringing her hands.

She was the wife of a retail hosier named Ducoudray.

The neighbours gradually undid their doors at the sound of her cries, and at her gestures of despair ran up and collected round the door.

I was one of the first to arrive, and I learnt the reason for her cries and her despair.

At the approach of the Cossacks, the hosier had closed his door in fear and trembling, having opened it out of curiosity after their first passage. As they passed, one of the riders discharged his pistol at the shut door, just as though it had been a target. The bullet pierced the door and hit M. Ducoudray in the throat, breaking his spine.

He was lying on the ground, with his head resting on his daughter's knees, torrents of blood flowing from his wound, which had severed an artery.

Death had been instantaneous; he had already ceased to breathe.

Hence the cries, hence the despair of his wife.

As for the Cossacks, they had disappeared as they had come, and, if they had not left this bloody testimony in their wake, the town would have imagined their visit had been a bad dream.

Half from fear, and half in order to bear this important news, I ran back home full speed, and at the corner of the street I met my mother; she had already heard the news.

This time neither the haricot mutton nor the Soissonais wine appeared to her a safe shield against our impending dangers. She pictured the Cossacks passing in front of our door, instead of passing before that of M. Ducoudray; she saw the bullet flying through the door, and myself stretched, bleeding and dying from the pistol-shot before her eyes. We had a sort of housekeeper whom we called "the Queen." My mother left her third haricot mutton and her wine of Soissons to the Queen, bade her watch over the house, took me by the hand and dragged me at a frantic pace towards the quarry.

We turned as we left the town, and we saw the troop of Cossacks climbing a long hill at a gallop, the hill of Dampleux. They were a little detachment that had lost its way, and kept straying even further afield. I afterwards heard it said that not one of those twelve or fifteen men ever left the forest.

My mother and I fled on; running as only people can run under the influence of terror, hot and breathless. We told whom we met not only of the presence of the Cossacks, but also of the assassination they had perpetrated ten minutes previously.

Everyone who was not already in the quarry at once retreated to it; the last man who descended removed the ladder, and, for twenty-four hours, not one of the colony had the courage to go near the opening.

By degrees this first terror subsided, and people ventured to put their noses outside. The bravest ascended to the earth's surface, went to learn what was happening, and found that the Cossacks had completely disappeared, and that, except for the misfortune that had occurred the day before, the town was quiet.

My mother then decided to accept the offer made her by Madame Picot; to take me to spend the day at the farm, and only to return to the quarry to sleep there at night.

If anything fresh happened we were to be warned of it instantly by one of the many labourers employed on M. Picot's estate, who were to unyoke a horse from plough or harrow and to ride off in hot haste to give the alarm at the farm.

Five or six days passed in this fashion, during which we learnt in succession of the battles of Lizy, of St Julien, and of Bar-sur-Seine.

At length one day, as I have said, we heard from the farmyard the roaring of cannon.

There was fighting going on at Neuilly-Saint-Front.

The night after the battle, I went to sleep with my head filled with the noise of battle, and I dreamt that the Cossacks came down into the quarry.

When morning came, I repeated this dream to my mother, and it terrified her to such an extent that she made up her mind we should set off next day.

Where were we to go? She had absolutely no idea; but she fancied by changing places she might perhaps exorcise the danger.

CHAPTER X

The return to Villers-Cotterets, and what we met on the way—The box with the thirty louis in it—The leather-bag—The mole—Our departure—The journey—The arrival at Mesnil and our sojourn there—King Joseph—The King of Rome—We leave Mesnil—Our visit to Crespy in Valois—The dead and wounded—The surrender of Paris—The isle of Elba.

When the resolution was made, it was carried into execution that very day. My mother and I climbed to the highest elevation about the farm, we explored all round, and, when we could not discover any appearance of Cossacks, we ventured to return to the town.

We had hardly gone a hundred steps before we met a clerk called Crétet on horseback. He was a good sort of lad, who had been in my brother-in-law's employment.

He was going from house to house.

"What are you looking for?" my mother asked.

"I am hunting for a carriage, a cab, a wagon, a berlin, or any sort of conveyance to harness my horse to and set off in," he said; "Mademoiselle Adélaïde does not want to stay in Villers-Cotterets any longer."

Mademoiselle Adélaïde was an old, humpbacked spinster, possessing several thousand francs of income, towards which I suspect Crétet had leanings.

"Ah! now that is lucky!" exclaimed my mother; "it is exactly what we are looking out for too. May we leave with you? You are two in number, and we two; we shall travel at half the cost."

It is always cheaper to travel four, rather than two; so the offer was accepted.

A spring cart was found possessing a minimum of springs, and it was settled that we should leave the same evening.

My mother returned to Villers-Cotterets to collect some clothing necessary for our journey, and, first and foremost, to extract the famous treasure of thirty louis from its hole.

We entered the house, still guarded by "the Queen"; then we went into the garden; we recognised the spot where we had buried our treasure, and I took a spade and set to work to dig.

At the third or fourth shovelful of earth I began to be uneasy. I looked at my mother, and I saw that she shared my anxiety.

There was no more sign of the box than if it had never existed. I returned to the guiding mark, I measured the steps; no—I had not made any mistake.

Then I set to work to dig all round my first hole,—all in vain; it was lost labour.

I returned to the middle hole, and continued digging deeper and deeper.

Suddenly I uttered a cry of delight. I had caught sight of the strings of the leather bag.

I pulled the strings, and the leather bag came up—but ... it was empty!

A hole had been made in the bottom of it.

Affairs were growing mysterious. Why in the world, if they had stolen the box, had they troubled to make a hole in the leather bag to take the money out? It would have been much easier to have carried off the whole lot; receptacle and its contents together.

A brilliant idea occurred to me. I zealously continued my digging, and a foot and a half deeper down my spade hit at last against an obstacle.

"Here is the box!" I cried.

And the box it was indeed.

A mole, attracted by the smell of the leather enclosed, had burrowed to get at it. It had disturbed the soil, and the box, dragged down by its own weight, had fallen into the pit made by the blind miner.

My mother quickly opened the box, and found that not one louis was missing.

The cart was loaded that evening, the horse put into the shafts, and we set off along the road to Paris.

I was enchanted: we were about to pay a second visit to the capital of the civilised world, and, although it was in a deplorable condition, I was no less anxious to see it.

Unfortunately we were not rich enough, with our few louis, to stay in Paris. This was a matter that had not occurred to me.

It was decided to stop in a village where living would be cheap.

The first night we got as far as Nanteuil, and put up at an inn which my father used to frequent when we went to Paris. Then, next morning, very early, we resumed our journey.

About one o'clock we reached the steep ascent of Dammartin, and got down from our conveyance to ease the horse a little.

Fighting was going on somewhere; we could hear the firing distinctly, like the thunder of a distant storm.

We even seemed to be travelling in the direction of the roar of the cannon; but, so blind is fear, that if the enemy had been in front of us my mother would rather have continued her course than turn back.

We passed through Dammartin without stopping, except to ask the news. No one knew anything very definite. The Count d'Artois was at Nancy; the allied sovereigns at Nogent-sur-Seine. The enemy was advancing upon Paris from all sides—that was all they could tell us.

We baited our horse at Villeneuve-Saint-Georges; then, when we had dined, we continued on our way, and reached Mesnil about eight in the evening.

We stopped at a hotel whose name I have forgotten—but it was situated on the left, at the corner of a street opposite the posting-house.

Next day, to my great regret, nothing was said about continuing our journey; it seemed to be almost settled that we should not go any further.

How were we better off at Mesnil than at Villers-Cotterets, a dozen leagues from our starting-point and upon the same road? Neither my mother nor Mademoiselle Adélaïde could say with certainty.

However, it was settled that, unless some serious event occurred, we had reached our journey's end.

We arrived at Mesnil on the 22nd of March.

On the 25th everybody was talking of a grand review of the National Guard, which was to be held by King Joseph in the court of the Tuileries.

This function roused Mademoiselle Adélaïde's curiosity, for she had never seen Paris, and it was decided to put the horse to our cart, to start on the afternoon of the 26th, to sleep in Paris, to see the review on the 27th, and to return on the 28th.

My mother did not care to take this little trip; for Paris recalled memories that my thoughtless childhood had forgotten. She entrusted me to Crétet and to Mademoiselle Adélaïde, who took me with them.

I have but two clear recollections of this journey—although it was eight years later than the last one.

One, radiant and poetic: and the other impure and stained.

The first was when, at the flourish of brazen trumpets and the waving of welcoming flags, they lifted up above the heads of 50,000 of the National Guard, the rosy, fair, curly head of a child of three, amid cries of *Vive le roi de Rome? Vive la régence!*

He was that poor child who was born a king, but who was destined by fate not only to be disinherited of both his kingdoms, but soon to lose both his parents.

A painting of this child was sent to the emperor at Moscow, and another followed Napoleon to Saint-Helena.

The father of this little martyr-innocent had scarcely time to realise his existence, except as a heavenly vision appearing for a brief space in this world. He saw him after the Russian campaign, after the Dresden campaign, and never again save in the dreams and hallucinations of his solitude and his despair.

His mother,—as disastrous an influence on the fortunes of France as all other daughters of the Cæsars: Anne of Austria, Marie Antoinette, and now Marie Louise—stood behind him, but her face left an indistinct and insipid impression on my mind, and her features are lost in the mists of time; I can only remember her fair hair fastened up on the top of her head by a diamond comb.

They swore fealty to this poor child, and, if the flourish of trumpets and the shouting had ceased for a moment, if the murmur of Paris with her million peoples had been stilled, the booming of the enemy's guns could have been heard thundering only two leagues away from the place where they were making all that futile cheering, and swearing those hollow vows!

In his name it was promised that he should never quit Paris; that he, Marie Louise his mother, and King Joseph his uncle, should die among the French people. And the carriages that were to bear them away next day were standing ready with the horses harnessed, in the courtyards of the Tuileries!

So it fell out that the King of Rome left the château of Catherine of Médicis the following morning—that castle which survived days like the 20th June, the 10th August, the 29th July, and the 24th February. On the morrow he left to his successors, the Duke of Bordeaux and the Count of Paris, the royal cradle presented by the Hôtel-de-Ville; they too—both great-nephews of Louis XVI.—were destined not to rest in it any longer than he had done.

This, then, was the flash of light and poetry still present to my memory.

The second recollection was of the number of girls of the town who, at that period, called out from the windows of their apartments to passers-by their licentious invitations with gestures obscene.

Every few moments I would turn round and say to Crétet and Mademoiselle Adélaïde, "They are calling to us." Both laughed, and I wondered why they laughed.

We left Paris quite early next day, but not too early, however, to learn the ill-starred news.

During the night the King of Rome, the Empress, and King Joseph had left Paris and were speeding towards the Loire.

On learning this news, which meant the abandonment of the capital, my mother felt that the place where we were—a little village on the great highway, six leagues from the barriers—was the place of all places where we should be least safe, even though we might not be in any danger at all.

Paris, we heard, was preparing to defend herself, so if we remained at Mesnil we should be right in the line of attack.

Moreover, the enemy was at Meaux—their advance-guard had been seen as far as Bondy.

My mother determined to turn back, and we started on our return journey to Villers-Cotterets the next day.

I have completely forgotten what we did with Crétet and Mademoiselle Adélaïde, I only know they were not with us during the subsequent events.

When we reached Nanteuil, we learnt that the enemy had turned the position at Soissons, and were at Villers-Cotterets, marching upon Nanteuil. The Cossacks had discovered the quarry, had gone down into it and, according to rumour, had committed abominations in its dark depths such as the sun itself would have blushed to see had they been done in the light of day.

We heard behind us, from the direction of Paris, the sound of firing, and we were informed that the Prussian advance-guard was at Levignan, two leagues from where we then were. Therefore, if we wished to escape entirely from the enemy, there was only the road to Crespy available.

Crespy, being situated two leagues north of the road from Laon to Paris, leads nowhere, and might be overlooked.

So we made for Crespy.

My mother knew an old lady there, named Madame de Longpré—the widow of an old valet de chambre of Louis XV.

Concerning her I only remember that she was addicted to the terrible habit of brandy-drinking, and that in order to procure her brandy she sold every single article of a collection of magnificent china such as I have never seen since.

And at what price do you think she sold them? Thirty or forty *sous* the piece!

True, at that time Chinese porcelain was not so highly valued as is the fashion to-day.

We drew up at her house, but she had not enough room to take us in; and the sight of her perpetual drinking would have been repulsive.

She took us to a lady—Madame Millet—who had, she said, a spare room quite ready that she could let us have.

It was soon settled;—Crespy is so near Villers-Cotterets that my mother was perfectly well known there, and we installed ourselves that same day.

Madame Millet had two sons and two daughters:—one of these two daughters, Amélie, would have been very pretty had she not lost one eye, through an accident—it was always closed, and she hid it by a great mass of beautiful black hair.

I remember nothing at all about the youngest girl, not even her name.

The two sons were army surgeons like their father.

The eldest had already left the service some two or three years before, and practised medicine in Crespy.

The other was with his regiment, no one knew where. In the midst of this general *débâcle* nothing had been heard of him for six or eight weeks past, and the poor mother and his two sisters were very uneasy about him.

As we crossed the main square of Crespy, we came upon a kind of bivouac; we inquired about this garrison—a source of danger rather than a means of help, in a town which was as open as a market-place, and we learnt that it was composed of 100 infantry and 200 cavalry. This little corps was completely cut off from all communication with the main army, and was stationed there, under inferior officers, without any orders: there they awaited the tide of events.

The enemy lay all round Crespy: at Compiègne, at Villers-Cotterets, at Levignan. But by some curious chance, for which we were most grateful, Crespy had remained, like Péronne, if not quite inviolable, at least inviolate.

Our two or three hundred men kept splendid guard; they had pickets all round, their muskets were kept ever ready piled, and their horses were only unbridled when they had to be fed.

The activity of this handful of men was a remarkable contrast to the negligence of the duc de Treviso and of his army corps, who, as we have related, allowed themselves to be surprised one night at Villers-Cotterets.

One day, in spite of this vigilance, or rather because of it, an alarm was spread; the enemy had been seen filing out of the wood of Tillet, at the foot of the rise of Montigny.

This was the same hillock I thought so high, when I travelled to Béthisy with Picard and my cousin Marianne.

However that might be, the enemy was approaching, and the little troop resolved to defend vigorously.

Madame Millet's house was the second or third on the right as you came into the town from Villers-Cotterets—the same road that the enemy was taking.

The windows looked up that road.

We went up into the attics, which we turned into a general camping ground,—for Madame Millet, my mother, and the two daughters had settled not to stir out. From the windows of these attics we could see the approach of a little corps of about a hundred men.

Was it, we questioned, an isolated corps like ours at Crespy? or the advance-guard of a more considerable force? We were unable to tell, or rather to see, from our attic windows, as the road turned a few paces outside the town, was lost behind the houses that stood on our right, and completely cut off from sight a quarter of a league further by the wood of Tillet, which was large enough to conceal a much larger force than the one that had just passed through it.

It was Prussian cavalry. The men were clothed in short blue coats, tight-fitting round the chest, loose below and fastened at the waist by belts.

They wore grey trousers, with a blue stripe like their coats, and had small vizored helmets on their heads, fastened by a leather chin-strap.

Each man carried a sabre and two pistols.

I can still see the first rank, preceded by two trumpeters, holding their trumpets in their hands but not blowing them.

An officer marched behind the trumpeters.

They were fine-looking young fellows, fair, and of a more distinguished bearing than the ordinary soldier; no doubt they were of the voluntary levies of 1813, who came to Leipzig to try their prentice hands on us; officers of the *Tugendbund*, which had produced Staps and was to produce Sand.

They passed under our windows, and disappeared out of our sight; a moment later we heard a perfect hurricane of sound, and the house shook to the gallop of horses. At the end of the street the Prussians had been charged by our cavalry, and, as they were unaware of the size of our forces, they retreated at full gallop, hotly pursued by our hussars.

They all rushed past together pell-mell—a hurricane of smoke and noise. Our soldiers were slashing and firing, sabre in one hand and pistol in the other.

The Prussians fired back as they fled. Two or three bullets struck our house; and one of them broke the bar of the shutter through which I was watching.

Great was the terror of the women, who rushed downstairs at a break-neck pace to hide themselves in the cellar. My mother tried to drag me with her, but I held fast to the window-sash, and rather than leave me she stopped by me.

It was a terrible and yet a magnificent sight to witness.

When pressed hard the Prussians faced about, and there, only twenty paces from us, under our very eyes, as near as the first row of boxes at the circus is to the stage, a battle was taking place in deadly earnest—a hand-to-hand fight.

I saw five or six of the Prussians fall, and two or three of the French.

The first man who fell was a Prussian, who was flying with his head and body bent low over his horse's neck; one slashing stroke cut open his back, from his right shoulder to his left flank, and left a ribbon-like band of red across him.

The wound must have been twelve or fifteen inches long.

Of the others whom I saw fall, one fell from a slash which cut his head open; the rest were stabbed or shot.

Then, after ten minutes' struggle, the Prussians were beaten; they trusted afresh to the speed of their horses to save them, and set off at full gallop.

The pursuit began again.

The hurricane resumed its course, strewing three or four men on the pavement before it disappeared out of sight.

One of these men was certainly killed, for he never moved; the others got up, or dragged themselves away to the other side of the road. One of them sat up and leant with his back against the wall; the other two, who were probably more seriously wounded, remained lying.

Suddenly a drum was heard summoning to the charge—it was our hundred infantry coming up to take their share of the fight: they marched with fixed bayonets, and disappeared round the bend of the road.

Five minutes later we heard sharp firing, then our hussars reappeared, driven back by five or six hundred cavalry.

The pursuers were now the pursued: but it was quite impossible to see or to distinguish any details in this second flurry of fighting—we only saw three or four more corpses stretched on the road when all was over.

A deep silence succeeded this turmoil. French and Prussians had plunged forward into the town: and, though we waited, we neither saw nor heard anything more.

What had become of our hundred infantry men? Probably they had rushed out into the open country, and had been either killed or taken.

And as for our cavalry men, who knew the district round about the town, they had escaped, it would seem, by way of the mountain of Sery, in the valley of Gillocourt.

We saw no more of their pursuers; no doubt they left the town by some other route than the one by which they had entered, and had gone to rejoin their comrades, who were drawn up in the plain of Tillet to the number of about two or three thousand.

We were emboldened by the solitude and silence; moreover, our host, the military surgeon, came forward to attend to the wounded men.

I hung to his coat-tails, in spite of my mother's entreaties, and we opened the street door. A Prussian sergeant, who was leaning against this door, fell backwards when his means of support suddenly failed him.

He was wounded through the right breast by a sword thrust. Directly the women saw they could be useful to a poor wounded man their fears vanished. They rushed to the rescue, raised the young man (who would be somewhere between twenty-six or twenty-eight years of age) and carried him into the sitting-room, which they speedily turned into a hospital.

Millet continued his rounds, and, with the assistance of the neighbours, who began to appear at their doors, he brought back four or five of the wounded, one of whom was a Frenchman. The remainder were either dead or at their last gasp.

And now the bandaging began.

Here the women played the divine part heaven intended should fall to their portion. My mother, Madame Millet and her two daughters turned into true Sisters of Mercy, comforting and tending at the same time.

I held the basin full of water, while Millet washed the wounds and the servants prepared lint.

We then learnt from one of the Prussians who was least seriously wounded (he had received a sabre cut on his head), that he and his comrades belonged to a detachment of three thousand men, which had refrained from entering the town for fear of being surprised; they were following their instructions, which were to camp out as much as possible, their commanders always fearing a nocturnal massacre if they ventured to stay in the towns.

"However, it will all be over soon," added the wounded man, "since Paris surrendered the day before yesterday."

This was the first intimation we had received of that important event.

We were just on the point of crying out at the news, when a voice in the doorway said suddenly—

"That is not true, Paris will not surrender like that."

We turned round, and there we saw, leaning against the door, pale, one of the officers of our small detachment of infantry. He had one of the finest and most soldierly heads imaginable, gashed, now, with a deep wound over the left eye-brow—hence his pallor and the blood that covered him.

He had received a pistol-shot in his face, which had felled him; but, the fresh air soon reviving him, he had managed to get up, and, seeing the town a hundred steps in front of him, he had reached it, leaning against its walls for support.

The kind neighbours who had assisted our host had directed this officer to our house, and, mortally wounded, he had arrived just in time to give that truly patriotic denial to the news announced by his enemy.

The bullet was still in the wound; it was extracted very skilfully by Millet, but, as we have said, the wound was mortal, and the officer died during the night, about two o'clock in the morning, just when a dog began to bark.

Millet went into the yard and listened. Someone was knocking at the garden gate which led into the open country, and knocking so cautiously that it was plain whoever it was had to be wary.

Our host opened the gate himself, and he who knocked thus at a private door in the dead of the night was the second son of the house, about whom they had been so terribly anxious.

Our host came back into the house alone, went into one of the rooms, and bent over the bed where his mother and his two sisters were sleeping for a little while, after their good offices as sisters of charity. It was indeed good news God had sent them as a reward for their devotion.

They smuggled in the new-comer by a landing window, so that he could reach our attics without being seen.

For ten minutes the three women sobbed for joy, then he told them that Paris had indeed practically surrendered on March 30th.

Georges Millet—so far as I can recollect I believe Georges was his name— Georges Millet realised then that all was over. He left his regiment, and, at the risk of being taken a score of times, he managed to return to Crespy, walking by night and across country.

It had only taken him a night and a half, for Crespy was but fifteen leagues from Paris.

His brother gave him a razor to shave off his moustache, and for clothing they sent to Madame de Longpré, whose eldest son was the same size, and borrowed a coat, a waistcoat, and a pair of trousers, as the clothes of his elder brother (who was twice as stout as he was) would not have fitted him.

Next day the news came.

The Allies entered Paris on the 31st March.

On the 1st April the Senate appointed a Provisional Government.

On the 2nd, a decree of the Senate declared Napoleon to have forfeited his throne.

A fortnight later we returned to Villers-Cotterets, and settled down again in our home.

What a host of events had happened during that fortnight! The face of Europe had been changed.

On the 4th, Napoleon abdicated in favour of his son.

On the 6th he made his plans for retiring south of the Loire.

On the 10th a *Te Deum* was chanted in the place Louis XV. by the Allies.

On the 11th Napoleon signed the decree of abdication.

On the 12th he attempted to poison himself.

The same day, whilst he was struggling with the poison, which had been adulterated by Cabanis, the Count d'Artois entered Paris.

On the 13th the Senate nominated that prince Lieutenant-General of the kingdom.

On the 14th the Emperor of Austria entered Paris.

On the 19th the Emperor Napoleon, deserted by everyone, was left alone with only a single valet de chambre.

Finally, on the 20th, he said adieu to the Eagles of the Imperial Guard, and set out for the isle of Elba; on the same day, and almost at the same hour, Louis XVIII. reached Compiègne.

All this had passed during that fortnight; thus had history been made, and the noise of these exploits had been bruited abroad for all the world to hear, whilst I, in my careless and happy ignorance, was untouched by the sound thereof.

Who would have said then that one day I should visit the isle of Elba, whose very existence was unknown to me till I heard its name pronounced, and whose geographical position I forgot as soon as it was told me? Who would have said that one day I should visit this isle of Elba with the Emperor's nephew?

CHAPTER XI

Am I to be called Davy de la Pailleterie or Alexandre Dumas?—*Deus dedit, Deus dabit*—The tobacco-shop—The cause of the Emperor Napoleon's fall, as it appeared to my writing-master—My first communion—How I prepared for it.

Two or three days after our return to Villers-Cotterets, M. Collard came to see us, and my mother had a long talk with him; after which he left us, inviting her to join him that evening at M. Deviolaine's house.

My mother went to M. Deviolaine's and took me with her. There was a large company of officers with their sabres and epaulettes at table, as on the last occasion I had been in the house: only, this time they were Russian sabres and epaulettes: the same language and manners, perhaps rather more polished manners—that was the only difference.

I could not understand that these were they whom the people spoke of as "the enemy"—the enemy represents a principle, not actual men themselves.

My mother and M. Collard continued their conversation. Next day M. Collard was to leave for Paris, but he promised to look in at our house again before going.

That night, when we returned home, my mother took me aside, and, looking at me more seriously than usual, but with as loving a face, she said:—

"My dear one, the Count d'Artois, who has been appointed Lieutenant-General of the Kingdom, and Louis XVII., who is just about to be made King of France, are both brothers of King Louis XVI. Your grandfather, the Marquis de la Pailleterie, served under Louis XVI. as your father served under the Republic. Listen now, and attend carefully to what I say, for probably your whole future will depend on the resolution we are about to take. Would you rather be called Davy de la Pailleterie, like your grandfather, for you are the grandson of the Marquis Davy de la Pailleteril, who was Groom of the Bed-chamber to the Prince of Conti, and Commissary-General of Artillery; in which case we could obtain a commission for you, or you could become one of the pages; and in either case you would have a position made for you in the new reigning family? Or would you like to be called simply and briefly Alexandre Dumas, like your father? If you bear the name of the republican General Alexandre Dumas, no career will be open to you, for, instead of serving those who now reign, as your grandfather did, your father served against them!... M. Collard is going to Paris to-day; he knows M. de Talleyrand, who was in the *Corps Législatif* when he was; he knows the duc d'Orléans; in fact, he knows many people belonging to the new Court, and he will do his best for you according to your own decision. Think carefully before you reply."

"Oh! I don't need to think, mother!" I cried—"I will be called Alexandre Dumas, and nothing else. I remember my father; I never knew my grandfather. What would my father think, who came to bid me farewell at the moment of his death, if I should disown him in order to call myself by my grandfather's name?"

My mother's face brightened.

"Is that your opinion?" she said.

"Yes; and yours too, is it not, mother?"

"Alas! yes; but what is to become of us?"

"Nonsense!" I replied; "you forget that I can construe the *De viris*, and therefore I understand my father's motto: *'Deus dedit, Deus dabit*—God has given, God will give.'"

"Well then, my child, go off to bed after that: you aggravate me very much sometimes, but I am sure your heart is in the right place."

I went to bed without realising quite the importance of the decision my filial instinct had just prompted me to make, and that, as my mother had warned me, it might very probably mean the shaping of my whole future life.

Next day M. Collard came again, and it was settled he should ask nothing whatever on my behalf, but only apply for a tobacco-shop for my mother.

A strange anomaly this—the widow of the Horatius Codes of the Tyrol selling tobacco!

And my education was to be continued at the Abbé Grégoire's.

I say *at* the Abbé Grégoire's, but I should have said under the Abbé Grégoire. For, whilst all these things had been happening, the abbé had lost his certificate as master of the school.

Some decision of the University had forbade him to keep a school at his own house—although he was allowed to teach pupils in the town.

For the consideration of six francs a month, which my mother agreed to pay him, I became one of his town pupils.

I was, besides, to take lessons in arithmetic with Oblet—the town schoolmaster, and to continue my fencing lessons with old Mounier.

And as for riding, I had taught myself, as the Roman soldiers did, by mounting bare-backed any horses I could get hold of. My sole education then was limited to as much Latin as the Abbé Grégoire could teach me; to studying the four rules of arithmetic with M. Oblet; and to executing counter-stroke, feint and parry with old Mounier.

Oblet, I must say, had the least enviable task, for I have always had such a profound aversion towards arithmetic that I never have been able to get beyond multiplication.

And even to-day I am incapable of doing the slightest sum in division.

But if I did not learn how to calculate under Oblet—God, who watched over me, providentially saw that I learnt something else.

Besides a perfect knowledge of his *Barême*, Oblet wrote a splendid hand; he could make all the letters of the alphabet, like M. Prudhomme, with one flourish of his pen; and, furthermore, he could draw the most marvellous designs, ornaments, hearts, rosettes, *lacs d'amour*, Adam and Eve, the portrait of Louis XVIII., and I know not what else.

Now, handwriting was quite a different matter,—here I was gifted! When Oblet had given me my arithmetic lessons, and, to acquit his conscience, had dunned the three rules into me—(for, as I have said, I never got beyond multiplication)—we got out fine pieces of white paper, pared three or four quill pens in advance, to coarse or fine or medium points, and then began writing round-hand, flourishes and up-strokes galore.

In three months I had attained to Oblet's standard, and if I were not afraid of offending his pride, I should say that, in some points, I had even surpassed him.

My progress in writing gave my mother some pleasure, though she would much rather it had been in arithmetic.

"Writing, writing!" she would say; "it is something to be proud of, I must say, to write well. Why, any duffer can write well. But look at Bonaparte, you have a score of his letters addressed to your father; can you make out a single one of them?"

"But, madame, M. Bonaparté is now at the island of Elba," Oblet would reply gravely.

Oblet was a hot Royalist, so he always pronounced the name Bonaparté, and gave the ex-Emperor the title of *monsieur*.

The same honour or the same insult that Oblet offered to Bonaparte was offered me in the Chamber of 1847.

"Do you mean to say," my mother replied, "that he is at Elba because he didn't know how to write?"

"Why should I not say so? It is an argument that may be maintained, madame. They say that M. Bonaparté was betrayed by his marshals; but I say 'Providence willed this usurper should not be able to write clearly so that his orders should be illegible, and therefore they were not able to be carried out.' 'His marshals betrayed him! 'Nothing of the kind, madame; they read his orders wrongly, so they acted contrary to what he had ordered them. Hence have arisen our reverses and our defeats, and the taking of Paris and the exile to the isle of Elba."

"Well, we will drop Bonaparte now, M. Oblet."

"Madame, you yourself introduced the man into the conversation and not I; I never speak of the man."

"But suppose if Alexandre..."

"If your son, madame, one day becomes emperor of the French, since he will have, or rather as he already has, a splendid hand, his orders will be literally carried out, unless his marshals do not know how to read."

But my mother was not comforted for my lack of mathematical ability by this contingency, she sighed a deep sigh, and gave expression to the final word let fall by weary consciences, and exhausted intellects, and faith that has reached the doubting point—

"If only!..."

So I continued my five sorts of writing, my down-strokes and my up-strokes, my flourishes, my hearts, my rosettes and *lacs d'amour*, with Oblet.

Oblet, be it understood, was not the worst of those who treated the dethroned emperor badly: it was bad enough to call him M. Bonaparté, but many even contested his very name, saying that it never was Napoleon, but Nicolas, thus depriving him of his title of *The Lion of the Desert*,—fools that they were,—in order to call him *Conqueror of the Nations*.

While all these things were happening I attained my thirteenth year, and it became time to think of making my First Communion—a serious event in the life of every child, but specially so in mine.

For, young as I was, I had always felt deeply religious, apart from external observances. That sentiment is always ready to vibrate in my heart like a mysterious, hidden chord, but it never really thrills save under the influence of a vivid emotion of joy or sorrow. In both circumstances, my first impulse, whether of gratitude or of affliction, is always towards the Saviour. Churches I hardly ever enter, for directly I cross the threshold I feel, like Habakkuk, as though an angel were pulling me back by the hair. Yet churches are such sacred places to me that I feel it sacrilege to go there as others do, merely out of curiosity or from a religious freak.

No, it takes a deep access of joy, or some profound grief, to make me go into our northern churches, and then I always choose the loneliest comer or the darkest place—(though with God no dark places exist)—there I often prostrate myself, near a pillar against which I can lean my head; there, with eyes riveted, my being isolated from all others, I can bury myself in the one thought, that of a God, good, all powerful, eternal and infinite. I cannot find a word to say to Him, not a prayer to address to Him. What can one say to God, and what use is it to pray to Him, when He can see the face behind the mask, impiety behind hypocrisy? No, I prostrate my body, my heart, my soul, before His mercy-seat, I humble myself at the feet of His greatness. I bless Him for past mercies, I praise Him for the present, and I hope in Him for the future.

But all this is not very orthodox; all this may be Christian enough but hardly Catholic; it was therefore feared that I should not turn out a very edifying example of piety.

Those who thought so could not grasp the fact that my apparent want of religious feeling was really from my excess of religious emotion.

It was just the same with prayers as with the rules of arithmetic; I never could learn more than three: "Our Father," "Hail Mary," and "I believe in God." Moreover, I only knew these in French, and not word for word: they tried to teach me them in Latin, but, as I had not yet become at that time a pupil of the Abbé Grégoire, I declined to learn them, saying that I wanted to understand what I was asking God for, to which they replied that God understood all languages.

"Never mind!" I insisted; "it isn't enough for me that God understands, I must understand too."

And I obtained leave to learn my prayers in French.

But, in spite of my Gallican prayers and my imperfect attention to the instruction of the Catechism, there were two persons, my mother and the Abbé Grégoire, who never doubted my religious tendencies.

And, more than that, the Abbé Grégoire, who was only a curate, obtained for me, in spite of the strictness of the Abbé Remy, the priest of the church at Villers-Cotterets, the supreme honour of being allowed to renew my baptismal vows.

The matter had long been talked of, and the Abbé Grégoire had to make himself personally responsible for his pupil.

A week beforehand I was given the vows of baptism, copied in Oblet's very finest handwriting; the next day I knew them by heart.

The day before the ceremony, my mother found me absorbed in reading a book which seemed to cast a spell over all my faculties. She never doubted for an instant that the book I was thus so taken up with was the *Imitation of Christ*, or the *Pratique du Chretien*: she approached me gently and read over my shoulder.

I was reading the *Lettres d'Héloïse et d'Abeilard*, a poetical version by Colardeau.

My mother snatched the book out of my hands.

"That is a nice book to read," said she, "to aid you in your first communion!"

I tried to defend the book; I said that Abelard's exhortations were highly moral, and the lamentations of Heloise extremely religious. I wished to know how either the one or the other could mar my sincere contrition for the sins I had committed, for which I was to receive absolution on the morrow. My mother did not think it meet to give me any explanation on the subject, but as the Abbé Grégoire happened to pass by, she called him in. The Abbé Grégoire, constituted judge, took the book, read half a page, shook his head and said—

"Really, the verses are very poor."

And he handed the book back to my mother.

I need hardly say I differed in my opinion from the abbé, and thought Colardeau's lines splendid. Who was in the right, the abbé or I? I strongly incline to think my mother was.

That night the Abbé Remy took me aside, after preparation, and explained to me that it was because of the name I bore, my mother's social position in the town, and specially because of the Abbé Grégoire's recommendation, that he had consented to allow me to repeat my baptismal vows. He hoped then that I should realise the importance of the responsibility with which I was to be invested, and that I should prove myself worthy of it.

I confess I did not quite understand his admonitions. If, among all the candidates, there was one child ready for this solemn rite, by reason of his own convictions, it was myself. I bitterly resented this injustice, the first that had ever been offered me.

I have since become more accustomed to false conceptions of my feelings, my conduct, my character. I hardly slept the whole of that night: the idea that I was going to place myself in communion with the sacred body of our Lord moved me profoundly; the greatness of the act weighed heavily on me, and tears were very near. I felt utterly unworthy of the grace that was to be vouchsafed to me.

They dressed me in a new suit for this solemn occasion; I wore Nankeen trousers, a white quilted waistcoat, and a blue coat with metal buttons,—all made by Dulauroy, the first tailor of Villers-Cotterets.

A white necktie, a cambric shirt, and a wax candle weighing two pounds, completed my toilet.

A previous ceremony had helped to deepen the impression of this one. The day before it was discovered that one of our companions, whose real name was, doubtless, Ismaël, but who was called Maël for short, whom I strongly suspected of being a Jew, had not been baptized; so he was baptized conditionally, and I and a young girl, who repeated the Vows for him, were chosen to be his godfather and godmother.

My fellow-sponsor was a very pretty girl with fair hair, slightly inclined to be reddish in tone, which did not at all spoil the general effect of her prettiness.

Her baptismal name was Laura, even that of Petrarch's illustrious mistress; but I have totally forgotten anything about her family.

It was arranged that I was to communicate next day between my two godsons—Ismaël and Roussy.

I had been godfather to Roussy for ten months, with Augustine Deviolaine, who was nine months younger than I; and Ismaël was nine months older.

At last the hour arrived. We know what a festival was made of the communion of children formerly, in small towns: it was the counterpart of that grand festival of Corpus Christi, since suppressed. Popular instinct thought of the two together with almost equal reverence: extreme weakness and Supreme Power. All faces were radiant, every house was decked with flowers. At least, that seemingly was how it looked to me, through the eyes of a child of thirteen, my heart full of life and faith.

Hiraux performed marvellous things on his organ that day: he was, indeed, a great artist; his melodious chords seemed to represent that everything which was youthful, loving, and poetic in life, was poured forth at the feet of our Saviour.

I remember nothing of the details of the ceremony. I was wrapped in the deepest contemplation. I remember that everything around me seemed filled with light and hope. Whatsoever is granted to the eye of faith in contemplation of heavenly things, was granted that day to me. The feeling was so overwhelming, and so real, that, when the Host touched my lips, I burst into weeping and fainted away.

The Abbé Remy could not understand it at all.

Ever since that day I have felt a deep reverence for all that is holy, a religious worship for everything high and noble; each heavenly spark has kindled within me an inward fire, which has had its outward effect, like the lava in a volcano when the crater is full to bursting.

It took me two or three days to recover from this excitement; and, when the Abbé Grégoire came to see me, I flung myself, crying, into his arms.

"My dear boy," he said, "I would far rather your feelings were less intense, and that they would last longer."

The Abbé Grégoire was full of common-sense.

No, my dear abbé, it did not last. No; for, as I have said, I was not the type of man to practise religion. As a matter of fact, that first communion was the only one I ever made. But—I can say it to the dead as to the living—when the last communion shall come to me, as the pendant of the first, when the hand of the Lord shall have closed the two horizons of my life, and drawn the veil of His love between the nothingness that precedes and the nothingness that follows man's life, He can search every atom of the intermediate space with the most rigorous eye and He will not find in it one evil thought, or one action with which I can reproach myself.

BOOK IV

CHAPTER I

Auguste Lafarge—Bird-snaring on a large scale—A wonderful catch—An epigram—I wish to write French verses—My method of translating Virgil and Tacitus—Montagnon—My political opinions.

It would seem as though in response to this outburst of my spirit towards God He rewarded my mother by giving her the only thing she had ever been able to obtain in return for her twelve years of petitioning.

To provide for this great event we had moved to the rue de Lormet, and had taken up our abode in the place de la Fontaine, in a house belonging to a coppersmith called Lafarge, who had let us the whole of his first floor, and engaged besides to let us his shop if we needed it.

The license to keep a tobacco-shop having been obtained, he kept his promise, and we established ourselves on the ground floor, facing the street, in a large room furnished with two counters: one for the retail of tobacco and the other for the sale of salt.

Our future prospects all centred in this twofold trade, which we owed to the protection of M. Collard.

Some time after we were installed, the son of the coppersmith came to see his father. He was a fine, light-complexioned young fellow, who held a post as head clerk in Paris; he was looking out for a lawyer's practice, but wanted the capital wherewith to purchase one. He had returned to his family with all the attractions of the capital about him; a box-coat with thirty-six bands to it in the latest fashion, a watch-chain with massive trinkets, tight-fitting trousers, and boots *à la hussarde*. He hoped to dazzle a wealthy heiress;—no difficult task, perhaps, to one accustomed to charm the fair ones of Paris.

Poor Auguste Lafarge was at that period a fascinating youth, with fair, pink complexion as I have said; a complexion which, under the disguise of health, hid the germs of consumption, the disease he later fell a victim to. Moreover, he had intellectual tastes, having been thrown into the literary atmosphere of the time, and he numbered Désaugiers, Béranger, and Armand Gouffé among his friends; he composed dainty songs, and, as though born wealthy, he knew how to draw a gold piece out of his pocket and fling it down carelessly in payment for the smallest article he bought.

Such a man of fashion could not, of course, sleep at the back of his father's shop; so they borrowed one of our rooms, which we willingly gave up to him, and Auguste was established in our quarters.

Greedy after novelty, I was, of course, anxious to cultivate so personable a model, and I made advances to Auguste, whom, moreover, my mother held up to me as a pattern. Auguste accepted my overtures, and offered, what he thought might please me most, to take me on a grand bird-catching expedition.

I agreed. I had hitherto recognised Auguste's superiority in everything, but I quite hoped to bear away the palm in the matter of bird-catching.

I was wrong: we country people perform our bird-catching like artists; Auguste did his as a lord of the manor.

He sent for Boudoux, and asked him which were the best bird-snaring pools in the forest?

"Those near the Compiègne and Vivières roads," promptly answered Boudoux.

"How many other pools are there within, say, a league of this neighbourhood?"

"Seven or eight."

"So then, if we block all the other pools three or four days beforehand, the birds will be obliged to go to the two pools on the Vivières and Compiègne roads?"

"Yes, poor little things, unless it rains; in which case, instead of leaving their haunts, they will, as you know, drink out of the hollows of the leaves."

"Do you think it will rain, Boudoux?"

Boudoux shook his head.

"My aunt's barometer is at set fair, M. Auguste; it will not rain till the moon changes."

"Very well! Boudoux, take these ten francs, and block all the pools round about; on Saturday evening Dumas and I will come and draw the two pools near the Compiègne and Vivières roads. We ought to have a first-class hut near one or other of these two pools, to spend the night in."

"Very good, M. Auguste," said Boudoux, "I will attend to it."

"I want, besides, two thousand lime-twigs to-night, so as to get them smeared beforehand."

"You shall have them, M. Auguste."

"All right," said Lafarge, with the gestures of an emperor.

This was my first lesson in extravagance; the readers of *Monte-Cristo* can judge if it was lost on me!

On the Saturday night, all was ready, thanks to the ten francs Boudoux had received. When the robin's last song was ended we spread the two pools with snares. Then we wrapped ourselves up, Auguste in his greatcoat, I in my blanket, on a bed of ferns prepared by Boudoux, and we tried to sleep.

I say we tried to sleep, but, although the air around us was balmy, the forest quiet, the moonlight serene, the expectation of pleasure keeps one awake almost as much as pleasure itself. It is very rarely I sleep the night before a hunting expedition, and only when life is more seriously preoccupied do these pleasant attacks of insomnia cease.

It was then very rarely that I slept on fine nights, when excited by anticipation of a bird-snaring, or shooting, or hunting excursion. Those lonely vigils were not waste time, for I love solitude and silence and vastness, and I owe this love to those nights spent in the forest, at the foot of a tree, watching the stars through the canopy of leaves stretched between me and the sky, and listening to all the mysterious, incomprehensible sounds which are awake in the bosom of the wood while Nature sleeps.

Lafarge slept hardly more than I did. What was he dreaming of, I wonder? Probably of the face of a pretty grisette he had deserted in a Parisian garret; or, simpler explanation still, of that overweening ambition of his to become a solicitor, though only the son of a coppersmith.

At three o'clock in the morning the song of a robin, as it hopped among the bushes, announced to us that day had come, as it had announced night to us; next a blackbird fluted, then the tomtits and jays followed suit.

Each bird seemed to have his own special hour for waking and praising God. I never recollect to have taken part in or seen such a haul of birds as we took that day. We numbered jays, blackbirds, and thrushes by the dozen; redbreasts, tomtits, linnets, and warblers by the score; and we returned to the town bent down under the weight of our spoils.

Three days after, Auguste Lafarge returned to Paris. His attractions had failed; he had come to Villers-Cotterets to ask Mademoiselle Picot to marry him, and had been rejected.

The night he spent with me he was not dreaming of ambition, or of love, but of revenge: he was concocting an epigram, copies of which he gave to me and to twenty other persons when he left.

It ran as follows:—

"La fière Éléonor compte avec complaisance
Les nombreux soupirants qui briguèrent sa main,
Et que sa noble indifférence
Paya toujours d'un froid dédain.
Pourtant, à ces discours que votre esprit résiste;
S'il en fut un ou deux tenté par ses ducats,
Un volume in quarto contiendrait il la liste
De tous ceux qui n'en voudraient pas?"

I cannot say whether the epigram is good or bad; I will leave the question to be decided by the Academy, which is learned in such matters, since it accepted M. de Sainte-Aulaire because of a quatrain. But I know very well that all the people I had seen the previous day laughing at the Lafarge family, on the morrow laughed at the Picot family.

Since the death of Demoustier there had not been an unpublished verse circulated in our little town; so Auguste's eight lines made a great sensation for eight days after.

I confess that the stir made over an absent man dazzled me. I was fired with ambition to have the glory attached to me of being talked of when away, and at the Abbé Grégoire's first lesson I begged him to teach me to make French verses, instead of insisting so tiresomely on my making Latin ones.

These lines of Auguste Lafarge were the first rays of light thrown upon my life; he kindled in me ambitions vague and nebulous until then; things which had been dreams rather than definite ideas, aspirations rather than determinations.

And it will be seen that Auguste Lafarge's influence on me was continued by Adolphe de Leuven.

I asked Abbé Grégoire to teach me to make French verses, for he was the official poet of the countryside.

I have said that since the days of Demoustier not an unpublished poem had tickled the wits of my fellow townspeople; but I am mistaken; for at every festival, at all christenings or baptisms of any importance, the Abbé Grégoire was called upon in his capacity as poet.

I have never seen more worthy verses than his were; therefore, when I made this request, which would have been tolerably presumptuous made to Hugo or Lamartine, "Teach me to make French verses," the Abbé Grégoire was not in the least taken aback, but answered simply—

"I shall be delighted; but you will be tired of it, as you are of everything else, at the end of a week."

He gave me some *boûts-rimés* to finish, and I strove hard to compose French poetry. But the abbé was right; and at the end of a week I had had enough of it.

All my other lessons continued as usual. The Abbé Grégoire came at eleven o'clock every day to give me two hours' lessons, while the rest of the day I had pretty much to myself; and this is what happened.

My professor, to save himself trouble, had a Virgil and a Tacitus, with the translation side by side with the original. These two volumes he left behind him at our house each day, to save carrying them backwards and forwards, and he locked them up in a little cabinet, carefully taking the key away, knowing what a great temptation they would be to an idle boy like me.

Unluckily, I made the discovery that the box had hinges on the outside. With the help of a screw-driver I half opened the hinges, and extracted whatever I wanted through this half-open space, sometimes the singer of Æneas, at others the historian of the Cæsars; and, thanks to the help of the French translation, I produced versions which astonished even the professor.

As for my mother, she was charmed.

"Look at that child," she would say to all callers; "he shuts himself up, and in an hour the whole of his home lessons for the day are done."

I did indeed shut myself up, and with the utmost precautions. But, unfortunately, things did not prosper so well on composition days as on those of translation.

The exercises were dictated by the abbé, but, alas! there was no translation to their Latin locked away in any sort of cabinet; they had to be done by the help of a dictionary, and the result was that they were full of mistakes, which counterbalanced, in the mind of my teacher, the good effect of my translations, and eternally puzzled the poor man with the question as to how "The child could be so good in translation and so weak in composition." He died without finding the solution to it.

So it came about that on composition days the work took me four hours instead of two: but, even then, the two or four hours' work left me ten or twelve hours free each day. It will be seen that I had plenty of time at my own disposal.

I spent the greater part of my time at a gunsmith's who lived opposite us.

He was called Montagnon. He had a son who took lessons with me from Abbé Grégoire, and who died of nervous exhaustion. They let me see him when he was laid out, and the sight completed the cure begun by M. Tissot.

I did not give up frequenting the father's shop after the death of his son, my companion; for the firearms there were what I loved above all else.

Amongst these firearms I found the single-barrelled gun which I had taken down on the day after my father's death, with which to kill God. I was to have that gun *when I was big*;—now, this definition *when I was big* was utterly vague, and tormented me greatly. I thought I was by now quite big enough, for I was growing taller than the gun.

The consequence of my assiduous attendance at Montagnon's shop was that I became more learned in my knowledge of a gunsmith's trade than in translation; and I could take to pieces and put together again as complicated a mechanism as the breeching of a gun as well, and almost as ingeniously, as the cleverest gunsmith.

Old Montagnon would tell me that it was my vocation, and offered to take me free of premium as an apprentice; but he was mistaken, my enthusiasm did not go to that length.

The rest of my time was spent in making weapons with Mounier, or in going bird-snaring, or decoying, with my two best friends Saulnier and Arpin.

In these leisure times it was very rarely that a day passed without my receiving a dressing down on account of my political opinions!

Everybody had an opinion about the end of 1814 and the beginning of 1815, and generally each opinion was very strongly held; only, these opinions were not divided into as many shades as the colours in a rainbow, as nowadays, but were divided into two sharply defined colours—you were either a Royalist or a Bonapartist. The Republican party had passed away and Liberals had not yet appeared; there were no such parties as Saint Simonism, Fourierism, Democracy, Socialism, Cabétism.

I do not assert that my mother and I were Bonapartists, but we had been labelled such by other people.

We Bonapartists! It was a strange idea. Bonaparte had disgraced, exiled, and ruined us; Napoleon had forgotten, disowned, and left us to starve; and they dubbed us Bonapartists!

The feelings which made me resent this appellation, on behalf of my mother and myself, were so hearty, that whenever any children called me a

Bonapartist as we met in the streets, I would throw off my cap and my jacket and, considering myself insulted, instantly demand reparation.

If the offender were of a size to offer it me, satisfaction was given, sometimes too satisfactorily; but it did not matter, for if that happened I began again the next day.

The persistency with which people called us Bonapartists made my mother very uneasy on two accounts: first, because it earned me so many blows; I had never come home so often with a bleeding nose or black eye as since the Restoration; and, secondly, because she detected, underlying this accusation, a feeling of hatred, or rather of jealousy, which would cause her to lose her tobacco-shop license: they would certainly not fail to take it away from her if the charge of Bonapartism were believed.

CHAPTER II

The single-barrelled gun—*Quiot Biche*—Biche and Boudoux compared—I become a poacher—It is proposed to issue a writ against me—Madame Darcourt as plenipotentiary—How it happened that Creton's writ caused me no bother.

In this state of anxiety we passed the winter of 1814 to 1815, during which I began my first lessons in shooting, in spite of my mother's unwillingness.

My mother had positively forbidden Montagnon to give me the famous single-barrelled gun; but Montagnon thought me so skilful in handling guns that he had no sympathy with my poor mother's terrors; so he gave me (not the forbidden gun, for he was a native of Auvergne to the tips of his fingers, and was too honest a man to break his word; but) another single-barrelled gun that he had himself made for his son, and, consequently, felt able to guarantee its safe working. Moreover, as one could not go shooting without powder and without shot, he provided me with ammunition, and let me go abroad in the parterre.

This gun was the more precious in my sight since it was of the true poacher's pattern, with a barrel like a stick that one could carry in one's hand, and a butt-end that could be put in one's pocket; so if one saw a bird one could turn it into a gun and become a sportsman—or if anybody was about, it could be transformed into a walking-stick, and one became a pedestrian.

As nobody suspected me of having such a weapon in my possession, nobody distrusted me. When the keeper heard a shot he might come to me and ask me if I knew anything about it. Of course I had heard the firing,—I could not have done otherwise,—but I had never seen the culprit, or, if I had seen him, he had taken flight when he caught sight of me; and the direction he had taken was always opposite to the way I myself meant to go.

So it came about that I regulated my walks by those of the keeper, and, save for the evil accusation of Bonapartism, all was for the best in the best possible of worlds.

My usual hunting grounds were those which then went by the name of *les grandes allées*; four rows of limes, ranged about a quarter of a league in length, running from the castle to the forest. These four rows of trees faced the flat, open country to right and to left; so it was easy to see an enemy approaching from a good distance, and to fly as he came nearer.

In winter these alleys abounded in all kinds of birds, especially with thrushes; and my walking-stick gun, which was of small calibre, was an excellent weapon, and carried to the highest trees.

So, when my composition or my translation was finished, or perhaps left unfinished, I would pursue my way, under cover of going to Montagnon's; Montagnon would hand me the gun ready primed, let me out at his back door, and I was at the *grandes allées* in no time.

There I found Saulnier or Arpin, with a firearm mounted in a block of wood, or a short gun, or a long pistol, and the sport began.

And there, moreover, I discovered *quiot Biche.*

Cooper has dedicated five novels to Leather Stocking; therefore I ask my readers to permit me to dedicate some lines to quiot Biche, probably the only man in Europe who might, without disadvantage, be compared to the American hero.

Hanniquet, for I know not what reason, was nicknamed quiot Biche. He was, at the time of which I am speaking, a boy of about twenty years of age, of medium height, perfectly well made, strong as a well-balanced machine, and, more than all things else, a first-rate poacher.

Biche had begun by snaring and decoying birds, as should every true poacher, and in these two exercises he was, beyond doubt, to Boudoux what Pompey was to Cæsar; perhaps Biche might even have become Cæsar, and Boudoux Pompey, had not ambition led him away in the direction of poaching, a province Boudoux held in lofty and prudent disdain!

Nobody could distinguish a rabbit in its burrow in a spinney, or a hare in fallow land, better than Biche; nobody knew so well as Biche how to steal up carelessly to that hare or that rabbit, and to kill it with a stone or a blow from a stick.

The reader knows what pace a partridge can go when it runs. Well! Biche possessed the art of mesmerising partridges till he could walk up and kill one with a wretched old pistol, without cock or hammer, which he fired by means of a tinder-match.

I need hardly add that he never missed it: for when people are such keen lovers of sport as to shoot with such bad weapons they kill at every shot.

Biche was my professor, for he had taken a fancy to me.

He taught me all the tricks of hunter and animals; and, for every animal's trick he knew, he had one, and sometimes two, to cap it.

Later, his merits became appreciated, and, as he could not be prevented from poaching, he was made one of the keepers.

After a period of fifteen years' absence, not knowing what had become of him, I came across Biche once more as head keeper in the forest of Laigue, where I happened to be shooting by permission from the duc d'Orléans.

It was under his guidance that I had permission to shoot. We recognised one another, I greeted him with delight, and off we set. The great Saint Hubert alone knows what sport we had that day!

When the Revolution of 1848 caused shooting prerogatives in the royal forests to pass into the hands of private individuals, Biche gave up shooting. The privilege allowed to keepers in former days, of killing as many rabbits for their own private consumption as they liked, has now been taken away. Furthermore, they have now been deprived of their guns, and reduced to carrying only a stick by way of weapon.

On my last visit to Compiègne one of my friends, who rented a tenth part of the forest of Laigue, gave me all these particulars.

"Oh! heavens!" I cried, "my poor Biche; surely he has died of grief at being deprived of his gun?"

"Biche!" replied my interlocutor; "don't you be uneasy, he kills more with his stick than the whole lot of us with our rifles."

So I was partially comforted on Biche's behalf.

I profited marvellously under Biche's tuition, but such great happiness could not last long.

Impunity begets confidence, confidence tends to foolhardiness.

One fine day towards the end of February 1815, when the sun was shining brilliantly on a carpet of snow, about a foot in depth, I followed a thrush, which was flitting from tree to tree, with such close attention that I did not notice I was myself being followed. At length it seemed to settle in the middle of a bunch of mistletoe. I made a gun of my stick, adjusted it, and fired.

It had scarcely gone off when I heard these terrible words three steps from my side:—

"Ah! you little rogue, I have caught you!"

I turned round thoroughly scared, and I recognised a head keeper called Creton. His open hand was within half a foot of my coat collar.

I was too well acquainted with the game of prisoner's base to allow myself to be taken like that; I leapt on one side, and was soon ten steps from him.

"You may catch me, but I am not caught yet," I said.

He need not have taken the trouble to run after me, as he had recognised me, for the evidence of a gamekeeper is valid unsupported by other witnesses; but his pride was touched, and he rushed after me in pursuit.

My legs had grown since the day on which Lebègue had given me chase with such humiliating results to myself. Creton saw at the first glance that I was a hard runner, and that he would not get much change out of me, but he did not give up trying to overtake me. I made for the open plain, which was separated from me by a six-foot wide ditch. A six-foot ditch was nothing to me, and I more than cleared it.

Creton, carried away by his chase, tried to do the same, but his legs were four times older than mine, and years had taken away their elasticity. Instead of alighting on the other side, he fell on the near side; and instead of continuing his chase at top speed, as I was doing, he got out of the ditch on all fours, got up with great difficulty, and went hobbling on his way, leaning on the butt of his rifle.

He had twisted his ankle: this did not improve matters for me, and I returned to Montagnon and told him the whole story.

"Bah!" he said, "we have dealt with many another ogre such as he, and we are not dead yet."

"But, tell me, can't he put me in prison?"

To go to prison was the supreme fear of my childhood. One of my playfellows, Alexandre Tronchet, had been put in prison for twelve hours for pillaging. I had accompanied him to the end of the town, and only one thing had prevented me from being one of the party: I was wearing a long coat; they thought I should not be able to run easily in case of a chase, and that I should therefore be taken and compromise the whole band.

Therefore they hounded me back ignominiously.

I was not an accomplice in the fact, but I was in intention. When I saw Alexandre Tronchet put in prison I thought I should die of fear.

That was why I asked Montagnon so piteously if they would put me in prison.

"If they try to put you in prison, come to me, my boy, and I will prove to them that they have no law or right to imprison you."

"What else could they do?"

"They can fine you and confiscate your gun."

"Your gun, you mean."

"Oh! that doesn't matter, I will give you another worth thirty sous."

"Yes, but the fine, what will that come to?"

"Oh! as to that, the fine will be a matter of fifty francs."

"Fifty francs!" I exclaimed: "they will ask my mother for fifty francs! Oh! goodness! What shall I do?"

And I felt ready to burst into tears.

"Bah!" said Montagnon, "isn't there your cousin Deviolaine?"

I shook my head, for I had not such confidence as that in my cousin Deviolaine. I had asked him several times, in order to sound him:—

"Cousin, what would you do to me if you caught me shooting in the forest?"

And he had replied, in the gentle tones that characterised him, and with his usual charming trick of frowning his eyebrows as he spoke:—

"Do? I should fling you into a dungeon, you rascal!"

So Montagnon's efforts at consolation with regard to M. Deviolaine were not at all reassuring on that head; and I returned home, therefore, looking very down in the mouth. I kissed my mother more affectionately than usual, and turned to go towards my room.

"Where are you going?" she asked.

"I am going to do my composition, mother," I replied.

"You must do it after dinner; it is time for dinner."

"I am not hungry."

"What, not hungry?"

"No, I had some bread-and-butter at Montagnon's."

My mother gazed at me in astonishment; Madame Montagnon had not a reputation for such hospitality.

"Nonsense," she said.

Then she turned to an old friend of hers, who spent nearly all her time at our house, and whose life I worried with tricks, saying, half laughingly, half anxiously:—

"Oh! he must be poorly!"

"Don't worry yourself," the old lady replied; "the scamp has been up to some fresh mischief, and has probably an uneasy conscience."

Oh I dear Madame Dupuis, what a profound knowledge you had of the human heart in general, and of my heart in particular!

No, I hadn't a clear conscience, and so I remained standing at the window, half-hidden behind the curtains, exploring the square on all sides to see if a keeper or a policeman, or even Tournemolle, with whom I had already had a skirmish over my pistol, were coming to the house from some quarter or other.

One far worse than keeper, or policeman, or Tournemolle came into the square.

M. Deviolaine came himself!

For one moment I hoped he might not be coming to the house: we lived next-door to an old keeper on whom he called sometimes.

But there was soon no longer room for doubt; one might have said that a mathematician had drawn a diagonal from the rue du Château to the threshold of our house, and that M. Deviolaine had made a bet to follow this diagonal without stepping a single hair's-breadth out of the line.

My only hope lay in escape, and I had laid my plans in five seconds.

I flew rapidly down the staircase; through two glass doors at the bottom of the stairs one could see into the shop. Directly M. Deviolaine opened the shop door, I bounded through a door which communicated with Lafarge's house, and, from Lafarge's house into a path that led to the street; I gained the king's highway; I cleared the houses; I reached the place de l'Abreuvoir, by a back passage, and from the place de l'Abreuvoir I entered Montagnon's house by the famous back door, which until that moment I had looked upon only as a means of exit, but which I was to make use of twice in one day as a means of entrance.

From Montagnon's shop I could see across to our house, as much as one can see from one side of a street to the other.

There seemed to be a great commotion going on, as though they were looking for someone; I had no longer any doubt when I saw my mother appear behind the panes of the first landing window, open the window, and look out into the street.

It was evident that not only was someone being searched for, but that my mother was looking for this individual, and that this individual was myself.

I could not depute either Montagnon or his wife to go and make inquiries, for, although I came to them most days, they rarely visited our house: the sudden appearance of one or other of them would have seemed curious, and would assuredly have revealed the whole thing. So I kept quiet, under cover, as Robinson Crusoe said he did when he first saw the savages landing on his island.

After a quarter of an hour M. Deviolaine came out again, and I thought his face looked even angrier than when he went in.

I waited till it was dark, at five o'clock, and, night having fallen, I made myself as invisible as possible, and ran to my kind friend Madame Darcourt.

The reader may remember that when anything serious happened, I always had recourse to her; so once more I laid my case before her, confessed everything to her, and begged her to go to my mother's in order to learn how matters stood.

The good and worthy woman was so fond of me that she would humour my least caprice; so she hurried to the house, and I followed her at a distance; then, when she went in, I glued my eye to a corner of the window-pane.

Unluckily my mother turned her back to the window, so I could not see her face; but I saw her movements, which seemed to me dreadfully threatening.

After a quarter of an hour Madame Darcourt came out and called me, as she knew I was certain to be somewhere near. I let her call me two or three times; then, as I detected a more reassuring intonation in her third call, I ventured to draw near.

"Is that you, you naughty child?" said my mother.

"Come! do not scold him," interrupted Madame Darcourt; "he has been punished quite enough."

"Thank goodness if he has," said my mother, nodding her head up and down.

I heaved a sigh which shook the stonework against which I was leaning.

"You know that M. Deviolaine has been?" said my mother.

"Yes, I know he has, I saw him coming; that was why I ran away."

"He positively insists that you shall be sent to prison."

"Oh! he has no right to send me to prison," I retorted.

"What! he hasn't the right to do it?"

"No, no, no! I know he hasn't; I know what I am saying."

My mother made a sign to Madame Darcourt which I intercepted.

"Oh! you needn't wink like that," I said, "he has no right to do it."

"Well, but he has the right to prosecute you and to fine you."

"Ah! yes, that is true," I said; with a second sigh much heavier than the first.

"And who is to pay the fine then?"

"Alas, alas, dear mother, I know too well you must: but do not be anxious; I swear on my word of honour I will repay you the fifty francs when I earn any money!"

My mother could not keep from laughing.

"Ah, you are laughing!" I exclaimed, "so there is no more fear of a fine than of prison!"

"No; but there is a condition."

"What?"

"You are to go to M. Creton, you are to tell him you are sorry for what has happened, and you are to ask his forgiveness."

I shook my head.

"What do you mean by No?" cried my mother.

"No!" I replied.

"You dare to say No?"

"I say No."

"And why so?"

"Because I cannot go to him to tell him I am sorry he has sprained himself."

"You cannot say you are sorry that he has sprained himself?"

"Why, no! for I am glad he did. It would be a lie, mother, and you know you have often forbidden me to tell lies!... One day, when I was very little, you whipped me for lying."

"Did you ever see such a rogue!" said my mother.

"Nonsense, the child does not wish to lie," Madame Darcourt remarked laughingly.

"But the prosecution—and the fifty francs!" exclaimed my mother.

"Bah! what are fifty francs?" said Madame Darcourt.

"Oh, really! do you think then that fifty francs are a mere trifle to us?" my mother answered sadly.

The tone with which she said these words touched me to the heart, for it showed that the loss of the fifty francs was much, indeed too much, for my mother to bear.

I was just going to give in, and to say, "Very well, I will go to the man and tell him I am sorry he has sprained himself. I will say everything you want me to say!" ... when, unfortunately for my good intentions, Madame Darcourt, who had noticed the intonation in my mother's voice, even as I had, turned to me:—

"Listen," she said; "I haven't given you your Christmas box for this year."

"No, nor Léonor either."

"Nor Léonor either?" she repeated.

"Neither," I said again.

"Very well! if you are compelled to pay the fifty francs in question we will each give you twenty-five of it."

"Thank you, Madame Darcourt.... In that case I will run over to M. Creton."

"What for?"

"To tell him that everything has turned out well; that he only got what he deserved; that another time he is not to run after me; that—"

My mother caught me by the arm.

"Look here—go into the house and straight to bed," she said.

"It is all right; Creton will get something for his sprain, and M. Deviolaine for his writ; so it is all right.... Thank you, Madame Darcourt; please thank Léonor, Madame Darcourt.... Good-night all, I am off to bed. I am tired after my run; it is wonderful how sleepy running makes one.... Good-night—all."

And, running through the shop from one end to the other, I gained my room, enraptured to have got off so easily.

Creton issued his writ, and sent it in to M. Deviolaine, who, learning of my obstinacy, swore he would enforce it; he would assuredly have fulfilled his oath, had not news arrived on the 6th of March which no one expected, and which turned the world upside down to such an extent that Creton forgot his sprain and M. Deviolaine his writ.

CHAPTER III

Bonaparte's landing at the Gulf of Juan—Proclamations and Ordonnances—Louis XVIII. and M. de Vitrolles—Cornu the hatter—Newspaper information.

Bonaparte had landed on the noon of the 1st March, at the Gulf of Juan, and was marching on Paris.

People of another generation, who were not alive at that period, can form no idea of the effect this news produced when on the morning of the 7th March we read the following lines in the *Moniteur*:—

"PROCLAMATION.

"We adjourned the Chambers on the 31st of last December until the Session of May 1st, during which interval we have striven unceasingly in every way that could contribute to the tranquillity and the welfare of our peoples. That tranquillity is threatened, and that welfare may be compromised by *malevolence* and *treachery*."

Imagine, dear readers, one of those worthy citizens who subscribe to the *Moniteur*,—there are some who do, although not many,—imagine a mayor, a magistrate, a deputy magistrate; anyone, in fact, who by duty, by position, or by a sense of responsibility, is obliged to read Government prose: imagine one of these men, carelessly opening his official news-sheet, which he reads every morning from conscientious motives, falling upon this first paragraph, with its final disturbing expressions of *malevolence* and *treachery*.

"Dear, dear, dear, whatever is the matter now!"

And he goes on:—

"If the enemies to our country have founded their hopes in its divisions, which they are ever seeking to foment, its supporters, its legitimate upholders, will cancel that criminal hope by the invulnerable strength of an indestructible union."

"By all means let us crush such a criminal hope," says the worthy citizen, who does not yet know what they are driving at.

"By all means let us crush such a criminal hope," says the public functionary, who imagines it means some conspiracy among subordinate officers.

And the citizen turns to his wife, nods his head, and repeats—

"... 'By the invulnerable strength of an indestructible union! '"adding, "How well the Government puts it!"

Then the reader, whether citizen or public functionary, reads as follows:—

"Acting upon the advice of our well-beloved and faithful chevalier, Sieur Dambray, Lord Chancellor of France, whom we charge to carry out our orders, we hereby command as follows ..."

"Ah! now let us see what the king orders," says the reader.

"*Article 1.*

"The Chamber of Peers and that of the Deputies of Departments are specially convoked to meet at the usual place where their sittings are held.

"*Article 2.*

"Those Peers and Deputies of Departments who are absent from Paris must at once proceed there as soon as they become aware of this Proclamation.

"Issued from the Château of the Tuileries on March 6, 1815, twentieth year of our reign.

(Signed)

LOUIS."

"Well!" says the citizen, "it is odd that they do not state why the Chambers are convoked."

"Ah!" says the public functionary, "they convoke the Chambers specially, and do not indicate the day for meeting. Deuce take it! the situation must be very grave to cause such an omission."

"Ah!" they both exclaim, "here is an Ordonnance! let us read the Ordonnance, and perhaps that will enlighten us somewhat."

"ORDONNANCE.

"Acting upon the advice of our well-beloved and faithful chevalier, Sieur Dambray, Lord Chancellor of France, whom we charge to carry out our orders, we hereby command and declare as follows:—

"*Article 1.*

"Napoleon Bonaparte is declared a traitor and a rebel *for attaching himself to the main army* in the Department of Var."

"Oh! oh!" says the citizen, "what do they imply by that? They are deceived! Is not Napoleon confined to an island?"

"Why, of course," replies his wife "in an island called Elba."

"Very well, then, how could he get into the Department of Var; there is probably an *erratum* further on. Let us continue."

"What!" exclaims the public functionary, "what are they talking of? Napoleon has attached himself to the main army in the Department of Var? Goodness me! that is serious news; fortunately my wife's cousin is related to the usurper's valet de chambre, so that, if by any chance.... Let us read on."

And both continue:—

"It is therefore urged upon all Governors, Commanders of armed forces, National Guards, Civil Authorities, and even upon Private Citizens, to *seize him...*"

"To *seize him*," the citizen's wife here interrupts; "what does that mean? to seize him?"

"Why, it is plain enough; it means ... it means to seize him.... But you interrupt me just at the most interesting point."

"To seize him!" murmurs the public functionary; "I am glad I am not mayor, or deputy, or magistrate in the Department of Var."

Then both resume their reading:—

"...to seize and arrest him, to cause him immediately to be brought before a court-martial, which, after having proved his identity, shall *sentence* him according to the law.

"*Article 2.*

"Soldiers or *employés* of any rank who shall have accompanied or followed the above-mentioned Bonaparte shall be visited with the same punishment, and held guilty of the same crimes, unless they make their submission within a period of eight days.

" *Article 3.*

"All civil and military rulers, heads or employers of labour, or receivers of public trusts, or even private citizens, who shall offer assistance or help of any kind, whether directly or indirectly, to Bonaparte, shall be equally proceeded against and punished as abettors and accomplices in this rebellion.

"*Article 4.*

"Also all those shall be punished in the same way, who, by holding discourse in public places, or by issuing placards, bills, or printed matter, shall take part in, or incite citizens to take part in, the rebellion, or who shall abstain from repressing the revolt.

"Issued from the Château of the Tuileries, March 6, 1815, twentieth year of our reign. (Signed)

LOUIS."

The citizen re-reads it, and still he is in the dark.

The public functionary does not need to read it twice, he understands it all.

Imagine news like this, announced to France in such a fashion!

Whether the subscribers to the *Moniteur* understood it at first glance, or had to re-read it twice, the shock was just as startling and sudden in its character.

Ten minutes after the *Moniteur* had been opened by the Mayor of Villers-Cotterets, the event was known throughout the town, and every house divested itself of its inmates, who rushed out into the streets.

Every other journal kept silence.

This is how the news reached Paris, and led to the Proclamation and Ordonnance we have just read.

From Lyons, on the morning of March 5th, the news of the landing of Napoleon in the Gulf of Juan had been transmitted to Paris by telegraph.

The delay was explained by the telegraph lines stopping short at that period at Lyons. A courier had been sent off post haste from Marseilles on the 3rd, by the military commander, and had brought the news to his colleague of the Department of the Rhone during the night of the 4th and 5th.

The telegraph was under the jurisdiction of M. de Vitrolles, cabinet minister and State secretary. He it was who received the despatch, in the place Vendôme, where his offices were situated: he did not even wait to have his horses put to his carriage, but ran on foot to the Tuileries, to communicate the despatch to the king.

It was worded thus:—

"Bonaparte landed on the 1st March, near Cannes, in the Department of Var, with 1200 men and four pieces of cannon. He is marching in the direction of Digne and Gap, as though to take the road to Grenoble; all measures are being adopted to arrest and thwart this mad attempt. The utmost loyalty prevails in the Southern Departments, and public tranquillity is assured."

Louis XVIII. took the despatch out of M. de Vitrolles' hands and read it with the greatest calmness.

Then, when he had read it, he said:—

"Well?"

"Well, sire, I await your Majesty's commands," said M. de Vitrolles.

Louis XVIII. made a gesture with his shoulders as though to say, "Why should I be troubled over the matter?" Then aloud he said:—

"Go and see Marshal Soult, and tell him to do what is necessary."

M. de Vitrolles ran towards Marshal Soult's, but he did not need to go as far as the War Office, he met Marshal Soult on the *pont Royal.*

They both returned to the Tuileries.

The marshal doubted the truth of the news; and doubted it so thoroughly that he told the military commander he should receive his orders next day.

So one day—one whole day—was lost, when not one second should have been lost.

However, towards ten that night, it was decided that M. le count d'Artois should set off for Lyons, and M. le duc de Bourbon for la Vendée.

Next day, the 6th, the papers were silent; but the telegraph spoke again. It announced that Napoleon was definitely advancing towards Grenoble and Lyons *via* Digne and Gap.

It was only then at about two o'clock in the afternoon that it was decided to summon the Chambers and to draw up the Proclamation and Ordonnance we read in the *Moniteur.*

Villers-Cotterets was more inclined to Royalist than to Bonapartist feeling. The château which, under Louis XV. and Louis XVI., had been occupied by the duc d'Orléans and by Madame de Montesson and their court; the château where Philippe-Égalité spent his frequent exiles and pursued his finest hunting expeditions; the forest to which half the working population owed its livelihood, in which they worked, and from which three-quarters of the poor people got their beech-nuts and firewood; the forest which was part of the estates of the House of Orléans, since the marriage of Philippe, brother of Louis XIV., with Madame Henriette; the château and forest, we reiterate, had spread aristocratic traditions in the town, which the Revolution had done very little to efface, although it had placed its soldiers, and the Empire its beggars, in the dwelling-house of an ancient line of princes.

So the first impression this news of Napoleon's landing in the Gulf of Juan produced at Villers-Cotterets was more hostile than joyous.

The women specially distinguished themselves by a fiery outbreak of threats, which tended even towards imprecations.

Among these women there was one more fiery and energetic than all the rest: she was the wife of a hatter called Cornu.

Those, then, to whom this return of Napoleon was a hope (I will not say a delight, for at that period no one could guess the rapidity of the march which, thirteen days after the day on which we had learnt of his landing on the most distant point in France, was to take him to the Tuileries), instead of rejoicing, seemed more melancholy than ever, and entered their houses with lowered heads.

My mother was not, nor could she be, one of their number. Napoleon had not been so benevolent to us that his return could afford us the slightest pleasure; but we were perfectly well aware, both of us, that we were among the people who were menaced. What could a woman and a child do against these menaces?

We therefore entered our home with heads as bowed as though we were Bonapartists.

And indeed, from that time forth, so we were in the eyes of the inhabitants.

The situation was not exactly cheerful, and our position anything but reassuring.

It was true that not only the *Journal des Débats*, but all the other papers, spoke of Napoleon as a fugitive bandit driven back into the mountains, tracked by the inhabitants like a wild beast; who had failed in his attempt upon Antibes, and was repulsed by Digne, which had shut its gates against him; who was already repenting having risked such a senseless act as trying to reconquer France with only 1200 men, he who had lost it with 600,000!

All awaited, then, with impatience the papers of the 9th and of the 10th, when, no doubt, we should learn that the usurper had been taken, as the *Journal des Débats* desired, and, in accordance with the instructions of the Proclamation inserted in the *Moniteur*, a Court-martial had begun to try him.

Should it so happen, he would have been shot, twenty-four hours later, in a courtyard, a farmyard, a ditch, and all would be at an end.

Why, indeed, should his court-martial take longer than that of the duc d'Enghien?

The paper of the 9th came: but instead of the paragraphs we expected to find, we read that the fugitive had been at Castellane, at Barême, and for a short while at Martigny, where he had issued a proclamation to the inhabitants of Hautes-Alpes.

Incredible as the step might seem, when one considered that it was taken by so great a strategist as Napoleon, the fugitive was fleeing to Paris!

Meanwhile, M. le comte d'Artois had gone to Lyons.

It was indeed an honour to send the first prince of the blood to block the advance of such a man.

He was accompanied by the duc d'Orléans and the marshal duc de Taranto.

And, in addition to this, a royal proclamation, upon the advice of the duc de Dalmatia, minister of war, had called up the Royal Standard officers on half-pay in order to form a select corps, in all the principal places of each Department.

Another mandate, issued the same day, mobilized the Parisian National Guards.

On the 10th the news of a grand victory gained by the duc d'Orléans over the usurper spread over Paris, and so into the provinces. An officer of the king's household appeared on the balcony of the Tuileries, and, waving his hat, announced that the king had just received official information that the duc d'Orléans had attacked the usurper at the head of 20,000 men of the National Guard, in the direction of Bourgoin, and had completely beaten him.

Unluckily the papers of the 12th announced the return to Paris of the would-be conqueror.

The *Moniteur* even gave out that Napoleon had slept at Bourgoin on the night of the 9th; and that they expected he might *perhaps* enter Lyons on the evening of the 10th of March, but that it seemed certain Grenoble had not yet opened its gates to him.

This was the extent of our news at Villers-Cotterets, which was a day behind that of Paris, when a conspiracy broke out which, without seeming to be connected therewith in any way, yet gave rise to the feeling that there was an extraordinary coincidence between it and Napoleon's landing and march towards Paris.

We shall see in what fashion, child though I was, I was to be mixed up in this great affair, a matter of life and death.

CHAPTER IV

General Exelmans—His trial—The two brothers Lallemand—Their conspiracy—They are arrested and led through Villers-Cotterets—The affronts to which they were subjected.

May we be permitted to go back a little further, since our dramatic training has accustomed us always and in every detail to prefer the clearest and most lucid style of presentation?

We know what spirit of reaction had been abroad under the government of Louis XVIII., and what persecution during the first restoration the men who had served under the usurper (as Napoleon was called) had had to undergo.

The indiscretion of a few prominent people in the party called the ultra-Royalists had revealed the intentions of the monarchy; one of these designs, they said, was to exterminate the Bonapartists, as the Protestants had been exterminated under Charles IX.

The more absurd the rumours were, the more readily were they believed: the Bourbons were thought capable of the most outrageous projects. And there was—I will not say a great fright among those who were menaced (the old comrades of the emperor were not so easily alarmed)—but many rumours were abroad. Many left Paris, hoping to rouse less hatred by going far from that everlasting seething pot of intrigues; others rallied together, armed themselves, and resolved to sell their lives dearly. The Government grew uneasy at these gatherings, wished to dissolve them, and, in order to attain this end, forbade all general officers to remain at Paris without leave; ordering all those who were not natives of the capital to return instantly to their own parts.

We can understand what exasperation this would cause at a time of violent dissensions; the retired officers protested against the measure, and banded together to resist it. Compelled by the minister to choose between Paris and half-pay, several, although poor, preferred independence to submission.

The Government, annoyed by this resistance, looked out for some occasion to make a public example; one soon came.

A letter from General Exelmans to Murat was seized and opened. He congratulated the King of Naples on the preservation of his crown, and told him that thousands of brave followers would hasten to defend his throne if it were again threatened.

Marshal Soult was minister for war. He immediately placed General Exelmans on the retired list, and ordered him to put sixty leagues between himself and Paris at once, and to stay away until further orders.

Exelmans declined to obey. The minister, he protested, had no right to exile officers who were not on the active service list.

The marshal arrested him, and denounced him before a court-martial of the twofold crime of disobeying his chief and of holding correspondence with the enemies of the State.

General Exelmans was acquitted.

This was a terrible blow for the Government.

Military men who were not on active service *did not owe the Government obedience*. Then, comprehending from the hatred they bore it, that its hatred for themselves would show itself in some dreadful ebullition, they resolved to forestall it.

A meeting was held at the house of one of the generals who was most deeply compromised by his Napoleonic opinions,—Drouet d'Erlon, I believe, was the man. At this meeting, which was composed of officers on half-pay, as well as of officers in active service, it was decided that all those in active service who had a command should march on Paris at a given moment, with as many men as they could muster. Fifty thousand men would be found ready at the right moment in the capital; more than necessary to dictate terms. They would demand from the king the dismissal of the ministry, and they would compel him to drive out of France all those who were pointed out by public opinion as enemies to the Charter, and disturbers of the public welfare and peace.

This meeting had taken place, and these resolutions were drawn up before Napoleon's landing; but, as the movement broke out simultaneously with his return from Elba, the two events were connected together in people's minds.

The generals who took the leading part in this conspiracy were Drouet d'Erlon, whom we have already mentioned, Lefèvre-Desnouettes, and the two brothers Lallemand.

The duc de Treviso, under whose command the comte d'Erlon served, had the command of the 16th military division, whose headquarters were at Lille. Towards the end of February he was absent from his post, and as that moment seemed favourable the comte d'Erlon decided to take advantage of it. The moment was, indeed, particularly favourable, as it was just at the time when the telegraph wires transmitted the news of Napoleon's landing. The garrison of Lille, deceived by supposed orders, set forth on the 8th March, conducted by the comte d'Erlon; but it was met *en route* by the duc de Treviso, who, at Lille, had received the extraordinary news which was convulsing Europe; he questioned the generals who were leading the columns, guessed the plot, gave counter-orders, and re-entered the town with his army corps.

But all this time Lefèvre-Desnouettes had been acting too. Believing that the garrison of Lille had started on its way, and not knowing what had happened, he had moved the regiment of the old Chasseurs de la Garde, which he commanded; but when he reached Compiègne, about seven leagues from us, he found the 6th chasseurs—who bore the name of the duc de Berry—drawn up in battle array, with its colonel, M. de Talhouet, at its head. At this spectacle Lefèvre-Desnouettes was struck dumb, and did not know how to answer his officers and those of the 6th chasseurs, who asked the cause of his perplexity.

He left Compiègne abruptly, met General Lyom, major of the regiment of royal chasseurs, divulged a part of his projected plans to him, and suggested that they should join the conspiracy and help it forward. Major Lyom refused; Lefèvre-Desnouettes perceived that there was nothing further to be done in that quarter, and that he would but risk his life by persisting. He therefore exchanged his uniform for a peasant's dress, and set his face across country towards Châlons, where General Rigaut was in command, whom he knew to be a fanatical partisan of Napoleon.

The two brothers Lallemand had not been idle. One of them, a general of artillery, had gone to la Fère with the two other squadrons of royal chasseurs, and his brother had accompanied him. Their intention was to seize the arsenal and park of artillery. They first tried to seduce the gunners, then to entice General d'Aboville, who commanded the artillery school, to their cause; but both these attempts were unsuccessful—soldiers and general held to their posts. General d'Aboville, seconded by Major Pion of the 2nd regiment of artillery, ordered arms to be taken to the garrison, placed a portion of the troops in the arsenal and others at the gates of the town, armed them, and had cannons mounted in the battery. It was effort wasted, as that of Lefèvre-Desnouettes had been. The two brothers retired, followed by a little band of gunners who had come over to their side, but who dispersed when an organised pursuit began, so that the two brothers Lallemand were obliged to fly without even knowing, as Lefèvre-Desnouettes had done, where to go, and losing themselves in a country which was strange to them.

All this happened within only thirteen leagues of Villers-Cotterets.

The attempt was made on March 10th.

On the 12th the police force at Villers-Cotterets received orders to search the countryside; it had been reported that the fugitives had been seen in the direction of Ferté-Milon.

We saw the police pass by, and we knew the object of their expedition, through a friend of mine, named Stanislas Leloir, the son of an old sergeant who had been killed near Villers-Cotterets during the campaign of 1814.

It may well be believed that all this news—whether from Paris or from Compiègne or la Fère—put our little hole of a town into a great ferment. The epithet of *Bonapartist*, now used definitely as an accusation, sounded more often than ever in my ears, but under the circumstances my mother had strongly urged upon me not to resist it. I therefore let them call me Bonapartist as much as they liked. At night, gangs of street boys, twenty-five to thirty in number, would collect, open the doors of suspected persons, come right into the house and shout out "*Vive le roi!*": compelling the inmates to shout with them. Ten times a night our door, which opened on the street, would be assailed by hooligans in this way, and their cries sounded in our ears with an angry persistence which was most disquieting.

By day everybody collected in the squares. Villers-Cotterets, being on the high road from Paris to Mézières, by way of Soissons and Laon, is one of the vital arteries which feed Northern France; numberless carriages, diligences and couriers use it; each often bringing some bit of special news not given us in the papers. It was by these means we learnt, on the 13th and 14th March, of Napoleon's entry into Grenoble and Lyons, to which the papers either did not refer at all, or which they only mentioned to contradict.

Thus, on the 14th, we learnt that Napoleon had entered Lyons, that the comte d'Artois, even as the duc d'Orléans, had been forced to return without an army; and, suddenly, we heard a great noise towards the end of the rue de Largny. As the street forms a perfectly straight line, we turned to look in the direction from whence the noise came; we saw three carriages, harnessed like post-chaises and escorted by a strong piquet of police.

Everybody rushed towards these conveyances. In each carriage sat a general officer between two policemen, and besides these six policemen, seated opposite the three prisoners, were six more as escort.

The carriages came at a fast trot. So long as they were in the rue de Largny, which is quite wide, they were able to keep up the pace, but, when they reached the entrance to the rue de Soissons, a narrow and uneven street, they were obliged to go slower, on account of the hindrances they met.

We had asked and found out, in the meantime, that these general officers were the brothers Lallemand, for whom the police had been set to hunt the day before; that they had found them about six o'clock that morning, near a little village called Mareuil, riding on worn-out horses; they were harassed by a journey of three days' duration across country and through woodland, and had given themselves up without much show of resistance.

The two brothers Lallemand were in the first two carriages; the third, so far as I can recollect, was occupied by an ordinary aide-de-camp, captain, or orderly officer.

They were being taken to la Fère, we were told, to be shot.

They looked pale, but seemed collected.

When they entered our town they were greeted with furious cries, and the postilions, at a sign from the police, quickened the pace; but when, as I have said, they came to the rue de Soissons, they had almost to pull up, or to go at a foot pace; and the procession walked slowly in the middle of the population, which crowded each side of the street. The generals, who had doubtless believed that the whole of France would be unanimously in favour of Napoleon, seemed amazed that almost the entire population of that little town should surge round them in so hostile a fashion, and suddenly from the hatter's shop issued a furious woman, livid with anger, with dishevelled locks like one of the Eumenides; she scattered the people far and wide, dived between the horses of the police escort, sprang upon the step of the first carriage and spat in the face of General Lallemand, stretching forth, at the same time, her hand to tear off his epaulettes, and hurling the most indecent epithets at him in strident shrieks.

The general leant back in the carriage, and, in a voice charged rather with pity than with anger, asked:

"What is the matter with that unhappy woman?"

The police soon drove her away, but she began to run after the carriages, which would have to stop at the post, for fresh horses, about a hundred yards farther on.

However, her husband, her children and three or four neighbours caught hold of her, and prevented her from going farther.

This horrible scene, I need hardly say, had made a painful impression throughout the town, and from that moment the shouting ceased; the crowds still followed the prisoners and watched them with curiosity, but they kept silence.

The prisoners were being taken to la Fère, as we have explained, to be court-martialled and then shot, but they would have to spend the night at Soissons.

It was necessary to search the road in order to make sure that no seditious party was in waiting to carry off the prisoners.

In the midst of all this commotion and of all these painful scenes, as I was watching the carriages disappear along the Soissons road, I felt someone take hold of my hand, and, turning round, I found it was my mother.

"Come," she said in a whisper, making a sign with her head as she spoke, and I knew something important lay behind that word "*Come*," and her gesture.

She seemed terribly agitated, and she led me straight home.

CHAPTER V

My mother and I conspire—The secret—M. Richard—*La pistole* and the pistols—The offer made to the brothers Lallemand in order to save them—They refuse—I meet one of them, twenty-eight years later, at the house of M. le duc de Cazes.

My mother was the widow of a general, and she had not been able to witness the insult paid to men who wore the same uniform and the same epaulettes that my father had worn without being deeply distressed.

We were soon alone.

"Listen to me, my child," she said: "we are going to do something which will compromise us terribly, but I believe your father's memory demands that we should do it."

"Then let us do it, mother," I replied.

"You will promise never to tell a soul what we are going to do?"

"If you forbid me to do so."

"I do indeed imperatively forbid you."

"Then you can trust me."

"All right! put your things on."

"What for?"

"We are going to Soissons."

"What! Really?"

To go to Soissons was always a great treat for me. Soissons, a garrison town of fifth or sixth rank, was a capital in my eyes. Its gates had iron portcullises to them; the ramparts that I was going to see once more were riddled with the bullets of the last campaign; the garrison, the noise of arms, the odour of battle were all to my young mind intensely entrancing.

Besides, I had a dear friend in the son of one of the gaolers of the prison there (I ask my aristocratic friends of to-day to pardon me), who, when I went to see him, made me shiver by taking me into the most *delightful* dungeons under his father's care.

So my first call was always on him, and the thought that flashed across my mind was that, as soon as we were once more in Soissons, I would ask what had become of him, for I never liked to deviate from my old customs.

His name was Charles.

The news of our going to Soissons pleased me much. I ran upstairs to my room, I dressed myself as quickly as I could, and then I went down.

A little shabby carriage, half cab, half tilbury, belonging to a livery stable-keeper called Martineau, was waiting for us at the door.

My mother and I got in, and we took the way by the park. Behind the Castle wall we met (whether by accident or by design I know not) a lawyer of Villers-Cotterets, whose opinions were extremely Republican, and who clung to Bonapartism as a means of opposition. My mother left the carriage to speak to him, and she returned with a packet which she had not had when she got out, at least so it seemed to me; then we drove by *les grandes allées*, and in ten minutes' time we had reached the high road.

Three hours later we were at Soissons, which we entered about five o'clock in the afternoon—that is to say, two or three hours after the prisoners.

The town was in a great uproar, and they demanded our passports; it was, as the reader may guess, the very thing my mother had forgotten to bring with her.

As they insisted, we begged the policeman who had made this inconvenient request to come with us to the hôtel des *Trois-Pucelles*, where we always stopped on our visits to Soissons; there, the proprietor would answer for us.

We had also a distant cousin living in the town, a baker, whose name I have totally forgotten.

But he lived in the opposite suburb to that through which we had entered, while the hôtel des *Trois-Pucelles* was only a hundred steps away.

The policeman made no difficulty about accompanying us there.

As my mother expected, when we got there, the host burst out laughing in the policeman's face: he made himself answerable for us, and there the matter ended.

We asked for a room and dinner; and, although my mother had taken nothing all day but a cup of coffee, she ate very little; she was evidently greatly preoccupied.

After dinner, she sent for our host and asked him news of the prisoners.

It will easily be believed that they were the topic of the hour, and there was probably not a house throughout the town where a similar conversation to ours was not being held at that moment.

The arrival of the three carriages and their escort had made as great a sensation as it had in Villers-Cotterets; with this difference, however, that Soissons, instead of being Royalist like the county town, was Bonapartist.

This was not to be wondered at, for Soissons, being a fortified town, took its political opinions from the army.

Our host, in particular, greatly deplored the fall of the Government; he was therefore much distressed on account of the poor conspirators, and was able to give us the information concerning them which my mother wanted.

They had been taken to the town prison. My mother sighed, and I heard her say to herself:

"Oh! so much the better! I was afraid they would be in the military prison."

That was indeed where it was intended to take them; but the feeling among the soldiers was known. The defection of the 7th of the line, the rebellion of various corps which had been sent against Napoleon and had joined his standard, roused uneasiness which future events proved not to be exaggerated. So the authorities decided it was best to shut up the conspirators in the civil prison rather than in the military prison.

I listened to all these details with the greatest attention, for I felt quite sure our visit to Soissons had some connection with the event which filled everybody's mind, and the questions my mother put to our host confirmed me in this opinion.

I was not left long in suspense either, for he had scarcely left us when my mother, looking to see if we were quite alone, drew me to her and kissed me.

I looked at her, for there was something unusual and almost solemn in her embrace.

"Listen, my boy," she said: "I am perhaps wrong in lending my hand to such an enterprise, but when I saw those poor friends of ours go by, when I realised that mayhap in three days' time their bodies will be riddled with bullets, the sight of the uniform they wore, the same uniform that your father wore as a general, moved me to come to Soissons with you and to send you to play, as you have been accustomed to do, with the son of the prison warder; and, when inside—"

My mother stopped short.

"And when there?" I asked her.

"Tell me," replied my mother, "do you clearly remember the prisoners' faces?"

"Oh! mother, not only can I see them now, but I believe I shall always see them."

"Very well! it is probable that one or other of the three prisoners will sleep in the room called *la pistole*.... Do you know which *la pistole* is?"

My mother put me on my mettle. As though I did not know *la pistole,* I, who knew every nook and cranny of the prison!

"*La pistole,*" I replied, "I know well enough which that is! It is a room leading out of the keeper's dining-room, where they put prisoners who can pay forty sous."

"That is the one! Very well! it is probable, as I have told you, that one or other of the three prisoners will have been put in *la pistole*; it is also probable that the one to be put there will be the eldest of the brothers Lallemand, to whom the others will have conceded this luxury; it is also probable that the door of *la pistole* leading into the big room where the keeper has his meals may stay open.... Well, then, while playing with your little friend in the large hall, you must find an excuse for entering *la pistole*, and then, without being seen, you must give this packet to the one of the three prisoners who happens to be in *la pistole*."

"Indeed I will."

"Only, you will be very careful, my child."

"Of what?"

"Not to hurt yourself."

"Not to hurt myself—then what is there in the parcel?"

"A brace of double-barrelled pistols, ready loaded."

I understood that with the help of these pistols the prisoners might perhaps be able to escape, or at least, if the worst came to the worst, to blow out their brains.

"Mother," I said, "it seems to me that instead of carrying the packet, which might be noticed, and consequently taken away from me, it would be very much better if I were to put a pistol in each of my trousers pockets."

"But if you were to be wounded."

"Oh! don't be afraid; I can manage better than that," and in a trice I untied the parcel, and handled the triggers of the four barrels in a manner worthy of a pupil of Montagnon.

"All right," said my mother, somewhat reassured by the proof of my dexterity I had just given her; "I believe you are right; put the pistols in your pocket, and take great care the butts do not touch. Now here is a little roll."

This roll reminded me of the precious box whose cover the mole had eaten.

"Ah! there is gold inside?" I exclaimed.

"Yes," said my mother. "There are fifty louis in that roll—take great care not to lose it, for if the prisoners do not accept the money, I must give it back to the person who gave it."

"See, mother! I will put the roll in my fob."

I had no watch, but I had a fob.

I stuffed the roll in my fob, and flattened my waistcoat down over it.

Luckily, my poor mother always made my clothes too long and too large, to allow of my growing taller and stouter; so the pistols and the roll of gold could lie in my pockets and in the fob without appearing to bulge out too much.

"And now," I said, "I am ready."

Then my mother's courage seemed to fail her.

"Oh!" she cried, "if they discover what you are doing in that prison! if they were to arrest you!"

"I will not let them take me," I replied, drawing myself up with one of those braggart airs which made me so ridiculous when I affected them; "am I not armed?"

My mother shrugged her shoulders.

"My dear," she said, "the prisoners were armed also, and you saw them pass through Villers-Cotterets each between two policemen."

I would fain have replied; but my mother's argument was so obviously true that I had not courage to venture on another boast.

Besides, time was flying; it was nearly seven o'clock in the evening, and under the circumstances perhaps I might not be able to get inside the prison if I delayed any longer.

My mother gave a last glance to see that the pistols and the roll were not visible; she fastened round my neck a short cape which I used to wear in wet weather going to college, when the college existed, and we took our way towards the prison.

Although my dear mother tried to hide her emotion, her hand trembled in mine. As for me, I did not even suspect that we ran any danger whatever in doing what we were about to do.

When we reached the prison, my mother knocked at the door, and the wicket was opened.

"Who is there?" asked the voice of the keeper.

"My dear M. Richard," said my mother (as far as I can recollect, Richard was the good man's name),—"my dear M. Richard, here is Alexandre, who has come to play with your son, while I go and pay a call."

"Ah! is that you, Madame Dumas?" said the keeper. "Will you not favour us by coming in for a moment?"

"No, thank you, I am in a hurry; I will come back for Alexandre in about half an hour."

"All right—come when you like;" and the keeper began turning two or three keys in two or three different locks.

Then the door opened.

In a sort of entry which separated the street entrance from the keeper's room some guns and bayonets glistened.

My mother shuddered and pressed me to her.

"Do not be afraid," I said to her.

"Oh!" said my mother, *"oh!* It looks as though you had increased your garrison, M. Richard."

"Yes, do you know why?" said the keeper.

"I expect it is on account of the prisoners who came here to-night."

"Yes, as they are of high rank in the army, we could not refuse to put them in *la pistole*; but the guard has been doubled."

My mother squeezed my hand; I replied by pressing hers.

"Is there any news about them?" she asked.

"Nothing promising, Madame Dumas, nothing promising.... They are going to be taken to la Fère; then a Court-martial will try them, deliver judgment and, bang! all will be over."

The keeper made a gesture as though aiming a gun.

This horrid pantomime was but too intelligible.

"Could Alexandre have a look at them?" my mother asked.

"Why not? They are all three there in *la pistole,* on beds of sacking, as quiet as lambs. They have already asked for Charles a dozen times; he is as friendly with them as though he had known them for ten years."

"Oh! mother," I said in my turn, "I should much like to see them."

"All right, go with M. Richard and you shall see them—go."

My mother pronounced the last word with a swelling heart, but nevertheless with firmness; for she let go my hand at the same time and pushed me towards the keeper.

I nodded to her, and rushed into the lower room, shouting:

"It is I, Charles!"

Charles recognised my voice, and ran up to me.

"Oh!" he said, "if only you had come a bit sooner.... Hutin has just gone."

Hutin was a playfellow of ours, of whom I shall have occasion to speak later, with reference to the Revolution of July and my expedition to Soissons, where, more fortunate than the generals Lallemand, I carried off the town's supply of powder.

"Oh! what a pity he has gone ... but we can play just the same without him, can't we?" I said.

"Certainly."

"All right, come on."

And we went into the lower hall.

"We mustn't make too much noise," said Charles to me.

"Why not?"

"Because there are people in *la pistole.*"

"Oh! I know that—the prisoners.... I say, I should like to see them."

"They sent me out again just now, saying they wanted to sleep."

"Tell them I also am the son of a general. They must have known my father."

Charles went up to the door.

"Monsieur Lallemand," he said, "there is a playfellow of mine here who comes from Villers-Cotterets and who says you must know his father."

"What is his name?"

"He is called Alexandre Dumas."

"Is he the son of General Alexandre Dumas?" asked one of the brothers Lallemand.

"Yes, General," I replied, and I entered.

"Is that you, my lad?" said the general.

"Yes, General, here I am."

"Come, my boy, come, ... it is always a pleasure for a soldier to see the son of a brave man, and your father was brave. Is he dead?"

"Yes, General; he died eight years ago."

"And you have come to Soissons?"

"Yes, General."

Then in a low voice I added:

"To see you."

"What! to see me?"

"Yes ... send Charles away."

A single candle lighted *la pistole*; it stood on the table near the general's bed. He pretended to snuff it, and he extinguished it.

"Confound it!" he said, "I am clever.... Charles, go and light this candle again for us."

Charles took the candle and went into the lower room. We were left in the dark.

"What do you want with me, my lad?" asked the prisoner.

"General," I said, "I am commissioned by my mother and by friends of yours to give you a pair of double-barrelled pistols ready loaded, and a roll of fifty louis. I have them all in my pockets: will you have them?"

The general did not speak for a moment, then I felt him bring his face nearer to mine.

"Thank you, little friend," he said, and he kissed my forehead; "the emperor will be in Paris before our trial takes place."

Then he kissed me again.

"Thank you, you are a brave boy; go and play, and take care they do not suspect you came to see us."

"Are you certain, General, that you will not need either the pistols or the money?"

"No, thank you: the same offer has already been made me this evening, and I declined it."

"Then I may tell those who are frightened about you, that you have no fear?"

The general began to laugh.

"Yes, tell them that."

And he kissed me for the last time, and pushed me gently towards the door.

Charles returned with the light.

"Thank you, my boy," he said. "We really must go to sleep. Good-night."

"Good-night, General."

And I went out of *la pistole*.

Half an hour later, my mother came to fetch me. I embraced Charles, I thanked old Richard and I ran and threw my arms round my mother's neck.

"Well?" she asked.

"Well, mother, he refused everything."

"What! he refused everything?"

"Yes."

"What did he say?"

"He said that the emperor would be in Paris before they had shot himself or his companions."

"God send it may be so!" said my mother, and she led me away.

The next day we left at daybreak.

The fifty louis were returned to the lender; but, in commemoration of the courage I had shown in the undertaking, the pistols were given to me. They were splendid double-barrelled pistols, mounted in silver, and were, oddly enough, destined to play a prominent part in the same town of Soissons in 1830.

General Lallemand was not mistaken. Napoleon's march was so rapid that he got the start of the trial; besides, the judges themselves were not apparently sorry to delay matters, and so laid aside their responsibility.

On the 21st March, at six o'clock in the morning, a courier rushed into Villers-Cotterets at full speed. It was hardly light, but a good number of people were already at their doors to hear the news, and all thronged round the courier as he changed horses.

"Well?" they asked him, "what news?"

"Well, gentlemen," he said, "His Majesty the Emperor and King made his entrance into the Tuileries at eight o'clock last night."

A tremendous excitement ensued, and everybody flew off to tell the news; the postmaster alone remained.

"And you are going to spread this news through the department" he asked.

"No; I am carrying the order to set generals Lallemand at liberty."

The horse was saddled, he leapt up and rode off at a gallop.

The same day a barouche with four horses passed through at a great pace, making much commotion. It contained three superior officers. As the carriage drove along the rue de Soissons the window was let down opposite the house where the eldest of the brothers Lallemand had been so shamefully insulted. The woman who had spat in his face was on her doorstep when the smiling face of the general passed by her.

"Well, madame, here we are," he said, "safe and sound; every dog has his day."

And he leant back in the carriage, which continued its way towards Paris.

"Never you mind, you villain!" said the woman, shaking her fist at the retiring carriage,—"our turn will come again."

And indeed it did return. The assassinations of Marshal Brune, of General Mouton-Duverney, and of General Ramel testified to the fact.

In 1840 or 1842 I was dining at the house of M. le duc de Cazes with this same General Lallemand, whom I had never seen since the day he had embraced me in *la pistole* of the prison at Soissons. Twenty-eight years had passed since that day, and had carried away almost as many events in their train as days.

The man's hair had turned white, and the boy's hair had become grey.

After dinner, I went up to the general.

"General," I said, "do you remember March the 14th, 1815?"

"March the 14th, 1815?" repeated the general, trying to search his memory. "I remember it well! it is a date of great importance in my life. March 14th, 1815, was the day my brother and I were arrested after our attempt on la Fère.... Yes, I recall March 14th, 1815."

"Do you recollect passing through a little town called Villers-Cotterets?"

"Before or after my arrest?"

"After, General: you were in a carriage, seated between two policemen; your brother followed you in a second carriage, and one of your aides-de-camp was in a third. Six or eight other policemen accompanied you."

"Oh! I remember it perfectly, and this proves it: a woman climbed on to the step of my carriage and spat in my face."

"That was so, General; your memory is good."

"Oh! do you suppose one forgets things like that?"

"No, General, I do not say such things are easily forgotten.... May I ask you if you remember something else?"

"Proceed."

"Do you remember passing the night in the prison at Soissons?"

"I remember it perfectly—in a room adjoining the gaol."

"Do you recollect receiving a visit there?"

"Yes, from a boy of twelve or fourteen years of age."

"Who came to offer you from your friends—"

"Fifty louis and a brace of pistols! I remember it perfectly."

"You have forgotten to say, General, that you kissed that lad on the forehead."

"The deuce! and he deserved it indeed. Is it by any chance that boy—?"

"Was myself, General, a trifle taller, a trifle older since that day; but myself, all the same. That was why I would not be introduced to you, I wanted to introduce myself."

The general took hold of both my hands and looked me full in the face.

"Sacrebleu!" he said, "embrace me again!"

"Willingly, General."

And we embraced.

"What the deuce are you doing down there?" asked the duc de Cazes, who saw this welcome, and could not imagine what it was all about.

"Nothing," I replied, "nothing,—a mere trifle that occurred some time ago, between General Lallemand and myself."

Then turning to the general, I said, "General, who could have foretold on the 14th of March, 1815, at eight o'clock in the evening, that we should dine together one day at the table of M. de Cazes, an important official of the Chamber of Peers under Louis-Philippe."

"Oh! my dear fellow," said the general, with a shrug of his shoulders, "we shall see many more odd things yet, you may take my word for it!"

CHAPTER VI

Napoleon and the Allies—The French army and the Emperor pass through Villers-Cotterets—Bearers of ill tidings.

As the courier had said, His Majesty the Emperor and King had re-entered the Tuileries on the 20th March at eight o'clock in the evening, the birthday of the King of Rome.

Napoleon was as superstitious as the ancients, and would have his omens.

This one was somewhat incomplete. He re-entered the Tuileries on the King of Rome's birthday, but where was that crowned child who was to cost him so many paternal tears at St. Helena?

Alas! the very evening of the day on which I had seen him through Carrousel's palings he left never to return; and his empty cradle had been banished to a corner of the lumber-room. The man who in twenty days re-conquered thirty-two millions of men in so miraculous a fashion searched in vain among all the faces he cared so little about, for the beloved face of his child.

That face was to become pale and to fade away when he was far from it; Schönbrunn was endowed with two qualities which kill quickly: too chilly a sunshine and too fiery a love.

Was it in order to lull his own grief that this all-powerful man attempted to lie, by announcing to France that his child was to be given back to him? Did he stoop to feign an alliance with Austria to strengthen trembling hearts?

He had not yet finished his work; after re-conquering France, there was still Europe to fight.

The saying of the woman who had insulted General Lallemand when he passed through Villers-Cotterets free and triumphant, "Never you mind, you villain! our turn will come again!" was true enough.

Meanwhile a singular thing came to pass; my mother and I, who were daily threatened by the Royalists, had ended by desiring that the emperor should triumph, and, in fact, we, who had no reason at all for loving the man, delighted in his return to the Tuileries.

But justice should be rendered to the Bonapartists of the department of Aisne, and to those who had been compelled to become of that party: they exulted quietly, and, instead of making a great-to-do, as the Royalists would certainly have done, their behaviour wore almost the appearance of an apology.

Besides, no one knew what might be the upshot of all these events. At the first invasion the enemy had actually come from Moscow to Paris—that is to say, a distance of six hundred leagues; at the second it would only have to come from Brussels—that is to say, sixty leagues.

We were two days' journey from Paris upon that road, and only three days' distance from the Dutch and the Prussians.

True, the news received was good, and the emperor did not appear to be at all uneasy.

On the 4th April he had written an autograph letter to the allied sovereigns, in which he announced his return to Paris and his re-establishment at the head of the French people, with a charming ingenuousness, just as though it were not a European revolution he was proclaiming.

On the 6th he visited the Museum, probably for the purpose of seeing what sort of animals they had found to stuff during his absence. Then he paid a visit to David in his studio.

On the 7th he re-established the house of Écouen.

On the 8th the duc d'Angoulême was taken prisoner at Pont-Saint-Esprit.

On the 10th, he published the decree with reference to the armament of the National Guard.

On the 11th he ordered the duc d'Angoulême to be taken to Cette and there set at liberty.

On the 12th the business was of a more serious nature! He heard the report of the duc de Vicence on the armament of the foreign Powers.

On the 14th he received Benjamin Constant.

On the 17th he appointed Grouchy marshal of the Empire.

Finally, on the 20th, a volley of a hundred cannon proclaimed that the tricoloured flag floated over every town in France.

True, Louis XVIII. addressed his manifesto to the French nation on the 24th, and the Allies on the 25th entered into an agreement not to lay down their arms until after they had beaten Napoleon. Also, on the 30th, England offered to supply the Allies with a hundred million francs for three years; on May 3rd, Murat was defeated near Tolentino; on the 12th the Austrians entered Naples; on the 14th the King of Prussia issued his decree concerning the landwehr; on the 19th the Russians threw my father's old enemy, Berthier, out of the windows of his hotel at Bumberg; and, finally, on the 26th, the emperors of Russia and Austria and the King of Prussia left Vienna to march on France.

So there was no longer any hope of preserving peace, everything was again to be put to the test of war; and troops began to pass through Villers-Cotterets for Soissons, Laon, and Mézières.

It must be admitted it gave us great pleasure to see the old uniforms once again, and the old cockades moving along the road from the isle of Elba to Paris, and the grand standards, riddled with the bullets of Austerlitz, Wagram, and Moskova, in their cylindrical-shaped cases.

It was a wonderful spectacle to watch the Old Guard, a military type that has completely disappeared in our day, the very embodiment of the ten years of imperial rule we had recently passed through, the active and glorious spirit of France.

In three days' time, 30,000 men—30,000 giants—resolute, composed, almost gloomy in their attitude, passed by, every one of whom realised that a share of the responsibility of the great Napoleonic dynasty weighed upon him, to be cemented by his blood, and all of whom, like those beautiful caryatides of Pujet, which so frightened the chevalier de Bernin when he landed at Toulon, seemed proud of this responsibility, although they felt that they might break down under the weight that was one day to crush them.

Those men who marched thus with such a firm tread to Waterloo, to their graves, must never be forgotten! They typified the devotion, the courage, the honour of the noblest, the warmest, the purest blood of France! they embodied twenty years of struggle against all Europe; they were of the Revolution, our mother; they were of the Empire, our nurse; they were not the French nobility, but the nobility of the French people!

I saw them all pass by, all, down to the last remnants of the Egyptian army, 200 Mamelukes with their baggy red pantaloons, their turbans, and their curved sabres.

There was something more than sublime in the spectacle: it was a religious, sacred, and holy sight to see these men, for they were as surely and as irrevocably condemned to death as were the gladiators of old, and, with them, they could have said: *Cæsar, morituri te salutant!*

Only, these were going to die, not to serve the pleasures of a people, but for its liberty, and they went to their death not by compulsion, but of their own free will, by their own unfettered choice.

The gladiator of old was but a victim; in the case of our men it was self-sacrifice.

They passed through one morning; and the sound of their steps faded, and the last strains of their music died away in the distance. I remember that the music they played was the air of *Veillons au salut de l'empire*....

The next announcement that appeared in the papers was that Napoleon had left Paris on the 12th June, to join his army.

Napoleon always followed the road his Guard had taken; so he would pass through Villers-Cotterets.

I confess I had an intense desire to see this man, who, in making his heavy hand felt throughout France, had, in a peculiarly hard fashion, ground down a poor atom like myself, lost among thirty-two millions of human beings whom he continued to crush, while forgetting my very existence.

On the 11th we received official news of his passing; horses were commanded to be in readiness at the posting stables.

He was to set off from Paris at three o'clock in the morning; so he should pass through Villers-Cotterets about seven or eight o'clock.

At six o'clock I was waiting at the end of the rue de Largny with the most able-bodied portion of the population, namely, those who could run as fast as the imperial carriages.

But really the best way to see Napoleon would be where the relays were to be changed, and not as he drove by.

I realised this, and, as soon as I caught sight of the dust of the first horses, a quarter of a league away, I set off for the posting-house.

As I approached, I heard the rumble of wheels behind me coming nearer.

I reached the posting-house, and on turning round I saw the three carriages flying over the pavement like a turbulent stream, the horses dripping with sweat, their postilions got up in fine style, powdered and be-ribboned.

Everybody rushed for the emperor's carriage, and naturally I was one of the foremost.

He was seated at the back, on the right, dressed in a green uniform with white facings, and he wore the star of the Legion of Honour.

His face was pale and sickly-looking, as though his head had been clumsily carved out of a block of ivory, and it was bent slightly forward on his chest; his brother Jérôme was seated on his left; and the aide-de-camp, Letort, was opposite Jérôme, on the front seat.

He lifted his head, looked round him, and asked:

"Where are we?"

"At Villers-Cotterets, sire," someone replied.

"Six leagues from Soissons, then," he answered.

"Yes, sire, six leagues from Soissons."

"Hurry up."

And he relapsed into the semi-stupor out of which he had roused himself while the carriage was being got ready to proceed.

When the relays were in and fresh postilions were in their saddles, the stable lads who had taken out the horses waved their caps and cried: "*Vive l'empereur!*"

The whips cracked; the emperor made a slight inclination with his head in return for the greeting. The carriages set off at full gallop, and disappeared round the corner of the rue de Soissons.

The splendid vision had vanished.

Ten days passed by, and we heard of the crossing of the Sambre, the taking of Charleroi, the battle of Ligny, and the engagement at Quatre-Bras.

Thus the first echoes were those of victory.

We only learnt the results of the events of the 15th and the 16th on the 18th—the day of the battle of Waterloo.

We awaited further news eagerly. The 19th passed by without bringing any; the papers reported that the emperor had visited the battlefield of Ligny, and had ordered assistance to be given to the wounded.

General Letort, who faced the emperor in his carriage, was killed at the taking of Charleroi, and Jérôme, who had sat with them, had had his sword hilt broken by a bullet.

The 20th rolled by slowly and sadly; the sky looked black and threatening; it poured with rain for three whole days, and it was said that doubtless no fighting could take place in such weather.

All at once the rumour spread that some men who had brought bad news had been arrested and taken before the mayor; they declared, we were assured, that a decisive battle had been fought and lost, that the French army had been annihilated, and that the English, Prussians, and Dutch were marching on Paris.

Everybody rushed to the town hall, I, of course, one of the first.

And there we found ten or a dozen men, some still in their saddles, others standing by their horses, surrounded by the crowd, which was watching them; they were covered with blood, covered with mud, and were in rags.

They said they were Poles.

We could scarcely make out what they said; they spoke a few words of French, but with difficulty.

Some made out that they were spies; others that they were German prisoners who had escaped and who wanted to rejoin Blücher's army, pretending to be Polish.

An old officer who spoke German came up and interrogated them in German.

They were more at home in that language, and replied more coherently. According to them, Napoleon had engaged the English on the 18th. The battle began at noon; at five o'clock the English were defeated; but at six o'clock Blücher had marched *au canon*, arrived with 40,000 men, and decided the day in the enemy's favour: it was a decisive battle, they said; the retirement of the French army was a rout; they were the advance-guard of the fugitives.

No one believed such disastrous news; they only replied, "You will soon see."

We threatened to arrest them, to fling them into prison, and to shoot them, if they lied; they gave up their arms, and declared they were at the mercy of the authorities of the town.

Two of them who were badly wounded were taken to the hospital; the rest were put in the prison adjoining the town hall.

It was nearly three or four o'clock in the afternoon; these men had come from Planchenoit in forty-eight hours; they had ridden more than a league and a half per hour, for the bearers of ill tidings travel on wings.

When some of the men had been sent off to the hospital and others to prison, everybody dispersed to spread the bad news over the town.

As the posting-house is always the most reliable place at which to obtain news, my mother and I installed ourselves there.

At seven o'clock a courier arrived; he was covered with mud, his horse shook from head to foot, and was ready to drop with fatigue. He ordered four horses to be ready for a carriage which was following him, then he leapt on his horse and set off on his journey again.

It was in vain we questioned him: he either knew nothing or would not say anything.

The four horses were taken out of the stables and harnessed in readiness for the carriage: a rapidly approaching heavy rumble announced it was coming, soon we saw it appear round the corner of the street and draw up at the door.

The master of the post came forward and stood stupefied. I took hold of his coat tails and asked: "Is it he? the emperor?"

"Yes."

It was indeed the emperor, just in the same place and carriage, with one aide-de-camp near him and one opposite him, as I had seen him before.

But his companions were neither Jérôme nor Letort.

Letort was killed, and Jérôme was commissioned to rally the army by Laon.

It was just the same man, it was just the same pale, sickly, impassive face, but his head was bent a little more forward on his chest.

Was it merely from fatigue, or from grief at having staked the world and lost it?

As on the first occasion, he raised his head when he felt the carriage pull up, and threw exactly the same vague look around him which became so penetrating when he fixed it upon a person or scanned the horizon, those two unknown elements behind which danger might always lurk.

"Where are we?" he asked.

"At Villers-Cotterets, sire."

"Good! eighteen leagues from Paris?"

"Yes, sire."

"Go on."

Thus, as on the former occasion, when he put a similar question in almost the same words, he gave the same order and set off as rapidly.

That same night Napoleon slept at the Élysée.

It was exactly three months to the day since his return from the isle of Elba and his re-entrance into the Tuileries.

Only, between the 20th March and the 20th of June, an abyss had opened which had swallowed up his fortunes.

That abyss was Waterloo!

CHAPTER VII

Waterloo—The Élysée—La Malmaison.

I believe I was the first to say that Waterloo was not only a great political disaster, but a great blessing for humanity. Waterloo, like Marengo, was a providential event; only instead this time of being a victory it was a defeat, and we lost Waterloo from the same cause that made us gain Marengo. At Marengo, we were defeated by five in the afternoon. Desaix arrived, unexpected by the enemy; by six o'clock we had won.

At Waterloo we were victorious up to five o'clock in the afternoon, then Blücher came, unexpected by us, and by six o'clock we were beaten.

Never had the hand of God been more visibly extended over Europe, whose fate hung in the balance on that famous day of Waterloo, the 18th of June.

Napoleon, a man who gave his orders rapidly, clearly, and with precision, left Grouchy without orders.

Then, when he needed Grouchy, when he realised that the success of the day depended on Grouchy, he sent an orderly officer to hasten his arrival. The officer was taken, and Grouchy remained at Gembloux.

Why did he only send one orderly instead of ten or twenty? Was Napoleon short of orderlies?

And Grouchy heard the firing, but did not stir! Grouchy persisted in remaining where he was, in spite of the prayers and entreaties of his generals, and all the time Blücher was marching on.

There was one more cause, which I ought to have put first. I had it from his nearest relative, his most faithful friend, his last general, who never despaired, when everyone else despaired. True, the event is unworthy of a place in a historical account; but I am not writing a history, I am writing memoirs.

Have you remarked that at Ligny, Quatre-Bras, and Waterloo, Napoleon, who on days of battle never left his saddle, hardly mounted a horse?

Have you noticed that when, by a last and supreme effort, he tried to grasp the victory which was slipping from him, and put himself at the head of his Old Guard to charge the enemy himself, it was on foot that he charged?

Why was this? I will tell you.

When the battle was lost, when the English charge broke into the heart of our squares, when Blücher's batteries hailed bullets all round Napoleon; when the whole of that vast plain was like a furnace, a cemetery, or a valley of Jehoshaphat; when in the midst of all the shouts the fatal cry *Sauve qui peut!* was heard above all else; when the bravest were flying; when General Cambronne and the Guard alone stopped to die; Napoleon threw one last look on the vast extent over which the angel of extermination was hovering, and he called his brother Jérôme to him.

"Jérôme," he said, "the battle of Mont-Saint-Jean is lost, but that of Laon is won. Go and rally all the men you can, forty thousand, thirty thousand, even twenty thousand; stop at Laon with them; the position is impregnable, and I leave it to you not to let it be taken. In the meantime I will cross the country with twenty-five men and two good guides, and rejoin Grouchy, who is not more than five or six leagues from here, with thirty-five thousand men; then, while you arrest the progress of the enemy before Laon, I will fall on their flanks and scatter them into the centre of France: French patriotism will do the rest."

Then, like Richard III., after the battle in which he lost his crown and finally his life, he cried:

"A horse! a horse!"

His horse was brought him; he got up into the saddle with difficulty, selected his escort, called up his guides, and set his horse to a gallop.

But when he had gone about twenty-five steps he suddenly pulled up.

"Impossible," he said—"it hurts me too much!"

And he dismounted.

Jérôme ran to his side.

"Do your best," he said; "I cannot ride on horseback."

Napoleon, on his return from the isle of Elba, like François the First, had had his *belle Ferronnière*; the difference was, that she had not brought him the vengeance of a husband, but the advice of a diplomatist.

Man of destiny, thou hast finished thy work,—now thou must fall!

See him at the Élysée—the man with an eagle's glance, full of quick resolves, tenacious and masterful of purpose! Is this the hero of Toulon, of Lodi, of the Pyramids, of Marengo, of Austerlitz, of Jena, and of Wagram? Is this the hero of Lutzen and of Bautzen? Is this even the man of Montmirail and of Montereau? No, all his energy has been expended over his miraculous return from the isle of Elba.

At first he did not at all realise his defeat. He returned to that day unceasingly in St. Helena, drinking again the bitter cup to the dregs.

"An incomprehensible day! an unheard-of combination of misfortunes! Grouchy! Ney! d'Erlon! Had there been treason? Was it ill luck?... And though everything that skill could suggest had been done, everything failed just when it should have succeeded!"

It was the hand of Providence, sire!

"A strange campaign!" he murmured another time, "in which in less than a week I saw the assured triumph of France and the determination of her destiny slip thrice through my fingers! I should have annihilated the enemy at the beginning of the campaign, had not a traitor abandoned me; I should have crushed them at Ligny, if my left wing had done its duty; I should have crushed them again at Waterloo if my right wing had not failed me."

Sire, it was Providence!

Then, again, on another occasion:

"A singular defeat wherein, in spite of the most horrible catastrophe, the glory of the conquered did not suffer, nor was that of the conqueror increased! The memory of the one will survive in its destruction; the memory of the other may be buried in its triumph!"

No, sire, your glory did not suffer, for you struggled against fate. The conquerors called Wellington, Bülow, Blücher, were but mere shades of men, they were genii sent by the Almighty to defeat you.

Providence, sire, Providence!

Jacob wrestled a whole night against an angel whom he took to be a man; three times was he thrown down, and, when morning broke, as he pondered over his triple defeat, he thought he must have gone mad.

Three times, sire, were you also beaten down, three times did you feel the knee of the divine conqueror press upon your breast.

At Moscow, at Leipzig, and at Waterloo!

You, sire, who loved the poetry of Ossian so much, do you not remember the story of Thor, son of Odin? One day he reached a subterranean town, the name of which was unknown to him. He saw an arena in full play filled with spectators; a horseman clothed in black armour had thrown down his challenge, but had waited in vain since morning for an adversary.

Thor entered, rode straight up to the funereal rider, and said to him:

"I do not know thee, but I will fight thee nevertheless!"

And they fought from midday till nightfall. It was the first time Thor had encountered a champion who could withstand him. Not only could this adversary withstand him, but, every moment, Thor felt himself losing ground, and although his body trembled from head to foot with the blows he dealt, his blood seemed to freeze within his veins, and not a step was gained; then, when his strength failed him, when he felt himself falling, he fell on one knee, then on both, then on one hand, ever trying to fight, and he ended by lying in the dust of the arena, breathless, conquered, dying— he—Thor, he, the son of Odin!

"Because of thy courage and because thou hast done what none other has done before thee, I will spare thee," said the black rider. "But the next time you meet me and we wrestle together, you will not escape me."

"Who then art thou, conquering stranger?" asked the son of Odin.

"I am Death," said the dark horseman, raising the vizor of his helmet.

And it took Thor nigh a year to recover his strength after having struggled thus with Death.

It was with you, sire, as with Jacob and Thor; you thought you had lost your senses, and it took you a year to return to your old strength.

But let us return to him at the Élysee.

He arrived there at seven o'clock in the morning; later he saw what he ought to have done.

Listen to his own words:

"When I reached Paris I was exhausted, for I had neither eaten nor slept for three days. I had a bath whilst waiting for the ministers, whom I had summoned. I ought no doubt to have gone direct to the Chambers; but I was worn out with fatigue. Who would have believed they would have taken action so quickly? I reached Paris at seven o'clock; by noon the Chambers were in a state of insurrection."

Then, passing his hand slowly across his face, he added in a hollow voice:

"After all, I am but a man."

Cromwell and Louis XIV. were also but men, sire, and one entered Parliament with his hat on his head, the other with a whip in his hand.

But the one was full of faith, and the other was very young, whilst you, sire, had neither youth nor faith.

"I am growing old," he said to Benjamin Constant: "one is no longer at forty-five what one was at thirty. I ask nothing better than to be enlightened."

Sire, oh! sire, where had the fire of your genius gone that you should ask Benjamin Constant to enlighten you?

He arrived on the 21st, and on the 22nd he abdicated in favour of his son.

Why did he abdicate?

The Chambers demanded it. Think of Napoleon as a constitutional king hastening to yield to the wish of the Chambers!

Sire, was not the man of the 22nd June the same as the man of the 18th Brumaire?

But wait ... perhaps he believed all was lost? perhaps a ray of hope had sprung up, and it was to re-kindle the extinct light which caused him, in the darkness in which he found himself, to have recourse to the lantern of Benjamin Constant?

Jérôme arrived on the evening of the 22nd. It was high time, for Lucien had just insulted his brother. Lucien, the unambitious, the simple Republican, who had refused the title of King of Portugal, which the emperor had offered him, to accept that of Prince of Canino, offered him by the pope, had come to him and had made conditions at the Élysée, as Napoleon had made to him at Mantua.

"France," he said, "no longer believes in the magic of the Empire. She wants liberty, even if she abuses it; she prefers the Charter to the splendours of your rule; she, like myself, desires a Republic, because she has faith in it. *I will give you the chief command of the army*, and I will prevent a Revolution by the help of your sword."

You see, the moment was propitious. Jérôme was a young soldier, and had accomplished things which Napoleon would not have looked for from an old general. By dint of activity, perseverance, and determination, he had stayed the fugitives; he had rallied them under the walls of Laon; he had placed them under command of Marshal Soult, and he came, exhausted with fatigue, bleeding still from the wounds he had received, not like Lucien to impose conditions on his brother, but to inform the emperor of the reorganisation of the 1st, 2nd, and 6th corps, which, united to the 42,000 men under Marshal Grouchy, would make a total of over 80,000 men, an army with which he could begin operations immediately, and take a sanguinary revenge upon the Duke of Wellington.

Eighty thousand men was more than he had ever had during the campaign of 1814.

Sire, sire, we shall have to say, as was said at Montereau, "Come, Bonaparte, save Napoleon."

Napoleon listened to Jérôme, but made him no reply, and dismissed him; a moment later, a great tumult was heard on the terrace of the Élysee; two regiments of sharp-shooters from the guard of volunteers drawn from the working classes of the faubourg Saint-Antoine threaded their way through the garden in disorder; they were the forerunners of a vast column of men, the rank and file of the nation, who came demanding with loud shouts that the emperor should place himself at their head and lead them against the enemy.

These regiments were part of those of which General Montholon had just received command.

The emperor ordered him to make them return to their post, and he himself went out to them, not to excite but to calm their patriotic zeal.

One of these men called out:

"Sire, remember the 18th Brumaire."

You would think that at that word, that date, and that recollection, his heart would have leapt, his eye flashed? You would think that his horse would rear under him at the prick of his spur?

No.

"You recall the 18th Brumaire to me," he said; "but you forget that circumstances are different now. On the 18th Brumaire the nation was unanimous in desiring a change; it only needed a feeble effort to get what it wanted; to-day, it would take rivers of French blood, and I will never shed a single drop to defend my personal cause." He realised then that there were now two causes—his own, and the cause of France.

Ah! you are right this time, sire! You foresaw the first glimmerings of that great light which caused you to say at St. Helena:

"In fifty years Europe will be either Republican or Cossack."

The two regiments withdrew, murmuring, "What has come to the emperor? He no longer recognises us."

And, as a matter of fact, he was no longer recognisable. He fled from Paris on the 25th for Malmaison, where fresh dilemmas awaited him.

He seemed unconscious of anything around him. The calmness, or rather the dejection, he had shown at the Élysee terrified both friends and foes.

"The lion is sleeping," they said in low tones, for fear of awaking him.

His departure for Malmaison was looked upon as meaning something important. The emperor had left Paris to have a free hand; he would make a detour, he would reach the road to Laon again, by way of St. Denis and, before three days were over, the sound of cannon, of a fresh Montmirail, would be heard.

General Becker was therefore sent to watch his movements.

They might have kept calm, for he was only going as far as Malmaison! All the vanquished man wanted was a fast sailing vessel to take him quickly to America; he longed to retire into private life and to become a citizen of New York or of Philadelphia: to be a planter, a squatter, a labourer.

Sire, the stuff wherewith to build a consul, an emperor, and a king was in you, but you could not make a Cincinnatus.

The men who governed in your stead knew this well, and they issued order upon order to expedite your departure. Whilst you remained at Malmaison there was no security for the Bourbons, with whom they were already in treaty.

And yet they were mistaken; for what was the emperor doing at Malmaison? With his feet on the window-sill he was reading Montaigne.

All at once there was a great noise, and beating of drums and fanfare of trumpets, and the air resounded with cries of *"Vive l'empereur! Down with the Bourbons! Down with traitors!"*

"What is that, Montholon?" asked the emperor.

"Sire, it is Brayer's division: twenty thousand men who have returned from la Vendée; they have stopped in front of the Castle palings."

"What do they want?"

"They demand their emperor again, and if he will not come to them, they declare they will come and take him."

The emperor remained wrapped in thought for a moment; he was probably calculating that with the 80,000 men under Soult, the 20,000 men under Brayer, 50,000 of the federated army and 3,000,000 of National Guard, he would still have a splendid means of defence at his disposal, and could maintain a fine struggle.

He was told that General Brayer wished to speak to the emperor.

"Let him come in."

"Sire, sire, in the name of my soldiers, in my own name, and in the name of France, come, sire,—we are waiting for you."

"What to do?"

"To march against the enemy; to avenge Waterloo; to save France! Come, sire, come!"

A year later, his feet on the window-sill at Longwood, a book in his hand as at Malmaison, he said:

"History will reproach me for letting myself be taken too easily. I confess there was some spite in my decision. When at Malmaison I offered the Provisional Government to place myself at the head of the army in order to take advantage of the imprudence of the Allies and to annihilate them under the walls of Paris: before the end of the day, twenty-five thousand Prussians would have laid down their arms. But they did not want me. I sent the leaders away, and I left the place myself. I was wrong: my good countrymen have the right to reproach me for it. *I ought to have mounted on horseback when Braye's division appeared before Malmaison; allowed myself to be taken back by it to the army; fought the enemy and taken command of affairs, rallying round me the people of the faubourgs of Paris. That twenty-four hours' crisis would have saved France a second Restoration.*

"I should have destroyed the effect of Waterloo by a great victory, and I should have been able to make terms for my son, if the Allies had insisted on setting me aside."

Therein, sire, you were mistaken. No, your good countrymen had nothing to reproach you with. No, you were not wrong to leave. No, we needed the second Restoration, the Revolution of 1830 and that of 1848; we needed the Republic; degenerate though it is, it will be godmother to all the other European republics. And you needed the hospitality of the *Bellérophon*, the voyage in the *Northumberland*, the exile to St. Helena; you needed the persecutions at Longwood; you needed Hudson-Lowe; your long agony was as necessary to you as the crown of thorns and Pilate and Calvary were to Christ.

You would not have been so god-like had you not suffered your passion.

CHAPTER VIII

Cæsar—Charlemagne—Napoleon.

It now remains for us to explain why it was that this man was both so strong at the beginning of his career and so weak at its close; why, at a given hour, in the prime of life, at forty-six years of age, his genius deserted him, his fortune betrayed him. The reason is this: he was but an instrument in the hands of God, and when God no longer had need of him He broke him.

I must re-write what I wrote in 1832; eighteen years have rolled by: time has confirmed my judgment in every particular. The Duke of Reichstadt died at Schönbrunn, Louis-Philippe died at Claremont, France is a Republic, and if a Bonaparte is at the head of the French people he is so simply as the titular president, the elected magistrate, the removable head.

In the eyes of historians who simply relate facts, who watch the game of chance being played on earth and not the will of Providence working above, Napoleon was a madman like Alexander, or a despot like Cromwell.

Napoleon was neither the one nor the other. Napoleon belongs to the race of Cæsar and Charlemagne. Just as those two men each had his mission, Napoleon had his.

These three men made the modern world. Cæsar's was the first hand that worked therein, Napoleon's the last.

Cæsar, a pagan, prepared the way for Christianity; Charlemagne, a barbarian, prepared the way for civilisation; and Napoleon, a despot, prepared the way for liberty.

Not one of these three men knew what he did, for, the greater the genius, the blinder is it. It is the instrument of God, that is all: *Deum patitur*, as Luther said.

Cæsar, the general and dictator, passed across the world with his immense flood of an army, in which fourteen nations were absorbed like so many streams, making one watercourse by their junction, one people out of all their peoples, one language out of their many tongues, an organisation which only passed out of his hands to become under Augustus a single empire out of all the other empires.

Then, when the time was ripe, Christ, the Sun of civilisation, was born in an obscure corner of Judea, in the far East, whence rises the day, and He shone upon the Roman world. The rays of Christianity separated the ancient age from the modern age, and gave light for three centuries before Constantine was illumined by them.

Charlemagne, whom certain historians (whose fame is already secured to them) have presented to the world as a French emperor, was simply and solely of Northern descent; he was, as we have stated, a barbarian, who, having never learned to write even his name, sealed his treaties with the hilt of his sword, and made them respected with the point. His chosen state was Germany, the cradle of his race; his two capitals were Aix-la-Chapelle or Thionville; he spoke Teutonic by choice, and he dressed in the costumes of his ancestors. Eginhard tells us what that dress was. He wore a linen shirt and drawers under a tunic bound round by a silken girdle; socks and fillets round his legs; sandals on his feet. In winter, a jerkin of otter skin kept the cold from his body and shoulders. He was always protected by the *saye des Vénètes*. He despised foreign clothes, and the more sumptuous they were the less he liked to be dressed up in them. Only twice during the visit he paid to Rome, first at the request of Pope Adrian and then at the instance of Pope Leo, did he consent to don the chlamys and the Roman toga; and, when he saw the Roman tongue gain ground over his own, he gave orders for the collection of all his native songs, so that they should not be lost to posterity.

Those were his acts; now see what he was commissioned to do. We have indicated Cæsar's mission; Charlemagne's mission was to raise in the heart of the Europe of the ninth century, half-way between the time of Cæsar and of Napoleon, a colossal empire, against whose outposts those warlike nations, whose repeated inroads hindered the Word of Christ, and overturned all attempts at civilisation, should dash themselves in vain. Thus the long reign of that great emperor was dedicated to but one object: barbarian repulsing barbarian, driving the Goths back to the Pyrenees, and hounding out Huns and Alans as far as Pannonia. He destroyed the kingdom of Didier in Italy, and, after having overcome Witikind, who was hard to overcome, and being weary of a war that had lasted thirty-three years, anxious to put an end to all resistance, treason, and idolatry at a single blow, he went from town to town, and, planting his sword in the ground in the heart of each city, he drove the people into the public places, and cut off the head of every man who was taller than the height of his sword handle.

One people alone managed to escape him—the Normans, who, later, combined with other peoples already established in the plains of Gaul, were to form the French nation. Wherever they put their foot on the soil of his empire, Charlemagne quickly made his appearance as well, and as soon as he appeared they went back into their vessels, like frightened sea-birds flying along the coasts, skimming over the ocean with rapid motion.

Charlemagne, in ignorance of the future, wanted to exterminate them, and, when old, he wept to see them cast anchor in a port of Narbonnese Gaul. He rose from his table in great fear, and stood looking out of his window for a long time, with his arms crossed, weeping, and not even wiping away his tears; then, as no one dare disturb so deep a grief, he said: "My faithful followers, can you tell why I weep so bitterly? It is certainly not because I fear those men will harm me by their wretched raidings; but I am deeply afflicted because they have dared to approach this sea-board during my very lifetime; I am miserable and utterly wretched when I foresee what sorrow they will cause my children and their peoples."

These Normans whom you wished to exterminate, O noble emperor! those men whom you looked upon as savages and whose escape out of your hands caused you to shed tears of rage—do you know whom they were? They were the ancestors of William the Conqueror; those daring vessels were the embryo of that English navy, which was one day to cover the three oceans, whose thousands of ships and vessels were to put a girdle round the globe.

We have said that Cæsar prepared the way for Christianity and Charlemagne prepared the way for civilisation; let us now see how Napoleon prepared the way for liberty.

When Napoleon appeared before our fathers under the name of Bonaparte, France was just emerging, not from Republicanism but, from a state of Revolution. She had disturbed the balance of the world by feverish political conditions that had shaken her for nine years and put her far in advance of other nations. An Alexander was needed to tackle this Bucephalus, an Androcles to combat this lion. The 13th Vendémiaire placed them face to face, and Revolution was conquered. Crowned heads, who should have recognised a brother at the head of the struggle in the rue Saint-Honoré, believed they saw an enemy in the Dictator of the 18th Brumaire. They took the man who was already the head of a monarchy to be simply the consul of a Republic, and, in their stupid ignorance, they made war against him, instead of incarcerating his energies in a general peace.

Thus Bonaparte gave way to Napoleon with his double-edged instinct for despotic rule and warfare, his two-sided nature, democratic and aristocratic, behind-hand, according to French notions, but in advance of European ideas; conservative in home policy, but a creature of progress in foreign affairs.

He took all the youth and intelligence and strength of France; he formed armies of this material, and spread his forces over Europe; they carried death everywhere to kings, but the breath of life to their peoples. Wherever the genius of France went, liberty made gigantic strides in its wake, throwing revolutions to the winds as a sower scatters seed.

Napoleon fell in 1815, and only three years passed over before the crop which he sowed was ripe for harvest.

In 1818 the grand-duchies of Baden and of Bavaria clamoured for and obtained a constitution.

In 1819 Wurtemberg clamoured for and obtained a constitution.

In 1820 there was a Revolution and constitutional changes in Spain and Portugal.

In 1821 there was a Revolution and constitutional changes in Naples and Piedmont.

In 1822 occurred the insurrection of the Greeks against Turkey.

1823 saw the institution of Prussian States.

A single nation escaped this progressive influence on account of its topographical position, it was too far off for us ever to think of setting foot in it. Napoleon gazed at it so long that he became accustomed to its distance, till it seemed at first possible, and finally easy, to bridge that distance. He only wanted an excuse to conquer Russia as he had conquered Italy, Egypt, Austria, Prussia, and Spain! He had not long to wait for this excuse. In spite of the interview with Niémen, in spite of the fraternal greeting between the two emperors, a vessel entered a port on the Baltic, and war was speedily declared between Napoleon the Great, Emperor of the French, King of Italy, and his brother, Alexander I., Czar of all the Russias.

At first it seemed as though the foresight of God were fighting against the despotic influence of a man. France entered Russia but as a lance enters the body, by a wound: liberty and serfdom could have no contact with each other.

It was in vain for Napoleon to scatter abroad programmes and revolutionary proclamations, no seed could germinate on such cold soil; for, before our armies,-not only the enemy's armies retreated but the whole population. We invaded a desert country, and it was a burning capital that fell into our hands. When we entered Moscow, it was not only uninhabited, but in flames!

Napoleon's mission was fulfilled, and his downfall had begun; henceforth his fall was to be as serviceable to liberty as his rise had been. The czar, who had been so prudent before the conquering enemy, might be imprudent with a conquered enemy. He had retreated before the conqueror; perhaps he would pursue the fugitives.

The hand of God was withdrawn from Napoleon, and, although Divine intervention was this time plainly visible in human affairs, it was no longer men who fought against men. The order of the seasons was subverted: snow and cold stole a forced march; these were the elements that destroyed our army.

And now the events foreseen by the wise came to pass: Paris did not carry civilisation to Moscow, Moscow came to ask for it from Paris.

Two years after the burning of his capital, Alexander entered ours.

But his sojourn was of short duration. His soldiers scarcely touched French soil; our sun, which was to enlighten them, was too dazzling for them.

God recalled His elect. Napoleon reappeared, and fate's gladiator set forth, still bleeding from his last struggle, not to beat, but to be beaten at Waterloo.

Then Paris re-opened its gates to the czar and his wild army. This time, their occupation lasted three years. The men of the Volga, the Tanaïs, and the Don camped on the banks of the Seine. They became impressed with new and strange ideas, they stammered the unknown words of civilisation and freedom, they returned regretfully to their barbarous country; and, eight years later, a Republican conspiracy broke out in St. Petersburg.

Turn over the great book of the past, and tell me whether you can find in any other period so many tottering thrones, and kings fleeing along the great highways.

These imprudent folk had buried alive the enemy they had so badly beaten, and the modern Encelados shook the world every time he moved in his grave.

CHAPTER IX

The rout—The haricot mutton reappears—M. Picot the lawyer—By diplomatic means, he persuades my mother to let me go shooting with him—I despise sleep, food, and drink.

Had any doubt remained in the minds of the most obstinate of sceptics concerning the disaster at Waterloo, which had been announced at Villers-Cotterets by the fugitives whom we had seen bespattered with mud and blood, Napoleon's journey through would have dissipated them.

Besides, this advance guard of fugitives was merely the precursor of the rest of the army, which began to put in its appearance on the morning of the 22nd. They all passed through in a motley crowd, first those who had extricated themselves from that horrible carnage, safe and sound or slightly wounded, marching by in disorder, without drums, almost weaponless.

Next came those who were wounded more severely, but could yet manage either to walk or to ride.

It was a terrible yet an imposing sight, its very hideousness awe-inspiring.

And at the end came those who could neither walk nor sit on horseback: unfortunate creatures, who had lost their arms, or whose legs were broken, wretches with great wounds through their bodies, lying in waggons, either badly bandaged or else not bandaged at all, unhappy beings who lifted themselves up now and then, and, waving their blood-stained rags, cried, *"Vive l'empereur!"*

Many fell back dead: it was their last cry.

This funereal procession lasted for two or three days.

Where were all these men being taken? Why was their anguish prolonged by such an exposure to the burning June sun, by the jolting of waggons, and by the absence of proper medical attention?

Were there so many that all the towns between Waterloo and Villers-Cotterets were filled to overflowing?

Oh! what a hideous, mad, stupid thing war is, seen divorced from the blaring of trumpets and rolling of drums, the smoke of cannon and the fusillade of guns.

We could recognise among this débris the remains of those splendid regiments we had seen pass by so proud, so determined, whose bands had borne witness to their enthusiasm as they marched by playing *"Veillons au salut de l'empire!"*

Alas! the army was destroyed, and the Empire crushed.

Finally, fewer waggons went by, and soon there were no more.

Then the troops Jérôme had rallied under the walls of Laon began to file past; each regiment reduced by two-thirds.

Fifteen of the unfortunate Mamelukes had survived; the others had been either killed or scattered.

Two or three out of the twenty-five or thirty officers who had lodged with us called to see us as they passed through: the others were left behind, either at the farm of Hougoumont or at la Haie-Sainte, or in the famous ravine which served as a common ditch wherein ten thousand heroes were buried! My sister and her husband arrived in the midst of this rout. Thanks to M. Letellier's excellent conduct as mayor during the siege of Soissons, in 1814, his son had obtained promotion, and was made *contrôleur ambulant* at Villers-Cotterets.

They came in by the Paris road just as the enemy was expected from the Soissons road.

The cruelty was not so great this time, as no resistance was offered.

Napoleon had abdicated, and Napoleon the Second had been proclaimed. No one seemed to put serious belief in that proclamation, not even those who had brought it about.

One day we heard clarions playing a strange air, and saw five or six thousand men enter the main square of our town.

They were Prussians of the grand-duchy of Baden, clad in their elegant uniform, faultless, save that it is too elegant for military purposes.

An English regiment marched in along with them, and two English officers fell to our lot.

The famous haricot mutton reappeared; our guests were two fine hearty young fellows, who did ample justice to it.

They spoke no French. I, of course, knew no English at that time. One of them began to talk to me in Latin.

At first, I confess, I thought he was still talking to me in English, and I admired his perseverance.

Finally I discovered that he was offering to drink a glass of wine with me, in Virgil's tongue.

I accepted, and for the rest of the day we managed to understand one another or very nearly so.

The workhouse that we had abused so much saved us from having a strange garrison; and the great stream of English, Russian, and Prussian soldiers passed through without stopping.

Then news reached us from Paris, from the provinces, and from abroad; much of it was of terrible import to us.

On the 2nd of July, while the allied powers were declaring Napoleon to be a prisoner of war, Marshal Brune was assassinated at Avignon.

Alas! he was the only one of all my father's friends who had remained faithful to us! I vowed then that one day, when I grew up, I would go to Avignon, and in some way or other I would make his murderers pay for their crime.

I kept my word.

On the 19th of August, as Napoleon reached the Straits of Gibraltar, Labédoyère was shot.

On the 13th of October Murat was shot at Pozzo, and on the 7th December Marshal Ney was shot in the walk leading to the Observatoire.

After these events everything settled down into its usual course, and in our little town, far removed from public news, isolated in the heart of a forest, one might readily believe that nothing had been changed; one or two folk had had nightmare, like Mocquet, and that was all.

We were among the number. It will be well understood that Napoleon's return and the events of the Hundred Days had made M. Deviolaine forget all about M. Creton's prosecution, and there was no longer any talk about either the fifty francs compensation or about the confiscation of my gun.

Nevertheless, my gun had been almost as completely confiscated as though it had fallen into the hands of the Inspector of the Forest. It had been hidden. Not for fear the Prussians would seize it as a weapon of war, but lest they should make off with it because of its beauty. It became rusty during its concealment, so I had to take it to my good friend Montagnon to be put right again.

When there, as can be imagined, it was always at my disposition.

Among the people who frequented our house was a M. Picot, a solicitor— brother of Picot de Noue and of Picot de l'Épée, a great hunter before the Lord, and almost as much envied by me as a sportsman in the open country as M. Deviolaine was as a hunter in the forest. His brother was very proud of his preserves, although he did not shoot at all and his son shot but little, and as the farm ran to three or four thousand hectares, M. Picot, the solicitor, and his pointer, had the freedom of three or four of the best stocked preserves round Villers-Cotterets. So, although he was not considered one of the best shots in our parts, he made splendid bags, which filled me with envy when their bulging sides revealed what had happened as he passed by our house to "*return to his own fireside*," as he used to put it.

I made up my mind that it was not sufficient that M. Picot should be one of our friends, but that it was very necessary I should be one of his. When this resolution was well fixed in my mind, I began coaxing him.

How did I manage it? I can hardly say, for the man was not easy to seduce; I only know that after a month's wheedling M. Picot offered to take me shooting with him.

But he would not take me without my mother's consent, and there lay the difficulty!

I laid my request before her, M. Picot, be it understood, being present when I did so, and my poor mother turned quite pale.

"Oh, M. Picot!" she said to him, "when we have the examples of M. Denré and of your poor nephew Stanislas before our eyes, how can you have the heart to take him from me?"

"Good gracious! I am not taking him away from you," M. Picot replied. "I do not want to be accused of leading away a child under age: I wanted to give him a bit of pleasure; the boy is crazy after shooting, and you know whom he takes after in that respect.... If you do not want him to enjoy himself we will say no more about it."

Although I did not appreciate his meaning at first, his way of putting things was clever; for, though brief (a great virtue in a lawyer's phrases), it contained two irresistible arguments: "*You know whom he takes after in that respect*," and "*If you do not want him to enjoy himself we will say no more about it.*"

Now I "took after" my father, and to tell my mother that I was like my father, that I had my father's voice, that I had my father's tastes, was a great inducement.

My dear good mother would have given her last farthing to give me pleasure, and to suggest that she did not wish to let me enjoy myself was a great stab to her, and an additional argument in my favour.

Even his peroration was studied. The "we will say no more about it" was said in a careless manner, as though his thoughts ran thus: "Goodness me, keep your young rascal to yourself, if you wish; it was only out of good-nature I wanted to take him. And if you do not care for me to assist in his education as a sportsman, so much the less trouble for me; *we will say no more about it.*"

And, to my intense amazement, instead of accepting the "*we will say no more about it*" as final, my mother sighed, and after a moment's thinking she began:

"Ah well! I know true enough that if he does not go shooting with you, he will go shooting with someone else, or even all alone. Taking everything into consideration, then, I would much rather confide him to you, for you are cautious."

M. Picot winked at me out of the corner of one eye, as though to say, "Be quick, snatch this tardy consent as though it were whole-hearted."

I understood; I flung my arms round my mother's neck, kissing and hugging her as I thanked her.

"Ah, my dear Madame Dumas," said M. Picot, "let me tell you, to overcome all scruples, that he knows a gun like a gunmaker! What the deuce do you imagine will happen to him?—it is far more likely that I run the risk of his putting an ounce of lead in me."

"Oh! is that likely?" said my mother.

"Yes, but I am not really afraid. I will put him a long distance off me, so don't be anxious."

"And you will load his gun for him?"

"I will load his gun for him—yes."

"Then, since you wish it!"

My poor mother might more truthfully have said, "Since he wishes it!"

I have had many desires fulfilled, many vanities gratified, many ambitions attained or even exceeded, but none of these desires, vanities, realised ambitions ever gave me such joy as those few words of my mother—"Then, since you wish it!"

M. Picot did not keep me long in suspense: he arranged a shooting party for the following Sunday.

True, it was only to shoot larks, but still it was shooting.

Directly permission was granted, I ran over to Montagnon to impart my good news to him and to ask him for my gun; then I took it to pieces and cleaned it, although it was clean and well oiled; finally, I took it to my room at night and put it by my bed.

It may be guessed that I did not close my eyes that night; from time to time I stretched out my hand, to make sure that my beloved gun was still there. Never was adored mistress more caressed than that lifeless block of wood and iron and steel.

Unfortunately it was the month of November, and day was long in coming; but, if the day looked in upon me as it broke, it found me an earlier riser than itself, and already dressed in my shooting costume.

The effect produced was a singular combination of elegance and shabbiness.

The gun was everything that could be desired; fit for a duchess, with its gilt and fluted barrel, its touchhole and two pans of platinum, its velvety smooth butt-end.

My powder horn for priming it was an Arabian one which my father had brought back from Egypt; it was made of a small elephant tusk, damascened with gold, and seemed, like everything Oriental, as though the sun had left its mark upon it.

My powder horn for loading from was of horn, as transparent as glass, and mounted in silver. The charge, or rather the vessel that held the charge, was in the shape of a fox lying down, carved as though Barye had done it: it had belonged to the Princess Pauline. All the rest of my accoutrement was extremely modest, and contrasted ill with these three luxurious objects.

But as I did not yet know what love was, so neither did I know the meaning of art.

I slept in the same room as my mother; she got up the same time I did, feeling both glad and sorrowful at the same time: happy in my gladness, sad at this first escape, so to speak, from her maternal care.

I ran to M. Picot's house; he was not up; I made such a fine racket that I awakened him.

"Oh! oh!" he said, as he got into his corduroy breeches and fine leather gaiters, "you here already, lad?"

"It is late, Monsieur Picot; it is seven o'clock."

"Yes, but it has been snowing, and the larks will not rise before noon."

"What! must we wait till noon?" I cried.

"Well, not quite so long as that; but we will have breakfast first."

"What for?"

"Why, to eat, child," M. Picot replied. "I am far too old a sportsman to set out on an empty stomach; it is well enough at your age."

And when I came to consider matters I was not very averse to breakfasting, especially at M. Picot's, where they did things well.

So we had breakfast, M. Picot sipping his coffee from the first to the last drop, like a true Sybarite of the eighteenth century.

Voltaire had made this drink very fashionable by poisoning himself with it regularly three times a day.

My eyes never left the window; I saw clearly that it was the overcast weather that caused M. Picot to linger.

Suddenly I uttered a cry of joy: a ray of sunshine began to pierce through the grey and snowy atmosphere.

"Oh! look, look!" I cried, "there's the sun!"

And at that moment I felt as devout as a Brahmin.

"Come, let us start," said M. Picot.

And we set off; the servant following us carrying the lure and the parcel of twine.

M. Picot went through his garden, which led into a poor quarter of the town called les *Buttes*, or rather les *Huttes*, for it was composed rather of huts than of houses.

I was terribly disappointed. I had hoped we should go through the town, and I should be seen in all my glory by my fellow-citizens.

We set up our establishment on the highest point on the plain. We set our lure, and we waited for results.

CHAPTER X

Trapping larks—I wax strong in the matter of my compositions—The wounded partridge—I take the consequences whatever they are—The farm at Brassoire—M. Deviolaine's sally at the accouchement of his wife.

I wonder what learned ornithologist first discovered the vanity of larks? What profound philosopher guessed that by means of moving surfaces of bright metal or of glass larks would come and look at themselves, provided the surfaces shone, and the brighter the surface the more freely and quickly would they be attracted?

This delight in looking at themselves cost the life of twenty larks, and I was the executioner of six.

I fired quite thirty times in achieving this result, but M. Picot assured me that it was very good for a beginner and that I was a hopeful pupil.

M. Picot never attempted to take the trouble to load my gun, and no accident befell me.

When we came to the first houses on our return home, I left M. Picot; I was most anxious to go through the town with my gun under my arm and the larks round my neck.

No Pompey or Cæsar entered Rome with more triumphant pride than I felt.

But, alas! everything decays in this world, joy, grief, and even vanity! A time came when, like Cæsar, I gave up my triumphs to my lieutenants.

One thought and one only used to fill my mind: and that was the promised shooting for the following Sunday, if the Abbé Grégoire was satisfied with me.

We know how my translations were done; I did not think it wise to change my practices; but I paid so much attention to my compositions that the abbé declared that if I went on so well, I should, in a year's time, be able to enter the sixth form of any Parisian college.

I also learned, for my own satisfaction, two or three hundred lines of Virgil. Although I was very bad at Latin, I have always loved Virgil. His pity for exiles, his melancholy consciousness of death, his feeling after an unknown God, completely won me from the very first; the music of his verse and its metrical ease delighted me extremely, and often lulls me to sleep even now. I knew long passages of the *Æneid* by heart, and I believe I could still repeat from beginning to end Æneas's narration to Dido, though I could not construe a Latin sentence without making three or four grammatical errors.

The longed-for Sunday came at last! Again I spent a sleepless night, again I went through the same emotion in the morning, again I felt the same excitement at setting off. This time we did not use the mirror, but simply shot right and left; the partridges seemed to fly off to tremendous distances. No matter! I went on firing all the same; only, I hit nothing. But when we reached the crest of one of the high hills (called in our parts *larris*) I surprised a covey of young partridges, which rose within gun-shot. I fired off my gun at haphazard: one of the two partridges flew as far as it could, but by the angle of its downward flight I saw that it was wounded.

"Hit!" cried M. Picot.

I had, of course, seen that it was hit, and I set off after it.

Only when I felt myself rushing down the steep slope did I realise my rashness. When I had gone about twenty steps I was not running, I was leaping down; at the end of thirty I was no longer leaping, I was flying, and I felt I should lose my balance any moment; my speed increased in proportion to my weight; I became a living example of Galileo's squares of distances. M. Picot saw my break-neck pace, but was unable to save me, although I was rushing down headlong towards a spot where the mountain was cut into perpendicularly by a quarry-opening. I myself could see the direction in which I was going without being able to stop myself. The wind had already carried my cap away; I threw down my gun as I reached the open space. Suddenly the ground gave way from under me, I leapt or rather I fell a distance of ten or a dozen feet, and I disappeared in the snow, which happily the wind had collected in a soft eider-down quilt about a yard deep where I fell!

I was dreadfully frightened, I must confess; I thought my last hour had come. I shut my eyes as I fell; and, when I felt I was none the worse, I re-opened them; the first thing I saw was the head of M. Picot's dog looking over at me from the place where I had jumped, and where, more mistress of herself than I had been, she had pulled up.

"Diane," I cried, "Diane, here! look, look!"

And, getting up, I pursued my race after my partridge.

I saw M. Picot some distance away, standing up on the top of a rock, his arms raised to the heavens; he thought I had been smashed to atoms. I hadn't even a scratch.

He made such a figure against the landscape as I shall never forget.

I had lost sight of my bird, but I knew in what direction she had fallen, and I set off Diane on her track; she had hardly gone twenty yards before she found the scent, and started on it at a steady trot.

"Let her go," cried M. Picot; "let her go: she sees it again, she sees it."

I took no notice; I ran faster than she did, and before her. Finally chance led me to the partridge, which began to run.

"There it is," I cried to M. Picot,—"there it is! Diane, Diane! see, see, see, see, see!"

Diane saw it; and just in time, for my breath was beginning to fail me. I only had strength left to get to where she held it in her mouth: I pounced upon her, I snatched it from her, I lifted it up by a claw to show it to M. Picot and then I fell down.

I never felt so near dying or my last breath so close to my lips as then; four steps more, and my heart would have burst.

And all this for a partridge worth fifteen sous!

What a strange value passion puts upon things!

I very nearly fainted; but, the fainter I grew, the tighter did I squeeze the partridge to me, so that when I returned to consciousness I had never dropped hold of it for a single second.

M. Picot came up to me and helped me to rise. The partridge was still alive, so he knocked the back of its head on the butt of his gun and stuffed it in my bag, still fluttering in its death agony.

I turned the bag round so that I could gaze through the net and watch the poor creature's end.

Then I discovered that I had neither gun nor cap.

I began to search for my gun, and M. Picot sent Diane after my cap.

And that was the end of my hunting for that day. It was quite enough, thank goodness!

Levaillant could not have been happier than I was, after he had killed his first elephant on the banks of the Orange River.

My triumph was complete, for when I re-entered the house I found my brother-in-law just back from a tour of inspection.

I showed him my partridge, which had already made the acquaintance of half the town.

He made with the tip of his finger a cross on my forehead with my victim's blood.

"In the name of St. Hubert," he said, "I baptize thee a sportsman; and now that you are baptized—"

"What then?" I asked.

"Well, I invite you for next Sunday to a battue with M. Moquet of Brassoire."

I leapt for joy, for M. Moquet's battues were renowned throughout the department.

As many as forty or fifty hares were shot at a time.

"Oh! my child," murmured my mother,—"there is nothing he will like better!"

Besides making me feel my own master, this invitation of my brother-in-law was of far greater importance than it looked to be at the first glance.

The battue at Brassoire was really a shooting party, at which all the best guns in the district were present, M. Deviolaine above all, who, if he were once my shooting companion, and fraternised with me on the plain, would no longer be my enemy in the forest.

Virgil and Tacitus owed much to this invitation; the abbé was delighted with me, and he made no objection when M. Deviolaine's hunting carriole stopped in front of our door and I climbed in.

This was on Saturday evening: the farm of Brassoire is situated between the two forests of Villers-Cotterets and Compiègne, and is three and a half leagues from Villers-Cotterets, so we had to sleep there the night before, in order to begin shooting at daybreak.

Oh! how beautiful the forest seemed to me although it was leafless! I felt as though I took possession of it, as a conqueror. Had I not by my side the viceroy of the forest, who treated me almost as though I were a grown man, because I had gaiters on, a powder horn, and a gun?

M. Deviolaine still swore a great deal, but I thought his oaths delightful and full of spirit; I wished to swear as he did.

A month or two previously his family had been increased by the arrival of a little daughter. After a lapse of thirteen or fourteen years, it had occurred to his wife to make him this present.

M. Deviolaine had accepted it, grumbling, as he accepted everything. His eccentricity was made public by one of his queer sallies, which were peculiar to himself. Although the new arrival was no bigger than a radish at its arrival in this world, its mother had cried out a great deal in bringing it forth.

M. Deviolaine had heard the cries in his study; but as, with all his apparent brutality, he could not bear to see a pigeon suffer, he kept well out of the way, till the cries had ceased. When the cries were over, he listened with more unconcern to other noises; he heard steps on the stairs; his study door opened, and the cook appeared on the threshold.

"Well, Joséphine?" asked M. Deviolaine.

"Well, monsieur, it is all over. Madame has been delivered."

"Satisfactorily?"

"Satisfactorily."

"What is it?"

"A girl."

M. Deviolaine made a most significant groan.

"Oh! but," Joséphine made haste to add, "so pretty—as beautiful as the Cupids. She is the very image of Monsieur."

"In that case," growled M. Deviolaine, "she won't marry easily: the very image of me, so much the worse! so much the worse, good Heaven! So much the worse! I shall never have another!"

And he took his way to his wife's room.

My mother and I were there; Madame Deviolaine was in her bed, and a charming little pink and white baby girl, who, as Madame Davesne, is to-day one of the prettiest women in Paris, was awaiting M. Deviolaine's visit, dressed in swaddling clothes trimmed with lace.

He came in, with his head hutched on his shoulders, his hands in his pockets, looked round him, studied the topography of the room, and walked straight to the cradle, where he inspected the little occupant, puckering his great black eyebrows into frowns.

Then, turning to his wife, he said:

"Was it over that embryo you made so much racket, Madame Deviolaine?"

"Why, of course," she answered.

"Pooh!" said M. Deviolaine, shrugging his shoulders: "I can do better than that myself when I am not suffering from indigestion. Good-day, Madame Dumas; good-day, snotty," and, turning on his heels, he went out as he had entered.

"Thanks, Monsieur Deviolaine," said his wife. "Ah! I will take good care this shall be the last."

Madame Deviolaine has kept her word.

Ah! sweet, pretty Louise, see how you were treated on the day of your birth: but you took your revenge in remaining tiny and charming, and the last time I saw you you were as charming and sweet as ever.

CHAPTER XI

M. Moquet de Brassoire—The ambuscade—Three hares charge me—What prevents me from being the king of the battue—Because I did not take the bull by the horns, I just escape being disembowelled by it—Sabine and her puppies.

I ask pardon for this digression, although it leads us to Brassoire.

At the sound of our carriage wheels M. Moquet ran out to welcome us. He was one of those wealthy landowners of the old-fashioned school of hospitality, who when he entertained a large shooting party invited all the sportsmen in the district, and killed a pig, a calf, and a sheep for their delectation. He was, besides, a clever, cultivated man, both in theory and in practice, and was noted for possessing the finest merino sheep for twenty leagues round.

A splendid supper was prepared for us. I being, as it were, a raw conscript in the hunting-field, with only six larks and a partridge as the trophies of my term of service, was, of course, the butt of the jokes of the whole party—jokes in which M. Moquet, as my host, had the good manners not to take any part. Furthermore, when he rose from the table, he whispered to me:

"Never mind, I will put you in some good places, and it won't be my fault if you don't turn the tables on them to-morrow evening."

"You may be sure," I replied, with that naïve self-confidence which never deserted me, "I will do my best."

Next morning at eight o'clock all the shooters gathered together, and a score and a half of peasants from the countryside collected round the great door of the farmhouse.

These were the beaters.

The dogs were howling piteously; they, poor beasts, quite understood they had no part in this sort of shooting party.

One or two might perhaps be chosen from amongst the roughest of the retrievers, to send after a wounded hare which seemed about to escape into the forest, but that would be all.

These dogs usually had a man specially kept to look after them, and, except for the brief times when they were let loose, they were kept rigidly leashed.

The shooting began on leaving the farm. M. Moquet explained the general plan for the day to the head gamekeeper, deferring until later to tell him the particular plan of each battue.

I was placed a hundred paces from the farm in a sandy ravine where some children had dug a great hole in the sand when playing. M. Moquet pointed this hole out to me, and told me to crouch in it, assuring me that, if I did not stir, the hares would come towards me hot-foot.

I did not feel much confidence in the spot, but, as M. Moquet was commander-in-chief of the expedition, there was nothing to be said in the matter. I subsided into my hiding-place, determined to rush out into the open when occasion offered.

Then the driving began. At the first shouts uttered by the beaters, two or three hares rose, and, sitting up for a moment to see what course to take, began to make for my ravine at uneven distances from one another.

I declare that when I saw them coming as straight as they could in my direction, making a rendezvous of the hole where I was hiding, a mist came over my eyes. Through this veil, which spread between the hares and me, I could see them advancing rapidly; and, the nearer they came, the louder did my heart beat. Although the thermometer stood six degrees below zero, perspiration ran down my face. The hare that headed the column seemed determined to charge straight at me. I had taken aim at it the moment it started; I ought to have let it approach within twenty or ten or five paces; but I had not the strength: when it was within about thirty paces, I fired full in its face.

It turned head to tail in a significant way, and began a series of most remarkable contortions. It was evidently hit.

I bounded out of my hole like a jaguar, shouting:

"Here it is! I have got it! Slip the dogs, you rogue, you scoundrel, ... wait, wait!"

The hare heard me, and made the wildest gyrations; of its two companions, one turned back on its tracks and took the beaters by storm, the other continued in its course and passed so close to me that, my gun being empty, I flung it at her.

But this incidental hostility had not turned me from the principal pursuit. I rushed upon my hare, which was still performing the most incoherent and extravagant gymnastics, not advancing four steps in any straight line; it leapt from side to side; then bounded forwards, next backwards; deceiving all my calculations, as my father had deceived those of his crocodile, by running to right and then to left; it escaped just as I thought I had got hold of it; it gained ten steps on me as though it hadn't a scratch on it; then it suddenly doubled back, and ran between my legs—one would have said as though for a wager. I did not shout this time; I simply yelled; I picked up stones and threw them at it. When I believed I was just on it, I fell flat on my stomach, hoping to crush it between my body and the earth as in a trap. In the distance I could see through a sort of haze the other shooters, half laughing, half furious; laughing at the exercise I was giving myself, furious at the noise and stir I was causing in the centre of the battue, which was turning back all the hares. At last, after unprecedented efforts, I caught mine by one paw, then by both, then round its body: it uttered despairing cries, and I held it against my breast, as Hercules held Antæus, and I went back to my hole, taking care to pick up my gun, as I passed it, where I had thrown it down.

When I returned to my quarters I examined my hare attentively, and I discovered what had happened. I had put out its eyes without wounding it anywhere else.

I broke its neck by the famous blow which kills a hare, although Arnal calls it the *rabbit-blow*.

Then I re-loaded my gun, my heart still thumping and my hand shaking. It occurred to me that I was making the charge extra strong, but I was sure of the gun, and the excess of four or five inches would give me a chance to kill at longer range.

I had hardly got back into position before I saw another hare coming straight for me.

I was cured of my fancy for firing at its head; moreover, this one promised to pass me broadside on, within twenty-five paces, and it kept its promise. I aimed with greater calmness than might have been expected of me, and fired, convinced that I had now secured a brace of hares.

The priming burnt, but the shot did not go off.

This was a sad misfortune.

I tried to let off one of M. Deviolaine's expressive oaths, but it was a half-hearted attempt: they did not seem to suit me. I never could swear properly, even in my angriest moments.

I pricked my gun, I primed it, and I waited.

M. Moquet had certainly not deceived me: a third hare came in the wake of its predecessors, and, like the last one, it crossed at right angles to me, within twenty paces! As before, I aimed and, when I had covered it carefully with my gun, I pressed my finger on the trigger.

Only the priming burnt.

I was furious; I could have cried with rage; all the more as a fourth hare was coming along at a gentle trot.

It was the same with this one as with the two others. He was as obliging as possible, and my gun as perverse as can be imagined.

It passed within fifteen steps of me, and, for the third time, my priming burnt, but the gun did not go off.

This time I wept outright. A good shot would have killed four hares in my position; and, although I was only a beginner, I ought certainly to have killed two.

This was the end of the battue. M. Moquet came to me. Placed in a hollow, as I was, none of the other shooters had seen the triple misfortunes that had happened to me; but M. Moquet, having seen all the hares pass by me and hearing no reports, had come to find out whether I was dead or asleep.

I was simply desperate. I showed him my gun.

"The priming has burnt three times, M. Moquet," I cried, in woebegone tones; "three times over three hares!"

"A flash in the pan, eh?" asked M. Moquet.

"Yes, it missed fire.... What the deuce can be the matter with the breech?"

M. Moquet shook his head; then, like an old sportsman who is never at a loss, he took out of his bag a gun-screw, fitted it to the end of his ramrod, drew out first the wadding of my gun, then the shot, then the second lot of wadding, then the powder; then, after the powder, half an inch of earth which had got down the muzzle when I threw my gun after the hare, and which I had rammed to the bottom of the breech with my first wad on the powder.

If I had fired at a hundred hares my gun would have missed fire a hundred times.

Alas! so frail are human affairs! had it not been for that half inch of earth I should have killed two or three hares, and I should have been the king of the battue.

Every hare had passed my way, except one which had passed by M. Dumont of Morienval and been killed by him.

My good luck departed with that first battue. There were ten more, but not one hare came my way.

I returned to the house tired out. I had killed a hare a hundred paces from the farm; M. Moquet had offered to send it there at once, but I declined to be thus parted from it, and I carried it on my back some eight or ten leagues.

I need hardly say that amidst the jokes which always enliven a shooting party's dinner I came in for a large share. The evolutions which I had executed; all the hares coming my way from an instinct that my gun was loaded with earth; no more passing me after my gun was put right again; all these items, to say nothing of my face, which had been scratched by the hare during my hand-to-hand struggle with it, formed capital themes for jesting.

But one thing made me forget all these quips and jibes, and sent me into an ecstasy of unspeakable happiness.

The series of jokes of which I was the butt finished by M. Deviolaine saying:

"Never mind! I will take you boar-hunting next Thursday, to see if you will catch hold of those gentry, with your arms round their bodies, as you catch hares."

"Do you really mean it, cousin?"

"Honour bright."

"On your honour, really?"

"On my word of honour."

And my delight was so great at this promise that I left the table and went off into the foldyard, to tease a fine bull, who thought nothing of me or my games, but who, when tired of my teasings, would have disembowelled me, if I had not rushed back into the kitchen by jumping over one of the small latticework gates always to be found about farms.

The bull followed me so closely that he put his head over the low gate and bellowed fit to shake the house down.

Madame Moquet calmly took a burning brand from the hearth and put it under the bull's muzzle, whereat he jumped back five or six steps, gave a few tremendous bounds, and disappeared into his stall.

It was not my custom to boast of such feats as these; on the contrary, when anything of the sort occurred to me, I resumed my tranquillity as quickly as possible, and returned to the place from whence I had set forth, with my hands behind my back, like Napoleon, humming *Fleuve du Tage* or *Partant pour la Syrie*, airs much in vogue just then, in a voice almost as cracked as that of the great King Louis XV.

Unluckily, Mas, M. Deviolaine's groom, had seen me, with the result that for the next fortnight my agility in jumping gates was the subject of ironical congratulations from Cécile, Augustine, and Félix.

Fortunately Louise was not able to talk yet, or she would most certainly have joined in with the others.

Mas put the horse into his master's carriage; for, as M. Deviolaine had to be at his inspection very early next morning, he preferred to return over night: besides, it was a splendid moonlight night.

M. Moquet tried every possible argument to induce M. Deviolaine to remain, but he had made up his mind, and he asked that preparations should be made to set off that same evening.

There was a custom at M. Moquet's which I have rarely seen elsewhere, even in houses which pride themselves on their aristocratic habits: when the shooters had left, not a single morsel of game remained at the farm; each person took away with him in his carriage-box, in his basket, or in his game-bag, his share of the game, distributed by the master of the house: who alone was always forgotten.

When we reached Villers-Cotterets, we found seven hares under the carriage box-seat.

There had been thirty-nine, killed in all.

Here I may be allowed to relate a singular proof of the love of a bitch for her puppies.

When I first made the acquaintance of my brother-in-law he possessed an intelligent dog called Figaro, who could mount guard, dance a minuet, salute the police, and turn his back on the gamekeepers. This dog had been succeeded by a charming sporting dog called Sabine. She had none of the attractive talents of the late Figaro; but she could point and retrieve most wonderfully.

My brother-in-law had left her at home for two reasons: first, because a pointer is a more tiresome than a useful companion in a battue; secondly, because she was too far gone in pup to be active.

Great therefore was our astonishment when, on re-entering the farm, at the end of the shoot, Victor saw Sabine, who came quietly up to us; she had managed to escape, and with the wonderful instinct of animals had followed her master.

When we were leaving, Sabine was called; but she did not appear. She was searched for, and the poor beast was found in a corner of the yard, where she had just given birth to three pups.

As Victor had no desire to breed dogs, he begged M. Moquet's son to make a hole in a heap of litter which was by the gate and fling the three puppies in it.

The request was carried out, in spite of poor Sabine's winnings; she had to be tied to the seat of the carriage to make sure she would return to Villers-Cotterets with us.

Sabine howled for a little while; then, after a few minutes, she settled down between our legs, and seemed to have forgotten all about them.

But when we reached the gate we had to undo Sabine, who leapt from the carriage to the ground without touching the step, and took the road back to Brassoire at full speed.

It was in vain my brother-in-law whistled and called her; the louder he called, the more he whistled, the more Sabine quickened her pace.

He could not go after her at that hour: it was midnight. Victor consigned her to Diana the huntress, and we went in, taking care to leave the garden door open, so that Sabine could get in to her kennel, if by chance she took it into her head to return home.

Next morning the earliest riser amongst us found Sabine in her kennel, asleep, with her three pups between her paws.

She had sought them at Brassoire, and as she could only bring home one at a time in her mouth, she had evidently made three journeys for them.

It was three and a half leagues from Villers-Cotterets and Brassoire; so Sabine had run twenty-one leagues during the night.

Her maternal devotion was rewarded by being allowed to keep her three puppies.

BOOK V

CHAPTER I

The second period of my youth—Forest-keepers and sailors—Choron, Moinat, Mildet, Berthelin—La Maison-Neuve.

As I have now entered upon the second period of my youth, and put off the boy's toga to don that of adolescence, I must make my readers acquainted with the individuals who peopled the second circle of my life, as they have already become acquainted with those who peopled the first.

There exists in localities bordering great woods a peculiar people who, in the midst of the general population, keep their own stamp and character, and contribute a quota of poetry (which is the soul of the world) to swell the mass.

These are the forest-rangers.

I have lived much among keepers and much among sailors, and I have always been struck by the great similarity between these two races of men; both, as a rule, are unemotional, religious, and dreamers. The sailor or the forest-keeper will often stay side by side with his greatest friend (the one while forty or fifty knots are being sailed on the ocean; the other walking eight or ten leagues through big woods) without exchanging a single word, apparently without hearing or noticing anything; but, in reality, not a sound echoes in the air that the ear does not catch; not a movement stirs the surface of the water or the depth of the leaves that has been overlooked; and, as they both have the same ideas, similar instincts and similar feelings, as this silence has really been one long dumb conversation, it is not surprising that, when occasion demands, it is only necessary to utter a word, make a significant gesture or exchange a glance, and they will have managed to express more ideas by that glance, that gesture, that word, than others could in a long dissertation. But when they talk at night, round a woodland bivouac, or over their own fires, always well supplied with fuel and firewood, these reserved and silent dreamers can hold forth at great length, and picturesquely enough: the keepers about their hunting, the sailors about their storms!

The poetry of vast oceans and wide forests, which has descended upon them from the crests of the waves and the tree-tops, makes their language unadorned and yet imaginative. Their words are expressive and simple.

These people, one feels, are the elect of nature and of solitude, who have almost forgotten the language of human beings, and speak that of the winds, the trees, the torrents, and the storms of the seas!

It was into the hands of this remarkable people that I passed when I left the care of my womenkind. They were specially noteworthy at Villers-Cotterets on account of the extent of forest which isolated them from the town, to which they only came once a week to take orders from the inspector, whilst their wives went to mass.

As a matter of fact, my appearance among these people had been long looked forward to by them; nearly all had hunted with my father, who, as we know, had leave to go where he liked in the forest, and all kept a lively remembrance of his generosity. Some of them, too, were old soldiers who had served under him, and who had got into the forest administration through his influence: in fact, all these honest people, who thought they could trace the same disposition to be openhanded as the general had been,—for so they always spoke of my father,—had been most friendly to me, and had always asked me, when they met me by chance at *la pipée* or at *la marette*:——

"Well, when is our inspector going to invite you to a more serious hunt?"

The invitation came at last, and it was for the following Thursday.

The rendezvous was at la Maison-Neuve, on the Soissons road, at the house of a head keeper called Choron.

There are four or five men, belonging to the class which I have tried to sketch in general outline, who deserve particular mention on account of their skill and their originality, and Choron was one of these men.

I have already had occasion to speak of him more than once; but I have spoken of him under another name. To-day, as I am writing memoirs, and not a romance, he must appear under his true name, since they are actual catastrophes I am about to relate.

At the period at which we have arrived, namely, the beginning of the year 1816, Choron was a fine young man of about thirty, with an open, frank countenance, fair hair, blue eyes, his jolly face well framed with big whiskers; he was finely made, about five feet four inches in height; and, added to the symmetry of his limbs, he possessed Herculean strength, which was talked of for ten leagues round.

Choron was always ready. Until he got jealous ideas into his head,— miserable ideas which ended fatally for him,—no one could say he had ever seen Choron ill or gloomy.

It mattered not at what time of day or night M. Deviolaine might knock at his door to question him, he was always the same. He knew, almost to within fifty yards, where the wild boars' lairs were in his range of forest; for Choron, like Bas-de-Cuir, would follow a trail for whole days together. If the meet was at Maison-Neuve, if sport were desired a quarter of a league, half a league, or a whole league from there, if the beast had been diverted by Choron, it was known beforehand what sort of a beast they had to deal with, whether a *tiean*, a youngster or an old boar; a boar or a sow; if the sow was in pig, and how long she had gone. The most artful old boar could not hide six months of his age from Choron, who, by inspecting his footmarks, could verify his birth certificate.

It was wonderful to watch him, and it especially astonished the Parisian sportsmen who came to hunt in our forest from time to time. To us countrybred huntsmen, who had practised the same art, though in a humbler degree, the power did not seem so supernatural.

But, all the same, Choron was looked upon by his comrades as a kind of oracle in all matters connected with the hunting of big game.

Courage, too, soon acquires a mighty power over men. Choron did not know what fear meant; he had never shrunk back before either man or beast. He would hunt out the boar from the deepest lair; he would attack poachers in their safe strongholds. Truth to tell, Choron did receive some tusk thrusts in his thigh occasionally, or some grapeshot in his back; but he had a sovereign remedy for treating such wounds. He would bring up two or three bottles of white wine from his cellar, pull one of his dogs from its pet corner, lie down on a deerskin, make Rocador or Fanfaro lick his wound; and, meanwhile, to compensate for the blood he had lost, he would swallow what he called his *cooling draught*; he would not reappear that evening, but by the morrow he would be cured.

Yet, singularly enough, Choron was not a first-rate shot, and in what were called "hamper hunts "—that is to say, when the object was to send away smaller game, such as rabbits, hares, partridges, or venison, to the duc d'Orléans—Choron rarely supplied his quota.

On these occasions he yielded the sovereignty of the chase to Moinat or to Mildet.

Moinat was the best marksman with small shot, and Mildet the first at bullet firing, in the forest of Villers-Cotterets. If it was Montagnon who had taught me how to take a gun to pieces and put it together again, it was Moinat who had taught me how to use it. Montagnon had only made a gunsmith's assistant of me; Moinat turned me out an accomplished shot.

When Moinat's gun covered any animal whatsoever, from a snipe to a deer, it was, bar accident, as good as dead: and the same skill often extended to those who went hunting with him. M. Deviolaine invited Moinat to his special hunts, declaring that he never shot well unless he felt Moinat near his side.

Once, when I was third in one of these hunts, I discovered the secret: Moinat fired simultaneously with M. Deviolaine, and the prey fell. M. Deviolaine was under the supposition that he alone had killed it, and appropriated the game; but really it fell to Moinat's gun. Sometimes, however, he allowed M. Deviolaine to fire by himself; and it was rarely then that anything fell.

Moinat had the good sense never to boast of these coincidences, and he remained the inspector's favourite to the end of his days.

Moinat was sixty at the time of which I am writing; but in walking powers and in keenness of eye he could hold his own with the youngest. On the open ground he could walk his ten leagues without a stumble; in the marsh-land he would go into the water and mire up to his middle; he would trample over the thickest of the underwood in the forest, and over the thorniest of brambles. My father was very fond of Moinat, so he did me a great honour, which he would not have done for just anybody,—he constituted himself both my friend and my teacher. I may add that he has not had any cause to regret his offices, for I believe I proved myself a worthy pupil of him, until I was forbidden leave to hunt in the State forests because I killed too much game, and because of a blow I was so foolish as to give an inspector.

I quarrelled with Moinat almost in the same fashion as Vandyke quarrelled with Rubens: one day I killed a roebuck that he had just missed, and he never forgave me.

Although I have said that Moinat was the crack firer with small shot and Mildet first with the bullet, I do not mean thereby to imply that Moinat was not also first rate with bullet as with shot; but that Mildet had made a special study of bullet-shooting during a long residence in Germany. I have seen him nail a squirrel as it ran quickly up the trunk of an oak. I have seen him put a horseshoe on a wall and place six bullets in the six nail-holes of the shoe. I have seen him in carbine shooting, when there were twelve shots to be made, draw a cordon round the black with the first eleven balls and then hit the middle with the twelfth.

Berthelin, Choron's uncle, came next in the order of merit. He was certain of hitting three out of four tries; then, after Berthelin, we descend to the ordinary run of men.

From the days of the emperor the big game of the forest of Villers-Cotterets had been strictly preserved. During the first return of the Bourbons it had been sold as forest domain to the duc d'Orléans, but he had not time to turn his attention to it. After the second restoration—partly out of opposition, partly on account of actual losses—the adjacent property holders made many complaints because of the ravages caused by the larger animals; and as they took legal action in the matter, the most stringent commands were issued to M. Deviolaine to destroy the boars.

Orders of this sort are always looked upon very favourably by the keepers. Boar being royal game, the keepers have no right to shoot it, or if they shoot it by chance it is required of them for the table. Then they are simply paid twenty-four sous for the shot, I believe; but in case of exterminating the beasts each one shot belongs by right to its marksman, and we can well understand that a boar in the salting tub is a famous addition to the winter store.

These hunting expeditions had been going on for a couple of months, when M. Deviolaine gave me the famous invitation which put me into such a state of ecstasy.

Mixed with this joy there was the thought of danger in the background: these fine boars, which had been left at peace for three or four years, had increased and multiplied to such an extent that the old ones had grown to a tremendous size; and the youngsters simply abounded. They could be met in the forest in herds of twelve and fifteen, and they had even been killed in the town vegetable gardens that winter.

A kind of proverb, consisting of question and answer, had been improvised among those who lived on the edge of the forest.

Question: When potatoes are planted within five hundred steps from the forest, do you know what comes up?

Answer: Why, potatoes of course ...!

Reply to the answer: No! Boars come up.

And the most contentious questioner was obliged to grant the truth of the assertion.

Now these hunts lasted nearly four months from the 15th of September.

Choron performed wonders during those four months. When the rendezvous took place at Maison-Neuve, and Choron was deputed to drive the boar, there were high rejoicings indeed, for one was certain of not finding the game flown. It is true that there was a league and a half to walk before Maison-Neuve could be reached; but, when one reached that out-of-the-way place by a beautiful route cut right through the heart of the forest, there was

Choron standing a few steps from his doorway, with his hunting-horn on his wrist, saluting his inspector and his party with a spirited blast and flourish. It was meant to express that the beasts would die, or the inspector and his party would be indeed a stupid lot.

Inside Choron's house we found half a dozen bottles of his *cooling mixture*, as he dubbed his white wine, glasses rubbed scrupulously bright by a charming housewife, and a ten-pound loaf, which looked as white as though it had been kneaded of snow. We ate a slice of this bread with a piece of cheese; we paid our compliments to Madame Choron on her bread, her cheese and the beauty of her eyes; and then we set off a-hunting.

We must just add that Choron worshipped his wife, and grew more and more jealous on her account every day, without cause. His mates would sometimes twit him about this increasing jealousy, but their harmless merriment was short-lived: Choron would turn as white as death, he would shake his fine head, and, turning towards the person who had rashly touched upon the heart-sore that was beyond the cure of his dogs' tongues, he would say:—

"Stop, you—you had better hold your tongue; and that right quickly;—the sooner you stop the better it will be for you!"

The ill-advised joker would stop immediately. Folks gradually ceased to venture upon any allusion to this strong fellow's only weakness, and in a very short time it bid fair never to be mentioned at all.

CHAPTER II

Choron and the mad dog—Niquet, otherwise called *Bobino*—His mistress—
The boar-hunt—The kill—Bobino's triumph—He is decorated—The boar
which he had killed rises again.

We have now introduced our new actors. The Thursday had come; and it
was half-past eight in the morning when we filed out—M. Deviolaine, my
brother-in-law, myself, and a dozen keepers, gathered up from the town and
recruited on our way—at the turning of the forest road, about four hundred
steps from Maison-Neuve.

Choron was, as usual, on his doorstep, horn in hand; directly he caught sight
of us, he blew a most sonorous blast, and we knew there were no doubts
about our hunt taking place.

We redoubled our pace, and soon reached him.

The interior of the little house that M. Deviolaine had built some eight or ten
years ago, and called la Maison-Neuve, was most charmingly pretty and well
arranged.

I can still picture the interior as I saw it when I stepped over the threshold;
its bed hung with green curtains; the chimney-piece adorned with three guns
on the left; at the head of the bed a window brightened by a ray of winter
sunshine, at the foot of the bed another window, in order to enable one to
see both sides of the road without going out; a cabinet full of plates of a big
flowery pattern; and a complete collection of four-footed animals and of
stuffed birds.

Amongst these animals there was a terrible looking sheepdog, the colour of
a wolf, with its hair all on end, its eyes bloodshot, and its mouth open and
slavering. Choron said he had only been afraid once in his life, and he had
immortalised the cause of his fear.

The cause of his fear was this dog, which, before being a stuffed dog, was a
mad dog.

Choron was one day pruning the trees in his little garden in front of the
house, when all at once he saw this dog trying to get through his hedge; he
soon saw, from the feverish look of its eyes, and its foaming mouth, that the
animal was mad, and he ran for the house. But, although Choron ran well,
the dog ran still better; so that Choron had neither time to shut his door
behind him nor to take his gun down from the chimney-piece. The only thing

he could do was to leap on his bed and to roll the counterpane round his body, to ward off bites as much as possible. The dog leapt on the bed almost as soon as Choron did, and began haphazard to bite the bale of cotton which encased a man. All at once Choron spread the coverlet out as wide as it would go, rolled the dog in it, and whilst it was trying to get out he seized his gun, and in an instant fired twice into the counterpane, which began to be dyed With blood, then to heave convulsively for some seconds. But these undulations soon decreased, and finally ceased altogether, to give place to the last shudders of ebbing life. Choron unrolled the coverlet, and found the animal was dead.

He had the dog stuffed, and mounted it upon the blood-stained counterpane, which it had bitten finely.

One look at the beast, even stuffed as it was, was enough to make one understand Choron's fear.

I examined all the animals, one after the other. I acquainted myself with their history, from the first to the last; I asked questions while I munched my bread and cheese; I drank two glasses of wine while I listened to the replies, and still I was ready to start before the others.

As we went out M. Deviolaine pointed out to me a six-foot gate in Choron's garden, over which he had seen my father vault when the house was being built, ill though he was at that time.

This tradition had reached Choron's ears, who had more than once tried to do the same, but had never succeeded.

The special feature of these hunting-parties, which were principally composed of keepers, was the total absence of *craques* (= bragging: excuse the word, please, it is peculiar to sportsmen). Each person knew his neighbour too well, and was himself known too well, to try to impose upon him by any of those flagrant lies by which the frequenters of the plain of St. Denis enhance their prowess. Everybody knew who were the clever and who the duffers; due homage was given to the clever, and no mercy was shown towards the duffers.

Among these was a man called Niquet, nicknamed *Bobino*, because of his passion, in his boyish days, for the game of peg-top which goes by that name. He was looked upon as a lad of parts; but to this reputation there was added one, none the less deserved, of being the very clumsiest shot of the whole party.

So Choron's and Moinat's, Mildet's and Berthelin's fine performances were discussed, but poor Bobino was chaffed to death.

He would retaliate with some ludicrous cock-and-bull story, to which his Provençal accent gave a most diverting touch.

On this particular day, M. Deviolaine had thought it best to change the topic of the joke, without intending to change their point of attack. Bobino was still to be teased, but not on account of his clumsiness this time.

He was to be twitted about his mistress.

Bobino had a mistress.... Why not?

This mistress was not a beauty.... But tastes differ.

In fact this mistress was the woman who had climbed up on General Lallemand's carriage-step and had spat in his face.

"Look here, Niquet," said M. Deviolaine; "as you have a comely, stout wife, tell me what charm there can be in a woman as hard as a nail?"

"She is for fast days, M. *l'inspecteur.*"

"If she were pretty," insisted M. Deviolaine, "I could understand it ..."

"Ah! M. *l'inspecteur*, you do not know!..."

"But, think of red eyes ..."

"You do not know, M. *l'inspecteur.*"

"And black teeth...."

"What is the reason Bréguet's watches are so good, M. *l'inspecteur?*"

"The deuce! because of their action."

"Exactly, M. *l'inspecteur*, Bréguet's action!... action worthy of a gold case to it!"

Everybody burst out laughing. I laughed like the others, though I could not in the least understand Bobino's retort.

I was just going up to Bobino to ask him to explain his own joke, when Choron signed to us it was time to keep quiet.

We were five hundred steps from the place where a boar was in its lair.

Not a whisper was to be heard from that moment. Choron suggested the plan of attack to the inspector, who gave us our orders in a low voice, and we went to take up our places round; while Choron, with his bloodhound in leash, prepared to search the enclosure.

I apologise most humbly to my readers for making use of all these hunting terms, after the fashion of the baron in *les Facheux*. But these terms alone express my meaning, and besides I think they are sufficiently well known not to require explaining.

My mother had, as you may imagine, put me under M. Deviolaine's care: she would only let me go on condition M. Deviolaine would not let me out of his sight. He had promised her to do so, and in order religiously to keep his word he had put me between himself and Moinat, telling me to keep entirely hidden behind a large oak; then, if I shot a boar, and he turned on me, I could seize hold of one of the oak's branches, raise myself up by my arms, and let the beast pass under me.

All experienced huntsmen know that this is the method to adopt under such circumstances.

In ten minutes' time everyone was at his post. Soon the barking of Choron's dog, which had found a trail, echoed loudly and frequently, showing he was getting close to the animal. Suddenly we heard the crackling of the underwood. I saw something pass near me; but it had vanished before I had time to put my gun to my shoulder. Moinat fired at a guess; but he shook his head to signify that he did not in the least believe he had hit it. Next we heard the report of a second gun a little distance off, then a third, which was immediately followed by a cry of *Hallali!* uttered by Bobino with the full strength of his lungs.

Everybody ran at the call, although, recognising the voice of the shouter, each person expected to find himself the dupe of a fresh hoax devised by the witty wag.

I ran with the rest, and I might even say I ran much faster than the others. I had never been present at a boar kill, and I did not want to miss the sight. It was quite useless for M. Deviolaine to cry after me not to hurry—I heard nothing.

I have said that everybody expected a hoax—great, therefore, was the general surprise when, coming to the Dampleux road, which intersected transversely the part we had been posted in, like the top line of the letter T, we saw Bobino in the very middle of the roadway, calmly sitting upon his boar.

To complete this picture, which might have served as the companion to the death of the boar of Calydon, which Meleager killed, Bobino, affecting the indifference of a man used to this sort of prowess, his pipe in his mouth, was trying to strike a light.

The animal had rolled over like a rabbit at the first shot, and had never stirred from the place where it had fallen.

You may easily imagine the chorus of half-mocking congratulations which rose round the conquering hero, who donned an off-hand air, and, covering his pipe with a little paper cap to prevent the wind blowing out the spark, replied between the puffs of smoke:—

"Ah, now you see how we Provençals bowl over such small fry."

And, as the bowling over had been so successful, there was indeed no comment to make; the bullet had struck the animal behind its ear. Neither Moinat, Mildet, nor Berthelin could have done better.

Choron was the last to arrive on the scene, for he had not hurried himself in the least.

Directly he appeared out of the forest, with his bloodhound on leash, we saw him fix his astonished gaze on the group, with Niquet in the centre. When we saw Choron, we scattered so that he might see what we had seen without believing.

"What the deuce is this they are saying, Bobino?" he cried, when near enough to be heard; "they tell me that the boar has been idiot enough to throw himself in front of your gun!"

"Whether he threw himself in front of my gun or my gun put a shot into him, it is none the less a fact that poor Bobino is going to have fine steaks throughout the winter, and he isn't going to invite anyone to share them who can't return the compliment—saving, of course, M. *l'inspecteur*," Bobino added, raising his cap, "who will make his very humble servant proud indeed if he will ever condescend to taste Mother Bobine's cooking."

Niquet always called his wife Bobine, which, according to his idea, was the natural feminine for Bobino.

"Thanks, Niquet, thanks; I will not refuse that offer," M. Deviolaine replied.

"S'help me, Bobino!" said one of the keepers, named François, who was brother to Léon Mas, M. Deviolaine's servant, whom I have had occasion to mention several times already—"as such strokes of luck do not often happen to you, with M. Deviolaine's permission I must decorate you!"

"Decorate away, my boy," said Bobino. "There's many a one been decorated *in other times* who did not deserve it as much as I do."

Bobino was unjust: *in other times* decorations were not too lavishly bestowed: but hatred blinded him. Bobino, who had been a Terrorist in 1793, was a red-hot Royalist in 1815, sharing, in this respect, the opinions of his beloved of the rue de Soissons.

And Bobino went on smoking with the most ludicrous imperturbability, whilst François, drawing a knife out of his pocket, approached the back of the boar, took hold of its tail, and cut it off at a single stroke.

To the immense astonishment of the whole company the boar gave a low growl, although it did not move.

"What is it then, my little darling?" asked Bobino, whilst François fastened the animal's tail to the hero's button-hole, "you seem to set great store by that bit of string."

The boar gave another groan and kicked out one leg.

"Ho, ho," said Bobino, "he's got the nightmare, like poor Mocquet,"—Mocquet's nightmare had passed into a proverb,—"but it isn't Mother Durand who is seated on your stomach, it is old Bobino, and when old Bobino has fixed himself anywhere it is not an easy matter to dislodge him."

He had hardly finished the words when he was sent spinning ten paces off, his nose in the dust and his pipe broken between his teeth.

We all started up, thinking there must have been an earthquake.

Nothing of the sort. The boar, it seemed, had only been stunned by the shot, and had come to consciousness when François wounded it; it had then freed itself of the burden weighing it down, in the way we have seen, and stood up, though tottering on its legs as though it were drunk.

"Ah! good Heavens," cried M. Deviolaine, "let it go: it will be odd if it recovers!"

"No, no; oh, no! do not let it go," shrieked Choron, looking for his gun, which he had put in a ditch while he tied up his hound; "no! fire at him, fire at him! I know those fellows, they are as tough as possible. Fire at him; don't spare your shot, or, upon my word, he will escape us!"

But he was already too late. The dogs, when they saw the boar get up, flew at him, some held on to his ears, others to his thighs, all, in short, went for his hide, till he was so completely covered that there was not a place as big as a crown-piece on his body wherein a ball could be lodged.

The boar was quietly gaining the ditch all the time, dragging the pack with him: then he entered the brushwood; then he disappeared, followed by Bobino, who had picked himself up in a great rage, and was determined at all costs to have satisfaction for the affront he had received.

"Stop! stop!" yelled Choron; "catch hold of his tail, Bobino; stop him, stop him!"

Everybody was convulsed with laughter, and then we heard two pistol-shots.

"Come on, look sharp!" said Choron; "the beast will kill our dogs next."

But we did not hear any yell indicative of Choron's gloomy foreboding, and in a little time we saw Bobino reappear, looking very crestfallen: he had missed the boar both times, and it had continued its course, pursued by all the dogs, whose baying was rapidly becoming fainter.

We hunted that boar for the rest of the day; he led us five leagues away to Hivors copse, and we heard no more of him, although Choron informed all the keepers of the forest of Villers-Cotterets who were not present at the accident, as well as all those of the neighbouring forests, so that if by chance any one of them killed a tail-less boar, and he wanted to have the complete animal, he would find the tail in Bobino's button-hole.

The hunt had most certainly been more amusing than if it had been successful; but it had not fulfilled the inspector's intentions, who had received orders to destroy boars, and not to dock their tails.

So M. Deviolaine told the keepers, as they separated, that there would be another hunt on the following Sunday, and he gave orders that they were to turn as many boars in a given direction as they could, so that if the prey were lost in one keeper's territory recourse could be had to another.

Whilst returning home with M. Deviolaine I made such love to him that, with the support of my brother-in-law, of whom he was very fond, I obtained leave not only to go with him to the next hunt, but to all the remaining ones, at any rate until the Abbé Grégoire should find fault with and forbid me my pleasure by means of a similar veto to that which cost Louis XVI. so dear.

CHAPTER III

Boars and keepers—The bullet of Robin-des-Bois—The pork-butcher.

The Sunday rendezvous was settled to take place at St. Hubert, one of the most often used meeting-places, and also one of the most beautiful places in the forest.

M. Deviolaine and I arrived punctually to the minute; but my brother-in-law, being away travelling, had not been able to come.

Everybody else turned up at the rendezvous with the most exemplary punctuality. Three beasts had been beaten up,—two youngsters and a wild sow.

Of course not a single keeper failed to ask Bobino for news of his boar; but he had heard nothing about the matter, and he had the good sense still to wear its tail from his button-hole.

We had three boars to tackle. One came from Berthelin's preserve, and the others from Choron's and Moinat's.

We began on the nearest, which was one of the youngsters; it was routed out by Berthelin, but before it got through the ring Mildet killed it by putting a bullet right through its heart at a distance of fifty paces.

We went on to the second, on Choron's preserve; it was a short league's distance from the place where we killed the first. Choron first conducted us, according to his usual custom, to Maison-Neuve, to have a drop to drink and a bite to eat; and then we resumed our way.

The circle was made. I was put between M. Deviolaine and François, the lad who had decorated Bobino: then came Moinat, and I forget who came after Moinat.

We had to deal with the sow this time.

Choron went into the thicket with his boarhound, and five minutes later the sow was turned out of her lair. We heard her come, as we had before, grinding her tusks against each other. She passed by M. Deviolaine first, and he sent two shots after her but missed; I next fired my gun at her; but, as it was the first boar I had fired at, I too missed her; finally, François fired in his turn, and hit her full in the body. Immediately the boar turned at right angles, and with the rapidity of lightning rushed upon the shooter. François, who was quite sure of his aim, held his ground stoutly, and sent a second shot into her almost point blank. But, at that very moment, in the midst of the smoke which the wind had not yet blown away, we saw François and the boar in one shapeless mass, and we heard a cry for help. François was on his back, vainly endeavouring to draw his hunting-knife, whilst the maddened sow was rooting at him with her tusks. We all rushed to his help, but had not gone more than a few steps before an imperious voice cried out, which stopped even M. Deviolaine:—

"Do not stir!"

We all stopped dead, silent, immovable, where we were, though all eyes turned in the direction of the voice. Then we saw Moinat lower the barrel of his gun in the direction of the dreadful heap. For a moment the old man seemed turned into a stone statue; then he fired, and the animal, hit in the small of its shoulder, rolled over a few feet from its crouched victim.

"Thanks, old friend!" said François, jumping up briskly to his feet; "if ever you have need of me, I am yours for life or death!"

"Oh! it is not worth all that," Moinat replied, as he quietly began reloading his gun.

We all ran to François: he had a scratch on his thigh, and a bite on his arm, but that was all; it was nothing in comparison with what might have happened to him, if, instead of the encounter having been with a sow, it had been with a boar. When we had ascertained that there was nothing dangerous in either of his wounds, all our exclamations were turned into congratulations on Moinat's skill; but, as it was not the first time he had been the hero of similar adventures, Moinat took our compliments as though he could not understand why we made so much of such a slight matter, one so easy for him to carry through.

After devoting our attention to the human beings, we then turned to the beast.

The boar had received François's two bullets, but the one shot broadwise had been flattened against its thigh, almost without breaking the skin; the other, fired in front, had glided over its skull, in which it had dug a deep wound; whilst Moinat's ball had caught the animal in the small of the shoulder and had killed it stone dead.

The dogs were given their usual portion; then the beast was put on the shoulders of two foresters to be carried to la Maison-Neuve,—as the messengers of Moses brought the bunch of grapes from the Promised Land,—and hunting began again as though nothing had happened, without any prevision of the much more terrible event than the one we have related that was to come to pass before the day's end.

The third attack took place in Moinat's preserve, adjacent to the one in which Bobino had been decorated, three days before: it was reached after three-quarters of an hour's walking. The same precautions were taken as in the preceding battues; a ring was formed, and this time I was placed between M. Deviolaine and Berthelin; then, as Moinat had found the beast, it was his turn to go inside the enclosure to rout it out.

The barking of his dog announced in five minutes' time that the boar had been started.

Everyone was on the alert to have a shot at it as it passed, when suddenly we heard the report of a gun, and, at the same time, I saw a piece of rock, which was about forty paces from me, burst into splinters; then I heard a cry of pain on my right. I turned my head, and saw Berthelin clinging to the branch of a tree with one hand, pressing the other against his side, whence the blood gushed out between his fingers. Gradually he became too faint to hold himself up, bent over double, and sank to the ground with a heavy groan.

"Help! help!" I cried; "Berthelin is wounded."

I ran to him, followed by M. Deviolaine, while the whole string of huntsmen came rapidly up to us.

Berthelin had lost consciousness. We held him in our arms, the blood flowing in torrents from a wound in his left hip: the ball was lodged in his body.

We were all standing round the dying man, questioning each other with our eyes to know who had fired the shot, when we saw Choron, capless, issue out of the underwood, pale as a ghost, holding his gun, which was still smoking, in his hand, and shouting:—

"Wounded! wounded! Did someone say my uncle is wounded?"

No one made answer. We pointed to the dying man, who was freely vomiting blood.

Choron came forward with haggard eyes, the perspiration in beads on his brow, his hair standing on end, and went up to the wounded man; he went paler still, if such were possible, as he looked at him; then he uttered a piercing yell, broke the stock of his gun against a tree, and threw the barrel fifty yards off.

He next fell on his knees, imploring the dying man to pardon him, but the eyes had already closed for ever!

They quickly improvised a litter, and placed the wounded man upon it; then they carried him to Moinat's house, which was only three or four hundred steps from the scene of the accident. We all accompanied the litter, or, rather, we followed Choron, who walked close after it, his arms hanging down, his head lowered, speechless, dry eyed. In the meantime one of the keepers had mounted M. Deviolaine's horse, and had ridden off full gallop to find a doctor.

The doctor arrived in half an hour's time, but only to say what everyone knew for himself when he saw that Berthelin had never regained consciousness—namely, that the wound was mortal.

His wife was still in ignorance of the news, and someone would have to break it to her. M. Deviolaine offered to carry the sad message, and got up to leave the house.

Then Choron rose too, and going up to him—

"M. Deviolaine," he said, "I want it to be understood that as long as I live the poor, dear woman shall never want for anything; and if she will come to live with us, she shall be treated like my own mother."

"Yes, Choron," M. Deviolaine replied, his heart full; "certainly,—I know what a good, true-hearted fellow you are. We can't help these things. Every bullet finds its billet: it is not your fault—it was fate."

"Oh! *Monsieur l'inspecteur*" exclaimed Choron, "say that again, you do not know how your words comfort me.... I think my heart will break."

"Cry, my boy, have a good cry, it will do you good," said M. Deviolaine.

"Oh! my God! my God!" the wretched man exclaimed, bursting into sobs, as he fell back on a chair.

Nothing ever moves me so much as to see a great, strong man broken down by deep sorrow.

The sight of Berthelin, struggling in his death agony, his lifeblood welling out of him, moved me less than did the sight of Choron, struggling against despair and unable to shed a tear.

We left that death-chamber, one after another, leaving there only the dying man, the doctor, Moinat and Choron.

And in the night Berthelin died.

You can imagine my mother's state of mind when she heard all that had passed, and the tremendous oration she gave me on random shots. Choron's ball might just as easily have hit me as Berthelin, and then *she* would have been weeping over *my* dead body!

I had plenty to say against such reasoning. I told her that of course everything was possible, but that this was the first accident of its kind, within the memory of man, that had happened in the forest; that the fact of its having happened was a good reason why it should not occur again for a century or so; that, within this period, those who were not killed by bullets would be slain by the redoubtable hunter we call Time. In short, there was no reason why I should not form part of hunting-parties to come, as I had of those that had passed.... Alas! my poor mother hadn't a will of her own where I was concerned. I worried her until she gave in. Oh! poor mother mine! the deadly hunter was to slay thee before thy time, just when I was going to make thee happy and comfortable in return for all the sorrows and anxieties I had caused thee!

The following Thursday I went to the hunt in spite of the terrible accident of the Sunday.

The rendezvous was at *la Bruyère-aux-Loups* this time.

M. Deviolaine had summoned everybody except Choron, but, summoned or not, Choron was not the man to fail in his duty. He turned up at the same hour as the rest; but he had neither carbine nor musket.

"There he is!" said M. Deviolaine; "I was sure he would turn up!"

Then, turning to him, he said:—

"Why the devil have you come, Choron?"

"Because I am head keeper, inspector."

"But I did not summon you to come."

"Yes, I understood, and I thank you. But it must not be. I must do my duty before everything else. God knows I would gladly have given my life to have prevented this; but, if I were to stay at home lamenting, it would not lighten the earth over his body, poor fellow.... And one thing troubles me terribly, M. Deviolaine."

"What is it, Choron?"

"That he died without forgiving me."

"Why should he have pardoned you? He did not even know that it was you who fired the unfortunate shot."

"No, he did not know when he was dying, but he will know now he is above—they say the dead know everything."

"Come, come, Choron, cheer up," said M. Deviolaine.

"Cheer up! indeed; surely the fact of my being here shows that I am doing my best, *M. l'inspecteur*: but all the same I wish he had pardoned me."

Then he bent down and whispered in his chief's ear: "You will see some misfortune will happen to me, some mishap ... M. Deviolaine ... and because..."

"And because?"

"Because he did not pardon me."

"Don't be a fool."

"You will see."

"Choron!"

"Well—that is what I feel."

"Very well, keep it to yourself, and let us turn the subject."

"Just as you please, *M. l'inspecteur.*"

"Why have you come unarmed?"

"Because—do you not understand?—I could not touch a carbine or a musket to save my life, not to save my life."

"Then how do you propose to kill a boar?"

"What shall I kill it with?"

Choron took a knife out of his pocket—

"Well, I shall kill it with that!"

M. Deviolaine shrugged his shoulders.

"Shrug your shoulders to your heart's content, M. Deviolaine,—it shall be as I tell you. These wretched boars have been the cause of my uncle's death, and I should not feel as though I were killing them if I did it with a carbine or a musket—but with my knife it is a different matter! Besides, don't they cut pigs' throats with a knife? and what else is a boar but a pig?"

"Well," said M. Deviolaine, who knew he would never get the last word, "as you will not listen to anything you must be left to go your own way."

"Yes, yes; leave me to my own devices, *M. l'inspecteur*, and you shall see!"

"To the chase! to the chase, gentlemen!" cried the inspector.

The boar was in the preserve of a man named Lajeunesse, and we attacked it pretty soon, as the rendezvous was not more than five hundred steps from the lair.

But this time, although the boar, which was a three-year old, was hit four or five times, it led us a fine dance, and only after four or five hours' chase did it desire to turn round upon the dogs.

Everybody knows that, no matter how tired one may be, so tired as hardly to be able to stand, all fatigue is forgotten directly the boar turns at bay. We had hunted altogether, taking into account the ins and outs, some ten leagues. But, directly we recognised from the dogs' voices that they were at close quarters with the animal, each of us revived, and began to run towards the direction whence the barking was heard.

It sounded from out a young spinney of eight or ten years' standing—that is to say, a thicket of about ten or a dozen feet high, wherein the drama was being acted. As we drew nearer the sound increased, and from time to time we could see a dog flung above the young trees by a creature's tusks, its four paws in mid air, howling madly, but renewing the attack on the boar directly it touched the ground again. At last we reached a kind of clearing: the animal was pinned, as in a fortress, by the branches of a large tree which a storm had blown down. Twenty to thirty dogs were attacking it all at the same time; ten or a dozen of them were hurt, several had their stomachs ripped open. But, game beasts as they were, they did not notice their pain; they returned to the fight, with their insides hanging out, trampling on them. It was a magnificent and yet a horrible spectacle!

"Come on, come on, Mildet or Moinat, send a ball into that rascal! There are quite enough dogs killed—finish it off."

"Hah! what are you saying, *M. l'inspecteur*," cried Choron; "a gun-shot, a gun-shot for a hog? Nothing of the kind! A cut with a knife is good enough for him,—wait and you shall see."

Choron drew his knife, dashed at the boar, scattering the dogs, which quickly returned to the charge, making one moving, howling mass. For two or three seconds it was impossible for us to make out anything; then, suddenly, the boar made a frantic attempt to spring out. We all had our triggers ready, when we saw that the animal drew back instead of rushing out. Choron stood up, and held the beast by its two hind-legs, as he would have held a wheel-barrow, and stuck to it, in spite of all its struggles, with that iron grasp of his we knew so well; while the dogs, flying at it again, covered it with their bodies, till the whole thing looked like a mottled and moving carpet.

"Go for it, Dumas!" shouted M. Deviolaine. "Now is your chance,—pluck your first laurels."

I went nearer to the boar, which redoubled its efforts as it saw me coming, and gnashed its tusks, looking at me with bloodshot eyes; but it was caught in a regular trap this time, and none of its struggles could free it.

I put the end of the barrel of my gun into its ear, and I fired.

The shock was so violent that the animal tore itself out of Choron's hands, but only to roll over ten steps away; bullet, wadding, and powder had all entered its head, and I had literally blown out its brains.

Choron burst out laughing.

"Come now," he said. "There is still some pleasure left in life!"

"Yes," said M. Deviolaine, scared by what he had just seen; "but if you go on in that fashion, my boy, you won't enjoy it long, I can tell you.... What have you done to your hand?"

"Oh, it is nothing but a scratch; the beggar's skin was so tough that my knife shut up."

"Yes, and in shutting up it has cut off your finger," said M. Deviolaine.

"Clean off, *M. l'inspecteur*—clean off!" And Choron held up his right hand, from which the first joint of the index finger had gone.

Then, out of the silence that this sight produced, he said as he went up to M. Deviolaine:—

"It is quite right, *M. l'inspecteur*, that was the finger with which I killed my uncle ..."

"But that wound must be attended to, Choron."

"Take care of that? Bah! it is not worth making a fuss about! If the wind gets to it it will soon heal."

And with that Choron reopened his knife and cut the beast up as coolly as if nothing had happened.

At the following hunt, instead of a knife Choron brought a poignard, the shape of a bayonet, with a Spanish guard to it which covered the whole hand. It had been made to his order by his brother, who was the gunsmith of Villers-Cotterets. This poignard could neither break nor bend, and thrust by Choron's fist it could penetrate to the very heart of an oak tree. The same scene I have just described again took place, only this time the boar remained in its place, and had its throat cut like a domestic pig.

He did the same at all the other hunts; so that his comrades began to nickname him the pork-butcher.

The extraordinary thing was that where any other man than Choron would have lost his life, Choron did not get so much as a scratch!

One might have said that he cut off the only vulnerable part of his body when he cut off his finger-tip. But all this did not cause him to forget the death of Berthelin; he grew more and more melancholy, and from time to time he said to the inspector:—

"You will see, Monsieur Deviolaine, nothing will prevent some misfortune happening to me one of these days!"

Then his wife would complain of his jealousy, confidentially to her friends.

"Some fine day," she said, "the wretch will kill me as he killed uncle Berthelin!"

Ought I to finish Choron's lamentable history straight away? Shall I wait till the dénouement comes to pass in due course in its proper time and place?

No, we will clear away at once the sanguinary stain that left its mark on the early records of my youth.

CHAPTER IV

A wolf-hunt—Small towns—Choron's tragic death.

Five or six years had flown by since the events we have just related. I had left Villers-Cotterets, and I had returned there to spend a few days with my good mother.

It was in the month of December, and the ground was completely covered with snow.

My mother kissed me over and over again. Then, I ran straight off to M. Deviolaine's.

"Ah! there you are, boy," he said; "you have come in the nick of time!"

"A wolf-hunt, isn't it?"

"Exactly so."

"I thought there would be as I looked at the snow, and I am delighted I was not wrong in thinking so."

"Right; we have had news of three or four of those gentlemen being in the forest, and, as there are a couple of them in Choron's preserve, I sent him orders to-day to have them unearthed to-night, warning him that we shall be at his house by seven o'clock to-morrow morning."

"He is still at Maison-Neuve?"

"Yes."

"How has poor Choron got on? Does he still kill boars with bayonet thrusts."

"Oh! the boars are completely exterminated, I do not think a single one is left in the forest. He took an account of them all."

"Did their death comfort him?"

"Good gracious, no! as you will see; the poor devil is sadder and gloomier than ever: he is quite an altered man. I secured a pension for Berthelin's widow; but nothing can cure him of his grief, he is struck to the heart. Moreover, he has grown more and more jealous."

"As unjustifiably as ever?"

"The poor little wife is an angel!"

"Ah! then it is a monomania! But he is still' one of your best keepers, is he not?"

"One of the best."

"He will not disappoint us of our prey to-morrow?"

"You may be sure of that."

"That is all we want; as for his folly, well! we must leave that to time to cure."

"Oh! lad, I am afraid, on the contrary, that time will only make matters worse; and, by dint of hearing him repeat it so often, I have begun to believe some misfortune will happen to him."

"Really? has it come to that?"

"Yes, upon my word. I have done my utmost for him; I have nothing to reproach myself with."

"How are all the others?"

"Capital."

"Mildet?"

"He still cuts squirrels in half with a single flying bullet; not as they climb along the tree, but now as they leap from one tree to another."

"And his rival Moinat?"

"Oh! poor devil; don't you know what happened to him?"

"Was he too killed by a nephew?"

"When he was out wolf-hunting last winter his gun burst and blew off his left hand."

"How on earth did an accident like that happen to such an old sportsman?"

"As he was leaping a ditch the butt of his gun struck the ground without his noticing it, and by some means or other the gun exploded."

"Was there no way of saving part of his hand?"

"Not one finger! Lécosse had to amputate it within a few inches of the wrist."

"Can he not hunt any more now?"

"Oh, yes! we were out shooting yesterday in the marshes of Coyolle, and he killed seventeen out of the nineteen snipe we shot."

"How clever of him! I suspect Bobino would not have hit so many with the use of both his hands? That reminds me—what has become of him?"

"Bobino?"

"Yes."

"He has made a whistle out of the boar's tail to call his dogs, and he declares he will never rest, in this world or in the other, until he has laid hands on the remaining portion of the animal."

"Then everyone is all right with the exception of poor Choron?"

"That is so."

"You say the rendezvous is at ...?"

"Six o'clock prompt to-morrow morning, at the end of the big avenue, to enable everybody to reach la Maison-Neuve by seven o'clock."

"I will be there."

And I left M. Deviolaine to go and greet all my old friends; shaking hands with some, embracing others, and wishing good fortune to all.

It is one of the best pieces of fortune in this life to be born in a small town, where one knows every inhabitant, and where each household keeps you in remembrance. I know it always excited me warmly to return home—even to-day, after thirty years of work and struggle have passed since my early days, and taken the bloom of freshness from things—to that poor little hamlet, almost unknown to the world at large, in which I first stretched out my arms towards life's fantasies—fantasies which seemed crowned with haloes and adorned with flowers. Half a league before reaching the town I get down from the carriage and count the trees as I walk along the footpath. I know from which trees I cut branches for my kites, and those into which I buried my arrows or from which I stole birds' nests. I sit with closed eyes at the feet of some of these, and give myself up to pleasant day-dreams that take me back twenty years; there are some which I love as though they were old friends, before which I bow as I pass them by; there are others which have been planted since my departure, and these I pass by indifferently, as before things unknown and of no account. But when I reach the town it is quite another matter. The first person who catches sight of me utters an exclamation, and runs to the door of his house; and each one does the same as I go through the town. Then, when I have passed by, the people of the district join in welcoming me, talk of me, of my youthful escapades, of my present life so far away from theirs, so full of storm and stress, which would have flown by uneventfully and tranquilly if, like them, I had stopped at home where I was born; then, ten minutes after, my arrival is the talk of the town, and there is joy in my heart, and in the hearts of some two or three thousand persons besides.

One makes a home everywhere one goes, but, in Paris, streets change their name, increase or decrease in length, according to the caprice of the head road-surveyor. If you leave Paris for ten years you do not recognise either your street or your house on your return.

So I promised myself a high festival with all the keepers on the morrow, in honour of my return.

This festival began at six in the morning. I saw the old faces, with their beards covered with hoar-frost; for, as I have pointed out, it had snowed in the night, and it was horribly cold; we all shook hands cordially, then we started for la Maison-Neuve. It was still dark.

When we reached *Saut-du-Serf* (so called because once, when the duc d'Orléans was hunting in the forest, a stag had leapt over the road which was enclosed between two thickets), we saw traces of daylight beginning. The weather was capital for hunting: no snow had fallen for twelve hours, so nothing prevented us following the trail; should any wolves have been turned out of their lairs, they were certain to fall into our hands.

We went another half league farther, until we caught sight of the corner where Choron usually waited for us. He was not there.

Such an infringement of habit in a man so punctual in his engagements as Choron made us uneasy. We hurried our pace, and we soon struck the path whence we could see la Maison-Neuve about a kilomètre away.

Thanks to the carpet of snow over the ground, all objects were easy to distinguish, even at some distance off. We saw the little white house half buried in the trees; we saw a thin column of smoke which, rising from the chimney, mounted up into the air; we saw, too, a riderless horse, saddled and bridled; but we did not see Choron.

We heard the dogs making a dismal howling, and that was all.

We looked at one another and shook our heads sadly,—instinct told us something unusual had happened, and we quickened our pace.

As we drew nearer nothing changed from our first view of things.

When we got within a hundred paces of the house we unconsciously slackened our steps, feeling that we were on the brink of discovering some dreadful mishap.

We came to a standstill when within fifty paces of the house.

"We must know what it is all about," said M. Deviolaine; so we set off afresh, silently, with anxious hearts, not uttering a word.

As we approached, the horse craned its neck towards us and, with smoking nostrils, whinnied to us.

The dogs rushed at their chains, champing wildly to be released from their kennels.

Ten steps from the house we perceived a spot of blood on the snow, and a discharged pistol close by it.

A track of blood led towards the house from that spot.

We shouted: no answer.

"We must go in," said the inspector.

We went in, and we found Choron stretched on the floor, near his bed, the bed-clothes still gripped between his clasped fingers.

Upon a little table by his bed stood two bottles of white wine—one empty, the other opened and begun. A large wound was in his left side, which his favourite dog was licking.

He was still warm, and could not have been dead above ten minutes.

This is what had happened; we learnt next day from a postman from a neighbouring village, who had almost seen what had occurred.

We have spoken of Choron's jealousy of his wife, and, although nothing justified this jealousy, as the inspector had told me, it had increased as time went on.

He had taken advantage of a splendid moon to set out at one o'clock in the morning to turn out a couple of wolves which he knew were round about.

A quarter of an hour after his departure a messenger came to tell his wife that her father had been struck with apoplexy, and asked to see her before he died.

The poor woman got up and set out immediately, without being able to leave word where she was going; neither she nor the messenger could write.

When Choron returned at five o'clock and found the house empty, he felt the bed and found it was cold; he called his wife, he hunted all over; she had disappeared.

"So, she has taken advantage of my absence," said Choron, "to go to her lover, and she has not yet returned, thinking I should not be home so soon. She has deceived me—I will kill her!"

He thought he knew where to find her, so he took down his holster pistols, loaded them, put fourteen buckshot in one and seventeen in the other.

The fourteen buckshot were found in the undischarged pistol and the seventeen in Choron's body.

Then he saddled his horse, brought it out of the stable and led it in front of his door.

He put one of the pistols in the right holster, and it fitted perfectly: but the left holster happened to be narrower, and it was difficult to get the pistol into its place, so Choron tried to make it go forcibly: he took the holster in one hand and the butt end of the pistol in his other hand, and violently pushed the pistol into its place; the prod moved the trigger and the gun went off.

Choron had pressed the holster close to him to hold it steady, so the whole charge, shot, wadding, and powder, entered his left side, tearing and rupturing his internal organs.

The postman, who happened to be passing at the moment, ran up at the sound of the shot. Choron was standing, leaning against his saddle.

"My God, what have you done, M. Choron?" asked the postman.

"My good Martineau, that has happened which I have been expecting," answered Choron; "I killed my uncle with a gun-shot, and now I have killed myself with a pistol-shot. It says somewhere in the Scriptures that 'he who lives by the sword, shall perish by the sword.'"

"You are killed—you, M. Choron?" cried the postman; "there is nothing the matter with you."

Choron smiled and turned round; his clothes were singed, his blood flowed in a stream down his trousers, which were dyed red all down.

"Oh! my God!" exclaimed the postman, starting back. "What can I do for you? Shall I go for the doctor?"

"The doctor—what the devil do you suppose he can do?" replied Choron.

Then, in a melancholy voice, he added: "Did the doctor prevent my poor uncle Berthelin from dying?"

"At least let me do something, M. Choron."

"Go and fetch me two bottles of my cooling draught, from the cellar, and unchain Rocador for me."

The postman, who used to take a passing drink every morning with Choron, took the key, went down into the cellar, got two bottles of white wine, unfastened Rocador and then came back.

He found Choron, seated before a table, writing.

"Here it is," said the postman.

"Thank you, my friend," replied Choron; "put the two bottles upon the night table, and then you had better go on with your own work."

"But, M. Choron," the postman insisted, "tell me, at least, how it happened."

Choron reflected for a moment; then, in a whisper, he murmured: "Perhaps it will be as well that people should know." And, turning to the man, he said:

"Will you go when I have told you everything?"

"Yes, M. Choron."

Then he related "*the thing*", as the postman put it, in every detail.

"And now that you know what you wanted to know, please go."

"You wish me to go?"

"I do."

"Really?"

"Yes."

"Well, then, good-bye."

"Good-bye."

And the postman left, hoping with all his heart that Choron was wounded less dangerously than he thought; for he could hardly believe a man who could preserve his presence of mind with such coolness could be mortally hurt.

No one ever knew what passed after the postman left him. No human creature helped Choron in that dark hour of his mortal agony—he struggled alone with death.

He had probably drunk as much of the wine out of the two bottles as was missing; then he had tried to raise himself on his bed, but his strength failed him, and he fell on the floor, clutching hold of the bed-clothes, in which position he was when we found him dead.

A piece of paper was on the table: it was the same the postman had seen him writing upon when he returned from the wine cellar.

On this paper were traced these few lines in a hand still firm:—

"M. L'INSPECTEUR,—You will find one of the wolves in Duquesnoy Wood; the other has decamped.

"Farewell, M. Deviolaine.... I told you truly that some misfortune would come to me.—Yours devotedly,

"CHORON—Head Keeper."

What I said a while back about small towns and their pleasing memories can be said still more truly with regard to terrible recollections.

Such a catastrophe, happening in the faubourg Saint-Martin, in the rue Poissonnière, or on the place du Palais-Royal, might have left an impression for a week, or a fortnight, or a month at the most.

But in the little town of Villers-Cotterets, on the highroad leading to Soissons, which passed by the ill-fated house itself, through the beautiful arches of green foliage made by oaks and beeches, planted centuries before, beneath which keepers take their noiseless way, talking only in low tones, the event I have just recorded is as vividly remembered to-day as if it had just happened, and everyone will tell it you as I have done.

Alas! poor Choron! when I entered your house and saw you growing deathly pale, with those half-empty bottles by your side and your body still palpitating faintly, your dog licking the wound, I little imagined I should one day become the biographer of your obscure life and tragic death!

CHAPTER V

My mother realises that I am fifteen years old, and that *la marette* and *la pipée* will not lead to a brilliant future for me—I enter the office of Me. Mennesson, notary, as errand-boy, otherwise guttersnipe—Me. Mennesson and his clerks—La Fontaine-Eau-Claire.

Although all these hunting parties procured me a most delightful existence, one which might have been indefinitely prolonged had I possessed an income of 20,000 livres, they did not provide a future for a poor devil whose patrimony, in spite of maternal economy, was melting away day by day in a terrible fashion.

I was fifteen years old. It was considered quite time I learnt some profession, and it was decided I should become a lawyer.

At that period, when a veil hid my future from me, and I had not yet felt any of those ambitions which have since led me into other paths, every profession, with the exception of that of the priesthood, was equally indifferent to me.

My mother left home one fine morning, and, crossing the square diagonally, went to ask her solicitor if he would be kind enough to take me as his third clerk.

The solicitor replied that he would be most happy to receive me, but it appeared to him, unless he were mistaken, that I cared too much for *la marette*, *la pipée*, and hunting, ever to become an assiduous pupil of Cujas and of Pothier.

My mother heaved a sigh; this was probably her own opinion, too, but she persisted all the same, and the lawyer replied:

"Very well, my dear Madame Dumas, since it will give you so much pleasure, send him to me, and we will see."

So it was decided that I should go to Maître Mennesson the following Monday; polite folk would say in the capacity of third clerk—others in that of errand-boy or guttersnipe, *saute-ruisseau*, to give the rank its slang name.

It gave me some pain to give up my sweet independence; but it gave my mother great pleasure when I yielded to her decision; all her friends told her it was such a good opening for me; Lafarge (you remember the spruce and clever son of the coppersmith who lived near us) had carved a brilliant and lucrative career for himself in the same profession; the thought that my profession would lead to an income of 12,000 or 15,000 francs per annum, and that then I could give bird-snaring parties in grand style, as he had done, took my fancy so enormously that—I went to M. Mennesson.

M. Mennesson would be at that time a man of about thirty-five, rather under the average height, thick-set, sturdy, well proportioned throughout his frame, almost to massiveness; his hair reddish and short, his eyes sharp, his mouth inclined to teasing. He was a clever man; often short in his manner, always obstinate; he was a fanatic, a Voltairian and a Republican, before anyone had yet thought of becoming a Republican.

The poem of *la Pucelle* was his favourite reading; he knew whole passages of it by heart, and would repeat them in his good-humoured moments or after dinner.

Of course he selected the most impious and licentious passages.

I am told that he has since, without renouncing Republicanism, become extravagantly religious, and that he now takes part in processions, taper in hand, whereas previously he would keep his head covered when they passed.

May God have mercy on his soul!

Two members of that legal hierarchy stand out in my memory—the head and second clerks.

The first was called Niguet. He was a young man of twenty-six or twenty-eight, the son of a lawyer, grandson of a lawyer, nephew of a lawyer; one of those individuals who come into this world possessed of the equipment of spidery handwriting, an illegible signature, and a tremendous flourish after it.

The second was a lad of about my own age. He was fat and yellow-skinned; he had a pointed nose; he studied ten years to become a lawyer, and ended by being a forest keeper.

I never heard whether he ever raised himself above the grade of a common keeper, although he had influential connections in the administration of the forest lands, and three or four thousand livres income from his mother's family.

He was called Cousin.

My apprenticeship to the law was agreeable enough. M. Mennesson was not a bad sort of fellow, provided one did not in his presence say anything good concerning priests, or pronounce a panegyric upon the Bourbons.

If anybody did, his little grey eyes would flash; he would seize hold of an Old Testament or a History of France, open the Old Testament at the Book of Ezekiel, the History of France at the Reign of Henri III., and begin commenting on either after the fashion of the *Citateur* of Pigault-Lebrun.

I have said that I entered M. Mennesson's as errand-boy; at first the title caused me some feeling of shame; but I soon saw, on the contrary, that quite the pleasantest side of the profession of a lawyer's clerk fell to my share.

M. Mennesson drew up many deeds for the peasants of neighbouring villages. When these peasants could not make it convenient to come to him, I was commissioned to go and get their signatures to the deeds in their homes. I was told over night of the direction I was to be sent next day, and I made my plans accordingly.

If it was in the shooting season, I took an excellent companion for the wayside in the shape of my gun; if the season was over, I would go over night and set bird snares at all the pools which lay along my route.

In the first instance, it was very seldom that I did not bring back a hare or a couple of rabbits; in the second, half a dozen thrushes, blackbirds or jays, and a score of robins and other small birds.

One day my employer gave me notice that I was to go to Crespy on the day following, to collect information about a deed from his confrère, Me. Leroux.

As the distance was rather longer than usual (it is three and a half leagues from Villers-Cotterets to Crespy), I engaged a baker, who was a client of M. Mennesson, and who was concerned in the business I was going about, to lend me his horse.

It was always a treat to me to be on horseback, even though only astride a baker's steed.

I set off next morning with instructions to return the same evening, at all costs.

Besides the pleasure of the ride, there was yet another attraction for me at Crespy; I should be able to call and see once more that worthy family from whom we had received hospitality at the time of the invasion and also my friends the de Longprés.

I have related Madame de Longpré's story. She was the widow of a groom of the bedchamber to King Louis XV. She had gradually sold all her magnificent china, inherited from her husband. Her oldest son was a quartermaster in the chasseurs, a brave fellow all round, but one who would shake with fear and hide himself under the bed when there was a thunderstorm.

I set off, promising to return as quickly as possible: and I kept my word scrupulously.

First of all, I fulfilled my commission to Me. Leroux; then, when that was over, I began my calls.

I remounted my horse at seven in the evening, and started on my homeward way.

It was the month of September. The days were visibly becoming shorter; and, as the weather was gloomy on that particular evening, and almost raining, it was already dark when I set off from Crespy and put spur to my horse.

The road between Villers-Cotterets and Crespy, or rather from Crespy to Villers-Cotterets—to be topographically accurate in our descriptions—is almost a highroad, but nearly deserted by business traffic; half-way between Crespy and Villers-Cotterets it rejoins the highroad from Villers-Cotterets to Paris, describing a huge Y by its divergence.

A quarter of a league from Crespy, a portion of forest, called the Tillet Wood, extends to the roadside, but does not cross to the other side.

A league and a half farther on, the road, which hitherto is flat, drops into a kind of ravine, at the bottom of which runs a stream; the sides of this ravine are intersected on the left by quarries long since deserted and unworked.

The stream has given its name to the place, which is called *la Fontaine-Eau-Claire.*

Several of these quarries open their dark and deep mouths on the road, and give the place a solitary and threatening character, which inspires the people of the countryside with terror.

There are traditions belonging to this ravine of armed robbers and assassinations—connected with obscure periods, it is true, but which are handed down in popular couplets, like the traditions connected with the forest of Bondy.

We will content ourselves by quoting the following, which, although poor enough in rhyme, is a product of the locality, and is not given as an example of poetry:—

A la Fontaine-Eau-Claire,
Bois quand le jour est dans son clair."

The charming valley of Vauciennes crosses transversely that of la Fontaine-Eau-Claire, half a league farther on; this valley of Vauciennes leads to the mill of Walue à Coyolle, at the bottom of which winds a stream of liquid silver ending in the noted marsh where Moinat used to practise his skill on squirrels with M. Deviolaine.

The road descends here at a steep gradient and climbs up beyond at a still steeper slope. In frosty weather these two hills are the terror of drivers, who descend the one too quickly, and do not know how to ascend the other.

Yokes of oxen are stationed in the village on purpose to perform the office of haulers.

The summit of the second hill, from which Villers-Cotterets can be seen at about a league's distance, is crowned by a windmill belonging to M. Picot, who owes, moreover, also part of the plain of Noue, of Coyolle, and of Largny.

This windmill plays an important rôle in the remainder of my story—for it will have been gathered that I have not described the road between Villers-Cotterets and Crespy (a road which would little interest my readers) for the mere love of description. The mill is totally isolated from all other dwelling-houses, it stands well above Vouffly, nearly three kilomètres from Largny, and a league from Villers-Cotterets.

This then was the road I followed, at as fast a trot as my baker's horse would permit, the highway of His Majesty King Louis XVIII. resounding heavily under its hoofs.

Towards about eight o'clock, I reached the neighbourhood of la Fontaine-Eau-Claire.

I have already pointed out that the weather was gloomy; the moon, in its first quarter, was shrouded in large clouds, which sped rapidly across the sky, ending off in flecks of greyish, foam-like scud.

I had money about me, I was unarmed, I was barely fifteen years old; the traditions of Fontaine-Eau-Claire were vividly present to my mind; therefore my heart was beating slightly.

Half-way down the hill I urged my horse into a trot, and, by the help of an oak branch that I had gathered in Tillet Wood, I succeeded in making him pass from a trot to a gallop.

I got past the dangerous place, the *malo sitio*, as they say in Spain, without accident, and, although it was behind me, I decided that I must still keep my steed to his gallop.

I was obliged, however, to slacken his pace down the steep and up the rising of Vauciennes; but I had hardly cleared the top of the hill, when I urged him into a gallop again by the help of a dig from my spur, and a couple of good lashes with my switch.

Everything round me seemed asleep. The landscape, steeped in darkness, was not even rendered less sombre by a light on the horizon or by a falling star;

not even a dog bayed, a sound that would have indicated the presence, in the invisible distance, of a farmhouse, which I knew was there, and which my eyes searched for in vain.

The windmill seemed asleep with the rest of nature; its sails were stiff and motionless, and looked like the arms of a skeleton raised to the heavens in a despairing attitude.

Only the trees along the roadside seemed alive; they twisted and groaned in the wind, which tore their leaves off roughly, sending them flying away down into the plain, like flocks of dark feathered birds.

Suddenly, my horse, which was keeping to the middle of the road and galloping fast, shied to one side so violently, and so unexpectedly, that he sent me spinning fifteen paces off across the road; then, instead of waiting for me, he went on his way at double speed, snorting noisily as he went.

I picked myself up, stunned by my fall, which might have been my death, if, instead of falling on the wet side paths, I had fallen on the paved road itself.

My first thought was to run after my horse, but he had already gone so far that I decided it would be quite useless. Then, curiosity overcame me to know what object had so terribly frightened him.

I rose and tottered into the roadway.

I had hardly gone four steps before I perceived a man laid right across the road. I thought he must be some drunken peasant, and, congratulating myself that my horse had not trodden on his body, I stooped to help him to get up.

I touched his hand: it was stiff and icy.

I stood up, looked all round me, and thought I could discern a human form creeping in the ditch some ten paces away.

Then it occurred to me that the motionless man had been assassinated, and that the moving figure was very likely his murderer.

I did not wait to push my inquiries any further. I leapt over the corpse, and I took the road to Villers-Cotterets at full speed, as my horse had done.

Without stopping, without turning round, breathless, I did the remaining league of my journey in about ten minutes' time, and I reached my mother's house panting, covered with mud and sweat, just as the baker had come to tell her that his horse had returned to its stable without me.

My mother was already terribly alarmed, but her alarm was greatly increased when she caught sight of me.

I took her aside and told her everything.

My mother recommended me not to say a single word of what I had seen.

She reflected that if it were really a murdered man, there would be an inquest, an inquiry at Soissons, assizes at Laon; I should be involved in the whole thing, and compelled to appear as witness at both inquiry and assizes; and it would mean expense and waste time, and annoyance.

My mother made the excuse that I was very tired, and went herself to take the answer I had brought for M. Mennesson from Maître Leroux, whilst I changed my clothes throughout. My underclothing was saturated with perspiration, my suit was covered with mud.

My mother's visit to M. Mennesson was a brief one. She was in haste to return to me, and to ask me fresh details.

The return of the horse without its rider was put down to an ordinary fall, and as there was nothing unusual in such an occurrence the baker's suspicions were not roused.

We spent half the night without closing our eyes. My mother and I still slept in the same room, and even our beds were in the same recess. She did not give over asking questions, and I did not weary of repeating the same details over and over again, so profound was the impression they had left upon me.

Towards one o'clock we fell asleep; but that did not prevent us from waking at seven in the morning.

The whole town was in a flutter.

A carter, from Villers-Cotterets, whom I had passed half-way from the hill of Vauciennes, had come across the corpse, had put it in his waggon, had brought it to the town, and had reported the occurrence to the authorities.

CHAPTER VI

Who the assassin was and who the assassinated—Auguste Picot—Equality before the law—Last exploits of Marot—His execution.

***

The body was taken to the hospital, where it was exposed to view, as neither the justice of peace, the mayor, nor the chief constable recognised it. I very naturally wished to go and see by daylight the object of my fears of the night before. My mother made me promise not to say a word, for she knew that if I promised I should keep my word.

The body was sheltered under a shed and laid on a table.

It was that of a young man of fifteen or sixteen years of age. He was dressed in a poor suit of blue cotton, and a coarse shirt torn open down to his waist, leaving his chest bare.

The wound that seemed to have caused his death was a transverse cut right across the skull, and it seemed to have been made by a blunt instrument.

His feet and his hands were bare. His feet looked like those of a man used to much walking; his hands were those of a working man.

Beyond these details he was, as I have said, completely unknown in our district.

Two days passed, during which everyone held forth upon the event at leisure; then, all at once, the rumour spread abroad that the assassin had been arrested.

He was a shepherd in M. Picot's employ.

And next we saw a crowd rushing to the corner of the rue de Largny, where a man wearing a blouse, and handcuffed, was being brought in between two mounted policemen, armed with swords.

His type of face was that of a Picardy peasant of the lowest class, coarse and cunning.

He was taken to the prison, and the gate shut after him; but the crowd continued to besiege the gate in spite of its being closed. It was far too exciting an event not to bring the whole town out. The magistrate began the inquiry, and in his first examination the accused man denied everything.

But terrible proofs were brought against him. Shepherds, as is known, sleep in log huts, near their sheep-folds. The hut of the accused, during the day in which the murder had taken place, and during the night following that on which the body had been discovered, had been only a couple of hundred paces or so from the highroad.

Traces of blood had been found under a wretched mattress on the straw which covered the floor of the hut.

Besides this, the mallet with which the accused drove in the stakes of his sheep-pens was blood-stained on one side, and it appeared to have been the tool with which the deadly blow had been delivered.

In spite of all these proofs, the accused man—whose name was Marot—as we have said, completely denied the charge, and the magistrate and his clerk left without being able to get anything out of him.

But, about eleven o'clock at night, he changed his mind, called the gaoler, Sylvestre, who was also verger to the church, and begged him to send for the magistrate, as he had a confession to make.

The magistrate sent word to his clerk, and both repaired to the accused's cell.

He did not refuse to speak this time; on the contrary, he had quite a long story to relate—the upshot being a charge of murder against his master, Auguste Picot.

The man had built up a clever fabrication in the solitude of his cell, by the help of which he hoped to drag into complicity with himself a man too influential to have any dealings with him. But Marot shall tell his own tale.

On the day of the murder, a young man was walking along the highroad, looking for work, when he perceived Marot on the plain, busied over changing his flock from one place to another. The young man left the highroad and came straight to the shepherd, just when the latter was driving in his last picket.

He told his miserable story; he said he had no money to buy himself bread, he had tramped through the town without a bite, too proud to beg alms; but, seeing Marot was a working man, he had ventured to come and ask a bit of bread from a fellow-labourer.

Marot had brought out of his hut some of the small, round, thick loaves, such as farmers distribute each morning to their day-labourers, and he shared the loaf with the tramp, who sat down by him.

They both leant back against the hut and began their breakfast, when suddenly—it is Marot who tells the tale—Auguste Picot came up on horseback at full gallop, and cried out roughly to his shepherd:

"You scoundrel, do you suppose I give you my bread to have it eaten by beggars and by vagabonds?"

The stranger was on the point of replying to excuse the shepherd, when Picot—so said his accuser—urged his horse on with such brutality that the youth was obliged to raise his stick, to prevent himself being kicked underfoot by the horse. At this movement in self-defence, Picot's horse wheeled round, kicked out with his hind feet, and hit the youth in the chest with one of his hoofs.

The youth fell down unconscious.

Picot then, seeing he had become an unintentional murderer, decided to become one in intention: he turned an accident he was anxious to hide into a crime. He looked round him, he saw on the ground the mallet with which Marot had just been driving in the pickets of his fold, and then (please understand thoroughly that this version is not mine, but the accused's) he dealt him a violent blow on the back of his head, finishing off the wretched tramp, who had only fainted before.

Death was almost instantaneous.

Then he offered all sort of bribes to the shepherd if he would help him to conceal the crime.

The shepherd had been weak enough to be touched by his master's entreaties: he consented to conceal the body in his hut.

Hence the blood-stains on the straw and mattress.

When evening came, Picot returned to the hut to take the dead body, under cover of darkness, to the windmill, of which he possessed the key.

The two accomplices intended to go in, shut the door upon themselves and the body, dig a pit and there bury the unfortunate tramp.

But, as they were crossing the road, they were alarmed by the sound of a horse coming at full gallop; they let the body fall out of their hands, and both ran off to hide themselves.

They returned ten minutes later; but the waggoner with his cart appeared on the top of the hill of Vauriennes, and they were obliged again to abandon their ghastly work.

The waggoner had taken up the corpse and had carried it, as we have seen, to Villers-Cotterets. All hope of hiding the crime had gone, and all their thoughts had to be given to attending to their own safety.

Marot had been captured and had at first attempted to deny the charge; but, on reflection, he preferred to confess his passive part in the crime than to risk his life by a complete denial of all complicity in it.

We shall soon see that the fable was sufficiently skilfully conceived to necessitate the arrest of Picot, even if it did not carry conviction to the judge's mind.

So, when morning came, everybody heard of the shepherd's accusation and of his master's arrest.

The news made a great stir: Picot was not liked; he was a rich and good-looking young fellow, strong in physique, haughty in his manner—all qualities and defects which are fatal to popularity in a small town.

As a matter of fact, Picot had never done an injury to anyone. But, alas! at the first news of the misfortune that had befallen him, half the town sided against him.

The Picot family were cursed with ill luck, and the Almighty made them pay very dear for the wealth He bestowed upon them.

Four years previously Stanislas Picot, it will be remembered, was killed when out shooting. Two years before, the farm had been burnt down, and now to-day the eldest son was accused of murder.

The inquiry was actively pursued, and it was decided that a visit should be paid on the following day to the spot where the murder had taken place: the Government prosecutor had arrived from Soissons.

I shall always recollect the terrible effect the sight of that procession made upon me, as it crossed the great square. The town authorities marched at its head, with the representative of the king; next came Picot between two rows of police, some before, others behind him; then the shepherd between two more rows of police placed in the same way; after these the whole town either followed the procession or stood at their doors and windows.

They all walked fast, for it rained. People talked of equality in the eye of the law, and the justices had thought to carry out this precept by placing the two men on foot each exactly the same, with an equal number of police to guard them.

But they had forgotten the different impression this would make on two such different natures, the one belonging to the head and the other to the foot of the social ladder.

Most assuredly the man at the top of the scale suffered all the tortures of the situation.

The other man was almost triumphant; he had by a few words dragged down to the same level as himself a man who had been far higher in the social scale only a week before, a man whose bread he had eaten, whose paid servant he was, and before whom he never spoke save cap in hand.

So a debased light of exultant satisfaction radiated from the man's low countenance.

Besides, he had the sympathies of the men of his own class, who looked upon him as a victim, and even of some enviously disposed people of higher ranks in life.

Picot's expression was quite unmoved, although one could realise the fury, shame, and pride that were raging tumultuously in that massive frame.

No! Justice was not evenly dealt out to these two men, in the very fact of their being treated alike.

Next day there was another ceremony quite as lugubrious—they proceeded to exhume the body.

Most discussion took place over the bruised wound in the youth's chest. The shepherd contended that it had been caused by the horse's kick. Picot retorted that if it had been bruised by a kick from a horse and from one leg only, violent enough to make him faint away, the marks of the shoe would be imprinted on the chest, which, although bruised, was more probably marked by the clogs of the shepherd than by the horse's shoe. They were both sent to the prison at Soissons, and at the end of a month Picot was given his liberty on the grounds of there being insufficient evidence against him.

He returned to his people; but the blow had been violent enough to spoil his future life. He had been proud before, but now he became misanthropic; he shut himself up on his property at home, avoided all assemblies of young people of his own age, and ended by marrying the daughter of a policeman, who had been his mistress for some time.

Doubtless—as there is compensation in the end for all unmerited misfortune—Providence had led him by dark paths into simpler and happier ways. He had one real joy,—perhaps the deepest joy of this world,—his father and his poor mother, to whom he was devotedly attached, died near him at an extreme old age.

The shepherd was sentenced to twelve or fifteen years' imprisonment, I think, for *having stolen the clothes found on a dead man.*

A strange sentence, which established the fact that a crime had been committed without pointing out a culprit!

And here are some further details that I received after the trial.

The young man whom I found assassinated on the 13th September 1816 was called Félix-Adolphe-Joseph Billaudet; he was the son of François-Xavier-Léger Billaudet, court-crier to the *tribunal de première instance* in the arrondissement of Strasbourg; he was born at Strasbourg on the 1st April 1801, and was therefore, at the time of his death, fifteen years, six months, and twelve days old.

He was servant to M. Maréchal, forest inspector at Vervins, and had a passport upon him, at the time of his assassination, for Paris, signed at Vervins, 8th September 1816.

Probably the father and the mother of the poor lad are now dead, and I am perhaps the only person in the world who still remembers him, in thus going back to the days of my youth.

When Marot came out of prison, he returned to the country, and at first settled as a butcher in the village of Vivières. Then it seems things went badly with him, and he went to a little hamlet called Chelles, situated two or three leagues from Villers-Cotterets.

Some time after this change of residence, his wife died under mysterious and strange circumstances. While she was drawing water from a well, she leant against the pulley support, which broke; she was precipitated thirty feet deep into the well, where she was drowned.

Her death was regarded at the time as an accident.

Some time after that death, the body of a young carter was found buried only one or two feet deep, between Vivières and Chelles; he appeared to have been murdered by a pistol-shot, fired point blank in his back.

Some inquiry was set up, but no assassin or assassins could be traced.

Finally, some time after, Marot himself went before the magistrate to make a declaration concerning a new event that had just happened. A young glass-painter, who had come to ask hospitality of him, lacking the money needed for a stay at the inn (a request to which he had generously acceded), had died during the night of an attack of colic in the barn, where he had been given a truss of straw to lie on.

The young painter was duly buried.

Some days after, Marot's fowls were found dead in neighbouring yards and gardens.

They seemed to have been poisoned.

These facts were put together, and suspicions began to be aroused.

Marot was arrested. His own child gave evidence against him, and brought about his conviction.

The young painter had been poisoned by some soup into which Marot had put arsenic.

The young man complained that the soup had a queer taste; Marot's son took a spoonful, tasted it, and agreed with the painter.

"The soup," Marot replied, "tastes queer because it is made of pig's head. As for you, you greedy boy," he added, addressing this remark particularly to his son, "eat your own soup, and let this boy eat his—each dog has his platter."

But the taste of the soup was so acrid that the young painter left half of it. The rest was thrown on the dungheap; the fowls ate it, and, driven by pain, they scattered to right and left, their death revealing the fact of the poisoning.

The charges brought against Marot were this time too strong for him to deny them.

And, seeing there was no hope of salvation from the consequences of his latest crime, he confessed all the others.

He confessed that he had killed Billaudet, to steal some six or eight francs there were on him.

He confessed he had filed the screw that held the pulley, so that his wife, who was about to add to his family, should be flung into the well, wherein she was killed, either by the fall or by drowning.

He confessed he had shot the young carter whose body had been found between Chelles and Vivières point blank with a pistol, in order to rob him of thirty francs he had just received.

Finally, he confessed he had poisoned the young glass-painter, by putting arsenic in his plate, in order to steal twelve francs from him.

Marot was condemned to death, and executed at Beauvais in 1828 or 1829.

CHAPTER VII

Spring at Villers-Cotterets—Whitsuntide—The Abbé Grégoire invites me to dance with his niece—Red books—The Chevalier de Faublas—Laurence and Vittoria—A dandy of 1818.

"O youth! springtime of life! O spring! youth of the year!" So said Metastasio.

We have now reached the beginning of May 1818, and I should be sixteen in the month of July.

The month of May, the favourite month of the year, which is abundant in beauty and in promise everywhere, is even more beautiful and resplendent at Villers-Cotterets than anywhere else.

It is difficult to form any idea of what that fine park was like at that epoch of time and at that season of the year: my heart still mourns because of the order for its destruction given by Louis-Philippe.

The park was simple and yet great in its design. Two splendid stretches of grass—rather longer than they were broad—were attached like two wings to the immense Castle which overlooked the green sward: one end touched the Castle walls, and the other joined two avenues of gigantic Spanish chestnut trees, which first formed laterally the two sides of a great square, then approached one another diagonally till they nearly met, then continued right out of sight, leaving between their two lines a large open space until within a league of the mountain of Vivières, which stood out on the distant horizon, with its crumbling red sides tufted with yellow blossoming gorse.

It was all lifeless, sad, lonely, and silent in winter; the birds had migrated to more cheerful climes; only the rooks' nests remained, sole and persistent proprietors of the highest trees about that magnificent domain. It seemed as though hordes of savages had spoiled the grounds and laid waste the forests.

This state of desolation lasted four months of the year; but with the beginning of April the grass began to spring up, braving the hoar frost, which spread a silvery carpet over it every morning; the buds of the trees, which had looked so bare, so desolate, so dead, began to put on their velvety down. The sleeping birds—(where do birds sleep? we know nothing about them;—) wake up, hop about among the branches, and soon begin building their nests. Thence, each day of the month and every hour of the day brings its own changes, as part of Nature's great awakening. Chestnuts, limes, and beeches are the spring's advance guard. Daisies star the lawn; buttercups glow richly; and grasshoppers chirp in the long grass. Butterflies, flying flowers that blow in the air, come and kiss the flowers of earth. Pretty children come out of the town in their white frocks and their pink ribbons, and play on the grass: everything moves, and revives, and lives. Spring comes with the first breath of May, and we think we feel her touch as she passes in the morning mists, shaking her rose-filled hair and reviving the world with her sweet-scented breath.

It was at this joyous time of renaissance that our town held it's feast—a feast ever lavish and charming, for Nature took upon herself to defray its costs.

The feast, as I believe I have already said, lasted three days, and fell at Whitsuntide.

For three days the park was filled with pleasant sounds and happy murmurs, which began at early morning and did not die away until far on in the night. For three days the poor forgot their misery, and, much more extraordinary still, the rich forgot their riches. The whole town was gathered together in the park as one great family, and, as this family invited all its branches, relations, friends, acquaintances, the population increased fourfold. People came from la Ferté-Milon, from Crespy, from Soissons, from Château-Thierry, from Compiègne, from Paris! Every place in the coaches was booked for fifteen days in advance: and all kinds of other means of transport were devised; horses, cabs, tilburys, postcarts arrived and jostled each other in the only two hotels of the district, the *Dauphin* and the *Boule d'Or*. For three days the little town was like a body over full of blood, whose heart was beating ten times as fast as it should. But on the Wednesday it began to part with its surplus, which gradually dwindled away during the following days, until everything little by little resumed its ordinary aspect again. The large woods, which had been disturbed for three days even in their thickest depths, recovered their silence and their solitude once more: the chestnuts again became inhabited by birds, which, flying in and out among their branches, scattered a snow of flowers. Finally, the sward, which had been trodden underfoot and despoiled of its flowers, sprang up again by degrees, under the sun's influence, and once more offered a second harvest of daisies and buttercups to the devastating hands of children.

Two strangers came to the pleasant feast of Whitsuntide, this particular year.

One was a niece of the Abbé Grégoire, named Laurence—I have forgotten her surname.

The other was a friend of hers. She made out that she was of Spanish extraction, and was called Vittoria.

The abbé had told me of her coming. One morning, he came into our house and quite frightened me.

"Come here, boy," he said to me.

And I went to him, not feeling very sure what he was going to do to me.

"Nearer," he said—"much nearer still; you know I am shortsighted ... there—that will do."

The poor abbé was really as blind as a mole.

"You can dance, can you not?"

"Why do you ask me that, M. l'abbé?"

"Why! don't you remember you accused yourself in your last confession of having been to the theatre, to the opera, and to a ball?"

And, indeed, in one of those examinations of conscience that are sold ready printed, to aid idle and recalcitrant memories, I had read that it was a sin to go to a comedy, to the opera, and to a ball; therefore, as during my journey to Paris with my father when I was three years old, I had seen *Paul et Virginie* played at the Opéra Comique; as I had since been to plays, if by chance any strolling players passed through Villers-Cotterets; as, finally, I had been to a ball at Madame Deviolaine's on the birthday of one of her daughters, I had naïvely accused myself of having committed these three sins, much to the amusement of the worthy Abbé Grégoire, who, as we see, had revealed the secrets of the confessional.

"Well,—yes, I can dance," I replied,—"but why?"

"Dance an *entrechat* for me."

The *entrechat* was my strong point. People really did dance at the time I learnt dancing: nowadays they are satisfied to walk; which is much more convenient ... and much easier to learn.

I danced a few steps there and then.

"Bravo!" said the abbé. "Now you shall dance with my niece, who is coming at Whitsuntide."

"But ... I do not like dancing," I rudely replied.

"Bah! you must pretend you do, out of politeness."

"It is no wonder your cousin Cécile says you are a bear in manners," added my mother, with a shrug of her shoulders.

This accusation set me thinking.

"I beg your pardon, M. l'abbé," I said; "I will do just what you wish."

"Very good," said the abbé; "and, to make the acquaintance of our Parisian visitors, come and have lunch with us after high mass on Sunday."

There were eight days in which to prepare myself for my office of attendant cavalier.

During those eight days an important event occurred.

When my brother-in-law left Villers-Cotterets he left part of his library behind.

Amongst these books, there was a work covered in smooth red paper, comprising some eight or ten volumes. My brother-in-law had remarked to my mother:

"You can let him read them all except that work."

I shot a furtive glance at the work, and determined that on the contrary it should be the very one I would read.

I waited some days after my brother-in-law's departure, then I set myself to find the famous red books he had forbidden me to read.

But, although I turned all the books upside down, I could not lay hands on it, and I had to renounce the search.

Suddenly the thought that I had to be the cavalier of a young lady of twenty-two or twenty-four made me look through my wardrobe. Nearly all my coats had patched elbows, and most of my trousers had darned knees.

The only presentable suit I had was the one I had worn at my first communion: nankeen breeches, a white piqué waistcoat, a light blue coat with gilt buttons. Luckily everything had been made two inches too long, so that now everything was but one inch too short.

There was a big chest in the loft which contained coats and vests and breeches belonging to my grandfather, and coats and breeches belonging to my father: all in very good condition.

These clothes were destined by my mother to form my wardrobe as I grew up, and they were protected against vermin by bottles of *vétyver* and sachets of camphor.

I had never troubled over my toilette, and consequently never taken it into my head to pay a visit to this chest.

But, promoted by the abbé, who looked upon me as a dancer whom he need not trouble about, to the dignity of squire to his niece, a new idea entered my head.

I felt myself seized by the desire to look smart.

Without saying a word to my mother, for I had my own plans in mind, I went up to the loft; I locked myself in there, so as to be undisturbed in my search; and then I opened the chest.

It contained clothing fashionable enough to satisfy the most fastidious taste: from a figured satin vest to a scarlet waistcoat braided with gold; from rep breeches to pantaloons of leather.

But, of more importance still, at the bottom of that mysterious press, under all these clothes, were the famous red paper-covered volumes which I had been so expressly forbidden to read.

I immediately opened the first that fell into my hands, and I read:

"*Aventures du Chevalier de Faublas.*"

The title did not convey much to my mind, but the engravings taught me rather more.

A score of lines which I devoured taught me more than the engravings.

I gathered up the first four volumes, which I hid, carefully spread out over my chest, over which I buttoned my waistcoat; and I went down on tiptoe. I went along M. Lafarge's back lane rather than pass by the shop, and I gained the park at a run. I hid myself in one of the darkest and remotest parts of it, where I was quite certain I should not be disturbed, and then I began to read.

Chance had sometimes put obscene books in my hands.

A travelling hawker who ostensibly sold pictures, but who concealed forbidden literature under his cloak, used to go through Villers-Cotterets two or three times a year, hobbling along with difficulty on two wooden legs, and giving out he was an old soldier.

The money that I had managed to extort from my poor mother had more than once been spent in these clandestine purchases; but a feeling of delicacy which was innate in me, and by reason of which there are not four out of the six hundred volumes I have written that the most scrupulous of mothers need hide from her daughter—this sentiment of delicacy, for which I give thanks to God, always caused me to throw far away from me such books at the tenth page or at the second picture.

But it was quite a different thing with *Faublas*. *Faublas* is, without gainsaying, a bad book from the point of view of morality; a delightful romance from the point of view of fancy; a romance full of originality, depicting a variety of types, somewhat exaggerated, no doubt, but which had their counterparts in the days of Louis XV.

So I felt as great an attraction towards *Faublas* as I had felt repugnance towards *Thérèse philosophe, Felicia ou mes fredaines,* those dirty lucubrations which persistently polluted the press throughout the latter part of the eighteenth century.

From that moment I discovered my vocation—one I had never recognised or even suspected until then—I wanted to become a second Faublas.

It is true I soon renounced the idea, and that idiocy has never been put down on the list of the many failings with which I have been charged.

I had prepared a magnificent theory, all cut and dried, of seductiveness, by the time Sunday in Whitsuntide came, and I was introduced, clad in my light blue coat and nankeen breeches, to the two charming Parisian girls.

Mademoiselle Laurence was tall, thin, willowy in figure, and in character she was of a bantering and indolent disposition. She was fair-haired, clear-skinned, and possessed the graceful taste of a Parisian woman: she, as I have said, was the good abbé's niece.

Mademoiselle Vittoria was pale, stout, slightly pitted with smallpox, broad-bosomed, wide-hipped, bold in her looks, representing exactly the Spanish type from Madrid, with her dead white complexion, her velvety eyes, and her supple figure.

Although I knew it to be my duty, from M. Grégoire's previous choice of me, to give my special attention first to his niece, and although the expression of gentle candour on her face had won me from the very outset, it was to Mademoiselle Laurence that I first paid court.

It was to her I offered my arm for a walk in the park after dinner.

I will not hide the fact that I was dreadfully bored, and that I must therefore have behaved very awkwardly and very ridiculously. My appearance, besides, which was all right for a child attending his first communion in 1816, was slightly eccentric in the case of a young man making his first debut into society in 1818. Breeches at that time were only worn by old-fashioned people, who almost all belonged to the previous century, so it came about that I, almost a child still, whom no one would have been surprised to see in a turn-down collar, a round waistcoat, and fancy knickerbockers, was dressed like an old man—an anachronism that made the charms of the coquettish young lady on my arm stand out to still greater advantage. She knew well enough that the ridicule that was being poured on her cavalier could not affect her, so she kept as calm a demeanour in the midst of the smiles we met and the curious looks that followed us, as Virgil's divinities, who passed in the midst of men unmoved by the looks of men, because they did not deign to notice them. But it was a different matter to me; I could feel myself blushing all the time; and, when anyone I knew came by, instead of meeting his glance proudly, I simply turned my head away.

Like the stag in the fable, I discovered that I had very poor legs.

My poor mother imagined that because I was heir to my father's breeches, I had also inherited his calves.

They have developed since, it is true, but they are a superfluous luxury at a time when short breeches are no longer worn.

Worse than this was the fact that the presence of the two strangers made me a centre of curiosity. Mademoiselle Vittoria walked immediately after us, giving her arm to the abbé's sister, who was a little hunchback, a most excellent housekeeper to her brother, but whose plain dress and deformity of figure stood out most conspicuously against the elegant dress and ample voluptuous figure of the Spanish woman.

Every now and again the two young girls exchanged looks, and, although I did not catch them, I could feel, so to speak, the smiles that passed between them; smiles which sent the blood rushing up to my temples with shame, for they seemed to say, "Oh! my dear friend, what a bear garden have we stumbled upon!"

A word I heard increased my confusion and turned it to anger.

A young Parisian who had been employed for two or three years at the Castle, and who was gifted with all the qualities I lacked, that is to say, he was fair, pink, plump, and dressed in the latest fashion, crossed our path, and gazed after us through an eyeglass hung from a little steel chain.

"Ah! ah!" he said, "there is Dumas going to his first communion again, only he has changed his taper."

This epigram hit me straight to the heart; I went white, and almost dropped my companion's arm. She saw what was my trouble, no doubt, for she said, pretending she had not heard:

"Who is the young man who has just passed us?"

"He is a certain M. Miaud," I replied, "who is employed at the workhouse."

I must confess I dwelt on these last words with delight, hoping they might modify the good opinion my lovely companion seemed immediately to have formed of this dandy.

"Ah! how strange!" she said; "I should have taken him for a Parisian."

"By what?" I asked.

"By his style of dress."

I am sure the arrow was not shot intentionally, but, like Parthian barbed arrows, it went right to the depths of my heart, none the less.

"His style of dress!" So dress was a most important matter; by its means and in proportion to its good or bad taste, people could at the first glance at a man form an idea of his intelligence, his mind, or his heart.

This expression, "his style of dress," illuminated my ignorance at a flash.

He was indeed perfectly dressed in the fashion of 1818: he wore tight-fitting, light coffee-coloured trousers, with boots folded in the shape of a heart over his instep, a waistcoat of chamois leather with carved gilt buttons, a brown coat with a high collar. In his waistcoat pocket was a gold eyeglass fastened to a fine steel chain, and a host of tiny charms and seals dangled coquettishly from the fob of his pantaloons.

I heaved a sigh, and vowed to dress like that some day, no matter what it cost me.

CHAPTER VIII

I leap the *Haha*—A slit follows—The two pairs of gloves—The quadrille—Fourcade's triumph—I pick up the crumbs—The waltz—The child becomes a man.

We went along the promenade taken by all the townsfolk and by every stranger who came to visit the town: we walked under the grand, magnificent avenue of Spanish chestnut trees, all laden with flowers, as full as they could hold, right down to a tremendous wolf-leap, hollowed out of the ground, called the *Haha*: no doubt the word was derived from the exclamation it produces from walkers ignorant of its position when they suddenly come upon it.

I felt the moment had come to regain something of my lost dignity.

I was, it will be remembered, pretty clever at all kinds of physical exercise, and I could jump best of all.

"Do you see that ditch?" I said to my companion, pointing it out to her as something amazing. "Well, I can jump across it."

"Really?" she said with an indifferent air: "it looks very wide."

"It is fourteen feet wide.... I can tell you it is more than M. Miaud can do."

"He would be right not to try," she said: "what is the use of jumping it?"

I was struck dumb at the reply. When Pizarro was conquering Peru, one of his lieutenants, so I had read, when pursued by the natives, had leapt over a little river, which was 22 feet wide, by the help of his lance, which he stuck in the bottom.

I thought it a wonderful feat, and I had long dreamt of the possibility of doing a similar exploit if ever in great peril.

Now I had got as far as to be able to jump a distance of fourteen feet, with my own unaided strength and without the aid of any lance; this accomplishment of agility astonished my comrades, two or three only offering to compete with me. How was it, then, that the suggestion did not excite any enthusiasm in my fair Parisian?

I took it that her indifference arose from her incredulity.

"You shall see," I said to her.

And, without waiting for further remarks from her, with one bound, that Auriol himself might have envied, I reached the other side.

But Auriol performed his feats in wide trousers, whilst I did mine in tight breeches. When I alighted with doubled-up knees, I heard an ominous crack, and there seemed an airy feeling about my hind quarters—I had burst open the seat of my trousers.

This stroke was decisive; I could not take back my beautiful Parisian to the dancing hall, or give myself up to the least choregraphic exercise with her in the teeth of such a catastrophe; I could not tell her what had happened to me and ask to leave her for half an hour. So I made up my mind to take leave without asking; and off I set, at a mad run, without uttering a single word, or offering any explanation. I flew towards home, which was more than half a league away, through the astonished promenaders, who asked if my rapid flight through the crowd was on account of a bet, or whether I had suddenly taken leave of my senses.

I reached home almost in the same state as my father reached Jérémie when he came across an alligator and amused himself by throwing stones at it.

My poor mother was scared to see the state of excitability I was in. Breathless, voiceless, nearly suffocated, I could only respond to her questions by the disrespectful gesture the Neapolitan makes near Vesuvius when he thinks it is going to erupt; but my mother saw nothing in the gesture but the true facts of the case, namely, an appeal to her good nature to repair the accident that had happened.

Five minutes after, thanks to the quickness of a needle used to such mendings, the break in continuity had been repaired.

I gulped down a big glass of cider, which we made ourselves with dried apples, and I resumed my race back to the lawn as quickly as I had left it.

But, quick though I was, I did not succeed in reaching the dancing hall until ten minutes after my two Parisians; who were just taking their places: Mademoiselle Vittoria was going to dance with Niguet, and Mademoiselle Laurence with Miaud.

I have depicted the imaginary sorrows of Pitou in this very situation. I had but to draw them from actual experience. Throughout the whole of that quadrille I never took my eyes off the lovely Laure,—so she was called for short among her intimate friends,—at every smile she exchanged with her partner, a flush of anger and of shame rose to my forehead; I fancied I was the subject of their conversation, and that the conversation was not of a nature very flattering to my self-respect.

When the quadrille was over, Miaud led Laure back to her seat. I drew as near as I could to the bench on which the two Parisians sat, looking exquisite and beautiful in the midst of the most beautiful, most charming, and most aristocratic-looking young girls of our countryside.

I met Miaud near the centre of the space I had to cross to reach them.

"See what it is to wear breeches!" he said as he passed me, as though speaking to himself.

It may be guessed that this apostrophe did anything but soothe the feeling of dislike I had towards a man whom I already regarded in the light of a rival. But I knew what ridicule I should bring down on myself if I picked a quarrel with Miaud for such a cause, and I continued on my way.

"Here I am, Mademoiselle Laure," I said, when I stopped behind my Parisian.

"Ah! that is all right," she replied; "seeing you set off like that, I thought some accident must have happened to you!"

The conversation had taken a most embarrassing turn at the very beginning.

"Indeed, mademoiselle," I replied stammeringly, "I saw that—"

"That you had forgotten your gloves; I quite understood. You did not like to dance without gloves, and you were quite right."

I cast my eyes down to my bare hands, and I went purple. I mechanically thrust my hands into my pockets.

Alas! I had no gloves.

I stepped back and threw a wild glance round me.

Four steps from me stood a young man, named Fourcade, who had been sent from Paris to start and direct a Lancastrian school at Villers-Cotterets; he was busily engaged trying with difficulty to get into a pair of beautiful new gloves, which he had evidently purchased only a quarter of an hour previously.

Fourcade was a delightful young fellow who, in spite of the difference in age between us, had taken a fancy to me. He belonged as much to the century that had just ended as to the one we had entered upon; so he too, like myself, wore nankeen trousers and a pale blue coat.

Such a bond of similarity between us would alone have given me confidence in Fourcade, if this confidence had not already existed.

"My dear friend," I said, "will you do me an immense service?"

"What is it?"

"Give me your gloves."

"My gloves?"

"Yes, I have asked the young lady seated there, Mademoiselle Laurence, to give me a dance, and just as I went to take my place I found I had forgotten my gloves. You understand the awkwardness of the situation?"

"My dear boy, I will not say to you, 'You are luckier than being in love,' for it seems to me you are deeply in love; but I will say to you, 'My dear friend, you are in luck's way,' for I have two pairs with me."

And he drew a second pair of gloves from his pocket, as new as the first, handing me those he was trying to draw on.

Such unheard-of luxury astonished me.

"Why do you have two pair of gloves?" I asked.

"Because the first might perhaps split, as I put them on," he replied, with the utmost ingenuousness and as though surprised I should ask him such a question.

His reply staggered me;—it opened such vistas of unknown extravagance of living; there were actually people who took the precaution of having two pairs of gloves, while there were others who had not even dreamed of providing themselves with a single pair.

"Have you a *vis-à-vis*?" I asked Fourcade.

"No, I have only just come."

"Will you be mine?"

"With pleasure."

"Take your places for the quadrille!" cried the head fiddler.

I rushed up to Laure and proudly presented my gloved hand.

Fourcade invited her neighbour Vittoria, and we took our places.

Fourcade and I were the only two who wore short breeches at the ball.

We were both making our debut; Fourcade had hardly been a fortnight in Villers-Cotterets, and open-air dances did not begin before Whitsuntide.

This solemn rite, together with the appearance of both of us wearing short breeches, attracted a considerable number of looks. Our Parisians themselves stared as hard at us as anybody present.

The dance began.

I have said I was apt at all physical exercises. I had had a dancing-master just as I had had a fencing-master, by a lucky chance; my dancing-master's name was Brezette, an ex-infantry corporal, uncle of one of the prettiest girls in the town, to whom I had hitherto paid no attention.

I have made up for lost time since, and I shall have occasion to refer to her more than once.

I had therefore learnt, for my three francs per month, a rather eccentric style of dancing, but nevertheless it was not wanting in deftness or power. Fourcade led off first; Fourcade was one of Vestris' best pupils.

I repeat that people really danced at that time, and all the flourishes of choreography which are thought absurd to-day were then considered elegant.

At the first steps Fourcade took, there was an audible murmur of admiration. Those who were not dancing stood on their seats to look at him; while the dancers themselves lengthened their *chasses-croisés* or their *traversés*, to seize an *entrechat* or a *flic-flac*. Fourcade's debut was a triumph.

It was on this occasion that I discovered nature had endowed me with the gift of assimilation. During the short *avant-deux* made by my *vis-à-vis*, I realised the superiority of such dancing over my own. I picked out from among the complicated twinklings of his ankles and the crossing and uncrossing of his legs those evolutions which were within my compass if simply performed, and, when my turn came to take the lead, a kindly rumour reached me, in the wake of my partner's immense success, that I was doing better than had been expected of me.

From that moment I became crazy on dancing, and the frenzy lasted until it became the fashion for young men of twenty-four or twenty-five to declare that they were too bored or too busy thinking of other things, to take part in such a pleasure as dancing.

I have begun by revealing the follies of my childhood: the reader need not be uneasy, for I am not going to hide those of my youth; I will be more courageous than Rousseau, who only confessed his vices.

As I conducted my partner back to her seat, I reaped the fruits of my triumph.

"Do you know, you dance very well," my Parisian said to me; "where did you learn?"

"Here."

"What! here in Villers-Cotterets?"

I had a great mind to reply as did the baroness in *la Fausse Agnès*, my pride in my native town being so deeply wounded, "Do you take us provincials for simpletons, then?" but I contented myself by replying in rather a sneering tone:

"Yes, here in Villers-Cotterets;" adding, with the air of a man sure of his powers:

"Do you by chance happen to waltz?"

"No, it makes me giddy; but Vittoria there loves waltzing." I turned towards the Spaniard.

"If you are not engaged for the next?" I said.

"No."

"Are you inclined to venture?"

She looked at me.

"Why, certainly!" she said smilingly.

A waltz was being played.

If I were a fair dancer, I was first-rate at the waltz. The Spanish girl discovered this at the first round we made, and she gave herself up to it completely, feeling she was being well steered and had a good partner.

"You waltz very well," she said.

"You flatter me," I responded; "hitherto I have only had chairs to waltz with."

"Chairs?" she asked.

"Yes, I learnt to waltz the year I took my first communion," I said, "and the Abbé Grégoire forbade me to waltz with girls; so my dancing-master, thinking I really must hold something in my arms, gave me a chair; I was thus enabled to take my lesson without sinfulness."

My partner stopped short; I thought she would choke with laughter.

"You really are the funniest boy, I like you very much," she said, when she could regain her faculty of speech.... "Let us waltz again."

And we plunged afresh into the whirlpool, which carried us round with it.

This, as I have said, was the first time I danced with a woman; it was the first time I breathed a woman's perfumed breath, or felt her hair touch my cheeks; the first time my eyes had been riveted on bare shoulders or my arm had clasped a round, full, supple waist. I heaved a shuddering sigh of delight.

"Well? what is the matter with you?" my partner asked, looking at me with her Spanish eyes, which shone even through her lace mantilla.

I replied, while we waltzed on unceasingly: "It is far nicer to waltz with you than with a chair."

She escaped out of my arms this time, and went to sit near her friend.

"Well, what is the matter?" asked Laurence.

"Oh! my dear, he is so comic."

"It is strange he did not strike me in that light."

"That is because you did not waltz with him," she whispered. "I assure you I think him fascinating! Come on," she continued, placing herself of her own accord on my arm, "just one more turn."

I asked nothing better: and we resumed our places.

I will say no more of my own success, but my partner made quite a sensation. Her supple quivering figure, accustomed to such dances as the cachucha and fandango, managed to put some of the voluptuous energy which is such an essential characteristic of Spanish dancing into French waltzing; some electric influence seemed to radiate from her lithe, snake-like body; she had acquired that faculty from the Andalusians, who love the waltz for its own sake; who are so graceful because they let themselves go with complete abandon, and who are so beautiful because they do not think of their beauty.

The music stopped; we still stuck to our places, I with brow contracted, my teeth showing through my open lips, with a rapt expression on my face; she graceful, panting, excited.

An immense change was coming over me: the womanly breath and hair and perfume had made a man of me in a few short minutes.

"Shall we have another waltz together?" I asked her.

"As many as you like," she replied, as she went and seated herself by her friend, who leant over and whispered something in her ear. I both listened and watched them.

"Come," said Laure, with a smile that indicated some amusement in her remonstrance, "do not take my schoolboy away from me; my uncle gave him to me, you know."

"No," the Spaniard replied, showing her white teeth, which looked quite as ready to bite as to kiss—"but you must lend him to me for the waltzes. I will return him to you for the other dances."

Behind all this I could detect a spirit of raillery; it was evident I was but a trivial plaything in the hands of these two beautiful creatures, both so different in their style of beauty. I was but a shuttlecock which they flung from battledore to battledore as they chose, caring little if the violence of their blows broke some of its feathers.

I had grown much older within the last ten minutes; for it was no longer shame that I felt—this time it was a feeling of sadness; it was not a moist blush of confusion that mounted to my temples, but a sharp sting of pain that made my heart bleed.

I had stepped into the second circle of human life; I suffered.

And yet, in spite of this pain, a mysterious hymn, an unknown song, rose from the depths of my soul; that hymn extolled pain, and for the first time cried out to the child, "Courage! you are a man!"

The boon I craved above aught else was solitude.

The musicians were playing the first bars of a quadrille; everyone sprang up to take his partner's hand. Fourcade made an interrogative sign with his head, which signified "Will you be my *vis-à-vis* again?" I replied with a negative sign, and, as the two Parisian girls were going to take their places with two new dancers, I went away.

I could not possibly describe what passed through my mind during the hour I spent dreaming by myself. The whole of my childhood disappeared; just as towns and villages, valleys and mountains, lakes and rivers disappear in an earthquake: the present alone remained with me, an immense chaos, lit up by intermittent flashes which neither showed up the whole void nor its details: nothing seemed definite enough to get hold of, either with regard to my body or my mind. The only definite incontestably real actual thing was that during the last quarter of an hour I had fallen in love.

With whom?

With no one as yet ... but with Love.

I returned at the end of an hour.

"You are polite!" Vittoria said to me; "you asked me to waltz with you, and then you go away."

"Quite true," I replied: "I beg your pardon, I had forgotten."

"You are indeed polite!"

I smiled.

"I assure you," I said, "it was not intended for rudeness."

"Where did you go, then?"

"Do you wish to know?"

"It seems to me I have a right to know."

"Look there," I said, "do you see that beautiful dark avenue?"

"Yes—well...?"

"It is called the Avenue of *Sighs*: I came from there."

I had replied out of the simplicity of my heart; I had no intention of being clever or sentimental.

Those two failings came to me later.

"Did I not tell you how charming he was!" said Vittoria to Laure.

I did not understand how or why I was charming; so, instead of thanking the Spaniard for the compliment she had paid me, I made a face, which was greeted with shouts of laughter from both the two young girls.

I wanted to return to my Avenue of Sighs, but I had not the courage; I was already in the condition of Molière's lovers who always get as far as the door, but who never make up their minds to cross the threshold.

People were again preparing for the quadrille.

"Come," said Laure, "do not pout, young scholar; I invite you to dance this time.... Will you accept?"

"Alas! yes," I replied.

"Why alas?"

"Yes, I hear."

And I gave her my hand. The rest of the evening and part of the night passed in dancing and in waltzing. We returned home at one o'clock in the morning.

Niguet, who was above me in the lawyer's office, conducted Mademoiselle Vittoria home; I conducted Mademoiselle Laurence.

The hours that followed during the rest of that night were the most agitated I had ever spent in my previous life.

END OF VOL. I.

9 789357 961042